T0373206

THE ELIZABETHAN MIND

THE ELIZABETHAN MIND

SEARCHING FOR THE SELF IN AN AGE OF UNCERTAINTY

HELEN HACKETT

YALE UNIVERSITY PRESS
NEW HAVEN AND LONDON

LEVERHULME
TRUST _____

Published with assistance from the foundation established in memory of Oliver Baty
Cunningham of the Class of 1917, Yale College.

For information about this and other Yale University Press publications, please contact:
U.S. Office: sales.press@yale.edu   yalebooks.com
Europe Office: sales@yaleup.co.uk   yalebooks.co.uk

Set in Adobe Caslon Pro by IDSUK (DataConnection) Ltd
Printed in Great Britain by TJ Books, Padstow, Cornwall

Library of Congress Control Number: 2022931856

ISBN 978-0-300-20720-0

A catalogue record for this book is available from the British Library.

10 9 8 7 6 5 4 3 2 1

CONTENTS

CONTENTS

ILLUSTRATIONS

ACKNOWLEDGEMENTS

Heartfelt thanks are due to many people who have helped to bring this book to fruition. Heather McCallum of Yale University Press planted the seed and has patiently nurtured the book to completion, giving much sage guidance along the way. Marika Lysandrou, Katie Urquhart, Felicity Maunder, and Lucy Buchan of Yale have also been tirelessly helpful in bringing the book to publication, and Robert Shore has been an assiduous and exemplary copy-editor. Two anonymous readers for Yale gave invaluable advice.

The Leverhulme Trust generously granted a twelve-month Research Fellowship which was vital to completion of the book. Stephen Cadywold and Steve Morrison gave expert help with the funding application, while Lucy Razzall provided excellent cover for my teaching and other departmental duties during the Fellowship. Thanks are due to the UCL English Department for two terms of research leave during the period of work on the book, especially to those colleagues who covered teaching and administrative duties that would otherwise have fallen to me. My students and colleagues at UCL have been a constant source of stimulation and inspiration over many years. I'm especially grateful to members of the Early Modern English Reading Group (EMERG) and its organisers, Harvey Wiltshire, Luke Prendergast, Kate Kinley, and Fraser McIlwraith.

For help with research materials, my thanks go to the staff of the British Library; the Oxfam Bookshop, Muswell Hill (especially Sam Golding); the Senate House Library of the University of London; the UCL Library (especially Sarah Burn); UCL Special Collections (especially Gill Furlong, Dan Mitchell, and Mandy Wise); and the Warburg Institute Library. I benefited enormously from opportunities to present work-in-progress at venues including the Literary Society, Fitzwilliam College, Cambridge; *Early Modern Voices: A Symposium for Alison Thorne*, University of Glasgow; the 2018 conference of the Italian Association of Shakespearean and Early Modern Studies at the Università degli Studi di Cagliari, Sardinia; the Early Modern Research Seminar, English Faculty, Oxford University; the Literature and History Seminar, Oxford University; the Department of Linguistic and Literary Studies, Università degli Studi di Padova; *Elizabeth I, 1588–2018: The Armada and Beyond*, the Queen's House conference 2018, Greenwich; and the Women's Studies Group 1558–1837.

This book would not exist without the many kinds of generous help and support received from Katherine Duncan-Jones, Karen Hearn, Mary Ellen Lamb, Neil Rhodes, and Henry Woudhuysen. My debts to them are profound. For taking the time and trouble to read draft materials, I'm grateful to Shani Bans, Douglas Clark, Susan Doran, Angus Gowland, Antonia Hamilton, Sarah Howe, Paulina Kewes, Dana Key, Eric Langley, John Mullan, Alison Shell, Chris Stamatakis, René Weis, and Emma Whipday. The book has been greatly improved by their comments and counsel, though any remaining errors and deficiencies are of course my own responsibility. Expert assistance on particular topics was kindly given by Eoin Bentick, Stella Bruzzi, Marilyn Corrie, Katharine Craik, Gregory Dart, Avital Hahamy, Rachel E. Holmes, Simon Jackson, Conor

Leahy, Tess Lowery, Kate Maltby, Barret Reiter, Neil Rennie, and Simone Webb. Special mention must go to Shani Bans, Dana Key, and Chris Stamatakis for leading me to invaluable research materials, and to Margaret Healy, Chris Laoutaris, and Sasha Garwood Lloyd for showing me ways into early modern medical humanities. Many different kinds of assistance have been given by Kathryn Allan, Alison Findlay, Susan Irvine, Norman Jones, Alison Light, Katie McKeogh, Alexander Samson, Lindsay Smith, Brian Vickers, and John Watkins.

I have been sustained by the interest and encouragement of my family and friends, especially Lisa Clifford, Jeri McIntosh, John Davis, Dermot Doughty, Belinda Fox, Judith Tew, and Peter Tyler. Some work on the book was done while enjoying the generous hospitality of Paul Hackett and June Hammond at their house in France. The hard work over many years of Birute Gelumbauskiene freed me from domestic tasks and provided me with a comfortable working environment.

My greatest debts, as ever, are the hardest to express. My children, Ed and Marina Hackett, read parts of the book, had many conversations about others, and gave much sage advice. My husband, Stephen Hackett, has read every word of the book and has lived with it for longer than either of us expected. He has been on holiday with it many times (uncomplainingly) and has been locked down with it during Covid restrictions. Throughout the book's gestation he has sustained me with delicious food and drink, long walks, long talks, and everything else a person could need. By now he probably feels that he has an Elizabethan mind. The book could not be dedicated to anyone but him. For Steve, with love (and apologies).

A NOTE ON THE TEXT

All quotations from the Bible, unless otherwise stated, are from *The Geneva Bible: A Facsimile of the 1560 Edition*, introduced by Lloyd E. Berry (Madison: University of Wisconsin Press, 1969). All references to the *Oxford Dictionary of National Biography* (*ODNB*) are to www-oxforddnb-com.libproxy.ucl.ac.uk. All references to the *Oxford English Dictionary* (*OED*) are to www-oed-com.libproxy.ucl.ac.uk. All references to Shakespeare's works, unless otherwise stated, are to *The Norton Shakespeare*, 3rd edn, International Student Edition, gen. ed. Stephen Greenblatt (New York: Norton, 2016).

For personal names that have variant spellings, I have consulted the *ODNB* and *Early English Books Online* (*EEBO*, proquest.com/eebo), then chosen the most appropriate form according to my own judgement. Variant forms are given in parenthesis where helpful for reference. Titles of early printed books are modernised in the main text but given in their original form in the Bibliography (where very long titles are shortened as appropriate) and notes (in short form). Where appropriate, dates are given in the form CE (Common Era) or BCE (Before Common Era). All dates of plays after 1533, unless otherwise stated, are the 'best guesses' given in Martin Wiggins with

Catherine Richardson, *British Drama 1533–1642: A Catalogue*, 9 vols (Oxford: Oxford University Press, 2011–18).

Spelling in quotations from early or unmodernised editions has been modernised, and punctuation has been lightly modernised if necessary for clarity. However, Edmund Spenser's idiosyncratic spelling in his poetry has not been modernised, in accordance with standard convention. Glosses of obsolete terms are given in square brackets, and are based on *OED* definitions.

ABBREVIATIONS

CELM   *Catalogue of English Literary Manuscripts 1450–1700.* celm-ms.org.uk

EEBO   *Early English Books Online.* Proquest, 2021. proquest.com/ eebo

ESTC   *English Short Title Catalogue.* London: British Library. estc.bl.uk

MHRA   Modern Humanities Research Association

n.s.   new series

ODNB   *Oxford Dictionary of National Biography.* Oxford: Oxford University Press, 2021. www-oxforddnb-com.libproxy.ucl. ac.uk

OED   *Oxford English Dictionary.* Oxford: Oxford University Press, 2021. www-oed-com.libproxy.ucl.ac.uk

Introduction

'There is nothing either good or bad,' declares Hamlet, famously, 'but thinking makes it so.' He is verbally sparring with Rosencrantz and Guildenstern, the former university friends who have been enlisted to investigate his state of mind and intentions. Hamlet asserts that 'Denmark is a prison'; Rosencrantz retorts that 'We think not so, my lord', and ventures that ''tis too narrow for your mind'. This provokes Hamlet to exclaim, 'O God, I could be bounded in a nutshell and count myself a king of infinite space, were it not that I have bad dreams' (2.2.231.5–17).

It goes without saying that *Hamlet* is a play rich in ideas about the mind, and in this brief exchange alone there is much for us to contemplate. It explores what we might call psychological relativism, contending that there is a disjunction between the material reality of the world and how the mind perceives the world; and that each mind has its own distinctive perception, differing, perhaps widely, from those of other minds. Hamlet also suggests that the mind has vast, visionary powers – it can turn a nutshell into infinite space – but at the same time is volatile and vulnerable, liable to 'bad dreams'.

1

While complex and thought-provoking, the ideas contained in these lines might not at first sight seem strange to us; indeed, we might be tempted to describe them as remarkably modern. Yet we should not ignore the fact that *Hamlet* is a play of 1600, and was profoundly shaped by the thinking of its time. Both Hamlet and his uncle, Claudius, diagnose him as a sufferer from melancholy (2.2.520, 3.1.162). This was not just a vague state of wistful sadness, as we might think of it today; it was a recognised medical condition, and the subject of substantial and detailed discussion in print. Just a year before Shakespeare's play, Richard Surflet, a physician, had published his translation of a discourse on melancholy by André du Laurens, doctor to the King of France. Its description of a typical sufferer from the disease closely fits Hamlet: he 'haunts the shadowed places, suspicious, solitary, enemy to the sun, and one whom nothing can please, but only discontentment, which forgeth unto itself a thousand false and vain imaginations'.[1] His mind is 'violently set on the rack', yet the cause is physical, 'a cold and dry distemperature of the brain' (89, 88). Melancholy, according to Du Laurens, and to his contemporaries in general, was a physiological disorder which could be treated by a range of practical remedies, including the avoidance of certain foods, blood-letting, purgatives, broths, scented baths, potions, and ointments (105–17). Company was good; Rosencrantz and Guildenstern were following textbook practice in tailing Hamlet and bantering with him: 'Melancholic persons should never be alone [. . .] sometimes they must be flattered and yielded unto in some part of that which they desire, [. . .] somewhiles they must be chided for their foolish imaginations' (106–7).

As well as having a physical origin, melancholy was also believed to have a supernatural aspect: Du Laurens explains that the 'thousand vain visions, [. . .] fantastical inventions, and dreadful dreams' that melancholics were prey to might be the result of 'the intercourse or meddling of evil angels' (82, 100). Today, we are likely to interpret Hamlet's 'bad dreams' as the products of a troubled unconscious, but the common sixteenth-century understanding of them was as Satanic incursions into the mind. A treatise of 1583 by Henry Howard denying that dreams had prophetic meanings based its argument not on proto-modern secular scepticism, but on general agreement that dreams come from 'agitation of the mind, from sickness, and from the Devil'.[2] Hamlet himself fears that his father's ghost 'May be a dev'l' (2.2.517), a possibility, or even likelihood, supported by the fact that it is visible to others, not just to him.

We have a strong impulse to claim Hamlet as having a modern mind, like our own, that we can comprehend on our own terms; and, of course, psychoanalysis has found much to say about the effects of Hamlet's father's death and his mother's remarriage on his psychological state. Yet we miss vast and important dimensions of the play if we are unaware of Elizabethan theories of the mind. Shakespeare assumed an audience who would recognise Hamlet as a sufferer from a well-known disease with a complex multiplicity of symptoms, effects, and cultural meanings, and who would also be alert to the evidence that Hamlet may be a pawn of the Devil. Knowledge of the thought-systems of its time renders the play even more enigmatic and thought-provoking, since they intensify the ambiguity of Hamlet as a hero and make the complex moral landscape of the play even more challenging to navigate.

This is just one example of how investigating Elizabethan ideas about the mind, in all their difference from our own, can enrich and deepen our understanding of the literature of the period. It was a time of intense interest in the mind, when old and new intellectual frameworks intersected and clashed, and when Shakespeare was just one among many authors inventing new ways of representing the mind and its processes in writing.

'Know thyself': a preoccupation with the mind

Hamlet stands at the end of the Elizabethan period (1558–1603), a half-century that had seen extensive discussion of the nature of the mind and how to manage its disorders. In large part this was driven by one of the major cultural developments of the period: the growth of the book trade. Print technology had reached England in the late fifteenth century, but it was in the sixteenth century, especially its second half, that the commercial printing and bookselling industry became fully established and expanded rapidly.[3] A count of early printed books of which copies survive today has found that, in the decade to 1560, just over 1,500 books were published; but by the decade ending in 1600, this had doubled to almost 3,000.[4] At the same time, large numbers of publications were imported from thriving centres of book production in continental Europe.[5] This new availability of books was accompanied by increased access to education, especially through the foundation of numerous grammar schools, bringing literacy to more of the population.[6] More kinds of knowledge were accessible to more people than ever before.

This included knowledge about the mind and the body. There was a thirst for medical books: a tally based on surviving copies has identified some 153 such works in English published between 1486 and 1605, a number of which went through two or more editions, giving a total figure of 392 editions of medical publications over this period.[7] As with books in general, the number of publications increased through the sixteenth century: an average of one or two medical publications per year in around 1520 rose to an average of four or five in the early 1600s, many of which were available in affordable editions aimed at a relatively wide readership.[8] These were not necessarily new works: some medical books in English were translations from Latin of medieval works in manuscript; others were translations of more recent printed works from Latin, French, Italian, or other languages.[9] Books in languages other than English were also widely available. Around 10 per cent of all books published in England between 1550 and 1640 were in Latin; some of these were reprints of classical authorities, but many others were new works that used this international language of scholarship to announce their seriousness and to address a pan-European intellectual readership.[10] These neo-Latin publications included medical works, while imports from the continent included works both in Latin and in European vernaculars.[11] At the same time, the trend was towards increasing publication in English, contributing to the widening of access to knowledge in general and medical knowledge in particular.[12] Works of different periods and origins – classical, medieval, recent, and new; English and international – coexisted in English bookshops and libraries, offering a host of diverse and competing opinions on the nature and workings of the mind.

One of the leading authorities was Aristotle (384–322 BCE), the title of whose treatise *De anima* may be translated as *Of the Soul* or *Of the Mind*. This work propounded a theory of the mind as embedded in, and integrated with, the body; and this doctrine was reinforced from other sources by the theory of the humours: fluids (one of which was melancholy, or black bile) whose circulation in the body and relative proportions determined temperament and mood. Humoral theory originated in the Hippocratic Corpus, a body of ancient medical works by Hippocrates (*c.* 460–*c.* 370 BCE) and his followers, and had been developed by the widely influential Greek physician Galen (129–?199/216 CE). Meanwhile, Aristotelian medical teachings had been elaborated upon and transmitted by Islamic scholars including Avicenna (Ibn Sina, *c.* 980–1037) and Averroes (Ibn Rushd, 1126–98).[13] Paradoxically, one of the greatest innovations of the sixteenth century, the expansion of the book trade, made these ancient authorities even more accessible and influential as they became available in print editions.[14] Aristotle, in particular, remained central to university curricula and intellectual life, with numerous commentaries on *De anima* being published across Europe in the sixteenth century, as well as many books in the same tradition by other authors but with similar titles.[15]

Among original English medical works one of the most widely read was *The Castle of Health* by Sir Thomas Elyot, a court official under Henry VIII. *The Castle* aimed to make ancient Greek and Roman medical teachings, especially Galen's humoral doctrine, accessible in the vernacular, enabling readers to manage their own health. First published in the 1530s, it went through sixteen known editions up to 1595. Similar manuals on the management of body and mind included the *Regimen sanitatis Salerni* (*The Salernitan Rule of Health*), a medieval work supposedly originating in the famous medical school of Salerno, translated into English by Thomas Paynell in 1528; and *The Government of Health* (1558) by the physician William Bullein. Both of these also went through multiple editions, continuing to be read throughout the Elizabethan period.[16]

New publications during the Elizabethan period included *The Touchstone of Complexions* (1576), a translation of *De habitu et constitutione corporis* by Levinus Lemnius, a Dutch physician, where 'complexion' means the constitution or temperament produced by each humour. Information on the mind was also available in two widely read encyclopaedic works: *Batman upon Bartholome* (1582), an expanded version of a thirteenth-century sourcebook of knowledge,[17] and *The French Academy* (*L'Académie française*, 1577) by Pierre de La Primaudaye, a compendium of moral, philosophical, and scientific thought (translated into English in three parts, 1586–1601). The simultaneous circulation of medical works that were old or new, native or imported is illustrated by a 1585 inventory of Roger Ward, a bookseller in Shrewsbury, which among many 'books of physic' included an epitome (or summary) of Aristotle's *De anima*, Bullein's *Government of Health*, and *Batman upon Bartholome*, alongside various Latin works printed in Basel, Paris, Venice, and elsewhere on the continent.[18]

Melancholy became a particular preoccupation for the Elizabethans. Works specifically in this field included the 1586 *Treatise on Melancholy* by the English physician Timothy Bright, as well as Du Laurens's treatise discussed above (published in French in 1594). Another growing fascination was with the passions and affections (roughly equivalent to what we call emotions), which were addressed in *The Anatomy of the Mind* (1576) and *A Pattern of a Passionate Mind* (1580) by Thomas Rogers, a Church of England clergyman, and in *The Passions of the Mind* (1601, expanded 1604) by Thomas Wright, a Catholic priest, former Jesuit and controversialist.[19] Such works participated in a tradition of Elizabethan writing governed by the ancient saying *nosce teipsum* (know thyself), and directed towards understanding and managing one's own mind. In a similar vein was the hugely influential *Examen de ingenios* (1575) by the Spanish physician and natural philosopher Juan Huarte de San Juan, which went through fifty-five editions in six different languages in the sixteenth and seventeenth centuries, including in English *The Examination of Men's Wits* (1594).[20] This work classified different 'wits' or psychological types and matched them with different professions, almost like an early modern careers manual. Also in the *nosce teipsum* tradition were two philosophical poems about the mind published towards the end of the Elizabethan period, one simply called *Nosce teipsum* (1599), by Sir John Davies, the other *Mirum in modum* ('Marvellous in Means', 1602), by his namesake and emulator John Davies of Hereford.[21]

Why were the Elizabethans so interested in the mind, and so keen to read about it? We might hypothesise that growing numbers of them felt that they needed help with understanding and managing their minds because of the many social, political, and cultural upheavals of their period; that these had produced an age of uncertainty and what we might call (in the terms of our own time) a mental health crisis, making them turn to books on the mind just as we turn to self-help manuals today. Of these upheavals, one of the most traumatic was the Protestant Reformation, with its abolition of many of the beliefs, rituals, and social practices of the past.[22] At the same time, it directly increased attention to the mind, through new practices of private prayer (for direct spiritual communion with God) and self-examination (for signs of divine grace) – what Richard Rogers, a Protestant minister, called 'deep entering into consideration with myself'.[23] The response of the Catholic Church, the Counter-Reformation, also promoted disciplines of meditation and examination of conscience that required turning within. Theology was as important as medical writing in intensifying interest in the mind and providing new techniques for observing and regulating mental states.

Philosophy too encouraged this inward turn, with a revival of interest in theories of the mind deriving from Plato and the Stoics. Christianised Neoplatonism elevated the mind above the body and the material world, while Neostoicism promoted mental resolution in the face of worldly vicissitudes, bodily suffering, and the volatility of the passions.

In the 1980s, some influential literary critics questioned whether Elizabethan and Jacobean authors had a concept of the inner self, arguing that this was a later modern construct.[24] More recently, Stephen Prickett has offered a more comprehensive and nuanced account of the evolution of a sense of inner space and of consciousness.[25] Concepts of selfhood have undoubtedly evolved over time, but in broad terms the Elizabethans did not differ from us in distinguishing between their outward and 'inward selfe', as Edmund Spenser puts it.[26] Under the influence of religious and philosophical doctrines of withdrawal from the world and introspection, this inward self was closely identified with the mind: as Sir John Davies wrote, 'Myself am centre of my circling thought, / Only myself I study, learn, and know'.[27]

The many Elizabethan works in this vein also disrupt the contentions of some other modern scholars that the period held a view of mind and body as integrated and indivisible, and that they were not separated until the French philosopher René Descartes declared in 1637 *'cogito, ergo sum'* – 'I think, therefore I am'.[28] Concepts of the mind as embodied were certainly important in the Elizabethan period: they derived from Aristotle and from the linking of mind and body in humoral theory, and were prominent in concepts of the passions as intermediate between mind and body. They have enabled some productive analysis of the literature of the period through application of modern theories of 'embodied cognition'. These propose that mental processes are not abstract and immaterial, but are materially traceable in neurological events in the brain, conditioned by bodily experience and connected to the material environment.[29] Yet in the Elizabethan period ideas of the mind as embodied existed alongside, and in tension with, quite contrary doctrines that promoted detachment of the mind from the body and withdrawal from the material world to a place within. Elizabethan thinking about the mind was not stable or homogeneous, and cannot be reduced to a single framework. Rather, it was a rich, complex, tumultuous brew of competing ideas from diverse sources.

The Elizabethan mind in the world of its time

While many Elizabethan thinkers may have advocated withdrawal from the world into the mind, at the same time their ideas about the mind were profoundly shaped by the social and political conditions of the time. For instance, the extension of education mentioned above only applied in a limited way to women; while some elite women received an impressive humanist education, this was not accessible to most of their sex. The female mind was believed to be constitutionally inferior to the male mind, and even the most highly educated women were only able to contribute to intellectual culture in relatively circumscribed ways. Yet at the same time, the genre of 'female complaint' became popular, in which male writers impersonated female speakers and expressed their inner woes and conflicts, apparently finding in the supposed irrationality of the female mind opportunities to explore a greater emotional range.

The minds of those of other nations and races were also viewed as essentially different, largely because of humoral theory, which dictated that the environment affected both body and mind. This age of extensive exploration and travel brought Elizabethans into contact with many kinds of people who not only looked unlike themselves, but whose minds too they assumed to be different because of climatic conditions. This did not necessarily mean defining these other minds as inferior: there was a widely held theory, for instance, that the hot and dry conditions in which Africans lived made them particularly intelligent. Nevertheless, the minds of those considered 'Other' tended to be viewed with suspicion.

At the same time, the Elizabethans harboured many fears and anxieties about their own minds. They believed they were subject to various kinds of outside force: the influence of stars and planets; and incursions by the Devil and his agents, which at worst might take the dramatic form of demonic possession, but even in ordinary life presented the constant threat of implanted evil thoughts and sinful impulses that must be monitored and suppressed. The imagination was thought to be especially prone to such incursions, and to its own waywardness. The consequence was that the Elizabethans thought of the mental processes of literary and artistic creation in very different terms from how we think of them today. In general, they regarded the mind as full of potentially disruptive and rebellious forces – bodily temptations transmitted by the senses, turbulent passions, sinful impulses, and the deceiving inventions of the imagination – which must be firmly governed by reason. This made popular a widespread metaphor of the mind as a state where reason (or sometimes will) was monarch, an authoritarian hierarchy that reflected the structure of the Elizabethan polity and that must be maintained in order to avoid chaos.

All this concerted interest in the mind produced new literary genres and techniques for representing subjectivity and interiority in writing. Interest in the relations between thought and language intensified as the rhetorical treatises of antiquity were revived, especially those of Quintilian and Cicero, from which grew new works of rhetorical theory by Erasmus, Rudolph Agricola, and other humanist scholars. Rhetoric became a core part of Elizabethan education and culture, understood as a method of translating the thoughts of a speaker or writer into words as accurately and effectively as possible, and of influencing the thoughts and feelings of the auditor or reader.[30] As formulated by Richard Sherry, one of the earliest English authors of a rhetorical manual, *A Treatise of Schemes and Tropes* (1550), to master rhetoric was 'to utter the mind aptly, distinctly, and ornately'.[31] Among the new genres that emerged to 'utter the mind' was female complaint, as mentioned above; another was a body of poetry and prose that expressed the tormented passions of penitent sinners. New kinds of autobiographical writing emerged, while poets seized upon the opportunities offered by the sonnet to explore and express interiority, and prose fictions developed increasingly sophisticated forms of interior monologue. Meanwhile, the new commercial play-houses that sprang up in the latter decades of the sixteenth century offered the opportunity to participate in a communal emotional and imaginative experience of an unprecedented kind, while also presenting another new medium for representing the inner states and thought-processes of fictional characters, taking the device of the dramatic soliloquy to unprecedented levels of psychological depth and subtlety.

All these aspects of the Elizabethan mind will be explored in the following chapters. Obviously, Shakespeare will feature prominently as one of the leading innovators in dramatic and literary representation of the mind, while Marlowe, Sidney, and Spenser will also receive extensive attention. However, to achieve a fully rounded, immersive sense of how the Elizabethans engaged with the mind we need to look beyond well-known works, so the output of these authors will be placed alongside a wide and varied range of other writings that may be less familiar to the modern reader, but that were popular and influential in their own time, and contributed to new ways of understanding and depicting the mind and its processes.

Today, much investigation of the mind takes place in the field of neuroscience or other scientific disciplines. For the Elizabethans, however, it is arguable that greater advances were made in under-standing the mind through literature than through science. The seventeenth century would bring a scientific revolution, but only the earliest signs of this were visible in the reign of Elizabeth.[32] Francis Bacon began to form his thinking about empirical method in the 1590s, but it was not until 1605 that he began to publish it, in *The Advancement of Learning*. Copernicus's hypothesis of a heliocentric solar system was published in 1543 and is often thought to have had a fundamental effect on humanity's sense of itself, having been displaced, with Earth, from a central position in the cosmos. John Donne would famously lament that

> new philosophy calls all in doubt,
> [...]
> The sun is lost, and th'earth, and no man's wit
> Can well direct him where to look for it.[33]

However, this was not until 1611; Donne was possibly responding to the publication of Galileo's telescopic observations in 1610. Galileo's findings were unknown to the Elizabethans, and although Copernicus's theory was available to them, it did not become widely accepted until the second half of the seventeenth century.[34] (Thomas Trevelyon, for instance, in 1608 was still reproducing the Ptolemaic model of a geocentric cosmos; see fig. 12.) Even more significantly for thinking about the mind, there was a similarly slow adoption of the radical anatomical discoveries of Andreas Vesalius, coincidentally also published in 1543 as *De humani corporis fabrica* (*On the Workings of the Human Body*). Laying aside the ancient medical traditions handed down through multiple generations, Vesalius based his observations on human dissections and thereby disproved much established anatomical teaching, including theories about the structure of the brain – yet his findings did not dislodge the ancient authorities from university syllabuses until well into the seventeenth century (see Chapter 7 below).

In literary criticism the Elizabethan period is often absorbed into a generalised 'early modern period' reaching well into the seventeenth century. Yet its position before the scientific revolution – poised precariously on its brink, but not yet fully embarking upon it – is just one among many reasons why the second half of the sixteenth century, and especially its thinking about the mind, requires to be considered in its own right and on its own terms, as a specific phase in the history of ideas. Its distinctive combination of rooted beliefs with nascent ideas that were beginning to disrupt and dislodge them makes it intellectually heterogeneous and dynamic, and a fascinating territory to explore.[35]

'Man is but his mind': the meanings of the mind

We struggle today to pin down what we mean by 'the mind'. The *Oxford English Dictionary* offers a bewildering profusion of definitions, including: 'The action or state of thinking; a thought process'; 'State of thought and feeling; mood'; 'The seat of awareness, thought, volition, feeling, and memory'; and 'A person's cognitive, rational, or intellectual powers; the intellect'.[36] Broadly speaking, these definitions are linked by the concept that the mind is where thinking happens. But they provoke many difficult questions: is thinking produced by physiological processes in the brain, or is it an immaterial phenomenon? Do bodily processes and experiences affect the mind, and if so, how? Is selfhood located in the mind, and if so, what is it? The eminent cognitive neuroscientist Anil Seth in *Being You* (2021) defines 'consciousness' as 'any kind of subjective experience whatsoever'.[37] However, if we stop to consider what we mean by 'subjective' and turn again to the *OED*, we find the definition: 'Relating to the thinking subject, proceeding from or taking place within the individual consciousness or perception; having its source in the mind; belonging to the conscious life'.[38] While neuroscientists like Seth have made huge advances in our understanding of the brain and mind in recent decades, thinking about this topic can still leave us feeling that we are going around in circles.

Elizabethans wrestled with many of the same questions about the mind as twenty-first-century people, though they often came up with startlingly different answers. They also frequently – and surely forgivably – produced answers that were complex, incomplete, or self-contradictory. A good example is the essay 'The Man Is But his Mind' (1593) by the prolific author Thomas Churchyard.[39] 'Man is but [only, or no more than] his mind' was a favourite Elizabethan saying, for obvious reasons – it sounds satisfyingly aphoristic. But what did it actually mean? According to a 1569 translation of Cicero, it meant that 'the mind and soul of every man is he, and not that figure and shape which may be pointed and shown with the finger' – that is, that the mind cannot be read from the face or the body.[40] Yet according to Churchyard, it meant the opposite: that each man's mind determined his character of virtue or vice, and hence his behaviour; in other words, that the mind *was* precisely visible and legible. The main part of Churchyard's essay catalogues these types, such as the invincible mind, the cowardly mind, the studious mind, the ignorant mind, and so on. However, the essay is also a kind of patchwork of different ingredients, and begins with an eloquent passage on the nature of the mind that is not strictly relevant, but simply a kind of prose cadenza:

> The mind is so noble, watchful, and worthy, that it is never unoc-
> cupied whilst the man is awake, nor taketh any great rest when
> the body is asleep (as some dreams and visions manifesteth plain).
> For even as a cunning carpenter or smith is hammering and
> hewing some piece of wood or iron, to bring the same to such
> shape and perfection as the artificer would have it, so the mind
> (the harbour of all secrets and mover of all good and bad motions)
> can at no season be idle or wax weary of devices. The imagina-
> tions thereof are so many, and the innumerable conceits [concep-
> tions] therein are so mighty, the fire is of such vehement heat and
> operation, that it must needs burn or consume anything that long
> remains in it; so the mind is of such force and power, that it
> leadeth the man any way it listeth, and shapes all the senses and
> vital spirits in what form or fashion it pleaseth.[41]

There is a striking blend here of admiration and anxiety. The mind is a thing of wonder: it is 'noble' and 'worthy'; it never rests; it has mighty creative powers; and it commands the 'senses and vital spirits' of the body. Yet at the same time there is a distinct note of fear of this incessant 'hammering' force, this 'harbour of all secrets', this mover of

'bad motions' as well as good, and this 'fire' that burns and consumes.
It 'leadeth the man any way it listeth'; here, it seems not so much that
man is his mind, but that man is at the mercy of his mind.

It should not surprise us that Churchyard, and Elizabethans in
general, held many diverse and conflicting ideas about the mind,
given that our own understanding of it, several centuries on, still
includes so many gaps and unsolved problems. As we have seen,
Elizabethan England was a place where entrenched intellectual
traditions – some of which we would call superstitions – existed
alongside radical innovations, including new theologies and spiritual
practices, rediscoveries and reformulations of classical thought,
encounters with diverse regions of the globe and their peoples, and
new media for the dissemination of knowledge and ideas. All these
elements combined to form a rich and generative turmoil from which
sprang multifarious and often inconsistent ideas about the mind.
This may be among the reasons why the latter part of the period,
from around 1590 onwards, saw such an extraordinary explosion
of literary creativity, as heterogeneous intellectual frameworks
converged and clashed in a volatile but fertile mix.

The Elizabethan Mind proposes that we cannot fully understand
the works of Shakespeare and his contemporaries without knowledge of the differences between their ideas about the mind and our
own. Investigating Elizabethan concepts of the mind will take us
along many fascinating and surprising pathways, and will cast new
light on the literature of the period. At the same time, by throwing
our own very different ideas and assumptions into relief, it may give
us a clearer awareness of what the mind means to us today.

PART I
Mind and Body

✒ 1 ✒

The Mind in the Body
Medical Frameworks

According to *The French Academy*, a widely read compendium of philosophical and scientific knowledge, the state of a person's mind was clear just from looking at the shape of their head. 'They which have the head over-great and ill-favoured [badly formed], whom we commonly call great blockheads', were 'naturally unapt to conceive, and to bring forth any sensible and witty thing'.[1] *The Examination of Men's Wits* agreed that a big head indicated slowness and stupidity, because it 'consists all of bones and flesh and contains a small quantity of brain, as it befalls in very big oranges, which opened, are found scarce of juice and hard of rind'.[2] These ideas that the size and structure of the head reflected mental abilities formed part of an extensive body of sixteenth-century thought that linked body and mind.

'Airy substance': the embodied soul and the spirits

Aristotle's *De anima* remained prominent on university syllabuses throughout the Middle Ages and sixteenth century. It taught that 'the soul is not separable from the body', and that as 'the cause and principle of the living body' it had three levels.[3] The most basic level was the nutritive or vegetative soul, which was present in all creatures, including plants, and simply made them live and grow. The next level was the sensible or sensitive soul, a capacity for perception that was present only in animals and humans. Finally, the rational or intellective soul (often equated by Aristotle's successors with the mind) gave the capacity to reason and understand, and was exclusive to humans.[4]

The Aristotelian soul was a life-force that circulated around the body and animated its organs by means of a mysterious medium called 'spirit'.[5] Sir Thomas Elyot's *The Castle of Health* described this as 'an airy substance, subtle, stirring the powers of the body to perform their operations'. Like the soul, spirit was divided into three categories: natural spirit, which emanates from the liver; vital spirit, from the heart; and animal spirit, from the brain, which 'maketh sense or feeling'.[6] Lemnius in his *Touchstone of Complexions* explained that spirit 'spreadeth itself most swiftly throughout the whole body, carrieth and extendeth his powers into every part thereof universally, and beside this, doth manifestly change and alter the state both of body and mind'.[7] For Timothy Bright in his *Treatise on Melancholy*, the spirits were subordinate to the mind: 'the spirit itself without impulsion of mind lieth idle in the body'. However, if mental troubles in the form of 'sudden conceit [thought], study or passion' impaired or misdirected the spirits, the consequence was illness and death.[8]

Spirit was generally agreed to be invisible and intangible, but writers disagreed on whether it was entirely immaterial. For many, it was at once immaterial and material, as in Elyot's oxymoron 'airy substance': a mysteriously refined form of physical substance, often described as 'subtle', meaning at once 'difficult to understand', 'difficult to analyse or describe', and 'of fine or delicate texture or composition'.[9] Its paradoxical nature is at the heart of 'The Ecstasy' by John Donne. The speaker in the poem seeks to persuade his mistress that the perfect union of their souls should be consummated by the sexual union of their bodies, and ingeniously invokes the spirits as an analogy:

As our blood labours to beget
    Spirits, as like souls as it can,
Because such fingers need to knit
    That subtle knot, which makes us man.[10]

Spirits are engendered by the body, from the blood; they have the physicality of fingers, and of a knot binding together body and soul. At the same time, this knot is 'subtle', not wholly material, and the spirits are as like souls as a physical entity can be. Just as a human being is tied together by the semi-immaterial, semi-material spirits, so, argues Donne, a fusion of souls must be enacted and completed by a fusion of bodies. The poem leaves us with questions: is this a cunning seduction strategy cynically dressed up in philosophical discourse? Or does Donne sincerely believe in sexual union as a kind of spiritual mystery, which inspires elevated philosophical reflection? Just as the spirits are simultaneously physical and metaphysical, both readings of the poem coexist, brilliantly entwined together in a 'subtle knot'.[11]

While the spirits were challenging to define, the concept of the soul blurred with the concept of the mind. The Latin term *anima* could be translated as either soul or mind, and the Aristotelian concept of the rational soul could be readily equated with the mind (see Chapter 2 below). Hence, Aristotle's emphasis on the soul as embodied was often applied equally to the mind, and reinforced not only by the concept of the spirits, but also by humoral theory.

'The mixture and temperature of the elements': humoral theory

The Hippocratic Corpus of ancient medical works taught that each human being was formed of the four elements – earth, water, air, and fire – each of which was associated with a particular fluid or 'humour' in the body. The term 'humour' derives from the Latin *humor*, meaning moisture or liquid (also the root of our term 'humid').

Galen, among others, developed this theory which flourished through the Middle Ages, and was passed onto sixteenth-century readers by Elyot and subsequent authors of printed medical manuals.[12] The basis of the theory was that each humour created a particular 'complexion' or temperament, according to its proportion and state in an individual's constitution. Black bile was associated with earth, and was cold and dry, creating a melancholic disposition. Phlegm had the coldness and moisture of water, but blood was hot and moist, like air, producing a sanguine character. Finally, yellow bile had the heat and dryness of fire, creating a choleric personality (see Table 1.1).[13] Each humour was also associated with a particular planet – for instance, melancholy with Saturn – and with a particular group of zodiac signs, which were thought to exert astrological influence over bodies and minds (see Chapter 6 below).

Humoral theory dominated physiology and psychology well beyond the Elizabethan period. A recently compiled database of medical texts of the period 1500–1700 comprises around 230 works which between them contain more than 2,000 occurrences of the word 'humour'.[14] One of the attractions of the theory was the ability to classify patients, and people in general, according to the four humoral personality-types. Du Laurens's treatise on melancholy, for instance, characterised phlegmatic individuals as 'for the most part blockish and lubberlike [loutish], having a slow judgement, and all the noblest powers of the mind, as it were asleep, because the substance of their brain is too thick, and the spirits laboured therein too gross'. By contrast, sanguine persons 'are born for to be sociable

Table 1.1: Elements, their properties, and the corresponding humours and humoral types.

Element	Water	Air	Fire	Earth
Properties	Cold and moist	Hot and moist	Hot and dry	Cold and dry
Humour	Phlegm	Blood	Yellow bile	Black bile
Humoral type	Phlegmatic	Sanguine	Choleric	Melancholic

and lovers of company: they are as it were always in love, they love to laugh and be pleasant'. Choleric characters 'have a quick understanding, abounding with many sleight [crafty, clever] inventions: for they seldom sound any deep and hidden secrets, it fitteth not their fist to grapple with such businesses as require continuance of time and pains of the bodies, they cannot be at leisure'. Finally, the melancholic had the most complex psychology. He was

> out of heart, always fearful and trembling, in such sort as that he is afraid of everything, yea and maketh himself a terror unto himself [...] he goeth always sighing, troubled with the hicket [hiccup], and with an inseparable sadness, which oftentimes turneth into despair; [...] if he think to make truce with his passions by taking some rest, behold so soon as he would shut his eyelids, he is assailed with a thousand vain visions, and hideous buggards [goblins or bogies], with fantastical inventions, and dreadful dreams.[15]

Thus, humoral theory understood the mind as an organ of the body, governed by physical conditions and processes. *The Touchstone of Complexions* explained that intellectual ability depended on correct humoral balance: dryness and heat in moderation 'maketh a good and faithful memory, and highly furthereth toward the attainment of prudence and wisdom', but in excess would dry out the brain and make an individual 'very oblivious, blockheaded and heavy spirited'. Even worse was excessive moisture and coldness, which made the phlegmatic individual 'in mind and wit doltish and dull, slothful and lumpish'.[16] *The French Academy* confirmed that 'the quickness or slowness of man's wit' depended on 'the good or immoderate mixture and temperature of the elements, of which our bodies are compounded and framed'.[17]

At first sight humoral theory may seem schematic and reductive, assigning each individual to one character-type – phlegmatic, sanguine, choleric, or melancholic – and then expecting them to

conform to its definition. However, in its development and application, the theory was considerably more sophisticated than this. An
individual might be diagnosed with a predominant humour, but it
was also understood that each person had a distinctive *combination* of
humours. Fractional differences in their proportions could have
significant effects, and the humours, being fluids, were always in flux,
remingling and rebalancing in response to many factors, including
temperature, diet, exercise, sleep, and happy or sad events. Humoral
theory thus provided both a typology of character, and a potentially
infinite variety of combinations, permutations, and fluctuations. It
was simultaneously a basis for generalisations and a basis for recognition of individuality.[18]

The Examination of Men's Wits contained some of the most deter-
ministic applications of humoral theory in its advice on how to match
different types of intellect with appropriate occupations. It declared
that 'if a child have not the disposition and ability which is requisite
for that science [field of knowledge] whereunto he will addict himself,
it is a superfluous labour to be instructed therein by good schoolmas-
ters, to have store of books, and continually to study it'.[19] A child
with the wrong composition of the brain and humoral temperament
for a particular discipline or vocation was doomed to failure and
should simply give up. Yet while it was rigid in its prioritisation of
nature over nurture, the *Examination* also recognised the multiplicity
and diversity of humoral temperaments. Each individual's humoral
profile, it asserted, was as unique as their face:

considering that man's face, being composed of so small a number
of parts as are two eyes, a nose, two cheeks, a mouth, and a fore-
head, nature shapeth yet therein so many compositions and
combinations as if you assemble together 100,000 men, each one
hath a countenance so different from other and proper to himself,
that it falleth out a miracle to find two who do altogether resemble.
The like betideth in the four elements, and in the four first qualities (hot, cold, moist, and dry) by the harmony of which the life

and health of man is compounded. And of so slender a number of parts, nature maketh so many proportions that if 100,000 men be begotten, each of them comes to the world with a health so peculiar and proper to himself.[20]

Similarly, many representations of the humours in Elizabethan literature fluctuate between a model of fixed character-types and a model of infinite individual variations. This was especially marked in the 'humours comedies' which became popular in the London playhouses in the late 1590s.

'Variable humours in disguised shapes': the humours on stage

Two plays by George Chapman initiated the fashion for humours comedy: *The Blind Beggar of Alexandria* (1596) and *An Humorous Day's Mirth* (originally known in performance as *The Comedy of Humours*, 1597). They were huge hits, and Ben Jonson quickly capitalised on their success with *The Case Is Altered* (1597), *Every Man in his Humour* (1598), and *Every Man out of his Humour* (1599). A humours comedy was a play that offered satirical depictions of different humoral types. However, this was less simple than it might sound, as the buzzword 'humour' came to mean many different things. As we have seen, its basic meaning was a temperament conforming to a recognisable type: two examples in plays are Dowsecer in Chapman's *An Humorous Day's Mirth*, who is a typical melancholic, and Giuliano in Jonson's *Every Man in his Humour*, who is a textbook depiction of choler. Also in *An Humorous Day's Mirth*, Lemot, a young gallant, amuses himself and his friends by provoking and observing the humours of other characters. As various gentlemen gather at an inn, he can predict with complete accuracy what each of them will say in response to particular remarks.[21] Throughout the play the different humours characters are like clockwork toys that Lemot winds up and sets in motion, and whose interactions are like games that he directs.

Increasingly, however, the concept of a character-type dominated by a particular emotion produced the idea of a humour as an overpowering, irrational obsession. Piso in *Every Man in his Humour* defines it as 'a monster bred in a man by self-love and affectation, and fed by folly', such as Thorello's irrational jealousy in the same play.[22] This in turn led a humour to be understood less as conformity to a type than as *aberrant* behaviour: an eccentricity or idiosyncrasy. It could manifest itself as a quirky mannerism or affectation, sometimes even as superficial as a verbal tic, as in *An Humorous Day's Mirth* where Blanuel's politeness consists in idiotically repeating all courtesies addressed to him:

Lemot: I shall be exceeding proud of your acquaintance.
Blanuel: I shall be exceeding proud of your acquaintance.
Lemot: I have heard much good of your rare parts and fine carriage.
Blanuel: I have heard much good of your rare parts and fine carriage.[23]

And so on. In some cases, in drama, then, a humour involved conforming to a standard category; but it could also be something unique and deviant, a personal obsession or behavioural oddity, suggesting the infinite range and variety of human character.[24]

It even came to mean a fleeting mood or whim, the opposite of a fixed, predictable character. In *The Case Is Altered*, Rachel asks herself: 'What means my father? / I wonder what strange humour?', using the term to mean a transient, perplexing state of mind.[25] To be 'humorous' often meant to be mercurial, subject to randomly shifting moods and impulses. The title-page of the first edition of Shakespeare's *Henry IV Part 2* in 1600 offers audiences 'the humours of Sir John Falstaff',[26] suggesting both Falstaff's innate eccentricities of character and his capricious whims; the implication that these will be entertaining points towards the modern sense of 'humorous' as simply 'comical'.

These different meanings created ambiguity as to whether a humour was an innate, physiologically dictated psychological state, beyond the control of the person in whom it was manifest, or merely a superficial social affectation that could be assumed or discarded at will.[27] Pretentious and superficial eccentricities offered comical entertainment to playhouse audiences, but their presentation on stage also raised deeper questions about whether humours were perhaps always merely performed behaviours. It was easy to imitate and parody the social conduct of characters with aberrant psychological traits, especially when the behaviour of, say, a choleric or melancholic type was in effect scripted by medical works. In Chapman's *The Blind Beggar of Alexandria*, the play that began the whole fashion for humours comedies, the central character assumes four different personae: Irus, a blind beggar with prophetic powers; Duke Cleanthes, noble beloved of Aegiale, Queen of Egypt; Hermes, a 'mad-brain', pistol-waving Count; and Leon, a usurer.[28] The title-page of the first edition of 1598 promises to show the blind beggar's 'variable humours in disguised shapes', implying that a humour is a performative pose that can be put on and off like a costume (A1r). This concept of humours as theatrical takes on another layer when the beggar in the guise of the Count, 'a wild and frantic man', competes with Bragadino, a proud and pretentious Spaniard, for the affections of Elimine (B2v, l. 332). As the Count brandishes his pistol in his usual reckless fashion, Bragadino entreats, 'Put up thy pistol,'tis a most dangerous humour in thee', to which the Count replies, 'Oh, is that all, why see 'tis up again, now thou shalt see I'll come to her in thy humour'. He proceeds to imitate Bragadino mockingly: 'sweet lady, I love sweet words, but sweet deeds are the noble sounds of a noble Spaniard, noble by country, noble by valour, noble by birth, my very foot is nobler than the head of another man' (B3v–4r, ll. 433–8). In Bragadino, humour is mainly a matter of verbal affectations, such as excessive repetition of the words 'sweet' and 'noble', which are easily parodied. Here, performances of two kinds of humour are layered upon one another: the beggar performs a humour in the sense of a temperament, as the 'wild and frantic' Count; then superimposes upon this performance his imitation of

Bragadino's verbal style, a humour in the sense of an affected mannerism.

Shakespeare's *The Merry Wives of Windsor* was written in around 1597, early in the fashion for the comedy of humours, yet suggests that the term had quickly come to feel overused and worn-out. In striving to be modish, Nym repeats the term so persistently that it becomes meaningless: 'I like not the humour of lying. He hath wronged me in some humours: I should have borne the humored letter to her [...] I love not the humour of bread and cheese' (2.1.117–23). A couple of years later, in the Induction to Jonson's *Every Man out of his Humour*, Asper deplored ignorant abuse of the term and sought to restore a medical understanding of humours as bodily fluids:

> what soe'er hath fluxure and humidity,
> As wanting power to contain itself,
> Is humour. So in every human body
> The choler, melancholy, phlegm, and blood,
> By reason that they flow continually
> In some one part and are not continent,
> Receive the name of humours.

He accepts the understanding of this flux as producing singular obsessions or dominant character traits:

> when some one peculiar quality
> Doth so possess a man that it doth draw
> All his affects, his spirits, and his powers
> In their confluxions all to run one way,
> This may be truly said to be a humour.

However, he objects to the representation of humour as merely a mannerism or style point, such as 'wearing a pied feather, / The cable hatband or the three-piled ruff'. His companion Cordatus agrees that 'Now, if an idiot / Have but an apish or fantastic strain, / It is his humour'. Asper, who emerges as a persona for Jonson as author, resolves that he will 'scourge those apes' and 'oppose a mirror' to 'the time's deformity', implying that his satirical targets will be threefold: those who practise the kinds of trivial affectations that have come to be understood as humours; those who misunderstand and misrepresent humours; and, most importantly, the psychological imbalances and irrational errors that are true humours.[29] Jonson claims a lofty moral purpose for his play by reasserting a definition of humours as deeply rooted psychological and physiological states. At the same time, however, this passage demonstrates that, by the late Elizabethan period, stage comedy had done much to confuse the concept of humours and to reduce them to merely performative postures. Representing them as no more than theatrical guises had undermined their role as an intrinsic connection between mind and body, as asserted by ancient medical theories, and instead had come to imply that a humour could be a merely superficial social appearance, concealing the true nature of the mind within.

'So often happening in these miserable times': melancholy

Melancholy was the humour that most fascinated the Elizabethans, with numerous writers of the period agreeing that the affliction was ubiquitous.[30] The term 'melancholy' referred to both the humoral substance in the body – black bile – and the psychological state that it produced, which Bright's *A Treatise of Melancholy* defined succinctly as 'a certain fearful disposition of the mind altered from reason'.[31] Medical works abounded in case histories of the bizarre delusions of melancholics. *The Touchstone of Complexions*, for instance, vividly recounted how one sufferer thought that his nose was as big as an elephant's trunk, how another thought that frogs and toads in his belly were gnawing his entrails, while a third refused food because he was convinced that he was already dead. Yet another patient 'thought his buttocks were made of glass, insomuch that he durst not do anything but standing, for fear lest if he should sit, he should break his rump, and the glass fly into pieces' (for more on melancholy and the disordered imagination, see Chapter 7 below).[32]

Discussions of melancholy were often far longer and more detailed than those of the other humours, elaborating numerous subcategories and variations. As Bright declared, 'Of all the other humours melancholy is fullest of variety of passion'.[33] By the end of the sixteenth century, its ever-growing catalogue of symptoms included unsociability, suspicion, capriciousness, stubbornness, delusions, sleeplessness, lethargy, despondency, introversion, taciturnity, attraction to darkness, misanthropy, self-hatred, and suicidal tendencies. It could settle in different organs of the body, 'as brain, spleen, mesaraic veins,[34] hart, womb, and stomach',[35] and it was subdivided into natural melancholy, unnatural melancholy (also known as 'adust' or burnt melancholy), and genial or witty melancholy (of which more below). Du Laurens concluded that there were almost as many different kinds of melancholy as there were sufferers:

> The imagination of melancholic men bringeth forth such diversity of effects, according to the difference of the matters whereabout it is occupied, as that a man shall scarce find five or six among ten thousand, which dote after one and the same manner. [...] This difference ariseth either from the disposition of the body, or from the manner of living, or from such studies as the parties do most apply themselves unto, or from some other secret and hidden cause.[36]

On stage, melancholy was a humour that especially lent itself to be performed and parodied. In Chapman's *An Humorous Day's Mirth*, Labesha, a foolish gallant who has been spurned in love, aspires to be a melancholic. He enters musing, 'O silly state of things, for things they be that cause this silly state. And what is a thing? A bauble, a toy that stands men in small stead.' However, a group of tricksters, who look on gleefully from a concealed position, have laid out a tempting array of cake and cream, and as soon as he spies this Labesha struggles to maintain his solemnity: 'But what have we here? What vanities have we here?' He can't resist tucking in: 'Well, taste it, and try it, spoonful by spoonful [. . .] Choke I, or burst I, mistress, for thy sake, / To end my life, eat I this cream and cake.'[37] Another comical melancholic is Matheo in *Every Man in his Humour*, whose affectation is pouring out bad poetry:

> Oh, Lord, sir, it's your only best humour, sir. Your true melancholy breeds your perfect fine wit, sir. I am melancholy myself divers times, sir, and then do I no more but take your pen and paper presently, and write you your half-score or your dozen of sonnets at a sitting.[38]

Onstage melancholy, at least in comedies, seems especially prone to representation as a social performance more than a physiological state.

An important factor in this was a certain glamour which made melancholy a state to aspire to. Witty melancholy was a special variety of the condition that was accompanied by enhanced intelligence and creativity. As Du Laurens explained, in such melancholics 'conceit [conceptual power] is very deep, their memory very fast [. . .], and when this humour groweth hot, by the vapours of blood, it causeth as it were, a kind of divine ravishment, commonly called *Enthousiasma*, which stirreth men up to play the philosophers, poets, and also to prophesy'.[39] This is the elevated melancholic state to which the dim-witted poet Matheo deludedly aspires. The concept of 'genial melancholy', or the melancholy of genius, originated with Aristotle, who had asked, 'Why is it that all men who have become outstanding in philosophy, statesmanship, poetry or the arts are melancholic, and some to such an extent that they are infected by the diseases arising from black bile?'[40] This question was further explored in fifteenth-century Florence by the Neoplatonist philosopher Marsilio Ficino in his *Three Books on Life* (*De vita libri tres*) (1489). According to Ficino – who identified himself as a melancholic – black bile at once creates

31

a predisposition to intellectual pursuits, and is intensified by intellectual activity, because this is accompanied by solitude, a lack of physical exercise, withdrawal of the mind from the body, and over-agitation of the brain, which has a drying effect. Symptoms of melancholy hence became evidence of engagement in lofty philosophical contemplations, and also of poetic gifts, since Ficino added that 'the priests of the Muses either are from the beginning or are made by study into melancholics'. When black bile is in the right quantity and state, 'our mind explores eagerly and perseveres in the investigation longer. Whatever it is tracking, it easily finds it, perceives it clearly, soundly judges it, and retains the judgement long.'[41]

What made genial melancholy even more special was that only a few, and perhaps only fleetingly, could attain this elevated state. Ficino warned that too much black bile 'dulls the sharpness of the intellect', while too little produces 'an unstable wit and a short memory'. If adust or burnt, it brings madness, while if mixed with phlegm, it brings torpor and despair.[42] Even those who have the right kind of melancholy, in the right proportions, to enhance their intellect will suffer from physical and psychological afflictions such as insomnia, fearfulness, headaches, and poor eyesight; indeed, much of Book 1 of Ficino's *Three Books* is dedicated to advice on avoiding or managing black bile in order to stay healthy while pursuing a life of study.

This work had a wide influence across sixteenth-century Europe, leading many writers in Elizabethan England to represent the gifts of melancholy as inextricable from its afflictions.[43] *The Anatomy of the Mind* (1576), for instance, by Thomas Rogers, noted Aristotle's observation that melancholics 'are strong in imaginations, and for sharpness of wit they excel', but added they are 'continually vexed, both in mind and body', and 'very seldom well at ease'.[44] Similarly, Bright's *A Treatise of Melancholy* acknowledged that 'Sometime it falleth out, that melancholy men are found very witty, and quickly discern', but also cautioned that 'Such persons are doubtful, suspicious, and thereby long in deliberation'. It added that 'their dreams are fearful [. . .] partly through black and dark fumes of melancholy, rising up to the brain, whereof the fantasy forgeth objects, and disturbeth the sleep of melancholy persons.'[45]

Yet this idea of a select form of melancholy that combined exceptional intellectual gifts with martyr-like suffering only added to its allure, as did its association with elite social status.[46] In ordinary people, according to Bright, 'melancholy causeth dullness of conceit, both by reason the substance of the brain in such persons is more gross, and their spirit not so prompt and subtle as is requisite for ready understanding'.[47] In John Lyly's 1589 comedy *Midas*, written for performance at court, two pages, Licio and Petulus, mock Motto, a barber, who has described himself as melancholy: 'Melancholy? Marry, gup, is "melancholy" a word for a barber's mouth? Thou shouldst say "heavy, dull, and doltish". Melancholy is the crest of courtiers' arms, and now every base companion, being in his mubble-fubbles [depression of spirits], says he is melancholy.'[48] Sir Philip Sidney was often regarded as the epitome of courtly values. In his *Arcadia*, his own fictional persona, Philisides, lies 'upon the ground at the foot of a cypress tree, leaning upon his elbow with so deep a melancholy that his senses carried to his mind no delight from any of their objects'.[49] Two cabinet miniatures (small-scale portraits designed to be displayed in a cabinet) by Nicholas Hilliard confirm the identification of melancholy with aristocratic superiority and style. The *Young Man among Roses* (fig. 1) may be Robert Devereux, 2nd Earl of Essex, painted when he was on the rise to become Elizabeth I's chief favourite. He declares his political devotion to Elizabeth by posing as a love-melancholic with his hand on his heart. His black-and-white clothing uses Elizabeth's personal colours, while the white roses that surround him were one of her emblems. In this case the languid posture of the melancholic is deployed at the pinnacle of court politics, to stake a claim to a special place in royal favour. The other Hilliard cabinet miniature (fig. 2) depicts Henry Percy, 9th Earl of Northumberland, known as 'the Wizard Earl' because of his pursuit of arcane knowledge. The globe balanced by a feather in the top right-hand corner of the picture symbolises disdain for worldly things;

1. Melancholy was a mental and physical affliction, but also had social cachet. Here a courtier, probably Robert Devereux, 2nd Earl of Essex, poses as a melancholy lover of Elizabeth I. His hand on his heart and his languid posture are outward signs of inner melancholy.

combined with his black garb, his carelessly unbuttoned doublet, his head on his hand, and his book, they tell us that he is a melancholic scholar.[50] We learn from this image that Hamlet's 'customary suits of solemn black' (1.2.78) signify far more than just the conventional mourning costume of a bereaved son: combined with his later appearances with 'doublet all unbraced' (2.1.75) and reading a book (2.2.166), they identify him as a melancholic intellectual, with all the attendant gifts and afflictions of the condition. The young John Donne was not

2. This miniature of Henry Percy, 9th Earl of Northumberland, illustrates the aristocratic and intellectual glamour of melancholy, visually signified by his book, black clothing, and recumbent posture with head on hand in a private garden. Behind him the world is weighed against a feather as he retreats into the mind.

an earl or a prince, but had himself painted in a similar guise, demonstrating how the identity of intellectual and courtly melancholic had become fashionable and aspirational. In a portrait of around 1595, he sports black clothes, a wide-brimmed hat, and an unlaced shirt, folding his arms in a standard melancholy pose (fig. 3).[51]

Melancholy, then, had lofty associations with elevated rank and intellect; yet at the same time, medical works anchored it very firmly

3. This portrait of the young John Donne declares his social and intellectual aspirations by presenting him as a typical melancholic, with black clothes, an untied collar, a wide-brimmed hat, and folded arms.

in the body. As a bodily fluid, it was thought to have heavy, sinking properties and to thicken the blood: *The Touchstone of Complexions* compared its consistency with gelatin, being 'not unlike unto beasts' feet when they be sodden [boiled] and brought into a jelly, which in eating, cleave to the fingers and lips, as tough as birdlime'.[52] It was a waste product of the bodily processes that maintained vitality, described in *The Salernitan Rule of Health* as 'dregs and dirt removed apart from the principals of life, enemy to joy and liberality, and of near kindred to age and death'.[53] Indeed, at the opposite extreme from its associations with intellectual elevation and social cachet, melancholy was often linked with the lowest bodily functions of digestion and excretion.[54] For Bright, melancholy was an excess of black bile arising from disorders of the spleen, not only affecting the mind with a 'splenetic fog' of 'melancholy vapours rising from that puddle of the spleen', but also causing 'costiveness' (constipation) and 'hardness of stool'.[55] Du Laurens similarly identified a form of melancholy arising from the digestive organs which his translator, Richard Surflet, termed 'the flatuous or windy melancholy' or 'hypochondriac' melancholy (where hypochondria refers to the abdominal organs of the liver, gallbladder, and spleen, not to unfounded anxiety about illness).[56] This hypochondriac melancholy was distinguished from melancholy of the brain and love-melancholy, and its symptoms were primarily physical, including a rumbling belly, breathlessness, and palpitations. Even so, they also included 'fear and sadness [...] as common accidents [attributes] to all manner of melancholy'. Du Laurens regarded this windy melancholy as the most widespread form of the humour, 'so often happening in these miserable times, as that there are not many people which feel not some smatch [touch] thereof'.[57] According to this account, the world was indeed in the grip of a melancholic age, but this was a mass disorder of the bowels as much as of the mind.

The many diverse and even contradictory aspects of melancholy are explored in Shakespeare's *As You Like It* (1600). Orlando arrives in the Forest of Arden suffering from love-melancholy, having been smitten by Rosalind at first sight. Celia discovers him in a stereotypical melancholic posture: 'I found him under a tree, like a dropped acorn [...] There lay he, stretched along like a wounded knight' (3.2.216–17, 222). However, Rosalind (disguised as Ganymede) teases him for insufficient outward symptoms of the condition: 'A lean cheek, which you have not; a blue eye [i.e., eyes ringed with dark circles from sleeplessness] and sunken, which you have not [...]; a beard neglected, which you have not' (3.2.342–4). His affliction has inspired him to write verses, but of such a 'tedious' and 'lame' kind (3.2.143, 154) (the judgement of Rosalind herself, who is the subject of their praises) that they satirise the association of melancholy with creativity and wit:

From the east to western Inde,
No jewel is like Rosalind.
[...]
All the pictures fairest lined
Are but black to Rosalind. (3.2.77-8, 81-2)

And so on.

Melancholy and its manifestations are even more fully explored in the figure of Jaques.[58] He is addressed as 'Monsieur Melancholy' (3.2.272–3), but claims to be no stereotype:

I have neither the scholar's melancholy, which is emulation; nor the musician's, which is fantastical; nor the courtier's, which is proud; nor the soldier's, which is ambitious; nor the lawyer's, which is politic; nor the lady's, which is nice [fastidious]; nor the lover's, which is all these; but it is a melancholy of mine own, compounded of many simples [ingredients], extracted from many objects, and indeed the sundry contemplation of my travels, in which by often rumination wraps me in a most humorous sadness. (4.1.10–18)

This passage exemplifies how discussions of the humours often, paradoxically, combine generalising typology with individualising specificity: in repudiating established types of melancholy, Jaques simultaneously catalogues and acknowledges them. Rosalind retorts by reducing him to the stereotype of the melancholy traveller:

Farewell, Monsieur Traveller. Look you lisp and wear strange suits, disable all the benefits of your own country, be out of love with your nativity [birthplace], and almost chide God for making you that countenance you are; or I will scarce think you have swum in a gundello [ridden in a Venetian gondola] (4.1.29–33).

We mostly trust Rosalind's judgement, and here she clearly regards Jaques as yet another melancholic-as-poseur, like Chapman's

Labesha and Jonson's Matheo. Overall, though, he invites an ambivalent response from the audience. Jaques brings seriousness and depth to *As You Like It*, providing eloquent social commentary and philosophical reflection, most notably in his famous disquisition on the Seven Ages of Man beginning 'All the world's a stage' (2.7.139ff.). Yet at the same time he is a figure of fun, mocked by other characters and often outdone in his duels of wit with them. He is treated much like a court jester by Duke Senior, who says, 'I love to cope him in these sullen fits / For then he's full of matter' (2.2.67). This 'matter' may be wisdom, or may be something far more basic and physical: stripping melancholy down to its most fundamental bodily causes, Jaques's unsociability and malcontentedness may be no more than symptoms of constipation. This is hinted at by his name, an alternative spelling for 'Jakes', Elizabethan slang for a privy. In this play, and especially through this character, Shakespeare explores the 1590s fashion for melancholy in all its multifariousness and ambiguities. As he highlights, while all humoral conditions involved a combination of physical and mental symptoms, this was especially so of melancholy, whose properties and manifestations ranged from the loftiest activities of the mind to the lowest functions of the body.

'Winds, whirlwinds, or tempests': passions and affections

The complex humoral model of relations between mind and body was rendered even more intricate and variable by the workings of the passions, forces similar to the modern concept of the emotions. Elizabethan writers also called them 'motions of the soul', 'affections', or 'perturbations', drawing on various classical and medieval authorities including Aristotle, Cicero, St Augustine, and St Thomas Aquinas.[59] 'Perturbations' were obviously troubling, and so were 'affections': these were not necessarily the feelings of friendly or romantic attachment that we understand by this term today, but rather overpowering emotional states that 'affect' the mind, often in damaging ways. Tarquin, the villain of Shakespeare's *The Rape of*

Lucrece (1594), resolves to violate the heroine because 'nothing can affection's course control, / Or stop the headlong fury of his speed' (ll. 500–1). Far from feeling fondness or kindness towards Lucrece, he is rashly surrendering his reason to his passions, in this case unrestrained lust. *The French Academy* vividly conveyed the turbulence and danger of unregulated affections: 'there are not so many sorts of winds, whirlwinds, or tempests in the sea, as there is variety of motions that come from the affections in our hearts'.[60]

Passions could originate in bodily impulses that affect the mind, like Tarquin's lust, but could also be states of mind that affect the body. Elyot warned that 'affects and passions of the mind' could not only 'bring a man from the use of reason', but also 'annoy the body and shorten the life'. Moreover, if immoderate, harm could be done not only by 'ire or wrath, heaviness or sorrow', but also 'gladness or rejoicing'.[61] William Bullein explained this in *The Government of Health* (1558): in 'the passion of the mind called dread or fear [...] the blood and spirits be drawn inwardly, and maketh the outward parts pale and trembling'; whereas in 'the sudden passion of joy, or gladness' the opposite happens, 'for the heart sendeth forth the spiritual blood, which in weak persons, the heart can never recover again'.[62] Yet as interest in the passions increased through the Elizabethan period, there was a growing recognition that they could be beneficial as well as harmful, and had the potential to be turned to good. *The Anatomy of the Mind* (1576) by Thomas Rogers had two sections, one on 'Perturbations' (defined as 'affections of the mind, not obeying unto the rule of reason') and the other on 'Moral Virtues'. Rogers explained that 'the end of our affections makes them either good, and so to be commended, or bad, and therefore to be dispraised'.[63]

We will explore further in Chapter 3 how Elizabethan interest in and ideas about the passions developed, and the literary innovations that they produced. By 1601, when Thomas Wright published his treatise *The Passions of the Mind*, the body of thought on the subject had become sophisticated and nuanced. Wright used Thomas Aquinas's taxonomy of eleven passions, ten of which fell into antithetical pairs: love and hatred; desire and abomination; delight and sadness; hope and despair; fear and audacity; and ire.[64] However, these tidy categories became more complicated when brought into conjunction with humoral theory, as Wright explained: 'according to the disposition of the heart, humours, and body, diverse sorts of persons be subject to diverse sorts of passions, and the same passion affecteth diverse persons in diverse manners' (68–9). A provocation to anger, for instance, would be slow to take hold in a phlegmatic person, but would produce a rapid and violent response in a choleric person; and just as the humours fluctuated in individuals, so these effects would fluctuate too. Additional factors determining the kinds and degrees of the passions included age, sex, class – 'what affections rule rustics, possess citizens, tyrannise over gentlemen' (80) – and nationality, to each of which Wright said that he could devote a chapter. We have seen that humoral theory could be used for either reductive categorisation of character-types, or for a model of humanity as infinitely diverse and particular; interacting both with these intricacies of humoral theory and with social factors, theories of the passions could encompass multiple and complex forms of interaction between mind, body, and world.[65]

'Nought else but a fault of humour': an Elizabethan body-mind?

Wright took different positions on mind–body relations over the course of *The Passions of the Mind*. Sometimes he represented the passions as mental responses to sensory impulses, 'acts of the sensitive power, or faculty of our soul [. . .] a sensual motion of our appetitive faculty'.[66] Elsewhere, however, he represented the passions as holding sway over the body, via the spirits and humours: 'there is no passion very vehement, but that it altereth extremely some of the four humours of the body [. . .] the spirits and humours wait upon the passions, as their lords and masters' (6–7). Elsewhere again, he represented relations between passions and humours, mind and body, as reciprocal: 'passions engender humours, and humours breed passions' (109).

As mentioned in the Introduction above, some modern scholars contend that mind and body were understood as unified until Descartes declared in 1637 that 'I think, therefore I am'. Certainly, in Descartes the division of mind, soul, and self from the body is clear:

> I saw that I could pretend that I had no body and that there was no world or place for me to be in [. . .] Accordingly this 'I', that is to say, the Soul by which I am what I am, is entirely distinct from the body; and would not stop being everything it is, even if the body were not to exist.[67]

Building on the Aristotelian theory of the embodied soul, the mysteriously immaterial yet material nature of the spirits, and humoral theory, some recent scholars assert a pre-Cartesian integration of mind, body, and world, which they describe as 'psychological materialism', 'psychophysiology', or 'materiality of the passions'.[68] Recent interest in theories of embodied cognition – that is, thought as a neurobiological process within the mind, as formed by sensory experience of the material world, and as expressed in physical action – has also produced assertions of the existence of a holistic early modern 'body-mind'.[69] In early modern theatre, in particular, ideas from the period relating the passions of the mind to physical gestures and sensations have been fruitfully explored as a framework for understanding the performance of emotions and their transmission between actors and audiences.[70]

Much evidence of an integrated view of mind and body can be found in sixteenth-century medical books. The most frequently reprinted of these, Thomas Moulton's *The Mirror of Health*, prescribed two strikingly practical, physical treatments 'For him that hath lost his mind': he should either be dosed for five days with a potion of the juices of marigolds, sage, and wormwood, mixed in wine; or the top of his head should be shaved, a mat of plant fibre should be applied to the bald patch, and after a sleep 'he shall be right weak, and sober enough'.[71] The second most frequently reprinted medical work of the century was Elyot's *The Castle of Health*, which also connected the mind with the body.[72] Haemorrhoids, for instance, could cause not only 'feebleness, tearing of the body, alteration of colour, [and] great pains in the lower parts of the body', but also 'madness, frenzies, and diverse diseases of the head'.[73] Conversely, recommended treatments for 'dolour, or heaviness of the mind' were physiological, including adjustments to the patient's environment – melodious music, good light, and avoidance of 'all things that be noyous [annoying] in sight, smelling and hearing' – and abstention from a long list of foods, including old mutton, hard cheese, hare's flesh, and sturgeon.[74] Catalogues of foods to be consumed or avoided were typical in medical books offering advice on the treatment of melancholy and other afflictions of the mind, as were details of other physiological remedies such as blood-letting, enemas, herbal syrups, and exercise.[75]

Belief in the efficacy of corporeal cures for mental afflictions offered opportunities for self-improvement and self-fashioning: it seemed possible to achieve mental stability and fortitude, to cultivate a desired temperament and identity, and generally to become a better person, simply by adhering to a physical regime of diet and exercise.[76] It followed that, in reverse, mental discipline was necessary to regulate the humours and passions and so maintain physical health. Elyot warned of the 'fevers, [. . .] apoplexies, or privation of senses, trembling palsies, [. . .] frenzies, deformity of visage' afflicting one seized by rage, but these could be avoided if 'before he speak or do anything in anger, he do recite in order, all the letters of the A. B. C., and remove somewhat out of the place that he is in, and seek occasion to be otherwise occupied'.[77] Strength of mind could even repel physical illness: Thomas Lodge (a physician and the author of *Rosalynde*, the source for *As You Like It*) advised during the plague epidemic of 1603 that contagion could be resisted by maintaining 'quiet of mind' and 'avoiding all perturbations of the spirit'.[78]

The darker side of this reciprocity was that a diseased body impaired the mind and vice versa.[79] The French essayist Michel de Montaigne lamented that agues, fevers, and colds all affect our understanding: 'And by consequence, hardly shall a man in all his life find one hour wherein our judgement may always be found in his right bias [course, inclination], our body being subject to so many continual alterations, and stuffed with so diverse sorts of gins [snares] and motions'.[80] In the other direction, according to Andrew Boorde's *A Compendious Regiment or Dietary of Health* (1542, reissued several times up to 1576),[81] 'if the heart and mind be not pleased, nature doth abhor. And if nature do abhor, mortification of the vital and animal and spiritual powers do[es] consequently follow.'[82] Hence, Mosby in the anonymous play *Arden of Faversham* (1590) finds that 'Continual trouble of my moody brain / Feebles my body'.[83]

Yet integration and reciprocity, while a widely held sixteenth-century view of mind–body relations, did not constitute the only model available in the period. Some modern scholars find a separation of mind and body earlier than Descartes, in the years around 1600.[84] Others have highlighted various classical and Christian teachings that were extremely important in the period and that often diverged significantly from the Aristotelian view of the embodied soul and from Galenic humoral medicine.[85] In fact, if we look again at the evidence from sixteenth-century medical works, we find that Galenic thinking often sits alongside assertions that in some circumstances the mind is separate from and superior to the body, and can only heal itself. Although Elyot provided copious lists of dietary and herbal remedies for psychological troubles, he also advised that in such cases 'counsel of physic, as in relieving the body', was secondary to 'remedies of moral philosophy', such as 'the wholesome counsels found in holy scripture, and in the books of moral doctrine'.[86] Bullein's *Government of Health* made an even firmer distinction between ailments of body and mind:

physic unto an extreme troubled mind (say what they list) helpeth as little, as to apply a plaster[87] to the breast, or head, of a dead body, to revocate [call back] the spirits of life or soul again. The sickness of the body must have medicine, the passions of the mind must have good counsel.[88]

Such statements reflect difficulties in reconciling Christian doctrine with Aristotle and Galen, whose theories risked reducing mind–body relations to a kind of symbiotic mechanical system. To do so was to ignore the concept of spiritual health, and of a relationship with God as the essential context for management of both mind and body; it might even appear dangerously like atheism.[89] Bright in his *A Treatise of Melancholy* complained that humoral medicine 'hath caused some to judge more basely of the soul than agreeth with piety or nature, and have accounted all manner [of] affection thereof to be subject to the physician's hand, not considering herein anything divine'. Even 'vice, prophaneness, and neglect of religion and honesty' had been construed as 'nought else but a fault of humour'. However, the body, and even the semi-material spirits, were for Bright merely subordinate instruments of the mind: 'I place the spirit and body both to the mind, as the saw or axe in the workman's hand, or to the lute touched of the musician'.[90] Similarly, Du Laurens, while recommending dietary and other physiological treatments for extreme cases of melancholy, advised that in most patients the 'natural inclinations [...] which proceed of the temperature and shape of the body [...] may be reclaimed and amended by the qualities which we get unto ourselves by moral philosophy, by the reading of good books, and by frequenting the companies of honest and virtuous men'.[91]

It becomes clear, then, that while Aristotelian and Galenic models of the interdependence of mind and body were undoubtedly important in the Elizabethan period, they were only part of the intellectual landscape. Existing alongside them, and sometimes in tension or in conflict with them, were classical and Christian traditions that positioned the mind as detached from, and often elevated above, the body; as engaged in immaterial processes of thought and introspection; and as the location of consciousness and identity. These traditions were revived by the movements that made up the Renaissance and Reformation, and were also elaborated upon and taken in new directions. As we continue to investigate the Elizabethan mind, then, we must consider thought-systems that involved its detachment from, and often opposition to, the body, and that associated it with concepts of the soul and the self.

❧ 2 ❧

Mind against Body
Philosophical and Religious Frameworks

T wo sisters, Pamela and Philoclea, are imprisoned and tortured by their evil aunt Cecropia. They are the heroines of Sir Philip Sidney's prose romance *The New Arcadia*,[1] and they are both in love – Pamela with Musidorus, Philoclea with Pyrocles. However, Cecropia is determined to force one of them to marry her own son, Amphialus, and so subjects them to physical torments, including imprisonment, malnourishment, and bringing a band of 'certain old women (of wicked dispositions)' to beat them with rods. The sisters remain resolute: Philoclea, dwelling on her love for Pyrocles, 'almost forget[s] the pain of her body through the pain of her mind', while Pamela, an even stronger character, defiantly tells Cecropia, 'Thou mayest well wreck this silly [wretched] body, but me thou canst never overthrow.'[2]

Clearly the model of mind–body relations in operation here is not the Aristotelian and Galenic integration explored in Chapter 1 above. We have seen that in Galenic medicine states of mind were determined by the proportions and fluctuations of the humours, and that these were material substances in the body, meaning that many mental afflictions could be treated with physiological remedies. Yet we have also seen instabilities in the application and elaboration of Galenic theory: dramatic performances of humoral types often reduced them to social mannerisms and affectations, behind which a true, essential self might remain hidden, while some passions of the mind were thought to be curable only by mental, not physiological, treatments.

In this episode from the *New Arcadia* the mind is emphatically separated from the body: Philoclea is able to ignore her physical state by withdrawing into mental contemplation, while Pamela asserts an inner self – 'me' – which is distinct from and opposed to her body. The *Arcadia* was by no means exceptional in asserting this division. Thomas Rogers, for example, explained that he had written *The Anatomy of the Mind*, his treatise on the passions, because 'he which thoroughly would know himself, must as well know his body as his mind', but this was in order to assert the supremacy of the mind: 'The body to put him in mind of his slavery; the mind of his sovereignty. The body of his misery; the mind of his felicity. The body of his mortality; the mind of his eternity.'[3] These dichotomies drew on deep-rooted philosophical and theological traditions – including Platonism, Stoicism, and Christian spirituality – which gained new impetus and took on new forms in the sixteenth century, as we will explore in this chapter. In both their ancient and revived manifestations, these thought-systems encouraged the separation of mind and body long before Cartesian dualism. They attributed to each human being a defining inner essence that was distinct from, and elevated above, the body and the material world, denominating this sometimes as the mind (as in Philoclea's obliviousness to bodily pain because of the 'pain of her mind'), sometimes the soul, and sometimes the self (Pamela's 'me' who cannot be overthrown).

'Myself am centre of my circling thought': mind, soul, and self

In the Elizabethan period, the terms mind, soul, and self often overlapped. The mind, then as now, was the place where thought happens, a mysterious inner space whose workings may or may not be detectable in outward signs. A 1570s autobiography by the music tutor

Thomas Whythorne describes courtship strategies that depended on concealing his own intentions while attempting, mostly unsuccessfully, to read the equally hidden thoughts of the women concerned: 'she seemed that she would have me to think that she bare me some good will'.[4] Sir Philip Sidney's sonnet sequence *Astrophil and Stella* similarly describes how the 'curious wits' try to read, but misconstrue, his 'dull pensiveness' and 'dark abstracted guise' (both works are discussed further in Chapter 9 below).[5]

In both these cases it is implied that true thoughts and feelings lie within: that the mind is not only an inner space, but a kernel of personal authenticity which outward appearance might conceal or falsify. Similarly, Nicholas Hilliard's 1578 miniature portrait of the eighteen-year-old Francis Bacon is inscribed '*Si tabula daretur digna Animum mallem*' (fig. 4). This may be translated either as 'I would rather it were my mind, given a fitting portrait of it' (imagining Bacon as the speaker) or as 'Had I the gift of portraiture worthy of it, I would rather portray the mind' (with Hilliard as speaker).[6] Either way, the message is that even Hilliard's superlatively painted image of Bacon's face cannot depict his mind, where his true essence lies. Shakespeare's Lucrece finds an even harsher incongruity between face and mind when she compares the 'fair' face of Sinon, the Greek who deceived the Trojans into accepting the wooden horse, with his 'wicked mind' (ll. 1530, 1540).

Perhaps writing was more able than painting to represent accurately the inner workings of the mind. Sir William Cornwallis published two volumes of *Essays* which he presented as 'the inward discourse of an honest mind';[7] more intimately, Elizabeth Grymeston presented an advice book compiled for her son before her death as 'the true portraiture of thy mother's mind'.[8] The Elizabethans, like us, also used the word 'self' to refer to this authentic inner essence. Sidney in *The Defence of Poesy* (written *c.* 1580, published 1595) praises both the 'inward self' and 'outward government' of Aeneas, while Spenser in Sonnet 45 of his *Amoretti* (1595) asks his mistress to look into his 'inward selfe'.[9] Mind and self are closely related in

4. The Latin inscription on this miniature of the young Francis Bacon ('*Si tabula daretur digna Animum mallem*') asserts that the mind eludes depiction. It translates as 'I would rather it were my mind, given a fitting portrait of it', or 'Had I the gift of portraiture worthy of it, I would rather portray the mind'.

the 1555 play *Jack Juggler*,[10] whose title character imitates the clothes, looks, and behaviour of Jenkin Careaway, a page. At first Careaway is baffled to find himself doubled: 'How may it then be that he should be I / Or I not myself?' Yet Jack Juggler can only simulate his outward identity; Careaway feels 'sure of this in my mind / That I did in no place leave myself behind'.[11]

Careaway experiences an inner conviction of selfhood similar to that described by Spenser in *The Faerie Queene* (1590). He writes that we each have a 'Genius' or inner spirit which 'is our Selfe, whom though we doe not see, / Yet each doth in him selfe it well perceiue to bee'.[12] Spenser's self is self-aware: this Genius, or self, or mind, is able to regard itself. The maxim *nosce teipsum*, or 'know thyself', was said to have been inscribed on the temple of Apollo at Delphi, and was repeated in many of the Latin works used in Elizabethan grammar schools. It inspired a genre of moral treatises on the obligation to pursue self-knowledge, as well as Sir John Davies's philosophical poem *Nosce teipsum* (1599), in which he explains that affliction

> within lists [limits] my ranging mind hath brought,
> That now beyond myself I list not go;
> Myself am centre of my circling thought,
> Only myself I study, learn, and know.[13]

Shakespeare too participated in this cultural preoccupation: fifteen allusions have been identified in his works to knowing or not knowing oneself.[14]

Elizabethan writers frequently expressed this reflexive self-consciousness in phrases like 'myself myself', 'himself himself', or 'herself herself', where the self is both subject and object.[15] George Puttenham in *The Art of English Poesy* quotes approvingly from a poem by Sir Walter Ralegh: 'Yet when I saw myself to you was true, / I loved myself, because myself loved you.'[16] Another example is the unrequited lover Sir George Rodney, who asked in a versified suicide note in 1601: 'Where shall I fly, myself to shun? / [Ay] me, myself my self must kill'.[17] In such doubling formulations the mind seems enclosed and detached, mirroring itself or looping round on itself, while at the same time bifurcated and self-divided.

The linked concepts of mind and self were also associated with a third important term: the soul. In the seventeenth century, philosophical discourse shifted from the term 'soul' (in Latin, *anima*) to the more secular term 'mind' (*mens*) for the human sense of inner being; but for the Elizabethans the two frequently overlapped.[18] In Thomas Thomas's 1587 Latin dictionary, *mens* is defined as both 'the mind, the wit, understanding', and 'the highest and chief part of the soul' – that is, the rational or intellective soul as defined by Aristotle (see Chapter 1 above).[19] Defining features of the soul were its sacredness (implanting in the individual something of the divine) and immortality (outliving the body), properties that encouraged its identification with an authentic, immaterial inner essence, and hence with the self and mind. The two philosophical poems *Nosce teipsum* by Sir John Davies and *Mirum in modum* (1602) by his namesake John Davies of Hereford treat the soul as equivalent to the mind, not least in its self-awareness and self-scrutiny: 'the soul herself doth know, / Her own effects she to herself discloseth, / So to herself, herself herself doth show'.[20] For the Elizabethans, concepts of mind, soul, and self entwined, because of their shared associations with interiority, immateriality, and identity. To explore this further, we must look back to some of the earlier philosophical and theological traditions that laid the foundations for Elizabethan thought.

'The inner man': ancient traditions of mind–body division

Alongside the influence of Aristotle, many other sixteenth-century ideas about mind, soul, and self were built on foundations laid by his teacher Plato (*c.* 428–347 BCE). Plato discusses these concepts across various works, often in the persona of his own teacher Socrates (*c.*470–399 BCE), and in terms significantly different from Aristotle's theory of the embodied soul or mind. In *Alcibiades I*, Socrates discusses the Delphic injunction to 'know thyself', and argues that the essence of the self is the rational soul.[21] In *Phaedo*, as Socrates prepares for death, he again argues that the soul is the essence of a human being and transcends the body by surviving beyond death. These concepts of the essential, transcendent soul relate to Plato's general proposition that the material world is only a pale shadow of the real world, which exists on a higher, metaphysical plane only dimly perceptible to us. That higher plane is the abode of the true essences of goodness, beauty, justice, and so on, which Plato called the Ideas or Forms, and which can be approached by means of the intellect but not the senses.[22] In the *Symposium*, Socrates teaches that true love must look towards this higher plane and charts an upward trajectory for the mind, away from the body and material things, as the lover moves from physical attraction to one individual, to appreciation of all beauty in the material world, to spiritual understanding of the divine essence of beauty.

In these metaphysical contexts Plato defined the soul against the body, but elsewhere he explored tensions between rational and bodily impulses within the soul or mind itself, using various analogies and metaphors. In the *Republic*, the mind is a microcosm of the state: just as the state has three classes – the workers, the 'auxiliaries' or militia, and the rulers – so the mind has three parts – the bodily appetites, the passions, and their governor, the intellect. In another image, Plato compares the bodily appetites to a many-headed beast, the passions to a lion, and the rational part of the mind to 'the inner man', which, again, must govern the other parts.[23] In *Phaedrus*, the soul is a chariot driven by reason, who must control the dark horse of appetite that pulls against the white horse of will. Elsewhere, in *Timaeus*, the imagery is from human anatomy, as the immortal soul, residing in the head, must rule over the mortal soul, whose seat is the body.

Plato's teachings on the relation between mind, soul, and body were not entirely consistent across his works, but they established ideas of the soul as superior to the body, able to exist independently from the body, and made up of potentially conflicting faculties. The mind was identified sometimes with reason, the highest part of the soul, responsible for governing physical, sensual impulses, and sometimes with the soul as a whole, prone to its own internal warfare between higher and lower impulses. Either way, the mind in Platonism was consistently elevated above the body, and it was always through intellectual transcendence of the physical world that ascent towards understanding the Ideas or Forms was to be achieved.[24]

Although Aristotle differed from Plato in emphasising the embodiment of the soul and mind, even his thinking tended to distinguish the mind from the body in some of its details. As we saw in Chapter 1, he defined three levels of the soul: the vegetative or nutritive soul, serving basic functions of vitality, growth, and movement in all living things including plants; the sensitive soul, able to process sensory experiences, present in animals and humans but not in plants; and the rational or intellective soul, present in humans alone.[25] This rational part of the soul was readily identified with the mind; it was 'the part of the soul by which the soul both knows and understands', and was named by Aristotle *nous*, frequently translated into English as 'mind' or 'intellect'.[26] Its definition as the highest level of the soul implicitly elevated the mind over the body and made it its rightful ruler. Moreover, although in general Aristotle maintained that 'the soul is not separable from the body', he made an exception for its rational part: 'nor is it [...] reasonable for it to be mixed with the body, since then it would come to be qualified in a certain way, either cold or hot, and there would be an organ for it, as there is for the perceptual faculty. As things are, though, there is none.'[27] In a passage later seized upon by Christian commentators, he even seemed to assert not only the immateriality but also the immortality of this highest part of the soul: 'this reason is separate and unaffected and unmixed [...] having been separated, this alone is just what it is, and this alone is deathless and everlasting'.[28] Here, the mind or rational soul becomes a transcendent spiritual essence.

Aristotle's works dominated the arts courses in European universities well into the seventeenth century, while those of Plato were also widely known, especially following the reinvigoration of Neoplatonism in fifteenth-century Florence by Marsilio Ficino and Pico della Mirandola. Interest also grew in Stoicism, a school of philosophy founded in Athens in the third century BCE and transmitted to the sixteenth century mainly via the Roman authors Cicero (106–43 BCE) and Seneca (*c.* 4 BCE–65 CE)[29] and the Greek author Epictetus (55–135 CE).[30] For Stoics, everything happens according to the plan of divine reason, which we must accept and with which we must align our own reason. Happiness lies in the pursuit of virtue, and in treating as indifferent all things that do not contribute to virtue and are not under our control. Failures of reason produce the passions, which are errors of judgement and diseases of the soul, and must be eradicated.[31] As Seneca wrote in his essay 'De tranquillitate animi' ('On Tranquillity of Mind'), the best defence against mental agitation is 'to examine our own selves' and to bear all vicissitudes with resilience and wisdom: 'no state is so bitter that a calm mind cannot find in it some consolation [. . .] Apply reason to difficulties'. 'Most of all,' he went on, 'the mind must be withdrawn from external interests into itself.'[32] Epictetus similarly distinguished between external events, which are beyond our control and must be calmly endured with strength of mind, and our own conduct, which we should manage by rigorous self-examination and self-discipline. Central to this is *proairesis*, the power to make the right choices, informed by reason.[33] Epictetus had been born a slave, and while in slavery had his leg broken. In his *Discourses*, he imagines a dialogue that prefigures the exchange between Sidney's Pamela and Cecropia: ' "I will fetter you." What is that you say, man? fetter *me*? My leg you will fetter, but my moral purpose [*proairesis*] not even Zeus himself has power to overcome. "I will throw you into prison." My paltry body, rather!'[34]

Early Christian writers also embraced and developed the concept of the 'inner man'. St Paul (died *c.* 62–65 CE) urged mental resistance to sinful bodily impulses: 'For I delight in the Law of God, concerning the inner man: but I see another law in my members, rebelling against the law of my mind, and leading me captive unto the law of sin [. . .] I myself in my mind serve the Law of God, but in my flesh the law of sin.'[35] St Augustine (354–430 CE) similarly advocated government of bodily desires by the rational soul, and looking within to seek truth and wisdom;[36] while *De consolatione philosophiae* (*The Consolation of Philosophy*), written while its author Boethius (480–525? CE) was imprisoned for treason and facing execution, drew on Platonism and Stoicism to imagine a dialogue with Lady Philosophy, who teaches mental fortitude to transcend physical suffering and material adversity.[37]

These various strands of ancient thought about mind/body divisions intertwined to influence Elizabethan thinking. At the same time, important medieval traditions also had a continuing influence, though reshaped by the intellectual and religious innovations of the sixteenth century.

'Battle and combat': psychomachia

Allegory, especially the use of personifications to represent abstract moral qualities, was widely used in classical and medieval culture.[38] Prudentius's *Psychomachia* (*c.* 408–09), whose title means 'conflict of the soul or mind', inaugurated a particular Christian form of allegory that became popular in medieval drama: the combat between figures of good and evil for possession of a generic human figure. Examples include *The Castle of Perseverance* (*c.* 1400–25), *Mankind* (*c.* 1461–85), and *Everyman* (*c.* 1480–1500). When such plays made spiritual properties and mental faculties into externalised dramatic characters, they embodied them on stage, in one way blurring the distinction between mind and body. Yet at the same time the dramatised battle was typically between spiritual aspirations and physical, worldly appetites, constructing mind and body as antagonists.

Allegory and psychomachia continued to be prevalent in early Elizabethan plays – usually described as morality plays or interludes (short plays for performance in the intervals of banquets) – and remained in use in various forms throughout the period (see Chapters 9 and 10 below).[39] However, innovations arose from the influence of Calvinist theology, which taught that most of humanity were damned, that only a chosen few, the Elect, would be saved, and that these fates had been predetermined by God since the beginning of time. Some morality plays of the 1560s and 1570s accordingly shifted away from psychomachia within a single protagonist to two protagonists, one ascending upwards towards heaven, the other downwards towards hell, but still assailed by competing personifications of virtue (associated with transcendence of the body) and vice (associated with bodily appetites).[40] Thus, *The Trial of Treasure* (1567, attributed to William Wager) depicts the opposed fates of Lust, an unregenerate pleasure-seeker who succumbs to carnal and material temptations, and Just (Righteousness), a member of the godly elect who exercises self-control to achieve the treasures of the spirit. The difference between them lies in their state of mind: Lust is an example of 'evil men' who 'Are subjects and slaves to their lusts and affection', whereas Just has 'battle and combat / Against the cogitations that inwardly spring'.[41] God's Visitation, representing plague, finds Just immune to his attempts to inflict bodily pain because of his resolute mental state (E1v). Just is directed and supported by Contentation, who personifies the invincible state of mental and spiritual serenity achieved by the justified or saved; she declares,

Alas, should we not have that estimation
Which God hath prepared for his dear elect?
Should not our minds rest in full contentation,
Having trust in this treasure, most high in respect? (D1r)[42]

There were continuities between psychomachic drama and the emerging discourse on the passions of the mind. In Wager's *Enough Is as Good as a Feast* (1568), the two protagonists, Worldly Man and Heavenly Man, are accompanied by two opposed camps of corrupters and counsellors who resemble the 'Perturbations' and 'Moral Virtues' listed in the two sections of *The Anatomy of the Mind*, the 1576 prose treatise on the passions by Thomas Rogers. Indeed, two specific properties, Covetousness and Temerity, appear in both works.[43] Rogers's catalogues of good and bad passions also resemble the allegorical characters in another Wager play, *The Longer Thou Livest the More Fool Thou Art* (1569), where the false friends of Moros (Folly) are Idleness, Wrath, Incontinency, Ignorance, Cruelty, and Impiety, while his virtuous counsellors are Exercitation,[44] Discipline, and Piety. The influence of the psychomachic tradition on Rogers is clear when he writes: 'except there be passions and perturbations in man, there is no place for virtue; even as there is no victory, where there is no adversary'.[45] Perturbations and virtues were opposed types of passion, locked in combat: Dread, for example, was a perturbation and 'token of an abject mind and servile disposition', but all philosophers agreed that its opposite, Hope, 'of all passions was the sweetest, and most pleasant'.[46] The psychomachic model of strife between vices and virtues contributed to developing ideas of the passions as leading either downwards, to carnal vices, or upwards, to raise the mind above the temptations of the body and the world.

'Tranquillity of mind': the iconography of martyrdom

Martyrdom was another medieval theme that endured into the Elizabethan period while reflecting new religious and intellectual frameworks. The popular medieval genre of hagiography (saints' lives) offered sensational narratives that explored complex relations between mind (or soul, or self) and body. Many such stories were known from *The Golden Legend* by Jacobus de Voragine, compiled around 1265, and printed in an English version by William Caxton which went through six editions between 1483 and 1527.[47] Its tales of female martyrs presented particularly intense contrasts between the injured body and the pure mind or soul. St Lucy is typical: threatened with multiple rape, she declares to her pagan oppressor:

> The body is not defiled [...] unless the mind consents. If you have me ravished against my will, my chastity will be doubled and the crown will be mine. You will never be able to force my will. As for my body, here it is, ready for every torture. What are you waiting for?[48]

Pollution of the body is presented as irrelevant to inner sanctity, or even enhancing it; damage inflicted on a saint's body paradoxically serves as a legible sign of her inner strength and virtue.

The Golden Legend and other miraculous saints' lives were suppressed in post-Reformation England as idolatrous and superstitious. However, their models of heroism and of mind–body relations had laid down deep cultural roots and endured in various forms. Their influence was evident in the secular genres of female complaint and romance, in the sufferings of heroines like Shakespeare's Lucrece or Sidney's Pamela. In the *New Arcadia*, Pamela's constant and virtuous love for Musidorus is a kind of secular faith and endows her with powers like those of medieval virgin-martyrs: endurance of bodily torment, articulacy, self-righteousness, resistance to conversion, and assertion of an essential inner 'me'.[49] Yet the iconography of martyrdom was not merely secularised; it persisted and evolved in religious contexts too, fuelled by the tumultuous religious upheavals and persecutions of the sixteenth century. The martyr's inward imperviousness to physical suffering was a recurrent theme of John Foxe's *Acts and Monuments*, popularly known as the *Book of Martyrs*, one of the most widely read books in Elizabethan England. Foxe gathered accounts of persecuted Protestants, principally during the militantly Catholic reign of Mary I (1553–58), into a prodigious work that went through four editions between 1563 and 1583, successively revised and expanded to reach an extraordinary 3,800,000 words. Copies were available in parish churches alongside the Bible, and in schools, public institutions, and private libraries, and were standard reading in godly households.[50] The Protestant gentlewoman Lady Margaret Hoby, for instance, recorded in her spiritual journal hearing readings from Foxe by her servants while sewing or preparing for bed.[51]

Foxe asserted that, unlike medieval saints' lives, his narratives did not contain 'anything fabulous' but were completely true, deriving from documentary sources.[52] Even so, like saints' lives they represented true faith as manifested in endurance of violent assaults upon the body, often verbally described in gruesome detail and visually depicted in woodcut illustrations. Readers could marvel at such examples as Thomas Haukes, sentenced to burning at the stake, whose friends

> being feared with the sharpness of the punishment, which he was going to, privily desired that in the midst of the flame he would show them some token if he could, whereby they might be more certain whether the pain of such burning were so great, that a man might not therein keep his mind quiet and patient. Which thing he promised them to do, and so secretly between them it was agreed, that if the rage of the pain were tolerable and might be suffered, then he should lift up his hands above his head toward heaven before he gave up the ghost.

Sure enough,

> when his speech was taken away by violence of the flame, his skin also drawn together, and his fingers consumed with the fire, so that now all men thought certainly he had been gone, suddenly and contrary to all expectation, the blessed servant of God, being mindful of his promise afore made, reached up his hands burning on a light fire (which was marvellous to behold) over his head to the living God, and with great rejoicing, as seemed, struck or clapped them three times together. At the sight whereof there followed such applause and outcry of the people, and especially of them which understood the matter, that the like hath not commonly been heard: and so the blessed martyr of Christ, straightway sinking down into the fire, gave up his spirit, *anno* 1555, June 10.[53]

Haukes's unforgettable physical gesture, raising and clapping his flaming hands, was both a graphic means of making his inner fortitude externally visible, and an assertion of the independence of his resolute mind and departing spirit from the mere shell of his body (fig. 5).[54] As Foxe wrote in a summarising 'consideration of all the blessed martyrs', 'although they suffered in their bodies yet rejoiced

The defcription of the burning of Thomas Haukes in Effex,
at a towne called Coxehall. Anno. 1555. the. 10. of Iune.

O Lord, Receiue my fpirite.

5. Accounts of martyrdom emphasised the triumph of the mind over physical pain. Thomas Haukes, a Protestant burned at the stake in the reign of Mary I, raised and clapped his flaming hands to show his friends that 'in the midst of the flame' his mind was 'quiet and patient'.

they in their spirits, and albeit they were persecuted of men, yet were they comforted of the Lord with such inward joy and peace of conscience'.[55]

The mind was also central to Foxe's accounts of Catholic interrogations that sought to extract from Protestants incriminating confessions of their inward beliefs and 'heresies'. Anne Askew (born c. 1521), a radical Protestant, fell foul of a reversion to religious conservatism in the closing years of Henry VIII's reign. In 1545–46, she was twice arrested and cross-examined, then tortured on the rack in the Tower of London, and finally burned at the stake at Smithfield.

Foxe draws on her own account of her interrogation by Edmund Bonner, Bishop of London, and other priests, who 'tempted me much to know my mind'.[56] Askew responded by either quoting scripture, or claiming female incapacity ('I told him [that] I was but a woman and knew not the course of schools'), or remaining laconic ('I answered again that, that I have said, I have said'). Bonner exhorted her 'that I should utter all things that burdened my conscience [...] and therefore he bade me say my mind without fear. I answered him that I had naught to say: for my conscience (I thanked God) was burdened with nothing.' As her questioners sought to expose her inward thoughts and beliefs, Askew repeatedly frustrated them, instead protecting and defending her private conscience as answerable only to God.[57]

While Protestants were stirred by Foxe's stories of heroic endurance, the tradition of martyrdom became more important than ever to Elizabethan Catholics. A decade before Bishop Bonner strove to extract the hidden contents of Anne Askew's mind, Sir Thomas More had been executed for resisting all efforts to induce him 'either precisely to confess the Supremacy [i.e. that Henry VIII, not the Pope, was Supreme Head of the Church in England], or directly to deny it'.[58] His persecution for refusing to reveal the contents of his mind made him a saintly hero to Catholics, especially during the later decades of Elizabeth's reign. The Pope's excommunication of Elizabeth in 1570, exempting Catholics from obedience to the Queen, followed by the arrival of Jesuit missionary priests from 1580 onwards, led to the criminalisation of Catholics as traitors, and the state increasingly used interrogation and torture in efforts to extract their thoughts and plans. Cardinal William Allen's account (published in 1582) of the martyrdom of the Jesuit missionary Edmund Campion (1540–81) described how he 'was diverse times racked, to wring out of him by intolerable torments whose houses he frequented, by whom he was relieved, whom he had reconciled [converted], what he knew (a strange case) by their confessions, when, which way, for what purpose, by what commission, he came into the realm, how, where, and by whom, he printed and dispersed his books and such like'.[59]

English Protestants increasingly regarded Catholics as profoundly duplicitous, not only addicted to outward shows over inner truth in their forms of worship, but also outwardly protesting their political loyalty while inwardly concealing treasonous intentions. The Act against Recusants of 1593 accused them of 'hiding their most detestable and devilish purposes under a false pretext of religion and conscience' as they 'secretly wander and shift from place to place within this realm, to corrupt and seduce her majesty's subjects, and to stir them to sedition and rebellion'.[60] A drawing in a manuscript miscellany by Stephen Batman, a Church of England clergyman, gives visual form to this suspicion of the hidden minds of Catholics (fig. 6). A man and woman pose as if for a portrait of a respectable married couple, but their secret thoughts are sketched in as tiny figures and scenes. Above

6. This drawing from a manuscript miscellany shows an apparently respectable couple whose minds harbour treacherous, sinful thoughts and secret Catholic sympathies (above the man's ear, a tiny figure of a priest celebrates Mass). The man plots invasion and sedition; the woman dreams of appropriated estates and illicit sexual pleasures.

the man's ear is a priest celebrating Mass, and the accompanying verses confirm that the couple are 'of upstart gentility, oppressing clergy for Romish liberty'. The images in the man's mind of ships, a burning town, and people fighting presumably represent secret plots of sedition and invasion. A devil lets Discord down from his ear, below which Flattery holds a horse representing Will. Meanwhile, the woman dreams of appropriated estates (represented by buildings, trees, and a deer park) and lechery (represented by a couple in bed), while Deceit, in the form of a mouse, slips out of her lips. She and her husband are social-climbing gentry who conceal in their minds secret vices and secret sympathies with England's Catholic enemies at home and abroad: 'these faces deformed bid England beware'.[61]

There was particular Protestant distrust of the Catholic practices of 'reservation' and 'equivocation'. Some Catholics argued that if they were confronted with the 'bloody question' – whether, if there were a Catholic invasion of England, they would place loyalty to the Pope above loyalty to the Queen – it was justifiable to reserve their private thoughts to themselves, and to evade or withhold an answer. Allen deplored the hypothetical 'bloody question' as an 'unreasonable search of men's consciences', which were answerable only to God, and complained that Catholics were being tyrannically persecuted 'not only for our pretended deeds, words, or any exterior acts, which only are punishable by man's laws, but for our very cogitations gathered by false suppositions and undue means'. A marginal note on this passage protested succinctly: 'Thoughts punished by death.'[62]

At the same time Allen's account of the interrogations, tortures, and execution of Campion asserted his absolute truthfulness throughout:

The meaning of the words he both then and afterward, as well at the bar, as at his death uttered most sincerely: and for the rest if they had torn him in ten thousand pieces or [dis]stilled him to the quintessence, in that holy breast they should never have found any piece of those feigned treasons.[63]

Like both medieval hagiographers and Foxe, Catholic martyrologists read the scarred and broken bodies of the persecuted as simultaneously meaning-laden and dispensable: both texts of their inner truth and sanctity, and discarded husks from which their pure, unified, unbroken spirits ascended above.[64] Allen also quoted from the first-person account of another martyred priest, Alexander Brian, of how 'my hands and feet were violently stretched and racked, and my adversaries fulfilled their wicked lust, in practising their cruel tyranny upon my body', yet he felt nothing but 'quietness of heart, and tranquillity of mind'.[65] Both Catholic and Protestant martyrdom narratives offered striking images of the mind's transcendence of the body.

'In a secret closet': religious introspection

Despite these similarities in the genre of martyrology, there were of course many profound doctrinal differences between the Catholic and Protestant Churches. Among the most significant was the Protestant belief that since salvation, or justification, was in God's power alone, a sinner could not earn it by their own agency, such as by participation in church rituals and pilgrimages, or by charitable works. If justification came, it would be as a life-changing conversion experience, during which the chosen one was the passive object of divine grace.[66] Nevertheless, much spiritual work was required to acknowledge one's own sinfulness and dependence on God's mercy, and to make the soul fit and ready for justification; then to discern whether God had chosen to bestow justification and to achieve full conviction of salvation. These processes demanded both rigorous self-discipline and constant self-monitoring.[67]

The principal doctrinal work of Jean Calvin was *Institutio Christianae religionis* (1536, usually known in English as *Institutes of the Christian Religion*), whose English translation of 1561 went through multiple editions.[68] Calvin urged vigorous soul-searching to achieve consciousness of sin and submission to God's power to save or punish: 'let even the perfectest man descend into his own conscience, and call his doings to account [...] every man may be a witness to himself that will with a right eye behold himself'.[69] English followers of Calvin such as the prolific theologian William Perkins echoed this emphasis on scrutiny and management of the mind and soul. Perkins distinguished between outward sin, which was committed by the body, and inward sin, which was 'of the mind, will, and affection. The actual sin of the mind is the evil thought or intent thereof, contrary to God's law.' Divine grace was received in the form of 'an illumination of the mind, whereby it acknowledgeth the known truth of the word of God'. Each individual should search within for 'signs and testimonies in ourselves to gather what was the eternal counsel of God concerning our salvation'.[70]

This imperative to descend within made private prayer central to Protestant devotional practice, along with meditation, the practice of focused mental contemplation of religious themes, sometimes assisted by reading, and often shading into prayer.[71] An official homily on prayer – one of the homilies issued by the Elizabethan government to be read at Sunday church services – defined three kinds of prayer, each based on scriptural precedent: public prayer; prayer that was vocal but private ('the secret uttering of the griefs and desires of the heart with words, but yet in a secret closet or some solitary place'); and silent, private, 'mental' prayer ('that is to say, the devout lifting up of the mind to God').[72] Manuals for private prayer and meditation became extremely popular: by 1603, there were multiple editions of Katherine Parr's *Prayers or Meditations* (1545), John Bradford's *Godly Meditations* (1567), Henry Bull's *Christian Prayers and Holy Meditations* (1568), and Edward Dering's *Godly Private Prayers for Householders to Meditate Upon, and to Say in their Families* (1574).[73] Prayer was mental work: Bull repeatedly exhorted the practitioner of prayer to 'call to mind' examples of their sinfulness and God's goodness, and to implore God to enlighten their minds. Before meditating, the reader should 'Muse a while, how much the light and eye of the mind and soul is better than of the body [...]

beasts have bodily eyes as well as men, but men only have eyes of the mind, and that, such as are godly wise'.[74] Lady Grace Mildmay of Apethorpe in Northamptonshire was trained from early youth to meditate daily, and in 1617 as she looked back over her life described her method. Having retired to her chamber, she would empty her mind of all 'desire and remembrance of earthly things [. . .] and all loathsome, vain, and fruitless apprehensions and fears'. In response, God would sometimes give 'such plenty of divine matter unto my mind, as I was not able to comprehend'. Her meditations were not only 'the exercise of my mind from my youth until this date', but 'the consolation of my soul, the joy of my heart, and the stability of my mind'.[75]

This practice of withdrawal from company to a private closet for introspection was widespread, but even the public space of the church was redesigned to encourage inward reflection. In the early years of the Elizabethan Protestant Settlement, churches were visually transformed as statues of saints and other church fittings were taken down and often publicly burned. Colourful wall-paintings of religious scenes were whitewashed over, and some stained-glass windows were removed. Official church documents ordered that 'all images, shrines, all tables, candlesticks [. . .], pictures, paintings, and all other monuments of feigned miracles, pilgrimages, idolatry and superstition' were to be 'removed, abolished, and destroyed'. Places where there had been images were to be 'made smooth as though no image had been there', for example, by being 'pargetted over with lime'. This was a campaign not merely to remove the material trappings of pre-Reformation worship, but to intervene in the minds of parishioners, attempting to wipe the former contents of churches from their memories. In part, this reflected a new emphasis on words – the vernacular Bible, sermons, print publications supporting Protestant piety – as the instruments of faith. However, the new visual blankness of church interiors also encouraged withdrawal into the mind, from outer sensory stimuli to inner contemplation in pursuit of a personal relationship with God.[76]

In its emphasis on self-scrutiny and mental prayer, Elizabethan Protestantism asserted itself as a faith of the mind and spirit, and this often involved setting itself against Catholicism as supposedly mired in idolatry and ritual, materialism and sensuality. Yet Counter-Reformation Catholicism also developed its own rigorous disciplines of mental withdrawal and introspection, largely based on the *Spiritual Exercises* (1548) of Ignatius Loyola, founder of the Society of Jesus. This manual of structured meditation and self-examination offered a four-week programme designed to induce profound inner change. The programme was intended to establish ongoing daily habits of self-scrutiny and mental prayer, and could be repeated at any time.[77] It was an essential part of the training of Jesuits, and was used by the Elizabethan missionaries both as an aid in the conversion of others and to reinforce their own inner resources. One of their number, John Gerard, recorded both numerous occasions when he gave the *Exercises* to prospective converts, and several periods in prison when he maintained his own spiritual strength by working through them from memory.[78]

The *Spiritual Exercises* inspired a genre of meditation manuals that was popular across Counter-Reformation Europe, including Luis de Granada's *Book of Prayer and Meditation* (1554), Gaspar Loarte's *Exercise of a Christian Life* (1579), and *Spiritual Combat* (1589, attributed to Lorenzo Scupoli). They were distributed in England by missionary priests and inspired English translations and imitations, including the *Christian Directory* (also known as the *Book of Resolution*) by the English Jesuit Robert Persons. English Protestants craving guides to meditation formed an eager market for expurgated versions: there were numerous editions of a Protestant adaptation of Richard Hopkins's 1582 translation of Luis de Granada, and of Edmund Bunny's Protestant version of Persons's *Christian Directory*.[79] Although Protestant polemicists tended to castigate Catholic worship as excessively invested in ritual, material trappings, and external show, mental prayer was evidently just as important to Elizabethan Catholics as to Protestants, even to the extent that Protestant practices of mental prayer drew upon Catholic models.

'The beauty that is seen with the eyes of the mind': Neoplatonism

The aspects of Reformation and Counter-Reformation teaching that emphasised detachment of the mind from the body converged with revivals of compatible classical philosophies. Following the recovery of Plato's works by Italian humanist scholars, his ideas became widely available in Christianising commentaries, print editions of the Greek texts, and Latin translations (of which at least 145 editions were printed between around 1474 and 1600).[80] Erasmus referred frequently to various works by Plato in his *Enchiridion militis christiani* (*The Manual of the Christian Knight*, 1503), a guide to Christian living which went through multiple Latin and English editions over the course of the sixteenth century. It presented human life as a constant psychomachic struggle between 'outward and inward man', a 'war against thy self', in which 'the chief hope and comfort of victory is if thou know thyself to the uttermost', invoking the doctrine of *nosce teipsum*. The mind must be set above the body: 'If thy body had not been added to thee, thou haddest been a celestial or godly thing. If this mind had not been grafted in thee, plainly thou haddest been a brute beast.' As well as Plato, Erasmus cited St Paul to assimilate classical philosophy with Christian doctrine: 'That the philosophers call reason, that calleth Paul sometime the spirit, sometime the inner man, otherwhile the law of the mind. That they call affection he calleth sometime the flesh, sometime the body, another time the outer man and the law of the members.' The Christian goal, informed by Platonism, was to live 'inwardly in the spirit', not 'outwardly in the body'.[81]

Platonism also reached the Elizabethans via Baldessare Castiglione's *Il cortegiano* (1528), a discussion of courtly conduct which circulated extensively across Europe in various editions and languages, and was translated into English in 1561 by Sir Thomas Hoby as *The Book of the Courtier*. Castiglione's ideal courtier was required to pursue love by elevating his mind to a metaphysical plane, as advocated in Plato's *Symposium*: 'instead of going out of his wit with thought, as he must do that will consider the bodily beauty, he may come into his wit, to behold the beauty that is seen with the eyes of the mind'. He must ascend a metaphorical 'stair' from appreciation of the beauty of one woman, to appreciation of all beauty in the material world, to communion with heavenly beauty.[82] This Neoplatonic idealisation of a love that transcends physicality became a central theme of Elizabethan poetry. Petrarch (1304–74) had been an important figure in the rediscovery of Plato by Italian human-ists,[83] and under his influence Neoplatonism became especially prev-alent in English sonnets. In Spenser's 1595 sonnet sequence, the *Amoretti*, he inventories his mistress's outer beauties, but concludes that 'that which fairest is, but few behold' is 'her mind adornd with vertues manifold'. This 'vertuous mind' is

> true beautie: that doth argue you
> to be diuine and borne of heauenly seed:
> deriu'd from that fayre Spirit, from whom al true
> and perfect beauty did at first proceed.[84]

In other words, the beauty of the mistress's mind gives the lover a glimpse of the metaphysical essence of divine beauty, and thereby elevates his mind too above the physical plane.

'The mind alone is man': Neostoicism

Stoic ideas also had a resurgence as works by Cicero, Seneca, and Epictetus circulated widely in sixteenth-century England, both in Latin and in English translations.[85] Boethius's *Consolation of Philosophy* was also well known through Caxton's edition of Chaucer's translation, and through further English translations by John Walton (1525) and George Colvile (1556).[86] Another medium for the dissemination of Stoicism was William Baldwin's *Treatise of Moral Philosophy*, a compendium of wise sayings which aimed to make classical philosophy accessible and reconcile it with Christian morality. First published in 1547, the *Treatise* went through nearly twenty editions by 1603, making it one of the most popular books of the age. It included many Stoic maxims about the detachment of the virtuous mind from material things: 'Fix not thy mind upon worldly pleasure, nor trust to the world, for it deceiveth all that put their trust therein.'[87]

James Sanford translated Epictetus's *Enchiridion* or *Manual* in 1567,[88] and in 1573 declared his allegiance to both Stoicism and Platonism in a preface to another translation (of Lodovico Guicciardini's *Garden of Pleasure*). He asserted:

> Fortune beareth rule over the body, but not over the mind; she worketh her tyranny on outward things, and not on inward; and if the mind be with wholesome doctrine diligently prepared, the cruelty of fortune may be the better endured, nay rather nothing at all esteemed, if with the divine Plato, and after him with the Stoic Epictetus, we hold that the mind alone is man, and that the body is nothing else but the prison or sepulchre of the soul.[89]

'The mind alone is man': Platonic and Stoic works sharply contrasted with Galenic medical teaching on the organic integration of the mind with the body.

Recent continental works influenced by Stoicism also circulated, such as *Cardanus's Comfort* (1573), translated from an Italian work of 1542, which declared that 'man's mind is severed from all corporal or bodily matter'.[90] In France and the Netherlands especially, under the pressure of religious conflicts and civil wars, there developed a Neostoic movement that attempted to integrate Stoic and Christian thought. In France, Philippe de Mornay, seigneur du Plessis-Marly, Protestant friend of Sir Philip Sidney, wrote his *Excellent discours de la vie et de la mort* (1576), extolling death as a release from the body and the world, which was translated twice into English, first by Edward Aggas as *The Defence of Death* (also 1576), then as *A Discourse of Life and Death* (1592) by Sidney's sister Mary Sidney Herbert, Countess of Pembroke (see Chapter 4 below).

Even more influential was *De constantia libri duo* (1584) by the Flemish writer Justus Lipsius (1547–1606), which went through more than eighty editions in Latin, including two printed in England (in 1586 and 1592).[91] It was translated into all the major European languages, including English (*Two Books of Constancy*, by John Stradling, 1595).[92] In an imagined dialogue with his friend Charles Langius, Lipsius proposed leaving the Low Countries because the civil war was disturbing his mind. The wiser Langius rebuked him that rather than change countries he should 'change your own mind wrongfully subjected to affections, and withdrawn from the natural obedience of his lawful lady, I mean REASON'. He must cultivate 'a right and immovable strength of the mind', imagined as a 'castle of constancy' under assault by '*such things as are not in us, but about us, and which properly do not help nor hurt the inner man, that is, the mind*'. The castle of constancy was also besieged by the passions and affections, construed as diseases of the mind, even compassion for others, which was 'a very dangerous contagion [...] the fault of an abject and base mind'.[93]

Lipsius was a controversial figure, not least because after a Catholic upbringing he taught at the Lutheran university at Jena, then the Calvinist university at Leiden, then reconverted to Catholicism to teach at Louvain. His reputation for multiple conversions provoked satire against his doctrine of constancy, and rejection of his works by some Protestants.[94] Even so, others took up and developed his ideas, including Guillaume du Vair, author of *La Philosophie morale des Stoiques* (*c.* 1585), translated into English as *The Moral Philosophy of the Stoics* (1598). For Du Vair, too, the passions were dangerous and required suppression:

> Therefore let us be diligent and careful, that we do not suffer any such passions to arise in our minds: but as soon as anything doth begin to move us any whit, or touch us to the quick, let us pause and think upon it a while: for if we could but once find in our

hearts to reason the case with ourselves, we should be well able to stop the course of this cruel fever of the mind.[95]

Among English writers, Fulke Greville applied Neostoicism to the unfortunate situation of a noblewoman (probably Margaret Clifford, Countess of Cumberland) trapped in marriage to an unfaithful husband, to whom he addressed his 'Letter to an Honorable Lady' (composed some time between 1595 and 1601). This advised her to 'enrich yourself upon your own stock, not looking outwardly, but inwardly for the fruit of true peace, whose roots are there; and all outward things but ornaments'.[96] Neostoicism seems to have had particular appeal for elite Elizabethan women (see Chapter 4 below), and also for writers navigating the precarious social and political environment of the Elizabethan court. Although classical Stoic authors promoted indifference to worldly pains and pleasures, they also advocated fulfilment of civic duties while maintaining personal constancy, as did Lipsius.[97] However, an alternative tradition of Christian Stoicism deriving from Boethius advised complete withdrawal from the vicissitudes of public life into self-reliance and tranquillity of mind.[98] Various Elizabethan works debated these positions. In a 1598 exchange of verse epistles, John Donne sought to console his friend Sir Henry Wotton, whose patron the Earl of Essex had recently fallen from favour, by disparaging court life. Wotton agreed that retreat into the mind is virtuous:

> It is the mind that makes the man's estate
> Forever happy, or unfortunate.

> Then first the mind of passions must be free
> Of him that would to happiness aspire.

However, he converted this into a declaration of his readiness to return to the fray and continue pursuing his ambitions, armed with Stoic imperturbability and fortitude.[99]

Rejection of the court and withdrawal into the mind were more fully embraced in 'In Praise of a Contented Mind', one of the most popular poems of the period. Its author may be either Sir Edward Dyer or Edward de Vere, Earl of Oxford, and it first appeared in print set to music in 1588.[100] In this poem: 'My mind to me a kingdom is, such perfect joy therein I find, / That it excels all other bliss that world affords or grows by kind'. The speaker is absolute monarch in this inviolable inner realm, rejecting the 'princely pomp' and 'wealthy store' of the outside world. Instead, 'my mind doth serve for all', and 'No worldly waves my mind can toss, my state at one doth still remain'. It is implied that the speaker has abandoned the court to lead a humble, simple life: 'I seek no more than may suffice / [...] / I little have, and seek no more'.[101] Even in this case, however, this claim seems heavily ironic in relation to the biographies of both of the poem's putative authors: Dyer incurred massive debts in maintaining a position at court, while Oxford was notorious for extravagant dress, and his periods away from court were mainly caused by decidedly un-Stoic sexual misdemeanours, personal feuds, and intemperate behaviour.[102] In this poem, too, rejection of the court for a contemplative life looks like a poetic posture and may serve merely to advertise the author's fashionable cultural interests and qualifications for a courtly career.

Actual abandonment of the court does take place in Book VI of *The Faerie Queene*, where Sir Calidore enjoys a period of pastoral retreat. His host, the wise old shepherd Meliboe, teaches that men must submit to whatever befalls them, since

> It is the mynd, that maketh good or ill,
> > That maketh wretch or happie, rich or poore:
> [...]
> Sith each vnto himselfe his life may fortunize.

However, Calidore twists Meliboe's lesson to make it endorse not submission to his fate, but abandonment of his quest:

Since in each mans self (said *Calidore*)
  It is, to fashion his owne lyfes estate,
  Giue leaue awhyle, good father, in this shore
  To rest my barcke, which hath bene beaten late
  With stormes of fortune and tempestuous fate.[103]

There is profound ambivalence here, perhaps reflecting Spenser's own conflicted feelings about his remoteness from court as an English settler in Ireland. Sir Calidore, the Knight of Courtesy, whose mission is to exemplify courtly values, may be viewed as reprehensible for giving up his public duty; but, on the other hand, Meliboe's personification of Stoic virtue implies an indictment of the instability and immorality of the court, and Sir Calidore may be right to crave withdrawal into virtuous pastoral pleasures and mental tranquillity.

This was certainly the stance of Sir William Cornwallis the Younger, author of two volumes of *Essays* (1600, 1601) and a *Discourse upon Seneca the Tragedian* (1601).[104] Drawing extensively on Seneca and Epictetus, Cornwallis exalted the 'inward qualities of the mind', declaring that 'I prefer the freedom of my mind, before anything of the world'.[105] 'Fie upon these engrossing senses of ours', he went on. 'The mind, the mind is the magazine [storehouse] of contentment. It is the mind that can distill the whole world, all ages, all acts, all human knowledges within the little, little compass of a brain' (C4v). Corporal sense-impressions were of no consequence: 'The mind sees the mind, and gives the body leave to look how it will' (O5r). The lowering effects of the passions and affections must also be suppressed for the mind to rise to its full and extraordinary potential: 'the mind graspeth universalities; the mind's employment is about things firm, the affections momentary and fading. Who seeth not then, to be led by our affections is vain and bestial; who seeing this will neglect the mind, whose ample territory stretcheth even to the heavens' (Y2r).

Yet Cornwallis's doctrinaire Neostoicism was by no means embraced by all Elizabethan writers. We have seen that this was a period when Aristotelian and Galenic ideas of the embodied mind coexisted with branches of philosophy and theology that saw mind and body as in conflict, and sought to detach the mind from the body. For the writers we have just discussed, this meant suppressing the passions as unruly impulses arising from the body. Yet for other Elizabethan writers, the passions were a subject of fascination, and were important as intermediaries between mind and body. As we shall see in the next chapter, a literature of the passions emerged and expanded, asserting the virtuous potential of the passions, and exploring connections between feeling and knowing.

3

Knowing by Feeling
Writing the Passions

The year 1601 saw the publication of an anonymous poem entitled *The Passion of a Discontented Mind*. It opened with its
speaker bewailing a 'heart quite rent with sighs and heavy groans',
then spent nearly 400 lines dwelling on the speaker's sin, inner pain,
and desire to 'weep streams of blood to be forgiven'.[1] The second
volume of Sir William Cornwallis's *Essays*, with which our previous
chapter closed, was published in the same year. Both works were
concerned with what Cornwallis called the 'inward qualities of the
mind'; but while for him the affections and passions were 'momentary and fading [. . .] vain and bestial', for the poet the passions and
their bodily signs – sighs, groans, and tears – were essential to outward
expression of an inner state.[2]

The Passion of a Discontented Mind was well received, appearing
again in print in 1602 and 1621, and also in eight surviving manuscripts, as an expanded adaptation, and as extracts set to music.[3] It
typified a wave of penitential poetry and literature of the passions that
flourished in the 1590s and early 1600s, sitting somewhere between
the Galenic integration of mind and body that we considered in
Chapter 1 and the introspective movements that we encountered

in Chapter 2. As both Protestants and Catholics increasingly looked within, they frequently found not Stoic constancy, but inner strife. Both Churches emphasised conversion, not only in the sense of winning over others, but also as self-conversion: not turning to a different Church, but turning to God with deeper commitment. This entailed mental and spiritual turbulence, letting the passions surge and churn to achieve inner purification and transformation. Assurance of salvation and a contented mind could not be reached without first passing through this inner conflict, which passion literature expressed in terms of physical pain, staining and spotting of the sinful soul, and bodily manifestations of inner change such as sighs and tears.

We saw in Chapter 2 that looking within often involved overlap between the concepts of mind and soul. In passion literature the heart too was prominent as a site of inner conflict. In classical and biblical traditions the heart was sometimes identified as the seat of thought and feeling, and in the sixteenth century its properties continued to blur somewhat with those of the mind.[4] In 1548, Nicholas Udall, translating Erasmus on 'the most inward parts of man', wrote that 'the seat of the soul or mind is in the heart'.[5] *The French Academy* similarly located private thoughts in the heart: 'The heart [. . .] is like to a cellar or garner, wherein counsels and thoughts are locked and closed up.'[6] In medical theory the heart generated the vital spirits that carried heat and life to the body, and was the seat of passions such as love, anger, grief, and courage.[7] It was also another way of representing an essential inner self, as in the frequent image of lovers exchanging hearts, exemplified by Sir Philip Sidney's sonnet 'My true love hath my heart, and I have his'.[8] Hence, *The Passion of a Discontented Mind* is spoken not only from the mind and 'From saddest Soul consumed with deepest sins', but also 'From heart quite rent with sighs and heavy groans'.[9]

It is unclear whether the transgressions regretted in the poem are religious – it dwells on sins and mentions various biblical figures and scenes – or political. Four of the manuscripts associate it with Robert Devereux, 2nd Earl of Essex, and his imprisonment in the Tower of

London prior to his execution for treason in February 1601; but is the author Essex, or someone writing in his voice, or did the poem come to be associated with him some time after its composition?[10] Another puzzle: two versions of the poem invoke the Virgin Mary as intercessor, suggesting a Catholic author, but in other places it uses distinctively Protestant terminology. It is not even clear if the speaker is a man or a woman. This indeterminacy is characteristic of passion literature more widely, a genre centred in devotional poetry, but mobile between Protestantism and Catholicism, between religious, political, and erotic uses, and between verse and prose.

The passions have been at the centre of much recent research on the early modern period, as scholars investigate the history of emotions and their literary representation in the works of Shakespeare and his contemporaries.[11] *The Passion of a Discontented Mind* is a significant text in the Elizabethan phase of the history of the emotions, representing the emergence and development of an identifiable genre of passion literature over the course of this period. Attempting to solve some of the poem's mysteries will entail excavating its background and contexts; and this in turn will shed light on Elizabethan attitudes to the passions as intermediaries between mind and body. Representing passions in writing often involved articulating states of mind in physical terms, demonstrating an understanding of mind and body as neither inextricable (as in Chapter 1 above), nor divided (as in Chapter 2), but engaged in strenuous and dynamic interaction.

'Have them we must, and use them we may': turning the passions to good

Calvin complained in his *Institutes* that a Stoic was 'such a one as like a stone was moved with nothing', reviving questions asked in earlier centuries by St Augustine and St Thomas Aquinas about the compatibility of Stoic *apatheia* – the suppression or elimination of the passions – with Christianity.[12] He pointed out that Christ 'mourned and wept both at his own and other men's adversities', and manifested his passions in bodily symptoms of 'bloody tears' and 'quaking fear'. Like Christ, then, we should 'take cheerfully' 'the prickings of sorrow [...], mourning and tears'.[13] Other leading Protestants also critiqued Stoicism, including Heinrich Bullinger, a follower of Zwingli, whose *Decades*, a volume of fifty sermons, was translated into English in 1577, and in 1586 was prescribed as reading for all ministers. Bullinger too insisted that Christians must not be 'altogether benumbed like blocks and stocks and senseless stones'.[14]

Thomas Rogers in his *Anatomy of the Mind* used a different image, comparing Stoic *apatheia* to a stagnant pool: 'as that water which is always standing, and never runneth, must needs be noisome and infectious: so that man, which is never moved in mind, can never be either good to himself, or profitable to others'. The passions must be acknowledged, then turned to virtuous purposes: 'have them we must, and use them we may (and that abundantly) in honest wise. And therefore the end of our affections makes them either good, and so to be commended, or bad, and therefore to be dispraised.'[15] Both the *Anatomy* and *A Pattern of a Passionate Mind*, a condensed version that Rogers published in 1580, were divided into a section on 'Perturbations', then one on 'Moral Virtues', but this binary opposition often broke down in the discussion of individual passions that could be used for good or ill. 'Sadness', for instance, 'is to be condemned, but gravity is commendable'; 'To be wily, crafty, subtle are horrible if they be used to wicked purposes; so are they to be embraced when they be referred to honest ends.'[16]

Many Christian writers suspected Stoicism's emphasis on human powers of self-control as presumptuous and unrealistic. *The Touchstone of Complexions* agreed with Neostoics that the mind 'must be reined by reason, and curbed by temperance, that it yield not to affections, but procure to itself quietness and tranquillity', but quickly added that 'this is by no other means to be brought to pass but by a firm and assured trust and belief in God only'.[17] *The French Academy* similarly warned that to suppose that a fallen human, 'by the only study of philosophy, [. . .] may of himself, following his own nature, become master of all evil passions and perturbations' was to 'lift him up in a vain presumption, in pride and trust in himself, and in his own virtue', and meant 'painting out a picture of such patience as never was, nor shall be among men'.[18]

Spenser acknowledged beneficial as well as harmful passions in Book II of *The Faerie Queene*. Alma, the rational soul, dwells in a castle, the human body, which is besieged by a 'swarme' or 'troublous rout' of 'A thousand villeins'.[19] These are the external passions and affections aroused by the world and the senses:

> What warre so cruel, or what siege so sore,
>> As that, which strong affections doe apply
>> Against the forte of reason euermore,
>> To bring the sowle into captivity. (II.xi.1)

Yet other passions dwell *within* the House of Alma, indeed right at its centre, in its 'goodly Parlour', the heart (II.ix.33). Here, Prince Arthur and Sir Guyon encounter 'A louely beuy of faire Ladies' who dutifully serve and honour Alma, personifying feelings in the heart that serve the rational soul. Some sing, laugh, play, and 'ydly satt at ease', while others are less contented – 'This fround, that faund, the third for shame did blush, / Another seemed enuious, or coy, / Another in her teeth did gnaw a rush' (II.ix.35) – but even if irritable or recalcitrant, they can be governed to serve virtuous ends. Arthur and Guyon are each drawn to a particular lady who mirrors his ruling characteristic and will assist his quest: Arthur, boldly aspiring to the hand of Gloriana, woos 'Praysdesire', while Guyon, the Knight of Temperance, courts 'Shamefastnes' (II.ix.39, 43). In accordance with Christian anti-Stoicism, Spenser presents passions that can work for good under the direction of the mind (or rational soul), and therefore rightly dwell in the heart (or sensitive soul).

'Shaking and comforting': through inner
conflict to contentment

The words 'contentment' and 'contentation' were frequently used by Elizabethan Protestants to describe the inner assurance of salvation experienced by the elect. Translations of Calvin's sermons promised believers that 'if we have faith' we will find in Christ 'all things that are requisite to our joy and contentation', while the English preachers John Knewstub and Henry Smith also spoke of the 'ease, quiet, comfort and contentment' of the minds of the elect.[20] To achieve this state, a sinner must first pass through a cleansing process of mental grief and pain. In exhorting believers to 'take cheerfully' 'the prickings of sorrow [...], mourning and tears', Calvin not only represented spiritual and mental struggles as painful physical experiences, but also insisted that 'troubles are healthful for us'. We should 'receive them with a thankful and well pleased mind [...] to our own benefit', because 'how much our minds are grieved in the cross with natural feeling of bitterness, so much they be cheered with spiritual gladness'.[21] For Gervase Babington (chaplain to Mary Sidney Herbert, Countess of Pembroke), this meant that both 'feeling and faith' were necessary to achieve salvation. Dedicating to Pembroke[22] *A Brief Conference betwixt Man's Frailty and Faith* (1583), a book that would go through four more editions by 1602, Babington described the Word of God as not only 'a comforting grace unto his children', but also 'a mortifying sword', whose power should be felt 'piercing and mollifying, shaking and comforting our souls'. Full understanding should be an emotional and physical experience as well as a mental and spiritual one, as feeling becomes a way of knowing. A true believer should receive 'a touch, a taste, and a very rent as it were, in their hearts to feel'.[23]

William Perkins's *Discourse of Conscience* (1596) similarly emphasised the need for inner conflict and for this to be experienced in the passions and the body. He explained that conscience is both 'a part of the mind or understanding' and 'a power in the soul'.[24] Its accusations are felt physically as 'very forcible and terrible', as 'prickings [...] in the heart', 'the stripes, as it were, of an iron rod', and 'a worm that never dieth but always lies gnawing and grabbling, and pulling at the heart of man [...] and causeth more pain and anguish than any disease in the world can' (85). Yet this terrible pain is curative: a 'wounded or troubled conscience [...] serveth often to be an occasion or preparation to grace; as a needle, that draws the thread into the cloth, is some means whereby the cloth is sewed together' (154–5).

From self-accusation should follow confession, prayers for pardon 'made with groans and desires of heart' (162), and finally assurance of salvation: 'For then the Lord will send down his spirit into the conscience by a sweet and heavenly testimony to assure us that we are at peace with God' (163–4). Yet this assurance and contentment must also be felt not just intellectually, but through the passions. In *A Declaration of the True Manner of Knowing Christ Crucified* (1596), Perkins asserted the need for 'a lively, powerful, and operative knowledge' of Christ, and scorned a mere 'knowledge swimming in the brain, which doth not alter and dispose the affection and the whole man'.[25] Full conviction of salvation was only possible by fully feeling it.[26]

'The storms that the faithful feel': the Psalms and Protestant passions

Devotional poetry needed to find new directions in Elizabethan England. Much medieval religious verse had been devoted to lavish and elaborate veneration of the Virgin and saints, which to Protestants was just as idolatrous and unacceptable as the statues and shrines that had been removed from religious sites.[27] How, then, could Protestant poets express their faith in verse? Was it possible to use verse in the service of God? For Calvin, the Book of Psalms was a scriptural model for Protestant self-examination in poetic form: 'in this book, the prophets themselves talking with God, because they discover [reveal] all the inner thoughts, do call or draw every one of us to the peculiar examination of himself'. It was, moreover, a kind of encyclopaedia of the passions, the anatomy of all the parts of the soul, inasmuch as a man shall not find any affection in himself whereof the image appeareth not in this glass. Yea rather, the Holy Ghost hath here lively set out before our eyes all the griefs, sorrows, fears, doubts, hopes, cares, anguishes, and finally all the troublesome motions wherewith men's minds are wont to be turmoiled.[28]

No fewer than ninety English versions of the Psalms were published in the sixteenth century,[29] some for congregational singing (the only church music regarded as acceptable by many Protestants), but others as personal expressions of thought and feeling, capitalising on the Psalms' use of the pronoun 'I'. Particularly important were the so-called Penitential Psalms (6, 32, 38, 51, 102, 130, and 143), which voiced the self-accusations of conscience and craved God's pardon with the 'groans and desires of heart' described by Perkins.[30] Sir Thomas Wyatt had composed a version, probably while awaiting indictment for treason against Henry VIII in 1541,[31] while William Hunnis's *Seven Sobs of a Sorrowful Soul for Sin* (1583), a version of the Penitential Psalms designed to be read or sung in private and domestic devotions, was very popular and frequently reprinted.[32]

At their executions many of the Protestant martyrs memorialised by Foxe, such as Lady Jane Grey, had recited one particular Penitential Psalm, number 51, '*Miserere mei, Deus*' ('Have mercy upon me, O God' in the translation by Miles Coverdale that was used in the Church of England's liturgy).[33] This Psalm also inspired the first English sonnet sequence, 'A Meditation of a Penitent Sinner upon the 51st Psalm'. The author was probably Anne Lock, an associate of John Knox and Protestant activist; the 'Meditation' was published in 1560 with her translation of some sermons by Calvin.[34] In these, Calvin reiterates the benefits of spiritual struggle: we must 'offer ourselves to God, to send forth unto him our sighs and groanings', while in the Psalms, David (thought to be their author) expresses 'the storms that the faithful feel when God searcheth them earnestly and to the quick'.[35] Following the sermons, the 'Meditation' has five prefatory sonnets 'expressing the passioned mind of the penitent sinner' (one of the earliest recorded uses of 'passioned' as an adjective meaning 'affected with suffering or sorrow').[36] They express inner turmoil in visceral physical terms: God's wrath 'is sharper than the knife, / And deeper wounds than double-edged sword', while the speaker's eyes are 'Full fraught with tears and more and more oppressed / With growing streams of the distilled brine / Sent from the furnace of a grief-full breast'.[37]

The main sequence of sonnets proceeds through verse-by-verse expansions upon the Psalm, accompanied by marginal translations of each verse. Sonnet 3, on the verse 'Wash me yet more from my wickedness, and cleanse me from my sin', adds emotional urgency as well as imagery of physical infection and pollution:

Wash me again, yea wash me everywhere,
Both leprous body and defiled face.
Yea wash me all, for I am all unclean,
And from my sin, Lord, cleanse me once again.

This image of the sinful soul as spotted or stained derives from another biblical text, *The Song of Songs* (also known as *The Song of Solomon*), in which a female lover or bride, often allegorically interpreted as the soul or the Church yearning for Christ, describes herself as 'black [. . .] but comely [. . .] Regard ye me not because I am black'. The marginal gloss in the Geneva Bible explained: 'The Church confesseth her spots and sin, but hath confidence in the favour of Christ.'[38] As well as developing this image of sin as visible, corporeal disfigurement, Lock also frequently uses vivid metaphors of physical pain – her 'ripped heart' (Sonnet 5), 'bruised bones' (Sonnet 10), and 'straining cramp of cold despair' (Sonnet 17) – for mental and spiritual turbulence. As the sequence draws towards its close, it becomes apparent that this inner pain has been a necessary preparation for divine grace. The final sonnet reaches towards assurance of salvation:

Relieve my sorrow, and my sins deface:
Be, Lord of mercy, merciful to me:
Restore my feeling of thy grace again:
Assure my soul, I crave it not in vain. (Sonnet 21)[39]

In that phrase 'feeling of thy grace', Lock offers one of the earliest Protestant expressions of feeling as knowing. Not only is passing through an intensely 'passioned' state of mind an essential preparation for conversion and redemption; that desired assurance of salvation is itself a profoundly emotional experience as well as a mental and spiritual one.

Around two decades later, Sir Philip Sidney began a set of paraphrases – poems closely based on each Psalm, rather than literal translations – of the whole Book of Psalms. By his death in 1586, he had completed forty-three; his sister the Countess of Pembroke revised these and paraphrased the remaining 107 Psalms, finishing her task some time before 1599. Her skilfully crafted poems, using a variety of intricate stanza forms, rhetorical effects, and verbal patterns, circulated widely in manuscript and had a significant influence on religious poets of the next generation such as John Donne and George Herbert. She worked with a range of Protestant translations of and commentaries on the Psalms,[40] often expanding or intensifying their images, and may have known Lock's 'Meditation' on Psalm 51, whose metaphor of sin as physical disfigurement she also elaborates: 'cleanse still my spots, still wash away my stainings, / Till stains and spots in me leave no remainings'.[41] Like Lock, Pembroke is inspired by the Psalms to use vivid corporeal images for inner states: in Psalm 102, on grief, she writes: 'My bones as flaming fuel waste [. . .] My heart is withered like the wounded grass'.[42] Another influence was the intense introspection of her brother Philip's erotic sonnet sequence *Astrophil and Stella* (discussed in Chapter 9 below). Pembroke's version of Psalm 139, '*Domine probasti*' ('O Lord, thou hast searched me out'),[43] describes being known to the core by God: 'Yea, closest closet of my thought / Hath open windows to thine eyes'. God looks into the speaker's closet to see her at prayer, then penetrates further, into the 'closet of my thought', her mind – to which the reader is also given intimate access.[44] Pembroke invites the reader to think and feel with her as she thinks and feels with the Psalmist, and thereby finds a way to a Protestant poetry of private devotion.[45]

'Many tears and relenting': the inner struggles of Richard Rogers

The influence of the Psalms, especially their self-exposure to God, self-recrimination, and longing for divine mercy, is evident in a spiritual journal kept by Richard Rogers, a Puritan minister in rural Essex, between 1587 and 1590. Rogers spent much time in prayer, meditation, and study, either alone or with like-minded companions, desiring 'to make my whole life a meditation of a better life' and to achieve 'the benefit of keeping rule over my mind and bridling my rebellious heart'.[46] His journal often records how these efforts at inward reflection and self-improvement are frustrated by physical ailments: 'These two days my body is much diseased so that I cannot greatly study' (58); 'I have been also this month much troubled with a vehement cough and stuffing through cold, that it took away both delight and ability from every good duty' (83). Physical pleasures are just as obstructive: 'doubtless a filling of the belly [. . .] bring[s] great unfitness to all good duties' (85). Even more problematic is the waywardness of his mind: 'though I began well, yet I by little and little fell from the strength which I had gotten and became unprofitable in study, and prayer and meditation were not continued privately of me with such joy [. . .] What strugglings and yet apparent hindrances I feel about it, it is marvellous [extraordinary]' (55). He attempts 'a restraining of my mind from many things which it was wont to delight in [. . .] But this afternoon I felt a strong desire to enjoy more liberty in thinking upon some vain things which I had lately weaned myself from' (59). Writing the journal in itself is an attempt to master these wandering thoughts:

and if I had not either written this immediately, or by some other means met with it, I had almost been gone from this course and become plainly minded and idle as before. And thus I see how hard it is to keep our minds in awe and attending upon the Lord in some good duty or other, at least to be strongly settled against evil. (59–60)[47]

Even so, 'So many thoughts stuff my mind: on the one side, some lawful, but yet either out of season or too long or too deep, some fond [foolish] and fantastical; on the other side, unsettlings with journeys, comers to me, etc.' (84). Trivial and distracting thoughts 'stuff' his mind, like a physical sensation, just as he complains elsewhere of 'stuffing through cold'.

Rogers seems to have intended his journal both for his own later review as material for meditations, and for communal use in exchanges with fellow local clergymen, who shared their own journals with him.[48] They also held regular meetings: 'twelve of us met to the stirring up of ourselves [...], four or five hours, with much moving of our affections' (69). The moving of affections, like the 'feeling of thy grace' craved by Lock, was a way of deeply knowing God; while observing and recording this moving of affections was a means of determining progress towards salvation. As Calvin promised, Rogers's periods of spiritual turmoil and effort, both alone and with others, were sometimes rewarded with commensurate feelings of 'sweet peace' or 'very sweet blessing and comfortable [comforting] staidness' (54, 63). Often the turning point from mental turbulence to renewed communion with God was marked by tears. Weeping occurs regularly in the Psalter as an outpouring of penitence and prelude to spiritual relief: 'I am weary of my groaning, every night wash I my bed: and water my couch with my tears' (Psalm 6.6); 'Hear my prayer, O Lord, and with thine ears consider my calling: hold not thy peace at my tears' (Psalm 39.13).[49] Lock had emulated this in her 'Meditation', 'Simply with tears bewailing my desert'.[50] Tears were bodily effusions, yet at the same time, as cleansing water, they could be readily associated with baptism, the washing away of sins, and the dew of divine grace. Because they were semi-involuntary, they could be experienced and read as signs of God's intervention to save and transform.[51] For Rogers, successful prayers and meditations were often followed by Psalm-like weeping: 'delight exceeding [. . .] with many tears and relenting' (66), or 'meltings of heart, which sighs and plaints were more sweet to me than honey', when 'with tears I desired that I might sometimes before bed recover that sweet recourse to God' (101).[52] Purgative passions were prominent in this writer's spiritual life; and for him the body was not merely an impediment to spiritual progress, but a source of motions and effusions which made spiritual progress felt, seen, and measurable, as 'meltings of heart', sighs, and tears.[53]

'What afflictions of mind, what abundance of tears': Catholic passions

Interactions between mind and body, including the tears and heart-meltings of conversion, were at least as important for Elizabethan Catholics. Many aspects of Catholic worship involved integration of the spiritual and the physical, including belief in the transubstantiation of the bread and wine of the Eucharist into the body and blood of Christ, the use of images and ceremony, and an artistic tradition of depiction of the physical sufferings of Christ. Loyola's *Spiritual Exercises* and other Catholic meditation manuals further intensified this emotional and physical engagement, encouraging visualisation of Gospel scenes as if personally present, empathetic participation in the stages of Christ's Passion, and a profound sense of personal responsibility for Christ's suffering. Spiritual transformation was pursued by an excoriating passage through extreme emotions.[54] Jesuit missionaries aspired to such passionate penitence in both their own inner being and the inner lives of those to whom they ministered.[55] Robert Persons, Jesuit polemicist and author of *The Christian Directory* (see Chapter 2 above), rejoiced that by the 'zeal and industry' of the Jesuits 'many a separation is made between good and bad, many a heat enkindled in Christian hearts, where deadly cold occupied the place before [...], many a careless and earthly mind stirred up to apprehend and think of eternity'.[56]

Catholic poetry was strongly influenced by the *Spiritual Exercises* and other meditation manuals, but it also shared with Protestant poetry the influence of the Psalms, as well as a compulsion to look within, a desire to engage both heart and mind, and use of corporeal imagery to express inner states. John Donne's Jesuit uncle Jasper Heywood contributed 'The Complaint of a Sorrowful Soul' to *The Paradise of Dainty Devices* (1585), a popular Elizabethan miscellany of erotic and devotional verse. Imagining the Day of Judgement, the speaker dwells on his sins and describes his inner turmoil:

Whereon whilst I do muse, in my amazèd mind,
Froward [perverse] thoughts, familiar foes, most fierce assaults
  I find:
My conscience to my face, doth flatly me accuse,
My secret thoughts within my ears do whisper still these news.

At the same time, like Lock and Pembroke, he represents sin as a physical stain on the soul: 'My many spots and great, must needs increase my guilt, / Unless thou wash them in the blood that for my sake was spilt.'[57]

The most important and influential Elizabethan Catholic poet was Robert Southwell, also a Jesuit, whose poems were probably mostly written between his arrival in England as a missionary in 1586 and his arrest and imprisonment in 1592.[58] 'Man's Civil War' is in the psychomachic tradition, evoking a taut tension between the mind's spiritual and sensual impulses: 'My hovering thoughts would fly to heaven', but the world restrains them 'with jesses of delights' (jesses were the tethers used in training a hawk). In this poem the body is 'heavy poise of mortal load', dragging thoughts down;[59] but elsewhere Southwell frequently uses graphic corporeal imagery to represent inner states. In 'Mary Magdalen's Blush', the face and body are texts of the mind: 'The signs of shame that stain my blushing face', explains Mary, arise from 'my guilty thoughts'. She laments having deflected the arrows of divine grace while allowing Cupid's arrows to wound her heart: 'To pull them out, to leave them in is death: / One to this world, one to the world to come' (29). Southwell was fascinated by such images of the damaged body and exquisite, elevating pain. 'Christ's bloody sweat' offers a series of elaborate patterned metaphors for the dying Christ's bodily emanations: they are

Fat soil,	full spring,	sweet olive,	grape of bliss
That yields,	that streams,	that pours,	that dost distil.

Images are organised in columns as well as rows, embedding meaning in the visual shape of the poem on the page while identifying Christ's flesh, tears, sweat, and blood as sacramental wheat (or bread), water, oil, and wine, sustenance to both body and soul. As the poem proceeds it foreshadows the martyrdom that Southwell expects for himself as a mystical interfusion of physical agony and spiritual rapture: 'How burneth blood, how bleedeth burning love; / Can one in flame and stream both bathe and fry?' (17).[60]

'A Vale of Tears' finds a different way to give palpable form to spiritual experience by imagining a gloomy, craggy landscape:

A vale there is enwrapped with dreadful shades
Which thick of mourning pines shrouds from the sun,
Where hanging cliffs yield short and dumpish glades
And snowy flood with broken streams doth run. (36–8)

The poem's title partly derives from Psalm 84.6 (or, in the Vulgate Bible, Psalm 83.7, 'in valle lacrimarum'), a phrase often interpreted as the soul's exile on earth as it aspires to heaven.[61] However, it also comes from the ancient Marian anthem 'Salve Regina', widely used in the Catholic Church, which includes the line 'Ad te suspiramus *gementes et flentes in hac lacrymarum valle'* ('We sigh to you, mourning and weeping, in this vale of tears').[62] Southwell's gothic vista is at once a topographical materialisation of the inner turbulence of a penitent sinner, and a political allegory of the melancholy and fallen state of England, bereft of its true Church:

> A place for mated [confused, bewildered] minds, an only bower
> Where everything doth soothe a dumpish mood;
> Earth lies forlorn, the cloudy sky doth lour,
> The wind here weeps, here sighs, here cries aloud.

Characteristically, Southwell takes the tears of the Psalmist to a new extreme: in this poem, a whole imaginary world is weeping.[63]

Just as the Protestant spiritual journal of Richard Rogers shared themes and images with Psalm-based devotional poetry, so a prose conversion narrative by a Protestant turned Catholic, William Alabaster, had much in common with Catholic poetry. Alabaster was himself a poet: before his conversion he composed *Elisaeis*, an unfinished neo-Latin epic celebrating Elizabeth I's defeat of Catholicism. He converted in 1597, and in around 1599 wrote an account of this experience and his subsequent imprisonment, escape, and flight to Rome.[64] Before his conversion he felt 'what afflictions of mind, what abundance of tears', with 'spiritual misery' and 'inward motions' towards Catholicism.[65] The conversion itself came in a flash: 'so was I lightened upon the sudden, feeling myself so wonderfully and sensibly changed both in judgement and affection as I remained astonished at my true state. I found my mind wholly and perfectly Catholic in an instant' (118). He then spent a period in introspection, during which, as for Rogers, steps forward in penitence and self-transformation were marked by passions and tears: 'when the floods of tears came down upon me, I could do no less but open the gates to let them pass' (122). He appropriates the term 'contentment', used by Protestants for the inner peace of the elect, to contrast his former Protestant mental perturbations with his new Catholic inner serenity:

'by Protestants' doctrine I felt my head filled only with a dry spirit of pride, *contention*, and contradiction', but 'so soon as I was a Catholic, I felt such illustrations [enlightenings] and illuminations of mind, such joy, such *content*, such abundance of tears, such tender devotions' (130, my emphases). A change of passions authenticates his change of confessional allegiance and spiritual state.

Later in life, in the 1610s, Alabaster would reconvert to Protestantism and become a Church of England priest. A contemporary described him as 'A papist formerly, now a zealous Protestant against them', and as 'antic and fantastical in some things'.[66] He was to some extent an eccentric, but he was also part of a 1590s wave of conversions that included fellow poets Henry Constable and Ben Jonson (from Protestantism to Catholicism), and John Donne (from Catholicism to Protestantism). The significant similarities between Alabaster's spiritual narrative and that of Richard Rogers reveal that, despite the deep doctrinal differences and fierce political hostilities between the Catholic and Protestant Churches, their members were not far apart in the ways in which they experienced and represented penitence and conversion. Both Rogers and Alabaster chart 'afflictions of mind' and periods of introspection as essential to spiritual progress, and both present tears as outward evidence of inner transformation.

'He that his mirth hath lost': passions, poetry, and politics

During the early to mid-Elizabethan period, aside from Psalm-based works, Protestant devotional verse was scarce as poets began to work out a theologically acceptable aesthetic. Yet secular poems from these years sometimes read like religious verse, as if the self-accusation and anguish of the Psalmist were spilling over into other genres. A prime example is Sir Edward Dyer's widely circulated manuscript poem 'He that his mirth hath lost', also known as 'A Fancy'. It begins by expressing extreme melancholy for an unspecified cause (although faith is mentioned):

He that his mirth hath lost, whose comfort is dismayed,
Whose hope is vain, whose faith is scorned, whose trust is all
   betrayed,
If he have held them dear and cannot cease to moan,
Come let him take his place by me, he shall not rue alone. (1–4)[67]

Deepening the psychological intensity, the speaker claims that he would welcome physical death, but 'my death is of the mind' (11). He sounds increasingly like a religious penitent with a troubled conscience: his heart is an 'altar', his spirit is a 'sacrifice', and his thoughts are 'no thoughts but wounds' (15, 23).

The poem continues in this vein for roughly half of its eighty lines, until at last the speaker reveals the cause of his woe. It is not, it turns out, a sense of his own sin:

Oh frail inconstant kind, oh safe in trust to no man,
No women angels be, and lo, my mistress is a woman;
[...]
I cannot blot out of my breast what love wrought in her name.
                                              (47–8, 54)

Despite this eventual revelation, mystery remains as to the occasion and genre of the poem. One manuscript titles it 'A complaint of one forsaken of his love', which seems straightforward; but in another, it is headed 'Bewailing his exile he singeth thus', leading some scholars to think, plausibly, that it relates to a period in 1572–75 when Dyer fell from the Queen's favour and was banished from court.[68] This would not be inconsistent with the idea of being forsaken in love, since Elizabethan courtiers habitually represented their relationships with Elizabeth as a Petrarchan lover's dependence on the elusive favour of an unattainable mistress.[69] All we can conclude is that the poem mobilises the religious language of disturbed passions and inner turmoil for purposes that are erotic or political, or both.

In the late 1580s and early 1590s, Southwell repeatedly declared a mission to reclaim poetry from erotic love to love of God. Dyer's poem was an obvious candidate for 'sacred parody' – the religious revision of a secular poem, not necessarily humorous – which Southwell carried through in 'Dyer's Fancy Turned to a Sinner's Complaint'.[70] He brings the poem even further into the penitential genre by adding tears (15, 133) and making explicit the devotional – and specifically Catholic – potential of the diction and imagery. Dyer's speaker's heart is an altar; so is that of Southwell's speaker, but it is also the 'host a God to move' (30), a Eucharistic offering, identifying with Christ's bodily sacrifice and seeking God's transforming mercy.[71] Where Dyer retails 'My exercise nought else but raging agonies, / My books of spiteful fortune's foils and dreary tragedies' (69–70), Southwell exploits the Ignatian connotations of the word 'exercise':

My exercise remorse
  And doleful sinner's lays,
My book remembrance of my crimes
  And faults of former days. (137–40)

It is striking, however, how little Southwell needed to change, especially in the first part of the poem. His opening lines are almost identical to Dyer's:

He that his mirth hath lost,
  Whose comfort is to rue,
Whose hope is fallen, whose faith is crazed,
  Whose trust is found untrue,
If he have held them dear,
  And cannot cease to moan,
Come let him take his place by me,
  He shall not rue alone. (1–8)

95

Southwell may have intended to satirise the hollow posturing of fashionable courtly melancholy by setting it against true, spiritual causes for inner grief, or simply to appropriate the poem for devotional use, but either way Dyer's poem is already so close to penitential religious verse that only the lightest of touches is needed to convert it.[72]

Southwell may also have intended another poem, 'Content and Rich', as a sacred parody of a courtly poem by Dyer (or Oxford – see Chapter 2 above): the Neostoic composition that opens 'My mind to me a kingdom is'. Southwell's poem celebrates victory in the psychomachic struggle and trumps the inner monarchy of the original poem's courtier-speaker: 'My mind to me an *empire* is' (my emphasis). His inner strength is grounded not in secular Neostoic fortitude, but in faith in a kingdom beyond this world: 'I have no hopes but one / Which is of heavenly reign'. He even appropriates the key Protestant terms 'conscience' and 'contentment': 'My conscience is my crown, / Contented thoughts my rest'. At the same time, the image of his mind as an empire asserts his right as a Catholic to dominion over his own thoughts and beliefs, beyond the oppressive efforts of law and politics.[73] While raising the poem above the courtly, worldly politics of the original, Southwell gives it a different kind of political edge.

'All weeping eyes resign your tears to me': Southwell's Mary Magdalen and St Peter

A prose work by Southwell, *Mary Magdalen's Funeral Tears*, appeared anonymously in print in 1591 and was a huge success, with six editions by 1609.[74] Its preface placed Southwell's religious reclamation of literature in the context of debate about the passions:

> Passions I allow, and loves I approve, only I would wish that men would alter their object and better their intent. [. . .] Sorrow is the sister of mercy, and a waker of compassion, weeping with others'

tears, and grieved with their harms [...] There is no passion but hath a serviceable use either in the pursuit of good, or avoidance of evil, and they are all benefits of God and helps of nature, so long as they are kept under virtue's correction.[75]

Having established this anti-Stoic position (not dissimilar to that of Calvin and his followers), Southwell vividly describes the tumultuous emotions of Mary Magdalen as she found the empty tomb, then met the risen Christ. Her grief is physically felt and expressed: 'the fire of her true affection enflamed her heart, and her enflamed heart resolved into incessant tears, so that burning and bathing between love and grief, she led a life ever dying, and felt a death never ending' (1r–v). The word 'heart' occurs nearly fifty times in this work, and 'tears' even more frequently. Southwell integrates the penitential grief of the Psalms with the intense passions of the Petrarchan love-poet, who conventionally burns in ice and freezes in flames. He also adds a further influence: a Counter-Reformation, continental genre of tears literature which represented penitential remorse with unprecedented and extravagant sensuality.[76] In its extremity, Mary's agony is also a kind of ecstasy: 'And though tears were rather oil than water to her flame, apter to nourish than diminish her grief, yet being now plunged in the depth of pain, she yielded herself captive to all discomfort, carrying an overthrown mind in a more enfeebled body' (4r). She is in 'a consuming languor' (14v), 'wholly possessed with passion', such that her 'reason is altered into love' and becomes a transcendent spiritual state in which Christ alone occupies her mind: 'Yea, she had forgotten all things, and herself among all things, only mindful of him whom she loved above all things' (6v–7r).

Southwell also wrote two short poems in the voice of Mary Magdalen ('Mary Magdalen's Blush' and 'Mary Magdalen's Complaint at Christ's Death'),[77] but was even more fascinated by St Peter, whose penitent voice he used in the short poems 'Saint Peter's Afflicted Mind' and 'Saint Peter's Remorse', and in short and long versions of 'Saint Peter's Complaint'.[78] He was influenced by a particular example of tears literature, the poem cycle *Le lagrime di San Pietro* (*The Tears of Saint Peter*) by Luigi Tansillo, but was also drawn to St Peter by his narrative of fallibility, contrition, and redemption. Although a leading disciple, Peter failed Christ by denying him three times on the night before his crucifixion. He redeemed himself to found the Church and become its first Pope, then emulated Christ in his own martyrdom. Identification with him offered rich opportunities for meditation of the kind prescribed by Loyola's *Spiritual Exercises*: imagining oneself present at a crucial scene in Christ's Passion, then contemplating personal responsibility for his sacrifice, and gratitude for his undeserved mercy. Moreover, Peter's contrition for his denial of Christ particularly spoke to the situation of English Catholics who were outwardly conforming to Protestant practice or wavering in their faith.[79]

While *Mary Magdalen's Funeral Tears* described Mary's passions in the third person, all Southwell's Magdalen and St Peter poems are in the first person, intensifying their emotional impact and inviting the reader's participation in self-recrimination. Several of them also use a stanza form of iambic pentameter lines rhyming ababcc, known as the 'sixain stanza' or 'heroic sestet'.[80] Each of these stanzas tends to explore a thought in the quatrain, then distil it in the couplet, before opening up a new thought in the next stanza. They lend themselves to the representation of an unfolding thought-process, especially when they accumulate over the course of a long poem, as in the long 'Saint Peter's Complaint' of nearly 800 lines.

This poem has three sections, of which the first takes up the widely used imagery of the sinful soul as 'spotted', to be cleansed by sacramental water in the form of tears. The speaker urges his soul to

Give vent unto the vapours of thy breast,
[...]
Thy trespass foul, let not thy tears be few:
Baptise thy spotted soul in weeping dew.[81]

However, Southwell goes on to magnify this imagery to an unprecedented scale, in sea imagery that befits Peter's occupation as a fisherman:

All weeping eyes resign your tears to me:
A sea will scantly rinse my ordured soul:
Huge horrors in high tides must drowned be,
Of every tear my crime exacteth toll.
These stains are deep: few drops take out no such:
Even salve with sore: and most, is not too much. (43–8)

Here, tears become a turbulent, unfathomable ocean of grief. This is emotionally powerful, but the extreme amplification of tears imagery also suggests that Peter's self-accusation at this point is excessive and self-indulgent, and verges on despair.

He is unable to progress in penitence until the second section of the poem, when Christ's eyes look upon him, inspiring twenty richly metaphorical stanzas on their beauty and power: they are 'blazing comets', 'living mirrors', 'baths of grace', and 'little worlds' (325–444). By the third and final section Peter understands that he is loved and saved by 'Christ, health of fevered soul, heaven of the mind' (751). He continues to express his contrition in physical terms: 'Prone look, crossed arms, bent knee, and contrite heart / Deep sighs, thick sobs, dewed eyes, and prostrate prayers / Most humbly beg relief of earned smart' (769–71). However, his tears have changed in purpose and meaning as he turns from inconsolable self-hatred to hopeful and trusting supplication for divine mercy: 'Let tears appease when trespass doth incense: [...] Let grace forgive, let love forget my fall' (783, 785).[82]

Southwell's explorations of the penitence of Mary Magdalen and St Peter may be aptly termed passion literature, on two counts. They invoke Christ's Passion as a focus for personal guilt, as a sinner recognises the painful sacrifice endured by Christ for their sake and aspires to emulate his model of martyrdom. At the same time, they understand penitence as involving deep, excoriating passions and seek to express these to the full.

'I sit / With Mary at the grave': new passions in Protestant poetry

Southwell was careful throughout *Mary Magdalen's Funeral Tears* to avoid anything doctrinally objectionable to Protestants, and pointed out in a preface that writing about a saint was not necessarily idolatrous: his subject was 'not unfit [...] the ground thereof being in scripture' (A8r–v). He opened up fresh literary possibilities not only in his uninhibited use of the body and the passions to express inner states, but also in using saints to explore their humanity, rather than for veneration, drawing on their roles in the narrative of Christ's Passion to explore spiritual and emotional crises. These innovations were timely, as a group of Protestant poets whose patron was the Countess of Pembroke began to look beyond the Psalms for scriptural inspiration. In 1591, the same year as *Mary Magdalen's Funeral Tears*, Abraham Fraunce published *The Countess of Pembroke's Emanuel*, comprising not only versions of several Psalms, but also poems on the nativity, Passion, burial, and resurrection of Christ. Meanwhile, there was also a Protestant revival of interest in the late medieval work *The Imitation of Christ*, and in forms of piety that sought personal renewal through contemplation of Christ's Passion.[83]

In 1592, another of Pembroke's client-poets, Nicholas Breton, published 'The Countess of Pembroke's Love'. This long penitential poem was clearly influenced by *Mary Magdalen's Funeral Tears*, and perhaps also by Southwell's lyric poems on the same theme. As mentioned above, Southwell's poems were probably mostly written before his arrest in 1592, and until 1595 circulated only in manuscript and mainly among Catholics, but may have been known to some Protestants too.[84] John Wolfe, for instance, the Protestant printer of *Mary Magdalen's Funeral Tears* and later of Southwell's poems, may have had a manuscript of them as early as 1591, and had connections with one of Breton's printers, Richard Jones.[85] A possible sign of influence is Breton's adoption of the sixain stanza for both 'The Countess of Pembroke's Love' and its companion-poem in the same volume, 'The Pilgrimage to Paradise'. In any case, the influence of *Mary Magdalen's Funeral Tears*, already in print, on 'The Countess of Pembroke's Love' is manifest. Somewhat disconcertingly, Breton introduces his patron Pembroke as 'This true love's saint', and ventriloquises her as a Magdalen-like penitent.[86] 'And who more sinner than this soul of mine?' she asks Christ, 'Which doth with tears of true repentance move / Thy gracious help to glorify thy love' (78).

Just as Southwell's Mary Magdalen 'had washed his [i.e. Christ's] feet with her tears, bewailing unto him the death of her own soul',[87] so Pembroke (Mary Sidney Herbert) as voiced by Breton implores Christ: 'Look on thy Mary with her bitter tears, / That washed thy feet and wipteth [*sic*] with her hairs' (92). She weeps, sighs, and sobs, physically experiencing her violent passions:

> But my heart pants, my soul doth quake for fear,
> And sorrow's pain possesseth every part:
> My heap of sins, too heavy for to bear,
> Press down desire with terror of desert. (91)

In its sensuality and extremity, the poem resembles Southwell's writing and feels aesthetically Catholic, though it is possible that Breton understood himself as merely extending the penitent passions voiced by Pembroke in her Psalm paraphrases, and as working within Protestant doctrine on conscience and contrition. By the end of the poem Pembroke has moved through the Protestant sequence of self-examination, self-recrimination, and penitence towards assurance of salvation:

> 'Behold,' quoth she, 'the true repentant hart,
> Which bleeds in tears with sorrow of her sin:
> What passions have perplexed every part,
> Where penitence doth pity's suit begin:
> Where true confession doth submission prove,
> And true contrition cries to me for love.' (101)

Southwell had provided Breton with both a way forward for Protestant devotional poetry and a means of representing a mind in process, working its way through painful confusions, doubts, and problems to achieve transformation and resolution.

Breton's poem also belongs to the genre of 'female complaint', in which male poets imagined themselves in the minds of women and voiced their woes (see Chapter 4 below). The genre had deep roots, from Ovid's *Heroides* through various medieval and early Tudor works, and became particularly popular in the early 1590s: examples include Samuel Daniel's *Complaint of Rosamond* (1592), dedicated to the Countess of Pembroke, and Shakespeare's *Rape of Lucrece* (1594).[88] Breton wrote another female complaint in Pembroke's voice: *The Passions of the Spirit* (*c.* 1592), also known in manuscript as 'The Countess of Pembroke's Passion'.[89] Again he enumerates 'words dissolved / To sighs, sighs into tears, / And every tear / To torments of the mind', and again the speaker is identified with Mary Magdalen: 'I sit / With Mary at the grave'.[90] By 1597, Breton had fallen from Pembroke's favour, perhaps because she was not entirely pleased to be represented as a sinful Magdalen-figure.[91] However, his passion poetry was an important innovation as a Protestant adoption of Southwell-like techniques, tracing the psychological process through grief and remorse to spiritual relief, and taking to new extremes the physical representation of turbulent inner states.

Henry Lok also made innovations in passion literature while looking back to his mother Anne Lock's 'Meditation'.[92] His *Sundry Christian Passions* (1593) were 200 sonnets organised into two sections, the first 'Consisting Chiefly of Meditations, Humiliations, and Prayers; The Second of Comfort, Joy, and Thanksgiving'.[93] This division both continued the psychomachic tradition, and represented the Protestant believer's progress from self-examination and self-accusation to assurance of salvation and inner contentment. Lok's preface explains that he has 'thought good to set down these abrupt passions of my passed afflictions' because they 'may serve for precedents for myself in the like future occasions, and not be altogether unprofitable for others to imitate' (A5r). This resembles the way in which Richard Rogers wrote down his spiritual struggles in order to manage them, to meditate on them in the future, and to offer them to others for reflection on their own spiritual journeys. The word 'sundry' in the title conveys a deliberate randomness. Lok explains that, within the two sections, he has not organised the sonnets, because he is 'persuaded their disorder doth best fit the nature of mankind, who commonly is delighted with contraries, and exercised with extremes, and also as they were by God ministered to my mind, to set down by sundry accidents in my private estate and feeling' (5v–6r). Just as his mother craved from God 'the feeling of thy grace', he too explores feeling as a route to knowing, and charts his shifting passions as a means of understanding himself, his relationship with God, and his progress towards salvation. He also follows Anne Lock in writing sonnets inspired by the Psalms, in his case imitating both the Psalter's emotional range as noted by Calvin and its often abrupt shifts between different themes, moods, and registers, capturing dissonant emotional moments rather than stages in a narrative.[94] Lok believes that 'God's direction (by that which men call chance)' will enable his poems to 'hit the affections of every reader' appropriately and usefully, according to what happens to fall into view as they turn the pages (A6r). He has sought to combine this lack of arrangement with a plain, sincere style, having 'rather followed the force of mine own inward feeling, than outward ornaments of poetical fictions or amplifications' (A6r–v). The sonnets, then, are presented as an authentic and almost stream-of-consciousness-style record of thoughts and feelings.

Lok also emulates his mother in using intense physical imagery for inner conditions. A 'regenerate soul' is 'sick with sin, sometimes (ague-like) shivering with cold despair, straight-ways inflamed with fervency of faith and hope' (A5r), and sin is a visible disfigurement: his 'corrupt mind [. . .] seeks with simony my soul to stain [. . .] lo, I see soul's leprosy herein' (p. 18, Sonnet 33). A melting heart and penitent tears were by now mandatory in passion literature: 'But now

my heart with tears my cheeks doth wet, / In sorrow of my so inconstant faith' (p. 49, Sonnet 95). However, Lok also embraces the new
trend of expressing contrition in the voices of scriptural figures,
including Mary Magdalen:

> The precious oil of penitence will I
>   Pour forth with tears from out my melting eyes,
>   [T]o bathe thy feet, and after will I dry
>   Them with my hairs (which balms no treasure buys).
>
> (p. 11, Sonnet 19)

Meanwhile, following his arrest in June 1592, Southwell had been
held in solitary confinement and experienced all-too-real physical
tortures. He was finally tried for treason in February 1595, and hanged,
drawn, and quartered at Tyburn.[95] Two collections of his poems were
rushed into print: *Saint Peter's Complaint* (containing the long version
of 'Saint Peter's Complaint' and some shorter poems) and *Moeoniae*.
Both collections omitted overtly Catholic pieces and achieved rapid
popularity, going through multiple editions over following years.[96]
The Protestant penitential poetry that Breton and Lok had begun to
develop now became fashionable and profuse, as poets and readers
relished its capacity to show a mind in process and chart its fluctuating passions. Protestant imitations of 'Saint Peter's Complaint'
included the anonymous *Saint Peter's Ten Tears* (1597), W. Broxup's *St
Peters Path to the Joys of Heaven* (1598), and Samuel Rowland's *The
Betraying of Christ* (also 1598), while works about Mary Magdalen
included Breton's *Mary Magdalen's Love* (1595) and *The Ravished
Soul, and the Blessed Weeper* (1601), and Gervase Markham's *Mary
Magdalen's Lamentations* (also 1601).[97] The passion literature that had
begun to emerge from the combined influences of the Psalm tradition, female complaint, and Southwell's *Mary Magdalen's Funeral
Tears* was catalysed by the publication of 'Saint Peter's Complaint'. In
the closing years of the Elizabethan period Protestant lamentations
became more numerous and more passionate than ever.[98]

'Never-drying tears': a fluid genre

Dyer's 'Fancy', as we saw earlier, had blurred the lines between religious, erotic, and political complaint. These genres overlapped further in the 1590s, as love poets addressed their mistresses as enshrined saints and petitioned them for mercy, and as praise of the Queen increasingly borrowed from both Petrarchan love poetry and the iconography of the Virgin Mary.[99] At the lovers' first meeting in Shakespeare's *Romeo and Juliet*, a play of around 1595, they speak a sonnet in which Juliet calls Romeo a 'pilgrim' and he calls her a 'saint', culminating in a kiss (1.4.204–18). In 1599, William Jaggard opportunistically published *The Passionate Pilgrim by W. Shakespeare*, probably intending to allude to this scene in the volume's title, and evidently hoping to cash in on the growing fame of the supposed author, even though only a few of the poems in the volume are actually by Shakespeare. Jaggard's title also aimed to exploit the current commercial success of passion literature, although any purchaser of his *Passionate Pilgrim* who expected a work like Breton's *Pilgrimage to Paradise* or *Passions of the Spirit* would have been startled by its erotic contents.[100]

The passions continued to be especially prominent in Catholic writing. Thomas Wright, author of the prose treatise *The Passions of the Mind* (1601), was a Catholic priest and former Jesuit who had been involved in the conversion of William Alabaster and perhaps also that of Ben Jonson.[101] Wright followed Aquinas in dividing the passions into damaging perturbations and virtuous affections.[102] A chapter on 'How the passions may be well directed and made profitable' took a position similar to that of Calvinists, arguing that Christ was moved by passions, that Scripture exhorts us to virtuous passions, and that the passions are 'not wholly to be extinguished (as the Stoics seemed to affirm)'.[103] At the same time, however, Wright's acceptance of the passions and affections, like Southwell's, arose from a distinctively Catholic openness to the full involvement of the senses and emotions in worship and in drawing closer to God.[104] The short poem 'The Passionate Man's Pilgrimage' was probably written around this time by an unnamed Catholic, although it later came to be attributed to Sir Walter Ralegh awaiting execution.[105] Although its title linked it to the current wave of passion literature, it looked beyond the well-worn tears and sighs of the genre to achieve a more visionary effect, as the speaker imagines his soul travelling 'to the land of heaven, / Over the silver mountains, / Where spring the nectar fountains'.[106]

The Passion of a Discontented Mind, the poem with which this investigation of passion literature began, was published in 1601. It is typical in its use of the sixain stanza, established by Southwell and Breton as the standard form for penitential verse. Also typical is how the speaker (probably male – he laments the pressure on the 'sociable man' to 'keep accursed company') describes his 'heart quite rent with sighs and heavy groans', his 'grief and sorrow', and the 'staining filth' of his sins which 'so spotted hath my soul'.[107] However, other aspects of the poem are unusual. Though tears are extolled as a medium of penitence – 'Tears are the key that ope the way to bliss' (211) – the speaker repeatedly laments his inability to weep, often understood as a symptom of insufficient spiritual contrition.[108] Though Mary Magdalen is invoked, this speaker is unable 'To play a poor lamenting Magdalen's part' and 'cannot strain one true repentant tear' (63, 97). He feels more like Judas, unable to free himself from sin: 'For even now, in this my sad complaining, / With new made sins, my flesh my soul is staining' (109, 257–8).

The print edition and one manuscript include a stanza soliciting the intercession of the Virgin Mary, 'fair Queen of mercy and of pity' (25–30); another manuscript includes the inscription IHS (a monogram representing Christ), usually employed by Catholics.[109] However, other lines echo the image used by the Protestant theologian William Perkins for a troubled conscience (see above): 'The worm of conscience still attendeth on us' (151). The word 'discontented' in the poem's title may refer to the Protestant concept of contentment as the assurance of salvation enjoyed by the elect, or may be a Catholic reappropriation

of the term like those of Southwell and Alabaster. However, whichever Church the discontented speaker belongs to, he knows that
heaven is 'the place wherein all sorrows die, / [...] / The mind set
free from care, distrust, or fear; / There all receive all joyful
contentation' (139–43). Most speakers of passion poems, whether
Protestant or Catholic, achieved by the end contented certainty of
divine grace, but the ending of this poem is provisional and equivocal:
the speaker's future intention is to 'spot my face with never-drying
tears' (350), but he may need to contemplate Christ's 'death and
torments' if 'my tears should fail me at most need' (364, 361). In the
closing lines he still has a 'sin-sick soul', and just as at the poem's
opening, 'A guilty conscience this sad passion bears' (382–3). His
passions remain still in process; but if anything, this intensifies the
self-observation and sense of unfolding self-knowledge that are
endemic to passion literature.

Although four of the manuscripts of *The Passion of a Discontented
Mind* associate it with the Earl of Essex awaiting execution, there is
also a strong case for attribution to Breton.[110] By 1601, works published
under his name included not only the penitential poems discussed
above, but also the secular anthology *Melancholic Humours*, which
participated in the craze for passion literature with verses entitled 'A
Doleful Passion', 'An Extreme Passion', and 'A Testament upon the
Passion' (not a poem on Christ's Passion, but a complaint of 'care, that
crucifies my heart').[111] Perhaps Breton wrote *The Passion of a
Discontented Mind* in the persona of Essex, just as he had used the
Countess of Pembroke's voice in other passion poems. Be this as it
may, it is striking that readers wanted to associate the poem with Essex
and his downfall. Passion literature was not only a devotional genre,
but could voice 'discontented minds' in political scenarios, whether
those of disfavoured courtiers (as in, probably, Dyer's 'He that his
mirth hath lost'), or of members of a persecuted community (as in
Southwell's 'Vale of Tears'). As such, it could be readily associated with
fallen oppositional figures, especially those like Essex and Ralegh who
accrued posthumous followings. The genre was remarkably fluid,

moving between Protestant and Catholic, between the devotional and the erotic, and between the inner spaces of the mind and the outer world of political events. What remained consistent across all these uses was a complex relationship between the troubled mind working through its problems and confusions, and the writing mind observing and recording this process and shaping it into a psychological narrative; a relationship made even more complex in the many cases where the writer was not using their own voice. Another defining characteristic of passion literature was a dynamic relationship between mind and body, as inner conflicts were physically signified by the stains of sin and the tears of contrition, and feeling became a way of knowing.

The fluidity of passion literature included gender ambiguity. As we have seen, it was often written by men adopting female voices; of seven penitential poems certainly attributed to Breton, five are dedicated to female patrons and use female personae.[112] The speaker of *The Passion of a Discontented Mind* compares himself to Judas, David, and the prodigal son, but also to Mary Magdalen and an unfaithful wife.[113] For Southwell in *Mary Magdalen's Funeral Tears*, 'the wit of one (and she a woman), wholly possessed with passion', took precedence over 'two wits of two men', the two male disciples who came to Christ's tomb, because of her absolute, self-erasing love of Christ.[114] It seems that women were thought to be especially open to, or prone to, the passions. The following chapter will explore this further, and how attitudes to the female mind affected writing by both women and men.

PART II
Marginalised Minds

℘ 4 ℘

In Other Voices
Female Minds

Katherina, heroine of Shakespeare's *The Taming of the Shrew* (1592), undergoes numerous humiliations and privations at the hands of her new husband, Petruchio. Having been crossed by him at every turn – dragged away from her own wedding party, deprived of food and sleep, and tantalised with fine clothes that are then snatched away – she insists that she will 'say my mind':

> My tongue will tell the anger of my heart,
> Or else my heart, concealing it, will break,
> And rather than it shall, I will be free,
> Even to the uttermost as I please in words. (4.3.76, 78–81)

Though this speech may invite our sympathy, Petruchio persists in 'taming' her, and soon appears to succeed when Kate agrees to comply with whatever he says, however erroneous or absurd. She will call the moon the sun and the sun the moon, if he desires: 'What you will have it named, even that it is, / And so it shall be so for Katherine' (4.6.22–3). She appears to become the ideal wife of early modern marriage manuals like Edmund Tilney's *The Flower of Friendship*,

111

which had five editions between 1568 and 1587, and instructed the virtuous wife that her husband's face 'must be her daily looking glass, wherein she ought to be always prying, to see when he is merry, when sad, when content, and when discontent, whereto she must always frame her own countenance'.[1] She must have no thoughts or feelings of her own; or, at least, she must suppress and conceal them.

The Taming of the Shrew culminates, notoriously, in Katherina's oration on the theme that 'Such duty as the subject owes the prince / Even such a woman oweth to her husband' (5.2.155–6). Bianca and the Widow have just disobeyed their new husbands; Katherina admits that 'My mind hath been as big as one of yours', but now, as a reformed character, she places her hand under her husband's foot and urges her fellow wives to follow her example (5.2.170, 177). Her eloquence suggests that her mind is as strong as ever, but now under control, detached from 'the anger of my heart'. She appears, then, to subject her mind entirely to her husband's – but questions remain. Does she submit to Petruchio out of desperation? Or – since he is just as socially disruptive as her – does she recognise that they can make a partnership against the world, and collude in a private joke to startle their friends and relations (and win a wager)? Is her final speech a strategic performance, behind which she secretly persists in her independence of mind? Or has she been brainwashed, her mind broken by Petruchio's mistreatment? Whichever is the case, this comedy's happy ending seems to leave no possibility for the new Katherina to 'say my mind' and 'be free, / Even to the uttermost as I please in words', as the old Katherina used to do.

Katherina's final speech can be problematic for modern audiences, unless delivered with a large dose of irony. Would it have troubled Elizabethan audiences too, or would they have taken it 'straight' as a happy ending? How possible or acceptable was it for real women to 'say their minds' or, if literate, to write their minds? The spiritual journal of Lady Margaret Hoby might seem at first sight to be a good place to look. Hoby made entries in her manuscript for most days from August 1599 to July 1605, and we might expect these to resemble the tears, sighs, and heart-meltings recorded by Richard Rogers in his spiritual journal a few years earlier (see Chapter 3 above). However, entries typically read like this:

> After private prayer I did take order for things in the house, then I brake my fast and went to church; then I came home and privately prayed; after I had dined I wrote to my mother and Mr Hoby, and dispatched one away to him, then I saw some things done in the house; after, I wrote notes in my Bible, then I prayed with Master Rhodes [her chaplain, Richard Rhodes], and then walked till almost supper-time, and then examined myself and prayed.[2]

We learn that Hoby spent much time looking within, but little about what she found there. On rare occasions she alludes to inner turmoil, but gives little detail: after a visit to her mother, for instance, 'where I was much grieved touching her weakness in receiving false reports', she went to bed 'with tears and prayers' (xlvi, 166). She frequently records physical ailments, which she interprets as judgements from God, but we might interpret as symptoms of psychological troubles: on one occasion she 'went to bed, God having a little afflicted me with sickness for a great desert: the Lord grant me true repentance for all my sins, Amen, Amen' (45). Intriguingly, she records reading Bright's *A Treatise of Melancholy* (xlv, 28). However, such hints at her mental state are scarce (for a few more examples, see Chapter 6 below), and leave the causes and nature of her mental afflictions largely opaque. Hoby's journal is governed by rigorous self-discipline, in both her regular acts of introspection and her austere record of their dates and frequency, but not their content. It is a kind of spiritual account book, not a repository for thoughts and feelings, which Hoby seems reluctant to set down even for herself.

What made Hoby so reticent? No doubt it was partly a matter of her personal temperament, but we can also find good reasons in the pervasive cultural view of women as intrinsically unable to control their minds and emotions. It is instructive to compare Arbella Stuart, who wrote her mind without restraint.[3] In early March 1603, in the weeks leading to Elizabeth I's death, Stuart was confined at Hardwick Hall in Derbyshire by her formidable grandmother Elizabeth Talbot, Countess of Shrewsbury, known as Bess of Hardwick. Stuart was the Queen's cousin, descended from Henry VIII's sister Margaret, and had been raised by Bess as a princess and prized family asset, but now, in her late twenties, she increasingly chafed against her grandmother's controlling behaviour. She also found herself in both political and personal stasis, as the Queen neither invited her to court, nor clarified her place in the order of succession, nor arranged a marriage for her (having royal blood, Stuart could not choose her own husband). Stuart may well have feared green sickness, a physical and psychological disorder that was supposed to afflict young women who retained their virginity for too long.[4] In the winter of 1602–03, she had taken matters into her own hands, secretly writing to Edward Seymour, Earl of Hertford, to propose her marriage to his grandson, also Edward Seymour, another potential claimant to the throne. However, Hertford had exposed her plot, and Stuart was even more strictly confined by Bess as her actions and intentions were investigated by the Secretary of State, Sir Robert Cecil, and his agent Sir Henry Brounker.

In a series of letters to Brounker, Stuart poured out her grievances and frustrations. Her longest letter – nearly twenty pages in a modern edition – took all day: 'Now I have spent this day in portraying my melancholy innocence'.[5] She appears to have been driven by combined motivations of self-vindication, revenge on Brounker for remarking 'that the more I writ, to the less purpose it was' (167), and the emotional release gained by writing. As she dwells on her 'most bitter tears of discontent', 'melancholy thoughts', and 'fear, despair, grief, mistrust' (161, 167, 170), she often sounds as if she has been steeping herself in the passion literature discussed in Chapter 3 above. Yet she realises that the more she writes, the more she damages her cause. Brounker should not think 'that my troubled wits cannot discern how unlooked for, how subject to interpretation, how offensive almost every word will be even to you' (167). Nevertheless, 'I think

the time best spent in tiring you with the idle conceits of my travelling mind, till it make you ashamed to see into what a scribbling
melancholy (which is a kind of madness, and there are several kinds
of it) you have brought me' (168). Stuart at once unreservedly
expresses her inner turmoil and self-consciously observes herself
doing so, repeating (in this and another letter) the eloquent phrase
'my travelling mind' (156, 168, 172). Her analytical intelligence is
applied to both her own mental state and how it will be received: it
will be 'subject to interpretation', which will not be favourable. This
expectation was completely accurate; indeed, already, on a letter that
she had written a few days earlier, Cecil had inscribed, 'I think that
she hath some strange vapours to her brain' (149).

Stuart's letters are sometimes rambling and incoherent, and she
was evidently in a disturbed mental state, probably exacerbated by
her refusal, as reported by Bess, to eat or drink (34–5). Yet she is
remarkable as an Elizabethan woman who freely expressed her mind
in writing, 'Even to the uttermost as I please in words', to quote
Katherina – even though keenly aware while doing so that she was
reinforcing stereotypes of the female mind as prone to disorder and
unruly passions. The general Elizabethan theories about connections
between mind and body that we explored in Chapter 1 were applied
with particular force to women: Cecil's phrase 'strange vapours'
epitomises widely held beliefs that the female body was weak and
unstable, and that this made the female mind equally unruly. Because
their minds were widely assumed to be out of control, many female
writers chose forms, genres, and subjects that exemplified control
and demonstrated their conquest of the supposed irrationality and
waywardness of their sex.

Spenser's characterisation of chaste Canacee in *The Faerie Queene*,
although a favourable portrait of a virtuous woman, underlines the
restrictive alternatives open to women. Canacee 'Ne euer was with
fond affection moued' – and we must remember that in Elizabethan
terms 'fond' can mean 'foolish' and an 'affection' can be an affliction of
the mind. Instead she 'rul'd her thoughts with goodly gouernement,

/ For dread of blame and honours blemishment'. Any failure, or apparent failure, in self-government in a woman incurs blame and blemished honour; hence, many women writers of the period seem to regulate their thoughts much as Canacee regulates her looks, which 'none of them once out of order went, / But like to warie Centonels well stayd, / Still watcht on euery side, of secret foes affrayd'.[6] We can understand such self-regulation more fully if we look further into what men wrote about the female mind.

'The imbecility of their understandings': men disparaging the female mind

'A woman's reason' was a proverbial Elizabethan phrase meaning a statement of the obvious, or an explanation in the form of a tautologous reiteration. In Shakespeare's *The Two Gentlemen of Verona* (1594), Lucetta advises Julia to favour Proteus over her other suitors, because 'of many good, I think him best'. When Julia asks, 'Your reason?', Lucetta simply replies, 'I have no other but a woman's reason: / I think him so because I think him so' (1.2.21–4). John Manningham, a law student at the Middle Temple, noted in his diary in 1603 that 'I will not believe it, because I will not' was 'a woman's reason'.[7]

Behind this flippant concept of 'a woman's reason' lay beliefs grounded in humoral theory that women had less reason and wisdom than men. As we saw in Chapter 1, men could not only belong to different humoral types, but could also have temperaments formed of potentially infinite combinations and variations of humours, creating a multiplicity of diverse individuals. The female constitution, however, was defined as always cold and moist – that is, phlegmatic. This made women fertile, but deprived them of the heat and dryness essential for intellectual aptitude. As *The Examination of Men's Wits* explained, 'verily it is impossible that a woman can be temperate or hot, but they are all cold and moist'; and 'cold and moist are the qualities which work an impairment in the reasonable part'.[8] A normal, healthy woman could not be 'hot and dry, or endowed with a wit and ability conformable to these two qualities', because if she were formed of a hot and dry seed, 'she should have been born a man, and not a woman' (283). Eve was the prime example: 'So then this defect of wit in the first woman grew for that she was by God created cold and moist, which temperature is necessary to make a woman fruitful and apt for childbirth, but enemy to knowledge' (283).

All this had obvious consequences for the social role and position of women: 'On this nature, St Paul grounded himself when he said: "Let a woman learn in silence with all subjection." Neither would he allow the woman to teach or govern the man, but to keep silence' (283–4). At the same time, the *Examination* recognised degrees of coldness and moisture in women, and that a woman who was less cold and less moist would have 'a sharp wit'. However, she would also be 'froward [perverse], curst [bad-tempered], and wayward', 'insupportable' to live with, and physically repugnant: 'shrill voiced, spare fleshed, [. . .] hairy and evil favoured [of ugly features]' (284, 290).

Such biologically determinist views of the female mind occur widely in Elizabethan writing. *The Haven of Pleasure* (1597), a conduct book, refers to 'the weakness of [women's] minds, and the imbecility of their understandings and judgements'. Women lack the mental faculties required to control their passions: 'a woman incensed with anger will be stark mad with rage, and purposing or presuming beyond her power can neither tame her lusts, nor bridle the troubled motions of her mind, no, nor in any mean sort resist them with wisdom and reason'. This mental chaos is exacerbated by menstruation:

I find there is nothing so much incenseth their anger as that venomous scum and filthy sink of humours, which they monthly gather and purge according to the course of the moon. For if a woman happen near the time of that disease to be provoked to anger (as small things then will greatly offend them), the whole sink of that filth being stirred doth fume and disperse itself over the body; whereby it falleth out that the heart and brain being affected and troubled with the smoke and sparks of that most odious excrement, the spirits both vital and animal that are serviceable to those parts are inflamed.

At this dangerous time of the month, women 'will bark and brawl like snarling dogs [. . .] because reason with them is of no force, their judgements weak, and their minds feeble and infirm, they brawl and brabble'.[9]

Women's supposed lack of reason meant that their imaginations too were out of control. Ludwig Lavater's treatise *Of Ghosts and Spirits Walking by Night* (published in Latin in 1569 and in English in 1572) accepted the existence of ghosts but dismissed many supposedly supernatural apparitions as the hallucinations of women: 'Women, which for the most part are naturally given to fear more than men [. . .] do more often suppose they see or hear this or that thing than men do. And so do young women, because commonly they are afraid.'[10] Reginald Scot in his sceptical treatise *The Discovery [i.e., Exposure] of Witchcraft* (1584) similarly blamed most apparently magical occurrences on 'poor melancholic women'. Because women had an intrinsically cold and moist constitution, any loss of moisture tipped them into the cold and dry condition of melancholy, whose effects included a disordered imagination. Scot asserted that 'the stopping of their monthly melancholic flux or issue of blood' in post-menopausal women caused a build-up of black bile, resulting in 'weakness both of body and brain', and making them 'the aptest persons to meet with such melancholic imaginations'. They could be readily persuaded that they could 'transform their own bodies, which nevertheless remaineth in the former shape', 'falsely suppose they can hurt and enfeeble other men's bodies', and 'hinder the coming of butter, etc. [. . .] what is it that they will not imagine, and consequently confess that they can do?'[11]

Scot's critique of superstition became an attack on older women, whereas the physician Edward Jorden hoped to detach women from negative associations with superstition when he published *A Brief Discourse of a Disease Called the Suffocation of the Mother* (1603). The previous year he had testified at the trial of Elizabeth Jackson for bewitching Mary Glover, arguing (unsuccessfully) that Glover's symptoms were actually caused by 'suffocation of the mother', a disorder of the womb.[12] His book likewise contended that supposed cases of demonic possession were more likely caused by uterine ailments. Jorden's stated intention was to defend women like Jackson from charges of witchcraft; yet the terms of his argument reinforced negative views of the connections between the female body and mind. According to Jorden, the womb was a dangerous, unruly organ whose disorders – what later ages would call hysteria – affected all other parts of the body and could produce bizarre symptoms, including breathlessness, animal noises, 'frenzies, convulsions, hiccups, laughing, singing, weeping, crying, etc.'. Loss of physical and emotional control in the sufferer was accompanied by impairment of the mental faculties of imagination, reason, and memory: 'very often there happeneth an alienation of the mind in this disease, whereby sometimes they will wax furious and raging deprived of their right judgement and of rest'.[13]

The idea of female mental disorders as rooted in the body, especially in the sexual organs, is epitomised in the differing mad states of Ophelia and Hamlet. Hamlet's madness hovers ambiguously between the real and the feigned, and does not prevent him from delivering profound soliloquies, philosophical reflections, and remarks that are surreal and nonsensical in manner but witty and satirical in effect. As Polonius observes, 'Though this be madness, yet there is method in't [...] How pregnant sometimes his replies are' (2.2.201–2, 204–5). Ophelia's speeches, by contrast, leave no doubt that she has entirely lost her reason and her mind is out of control, jumbling together fragments of proverbial sayings, ballads, folk songs, and social formulae ('Good night, ladies, good night, sweet ladies, good night, good night', 4.2.71–2). Throughout she harps obsessively on sexual matters:

Then up he rose and donned his clothes
And dupped [unlatched] the chamber door,

Let in the maid that out a maid
Never departed more [...]
Young men will do't if they come to't,
By Cock they are to blame. (4.2.52–5, 60–1)

Her persistent association with flowers – including the pansies, columbines, and daisies that she gives to her brother and other courtiers, and the garlands she weaves before her watery death – intertwines connotations of virginal innocence, youthful fertility, and defloration (4.2.171–7, 4.4.167–71). Jorden maintained that the 'suffocation of the mother' was frequently caused by a virgin's need for sexual initiation to release the 'congestion of humours' around the womb, or by 'the want of the benefit of marriage' – that is, lack of sexual intercourse – 'in such as have been accustomed or are apt thereunto'.[14] We are never clearly told whether Ophelia has slept with Hamlet: if she has not, then she may be suffering from the green sickness of a virgin; if she has, then she may be a sexually awoken woman suffering unsatisfied physical needs. Either way, although the immediate provocation for her madness is grief at her father's death, it is represented in terms of disordered sexual desires which have unleashed her speech from the control of modesty and reason. Her madness is pitiful, produced by the fluctuating states of the female body, consisting in a loss of rational control, and fundamentally different from the articulate, intellectual, madness of Hamlet, which by contrast seems purposeful and managed. The context for this difference is the persistent and pejorative Elizabethan association of women's minds with their disorderly and mysterious bodies.[15]

'Exercises of good learning': men praising the female mind (within limits)

The disparaging assessment of women's reason and wisdom by many Elizabethan writers, and the underlying humoral theory that women's constitutions invariably excluded them from intellectual activity, seem extraordinary in view of the impressive achievements of women of the period as scholars, linguists, and authors. Earlier chapters have already discussed or mentioned notable writings by various women, including Anne Askew, Katherine Parr, Anne Lock, and Mary Sidney Herbert, Countess of Pembroke. As well as translating sermons by Calvin and writing devotional sonnets, Lock also (as Anne Prowse, following her third marriage) translated Jean Taffin's *Of the Marks of the Children of God* (1590). Pembroke was also prolific: in addition to her translation of de Mornay's *Discourse of Life and Death* and her Psalm paraphrases, she translated Robert Garnier's neo-Senecan tragedy *Antonius* (1590) and Petrarch's *Triumph of Death*, and composed a dramatic dialogue and at least two original poems.[16] Nor were these by any means the only female scholars and writers of the period. Other authors of original works in English included Isabella Whitney, whose poems were published in *The Copy of a Letter* (c. 1566–67) and *A Sweet Nosegay* (1573), and Anne Wheathill, author of the prayer book *A Handful of Wholesome (Though Homely) Herbs* (1584). Meanwhile, there were also many other notable female translators. To pick out just a few: Lady Jane Lumley made the earliest known translation of any Greek tragedy into English, her version of Euripides' *Iphigenia* (in manuscript, probably made a few years before Elizabeth's accession in 1555).[17] Anne Cooke Bacon (sister of the equally learned Mildred Cooke Cecil, Elizabeth Cooke Hoby Russell, and Katherine Cooke Killigrew) made available to readers of English John Jewel's *Apology of the Church of England* (1564), an important founding text of Elizabethan Protestantism;[18] while Margaret Tyler's translation from Spanish of *The Mirror of Princely Deeds and Knighthood* (1578) initiated a boom in the publication of Iberian chivalric romances. According to Brenda M. Hosington, English women made twenty-five translations into or out of Latin between 1526 and 1600, and composed some 200 original neo-Latin poems over the Renaissance period, including *Poëmata* (1602) and *Parthenica* (c. 1608) by the prolific Elizabeth Jane Weston.[19]

The Queen herself was famed for her proficiency in multiple languages – her former tutor, Roger Ascham, extolled 'her perfect readiness in Latin, Italian, French, and Spanish' – which was displayed throughout her life.[20] In 1544, aged eleven, she translated Marguerite de Navarre's *Le Miroir de l'âme pécheresse* (*The Glass of the Sinful Soul*), declaring in a preface that 'the wit of a man or woman' will 'wax dull and unapt to do or understand anything perfectly unless it be always occupied upon some manner of study'.[21] Fifty-three years later, she showed that she had lived by this maxim when she delivered an *ex tempore* Latin speech of rebuke to an impertinent Polish ambassador.[22] Elizabeth also composed speeches, letters, poems, and prayers, and deployed her prowess in rhetoric, languages, and scholarship to assert her authority in the face of persistent doubts about female monarchy.[23] Her earliest portrait, as a thirteen-year-old princess, shows her holding one book and flanked by another on a lectern (fig. 7).[24]

The visible intellectual achievements of these women reflected the fact that some men took a more favourable view of their mental capacities, and hence of their entitlement to education. Earlier in the century, Sir Thomas More had been in the vanguard of this movement by giving his daughters a similar humanist education to that of his sons; Sir Anthony Cooke, father of the learned Cooke sisters mentioned above, emulated this model. Protestantism placed a particularly high value on learning as an essential part of piety, and this identification of erudition with virtue made it more available to women.[25] Ascham praised the intellectual aptitude not only of his former pupil Princess Elizabeth, but also of Lady Jane Grey, whom he recalled joyfully reading Plato while the rest of her family went hunting.[26] Another educationalist, Richard Mulcaster, headmaster of the Merchant Taylors' School, asserted in his treatise *Positions* (1581) that 'young maidens are to be set to learning, which is proved by the custom of our country, by our duty towards them, by their natural abilities, and by the worthy effects of such as have been well trained'.[27]

Yet a strong motivation for Ascham's praise of his illustrious female pupils was to promote his own excellence as a tutor;[28] and others who

7. The young Elizabeth I is depicted here as a studious Protestant princess, accompanied by books. Female erudition was associated with piety, virtue, and elite status. Throughout her life, Elizabeth would flaunt her impressive scholarship in refutation of persistent claims that women lacked the intellect and reason to govern.

wrote favourably of the female mind often did so in terms that were qualified or limited. Anne Cooke Bacon's translation of Jewel's *Apology* was felt to improve upon an earlier translation and so was adopted as the official version. A preface by Matthew Parker, Archbishop of Canterbury, praised her 'clear translation', avoiding 'the perils of ambiguous and doubtful constructions', and making this 'good work more publicly beneficial'. At the same time, however, he implied that this was almost miraculous in a woman's work and that few of her sex were so seriously minded: 'all noble gentlewomen shall (I trust) hereby be allured from vain delights to doings of more perfect glory'.[29] Mulcaster meanwhile seemed undecided whether to uphold Elizabeth and other learned ladies as evidence that girls could and should be educated, or to extol them for transcending the general inferiority of their sex:

> that young maidens deserve the training, this our own mirror, the majesty of her sex, doth prove it in her own person, and commends it to our reason. We have besides her highness, as under-shining stars, many singular ladies and gentlewomen so skilful in all cunning [knowledge] of the most laudable and love-worthy qualities of learning, as they may well be alleged for a precedent to praise, not for a pattern to prove like by.

He firmly maintained that girls' education must be at home and limited to appropriate subjects and skills. Boys' education should be 'without restraint for either matter or manner, because our [i.e. men's] employment is so general in all things', and royal women were exceptional cases who should be trained in government; but most girls should merely be trained in wifely obedience, or a skill by which to earn a living, or, if aristocratic, to enhance the honour of the family.[30]

The Examination of Men's Wits dismissed the achievements of female scholars as no evidence for their possession of reason or wisdom:

> the female, through the cold and moist of their sex, cannot be endowed with any profound judgement. Only we see that they talk with some appearance of knowledge in slight and easy matters with terms ordinary and long studied, but being set to learning, they reach no farther than to some smack of the Latin tongue, and this only through the help of memory.[31]

Other authors feared that the female mind, because of its intellectual and moral weakness, would turn a good education to bad ends.

Edward Hake's *A Touchstone for this Time Present* (1574) commended 'exercises of good learning, and knowledge of good letters' for women, but deplored the uses to which female literacy was being turned:

> No sooner is the daughter of age of understanding, but she straightway and therewithal learneth the high path to whoredom, and the principles of vanity and lewdness. [...] she is so nuzzled [nurtured] in amorous books, vain stories, and fond trifling fancies that she smelleth of naughtiness even all her life after.[32]

Thomas Salter's *Mirror of Modesty* (1579) advised that a woman's education should be wholly confined to 'the government of her household and family', not only because women had no part in public life, and so no need of training for it, but also because

> recreation by learning [...] cannot be granted her without great danger and offence to the beauty and brightness of her mind [...] in such studies as yieldeth recreation and pleasure, there is no less danger that they will as well learn to be subtle and shameless lovers, as cunning and skilful writers of ditties, sonnets, epigrams, and ballads; let them be restrained to the care and government of a family.[33]

Even the scholarly and literary accomplishments of women did not necessarily dispel views of female minds as too weak and irrational to control their wayward passions, imaginations, and senses.

'Waxen minds': men inside the female mind

The print pamphlet *Jane Anger: Her Protection for Women* (1589) appears to be the work of an Elizabethan woman defending her sex against charges of intellectual and moral incapacity. It responds to a lost attack on women called *Book: His Surfeit in Love* (i.e., *Book's*

Surfeit in Love), which, we can deduce, attacked women as seducers and deceivers. Anger puts forward a number of bold and cogent arguments in women's defence: for instance, that male writers rail against women when they run out of other ideas and to show off their rhetoric; and that 'we women are more excellent than men' because Adam was made of 'dross and filthy clay', whereas Eve was made of the 'purer' matter of 'man's flesh'.[34] This might look like a refreshingly spirited proto-feminist polemic – but all may not be as it seems. 'Jane Anger' is obviously a pseudonym and may well conceal a male author. In a preface to women readers, 'she' apologises that the work is 'that which my choleric vein hath rashly set down' – so 'she' has a hot and dry temperament, not the cold and moist constitution supposedly natural to women (31). She could be an unnaturally mannish and shrewish woman, or she may be a man, writing in this persona to create an extended satirical portrait of female anger and to capitalise commercially on a controversy instigated by *Book: His Surfeit in Love*. Like Chaucer's Wife of Bath, 'Jane Anger' may look to the modern reader like a cheeringly proto-feminist spokeswoman for her sex, but she could be the fictional creation of a male author, one that responds to the contexts of the time by presenting a misogynist stereotype of a stroppy, loud-mouthed woman.

If 'Jane Anger' is really a man, 'she' is one of numerous textual impersonations of women by Elizabethan men, in female dramatic roles, speeches, and interior monologues by female characters in prose fiction, and various kinds of female-voiced poems.[35] Indeed, it makes sense to locate Anger's *Protection* on a narrow borderline between the railings of a shrew and the popular Elizabethan genre of female complaint, in which a woman laments mistreatment by a man. As we have seen, Shakespeare's Katherina occupies this borderline between unruliness and pathos when, after much suffering at Petruchio's hands, she declares that 'My tongue will tell the anger of my heart / Or else my heart, concealing it, will break' (4.3.78–9). Jane Anger is similarly sympathetic when she protests that, far from seducing and deceiving men as *Book: His Surfeit in Love* had claimed, women are their innocent prey: men 'become ravenous hawks, who do not only seize upon us but devour us [. . .] we languish when they laugh, we lie sighing when they sit singing, and sit sobbing when they lie slugging and sleeping [. . .] If women breed woe to men, they bring poverty, grief and continual fear to women' (35, 37). The emphasis on the languishing and sobbing of pitiful women in these more plaintive passages is perhaps no less discordant with modern feminism than the stereotype of the railing shrew. However, it typifies a fascination in Elizabethan writing with female accusations against men, which could readily slide between the stridency of a scold and the senti- mental appeal of a victim.

The genre of female complaint stretched back through the Middle Ages to Ovid's *Heroides* and other classical sources, but particularly flourished in the Elizabethan period.[36] 'Shore's Wife' by Thomas Churchyard, in the voice of Jane Shore, the disgraced mistress of Edward IV, appeared in the 1563 edition of *A Mirror for Magistrates*, an anthology of tragic verse monologues by historical figures, then in expanded form in *Churchyard's Challenge* (1593). This second version formed part of a wave of female complaints in the early 1590s, including Samuel Daniel's *Complaint of Rosamond* (1592), Anthony Chute's *Beauty Dishonoured* (1593), Thomas Lodge's 'Complaint of Elstred' (1593), Michael Drayton's *Matilda* (1594), and more.[37] As in the contemporaneous genre of penitential poetry that we explored in Chapter 3, in which male authors such as Southwell and Breton frequently adopted female voices, male authors exploited the scope offered by a female persona to range through extremities of desire, remorse, and grief. Ironically, because they were not under the same pressure to prove their self-control, male authors had more freedom than female authors to explore the full emotional range of the female voice. The very volatility and unruliness that were attributed to the female mind, and used to justify women's exclusion from public life and intellectual endeavour, made it an appealing and productive site from which to write passionate poetry.[38] Moreover, because the female mind was supposedly particularly subject to bodily fluctuations, a female voice could be used for dynamic and complex explorations of mind–body relations. In particular, women's association with the private sphere and sexuality meant that female complaint often involved sensational erotic narratives of seduction, rape, or tragic death in the cause of chastity. Such situations imagined from the point of view of fallen, wronged, or desperate women gave male authors and readers voyeuristic access to women's secret thoughts and feelings.

Shakespeare often wrote female complaints. In his Elizabethan plays, Adriana in *The Comedy of Errors* (1592), multiple women in *Richard III* (1593), Julia in *The Two Gentlemen of Verona* (1594), Helena in *A Midsummer Night's Dream* (1595), and Viola in *Twelfth Night* (1601) all have speeches that participate in the genre. However, his fullest contributions were his non-dramatic poems *The Rape of Lucrece* (published in 1594) and 'A Lover's Complaint' (published with the Sonnets in 1609). The former in particular takes us deeply into the mind of its heroine as it retells the rape of Lucrece (or Lucretia) by Tarquin, son of the King of Rome, and her subsequent suicide. This tragic tale was well known in Elizabethan England from Livy and Ovid, from St Augustine's discussion of the morality of Lucrece's suicide, and from versions of the story by authors including Chaucer in *The Legend of Good Women*.[39] Her image was widely reproduced in paintings, tapestries, shop signs, printers' devices, and seals: Olivia in *Twelfth Night* uses a Lucrece seal (2.5.84–5). Fascination with Lucrece was evidently fuelled by the many ambiguities of the story: was it a titillating erotic narrative or a celebration of female purity? Was Lucrece's suicide an act of heroic self-mastery and sacrifice, or of surrender to despair? The relations between the female mind and the female body were at the heart of these questions, and were explored in depth by Shakespeare.

The rape occurs around a third of the way through the poem, where it is over in a moment and barely described (680–93). Most of the work consists of lengthy interior monologues, first as Tarquin debates 'in his inward mind' whether to commit the rape (185), then, at even greater length, Lucrece's debate after the rape. Her attempts at public utterance in encounters with her servants and with her husband and other Roman lords are hesitant and inhibited; but in her mind she is almost unstoppably eloquent as she articulates her inner turmoil and sense of shame, strives to understand the rape's effects on her mind and soul, and argues her way towards suicide. The poem contracts inwards: as a virtuous Roman wife, Lucrece is confined to the private space of the home, and within this to her chamber; within this again, we retreat with her into the 'cabinet' of her mind (442).

In the aftermath of the rape, Tarquin's soul is described as a 'spotted princess' (721), and much of Lucrece's inner debate revolves around the question of whether she too has been spotted or stained. Indeed, the poem is obsessed with staining: the word 'stain' and its derivatives are used twenty-one times, while 'spot' and 'blot' each occur seven times, and 'blemish' three. The sense of these terms is poised between the metaphorical and the literal: at some points Lucrece considers the 'sacred temple' of her own soul 'spotted, spoiled, corrupted' (1172); but she also worries that this inner stain is outwardly visible on her body: 'Make me not object to the tell-tale day; / The light will show charactered [inscribed] in my brow / The story of sweet chastity's decay' (806–8). Elsewhere, however, she defiantly proclaims her inner purity, especially in the moments before her suicide:

> Though my gross blood be stained with this abuse,
> Immaculate and spotless is my mind.
> That was not forced, that never was inclined
>> To accessory yieldings, but still pure
>> Doth in her poisoned closet yet endure. (1655–9)

As in the representations of martyrs discussed in Chapter 2 above, she contrasts the damage to her body with the inviolability of her inner being. After her death, her blood is divided into two kinds that give physical, visible evidence of both purity and staining, and leave

Lucrece's spiritual status troublingly ambiguous: 'Some of her blood still pure and red remained, / And some looked black, and that false Tarquin stained' (1742–3).

The poem also offers no easy answers to the question of whether Lucrece's suicide is a rational, considered act that proves her virtue and courage, or an irrational, passionate act of violent despair. Lucrece certainly uses many words and much rhetorical skill to argue herself and the reader towards it. Yet the narrator repeatedly asserts that she is overwhelmed by frantic passions:

> So she, deep drenchèd in a sea of care,
> Holds disputation with each thing she views,
> And to herself all sorrow doth compare.
> No object but her passion's strength renews,
> And as one shifts, another straight ensues.
>   Sometime her grief is dumb and hath no words;
>   Sometime 'tis mad and too much talk affords. (1100–6)

We are told that women have 'waxen minds', easily 'stamped' with 'th'impression of strange kinds [. . .] by force, by fraud, or skill' (1240–6). Tarquin may have imprinted on Lucrece not only the stain of dishonour, but also his own failure of self-government and surrender to his disorderly passions. He certainly seems to have communicated to her his self-division: first 'he himself himself confounds' (160), then she declares (addressing her absent husband, Collatine): 'Myself, thy friend, will kill myself, thy foe' (1196).

At the end of the poem, Brutus avenges Lucrece's death by leading a rebellion against the Tarquin dynasty. He tells Collatine, 'Thy wretched wife mistook the matter so / To slay herself, that should have slain her foe' (1826–7). This judgement is logical but feels brutal, partly because of the privileged access that we have been given to Lucrece's anguished inner debate, and partly because it has been made clear throughout that as a woman she is too weak to take physical action against Tarquin. In fact, one of her justifications for her suicide is that it will compel revenge on Tarquin, which is indeed the result when the Romans expel his tyrannical family (1177–1211, 1840–8, 1854–5). In this sense, her suicide is a well-reasoned plan with a successful outcome, and her assertion of personal autonomy – 'I am the mistress of my fate' (1069) – brings about the liberation of all the Roman people. She is a martyr not only to married chastity, but to the establishment of democracy. In this political message *The Rape of Lucrece* is typical of 1590s female complaints, which often involved sexual aggression by a male ruler and thereby linked the personal and political (for more on the politics of *Lucrece*, see Chapter 8).[40]

Yet like Arbella Stuart, Lucrece knows that as a woman she is 'subject to interpretation'. In writing to Collatine she manages her passions in order to present signifiers of righteous grief rather than guilty shame, keeping the letter short:

> the life and feeling of her passion
> She hoards, to spend when he is by to hear her,
> When sighs and groans and tears may grace the fashion
> Of her disgrace, the better so to clear her
> From that suspicion which the world might bear her. (1317–21)

This may sound unsettlingly calculated and performative, but our extensive access to Lucrece's inmost thoughts has authenticated her innocence and distress, so we understand that she simply wants to be read correctly. Because Lucrece is a defenceless victim, because we spend so much time inside her mind and because of the rhetorical cogency of her interior monologues, she wins our sympathy, and on the whole her suicide feels virtuous and heroic, an act of self-control, not lack of control. This is reinforced by the poem's invocations of Neostoicism and martyrology. Yet the poem never fully resolves the many ambiguities and problems that it raises around the meaning of rape and the morality of suicide, and behind these, relations between reason and the passions, and the mind and the body.[41] It gives us one of the richest, fullest, most sophisticated expressions of a female mind in Elizabethan literature – almost making us forget that this is in fact only a 'female' mind, simulated and ventriloquised by a male author.[42] There are potentially disturbing parallels between Tarquin's penetration of Lucrece's body and Shakespeare's penetration of her mind, in which he makes the reader complicit.

'Matter more manlike': speaking through translation

While Shakespeare and other male writers spoke in the voices of female characters, in female complaint and numerous other genres, many Elizabethan women writers spoke in the voices of men, as translators. According to Thomas Norton, translator of Calvin's *Institutes*, the goal of all translators was 'the true setting forth of a writer's mind'.[43] He meant, of course, the mind of the original author of the source text – in his case, Calvin – not the translator, who, he implied, should make him- or herself as unobtrusive as possible. Laurence Humphrey's treatise *Interpretatio linguarum* (*The Translation of Languages*, 1559) implied that women – virtuous ones, at least – might be particularly qualified for this literary disappearing act, and that in turn translation was an appropriate, decorous exercise for women. He listed exemplary female translators, including the daughters of Thomas More, Lady Jane Grey, the Cooke sisters, and, pre-eminently, Elizabeth I, and explained that a good translator must have fidelity supported by diligence, its 'handmaiden and servant', using feminine nouns for all these properties (*fides, diligentia, famula et ministra*).[44] Many conduct books and other sixteenth-century works instructed women that the chief virtues that they should cultivate were 'Obedience, Chastity, and Silence'.[45] The close fit between these virtues and those of the ideal translator at once opened opportunities to women in this kind of writing, and to some extent restricted them to translation as their main literary field of activity.

When authors praised female translators, they often did so by representing their achievements as the products of conscientious toil and piety, reassuringly distinguished from the potentially less conformist activity of original literary creation. Parker commended Anne Cooke Bacon's translation of Jewel's *Apology* as 'your studious labour of translation profitably employed';[46] while Thomas Bentley, editor of *The Monument of Matrons* (1582), a compilation of devotional works by female authors and translators, explained that the contributors

> have not ceased, and that with all careful industry and earnest endeavour, most painfully and diligently, in great fervency of the spirit and zeal of the truth, even from their tender and maidenly years, to spend their time, their wits, their substance, and also their bodies, in the studies of noble and approved sciences [forms of knowledge], and in compiling and translating of sundry most Christian and godly books.[47]

Translation was painstaking and useful labour in the service of others, not unlike needlework, one of the other chief occupations associated with female virtue in this period.[48] In the Argument to *The Rape of Lucrece*, the heroine fulfils her husband's boast of her 'incomparable chastity' when she is found 'spinning amongst her maids' while other Roman wives 'were all found dancing and revelling, or in several disports'. Salter's *Mirror of Modesty* recommended use of the 'distaff and spindle, needle and thimble' as safer for women than learning and writing, which might bring them into 'disfame and dishonour'.[49] Original literary composition might lead women into all kinds of waywardness, but translation was a profitable, diligent kind of labour more like the approved occupations of spinning and sewing.

Yet female writers found in translation various opportunities for literary influence and agency. The values attached to translation were in fact somewhat contradictory, as epitomised by the prefatory materials to John Florio's 1603 translation of Montaigne's *Essays*. In his dedication to two female patrons, Florio asserted that 'all translations are reputed females, delivered at second hand', associating both translation and femaleness with subsidiarity and inferiority. However, a few pages later, in an epistle to the reader, he asserted that 'from translation all science [knowledge] had its offspring [. . .] Why, but whoever did well in it? Nay, who did ever well without it?'[50] Translation was at the centre of Elizabethan literary culture: it was essential to the dissemination of Protestant teaching, the revival of classical learning, and the importation of new discoveries, ideas, and genres.[51] It has been estimated that in the period 1550 to 1660 nearly 3,000 works were translated into English, with a peak of activity between 1570 and 1600.[52] Although much writing by Elizabethan women was in the form of translation, most translations of the period were by men: it was a major, mainstream literary activity.

Also at the centre of literary culture was religion. It was the most important and contentious issue of the age, fundamental to both domestic and international politics, governing most aspects of personal life, and often a matter of life or death. The Bible in English, whether the authorised Bishops' Bible (1568) or the widely used Geneva Bible (1560), was of course at the doctrinal core of English Protestantism, but was surrounded by a vast and varied landscape of religious translation. In a recently compiled catalogue of translations printed before 1641, 49 per cent of entries are religious.[53] This general predominance of religious subject-matter was the context for translations by women. At least fourteen women executed major religious translations between 1500 and 1625, half of whom produced more than one work.[54] Of the twenty-five known translations by women out of or into Latin between 1526 and 1660, eleven were religious, including all of the seven such translations published in print.[55] To some extent this reflects cultural restrictions on women: religious translation was more open to them than other kinds of writing because it could be justified as a pious use of erudition in order to disseminate doctrinal truth and serve God. Yet at the same time, female religious translators were participating in ongoing national and international debates about both institutional religion and personal faith, and could achieve extensive influence. Anne Cooke Bacon's translation of Jewel's *Apology*, recognised as superior to the previous English version in its clear and vivid style, was ordered by the Convocation of 1563 to be placed 'in all cathedral and collegiate churches, and also in private houses'.[56] It was a landmark work in establishing the legitimacy and authority of the new Protestant Church of England, and in explaining and defending its doctrines.

Religious translation could also enable women to promote personal beliefs and engage in controversies, political as well as religious.[57] Even needlework, to which as we have seen translation was sometimes likened as a safe and decorous art for women, could be turned to subversive political ends by female minds. While a prisoner at Hardwick Hall, Mary, Queen of Scots made embroideries depicting a cat (representing Elizabeth) playing with a mouse (Mary herself), and of a barren vine (the childless Elizabeth) being severed so that a fruitful vine (Mary and her Stuart descendants) could flourish.[58] While not quite so combative, the Countess of Pembroke's Psalm paraphrases (exercises closely related to translation) also contained political messages. Pembroke was a member of the disaffected Sidney–Herbert faction which advocated more militant support for Protestant rebels in the Netherlands, the cause in which her brother, Philip Sidney, had died of a battle wound received at Zutphen in 1586. Many of her Psalm paraphrases, along with the dedicatory poem, 'Even now that care', which she composed for the presentation copy for Elizabeth, subtly but firmly instructed the Queen in her duty – so far not fulfilled – to emulate David as a godly ruler.[59]

Pembroke's 1592 translation of Philippe de Mornay's *Discourse of Life and Death* honoured her brother's friendship with this Huguenot writer, and also reinforced their family's affiliation with the international Protestant cause.[60] At the same time it exemplified the appeal that Stoic and Neostoic writing had for women. De Mornay integrated extensive borrowings from Seneca with Christian teaching to advocate disdain for the body and the liberation of the mind and soul from its constraints.[61] In an age when women were repeatedly told that their bodies made their minds deficient and unstable, it is easy to understand the appeal of this for a female translator. De Mornay, in Pembroke's version, represents the body as a 'foul and filthy prison', merely 'the bark and shell of the soul' from which it will be released at death: 'this body which thou touchest, is not man [. . .] Man indeed is soul and spirit: man is rather of celestial and divine quality, wherein is nothing gross nor material.'[62] True identity here resides in the soul, not the body – an affirmative doctrine for Elizabethan women. At the same time the act of translation makes Pembroke into a ventrilo-quist for de Mornay. In this role she temporarily occupies a mascu-line or gender-free subject-position (speaking of the nature of 'man'), and also wields de Mornay's authority, just as in their translations Anne Lock spoke in Calvin's voice and Anne Cooke Bacon in Jewel's voice.

Simply the choice of which work to translate was often in itself a statement by a female writer. Elizabeth I shared with Pembroke an attraction to Stoic works, which she evidently felt spoke to her and for her. Resolution of mind in the face of adversities is a strong theme of Epistle 107 of Seneca's *Moral Epistles to Lucilius*, which Elizabeth translated in around 1567, and of a choral speech from *Hercules Oetaeus* (*Heracles on Oeta*), a tragedy ascribed to Seneca, which she may have translated in around 1589 (though its attribution is uncer-tain).[63] In 1593, she translated Boethius's *Consolation of Philosophy*, with its message of resilient endurance and alignment of the rational soul with the mind of God. As in Pembroke's rendering of de Mornay, the body is disdained: 'But what should I speak of the body's pleasure, whose greedy desires be full of woe, and satiety of repentance?' The mind, however, by casting off physical constraints, can aspire to enter the presence of God: 'Grant that the mind, O Father, climb to Thy highest seat; / And, on Thy view, the clearest sight may set. / Away cast earthly cloud and weight of this mould.'[64] The translation was executed rapidly over just one month, apparently for Elizabeth's private satisfaction and for reassurance at a time of political turbu-lence following the conversion to Catholicism of Henri IV of France, England's main Protestant ally.[65] It may also have been a response to ongoing controversy about female rule and increasing criticism of

Elizabeth in these later years of her reign in terms of the stereotype of the unstable, capricious ageing woman. Sir Walter Ralegh, having fallen into disgrace, had recently complained of her:

Yet will she be a woman for a fashion,
So doth she please her virtues to deface,
[...]
So hath perfection which begat her mind
Added thereto a change of fantasy,
And left her the affections of her kind.[66]

In espousing Stoicism, Elizabeth asserted her inner constancy, and her ability, though a post-menopausal woman, to govern both herself and the nation.[67]

Margaret Tyler was unusual in ranging beyond religion and Stoic resolution to translate a Spanish chivalric romance, *The Mirror of Princely Deeds and Knighthood* (1578). It was so successful that it created a popular literary craze: male writers followed Tyler in translating sequels to the *Mirror*, and other Spanish and Portuguese romance cycles including *Amadis de Gaul* and *Palmerin*. In her preface, she was self-conscious about the transgressiveness of translating 'a story profane and a matter more manlike than becometh my sex', but she defended this radical literary act by brilliant deployment of conventional feminine gestures of humility. She reiterated the conventional view of translation as appropriate for women because it was 'a matter of more heed than of deep invention or exquisite learning', then used this to disclaim responsibility: 'The invention, disposition, trimming, and what else in this story is wholly another man's, my part none therein but the translation'. She also anticipated objections from strict readers who 'would enforce me necessarily either not to write or to write of divinity' by explaining that she had chosen to translate a secular work because 'neither durst I trust mine own judgement sufficiently if matter of controversy were handled, nor yet could I find any book in the tongue [i.e. Spanish] which would not breed offence to some'.[68] This combined a conventional admission of female intellectual incapacity with a shrewd recognition that religion was not in fact as 'safe' a topic for women as was often assumed.

As translator of *The Mirror of Knighthood*, Tyler wrote in the voices of lovelorn princesses and valiant warrior-women. Not only could translation enable women writers to ventriloquise male authors; it could also add another layer of polyphony, enabling female writers to speak through the fictional female personae ventriloquised by men. In translating Petrarch's *Triumph of Death*, Pembroke occupied the role of the poet's unattainable, idealised mistress, Laura, posthumously revealing not only that she secretly returned his love, but also that she had managed his passions as well as her own:

> For, if woe-vanquished once, I saw thee mourn,
>   Thy life or honour jointly to preserve
>   Mine eyes to thee sweetly did I turn.
> But if thy passion did from reason swerve,
>   Fear in my words, and sorrow in my face
>   Did then to thee for salutation serve.[69]

Pembroke also chose to translate Garnier's tragedy *Antonius*, in which the lovers Antony and Cleopatra, defeated in war, despair and kill themselves. This may be construed as a warning against the triumph of passion over reason, making the play a suitable work for a respectable woman to translate; but in doing so, Pembroke wrote at length in the voice of the distressed and sensual Egyptian Queen:

> What say I? Where am I? O Cleopatra,
> Poor Cleopatra, grief thy reason reaves [robs].
> No, no, most happy in this hapless case,
> To die with thee [i.e., Antony, already dead], and dying thee
>   embrace:
> By [*sic*] body joined with thine, my mouth with thine,
> My mouth, whose moisture burning sighs have dried:

To be in one self tomb, and one self chest,
And wrapped with thee in one self sheet to rest.[70]

While Shakespeare and other male authors of complaints used female voices to explore wide-ranging passions and depths of interiority, female translators sometimes practised a kind of double ventriloquism, speaking through the female characters impersonated by male authors to access a wider range of thoughts and feelings than was usually considered acceptable for their sex. Translation, far from involving the dutiful self-effacement of a female author to serve 'the true setting forth of a [male] writer's mind', offered various means of setting forth a mind of her own.[71]

'My mind is here expressed': original poetry by women

Translation, then, was open to women as a supposedly safe form of writing that involved diligence and service rather than independent thought; yet women used it to express their minds through purposeful choices of works to translate, and by speaking in the voices of male authors and assertive or passionate female characters. A few audacious Elizabethan women went further and wrote poetry in their own voices. In an age when men were making extensive use of the sonnet and other lyric forms to express interiority and subjectivity (see Chapter 9 below), women too put thoughts and feelings into verse. However, always detectable in their writing is a pressure to prove that they possessed reason and intellect, and were in control of their passions. This often produced displays of erudition or of harnessing the passions to a virtuous cause, two features that are both present in the funerary verse that Elizabeth Cooke Russell composed for members of her family. Her elegy for her first husband, Sir Thomas Hoby, who died in Paris in 1566, is full of emotional intensity:

O dulcis conjux, animae pars maxima nostrae,
Cujus erat vitae vita medulla meae,

Cur ita conjunctos divellunt invida fata?
Cur ego sum viduo sola relicta thoro?

(Beloved husband, greatest part of our soul,
Whose life used to be the marrow of my life,
Why are the malignant fates tearing apart people who were
     united in this way?
Why am I left alone in a widowed bed?)[72]

Writing in Latin, accessible only to an educated minority of readers, combined with the propriety of wifely mourning, gives Russell licence to express passionate grief.

Isabella Whitney was not an aristocrat like Russell, and all we learn from her poetry is that she lived in London, had siblings who were servants, and experienced financial hardship. Even so, she was the first woman under whose name (or at least initials) a printed volume of original secular poetry appeared in English. Her poem 'I. W. to her Unconstant Lover' (1567) is a rare example of a female complaint by a female author, as the speaker – identified by the initials in the heading with Whitney herself – berates a suitor who has abandoned her for a different bride. However, this is no torrent of unbridled passions. The speaker asserts her authority by flaunting her classical knowledge: she compares her predicament to those of Dido, Ariadne, and Medea, deserted respectively by Aeneas, Theseus, and Jason, thereby announcing that her epistolary poem is an imitation of Ovid's *Heroides* (translated into English by George Turberville in the same year). Just as female translators spoke through female characters created by men, so Whitney reappropriates the voice of the aggrieved woman from Ovid; but instead of the pathos that we might expect, the tone of the poem modulates between blunt plain-speaking, sarcasm, and even jauntiness. It even invites description as passive aggression:

But if I cannot please your mind
     For wants that rest in me,

Wed whom you list, I am content
    Your refuse for to be.[73]

The speaker tells her ex-suitor that she hopes his new wife will unite the beauty of Helen, the chastity of Penelope, the constancy of Lucrece, and the truth of Thisbe, an image of perfection so absolute that it seems impossible, and sarcastic. She then turns it around:

Perchance, ye will think this thing rare
    In one woman to find:
Save Helen's beauty, all the rest
    The gods have me assigned. (105–8)

She expresses satisfaction with her epistle as she bids her treacherous lover farewell: 'My mind is here expressed' (138). She might well be pleased with her deft, acerbic composition which conveys the speaker's 'mind' in multiple senses: her point of view, her embittered yet unperturbed psychological state, and her cleverness.

Whitney is exceptional as a non-elite Elizabethan woman writing and publishing original secular poetry. Elizabeth I, also a poet, was exceptional in different, obvious ways, and we may assume that as Queen she could write her mind freely. However, she was fond of saying that 'we princes, I tell you, are set on stages in the sight and view of all the world', and was highly conscious of the public reception of all her words and deeds.[74] In her manuscript poem 'The Doubt of Future Foes' (c. 1571), she appears to express her thoughts and feelings about Mary, Queen of Scots. Although Mary had been in confinement in England since her expulsion from her own throne in 1568, she was a threat to Elizabeth because of her rival claim to the English crown and her support from Catholics at home and abroad. The poem opens in a mood of unease and insecurity: 'The doubt of future foes exiles my present joy, / And wit me warns to shun such snares as threatens mine annoy, / For falsehood now doth flow, and subjects' faith doth ebb' (1–3). However, it builds to a declaration of defiance: 'No foreign banished wight shall anchor in this port / [...] / My rusty sword through rest shall first his edge employ' (13–15).[75] Here personal courage blends with the assertion of political authority. The courtier Sir John Harington narrated how a copy of the poem was stolen by Lady Willoughby, much to the displeasure of Elizabeth, who did not want gossip that she was 'writing such toys when other matters did so occupy her employment'.[76] Yet the poem circulated widely thereafter in both manuscript and print,[77] and since it presents an entirely favourable image of Elizabeth's imperturbable bravery and resolute dedication to the realm it seems likely that her annoyance was a performance. The poem itself also looks very like a strategic performance of her supposedly private thoughts intended for public consumption.[78]

Another poem attributed to Elizabeth also appears to give us a glimpse into her secret thoughts and feelings. This is 'On Monsieur's Departure', associated in some later sources with the departure from England in 1582 of Elizabeth's last marriage suitor, 'Monsieur', Francis, Duke of Anjou. The speaker uses a sequence of antitheses:

I grieve and dare not show my discontent;
I love and yet am forced to seem to hate;
[...]
  I am, and not; I freeze, and yet am burned,
  Since from myself another self I turned.[79]

This device derived from Petrarch and had become popular in England from the frequently reprinted anthology *Tottel's Miscellany* (1557), where male poets used it to express their painfully unrequited desire for an unattainable woman. Elizabeth's appropriation of it lays claim to masculine subjectivity and agency, and at the same time suggests that the reader is being granted privileged access to her inner state: she 'dare not show' and is 'forced to seem'. Especially striking is the reference to 'another self' who has been turned away. This is perhaps Anjou as potential husband, or perhaps the Queen's own private self – her 'body natural' as a woman as opposed to her 'body politic' as monarch[80] – sacrificed to political expediency, in the face of opposition from most of her counsellors and subjects to her marriage to a French Catholic. The fact that no manuscripts of the poem survive from Elizabeth's lifetime may indicate that it was not released into public circulation, and indeed represents Elizabeth's carefully guarded emotional secrets.[81] Yet like 'The Doubt of Future Foes', its contents were entirely to her political advantage. Elizabeth was playing a subtle political game with Anjou, distancing herself from him as a wooer while continuing to use him as a military ally in the Netherlands; to him the poem displayed tactful longing and regret, while to her subjects it declared her willingness to sacrifice her personal happiness to their wishes and the public good. We cannot be sure that the poem is not another strategic performance of Elizabeth's inner state. We cannot even be sure whether it was written by her or by a male author imagining her state of mind.

Whitney's 'To her Inconstant Lover' and Elizabeth's 'The Doubt of Future Foes' and 'On Monsieur's Departure' (if it is by her) all express passions while exercising impressive rhetorical control. Even Russell's elegy for her husband contains passionate grief by framing it in skilfully composed Latin verse. Almost all writing by Elizabethan women is shaped by the dominant cultural assumption that the minds of their sex were wayward, volatile, and in need of strict discipline, defined against the supposedly rational, stable, well-governed qualities of the male mind. Definition of the 'standard' mind against minds considered essentially 'Other' also applied when the English mind was compared with those of different nationalities and races. Some of these non-English Others had even fewer opportunities than the women we have been discussing to put their thoughts and feelings into writing – as we shall find in the next chapter.

~ 5 ~

The Minds of Africans
Imaginings and Encounters

In common with human habits throughout history, the Elizabethans often defined themselves against those they considered 'Other'. Many different categories of Other were available to them, spiralling outwards from those close at hand to those in far distant lands. As we saw in the previous chapter, men enhanced their sense of mental superiority by disparaging the supposed irrationality of women. Elizabethan Protestants defined themselves in relation to Catholics, while English Catholics did the reverse. Overseas, but still nearby, the English could find Others in Ireland, their only colony at this time (while England had bold imperial aspirations, these would not be fulfilled until the next century). Representations of the Irish as wild and primitive reinforced a sense of English civility and sophistication and justified English efforts to subdue and govern them, laying the groundwork for later global colonial ideology.[1] Looking instead towards European neighbours to the east and south, English writers vilified Italians and Spaniards as *too* sophisticated, to the point of decadence, characterising them as scheming Machiavels, sensualists, and papist idolaters. Meanwhile, this age of unprecedented global exploration and trade produced numerous more far-flung Others against whom English Elizabethans could position themselves, psychologically and culturally, including Turks, Africans, Indians, and Native Americans.

To explore how the Elizabethans defined their own minds against the minds of all these Others would require at least a whole book in itself, so this chapter offers a case study of one of the groups who seemed to the Elizabethans most different from themselves: Africans. The people of Africa were variously referred to by the English as 'Moors', 'blackamoors', 'Negros', or 'Ethiopians', terms that I will reproduce when quoting from works of the period, though I will use 'Africans' in my own prose. These terms reflected some understanding that Africa was inhabited by diverse populations (as discussed further below), but often collapsed into a single 'Othered' category. The Elizabethans perceived Africans as essentially different from themselves partly because of geographical distance – the southern parts of Africa, in particular, were little known in the sixteenth century – and partly because of skin colour, which was relevant to ideas about the minds of Africans because of sixteenth-century belief in the inter-relationship of mind and body. The term 'complexion' meant not only 'The natural colour, texture, and appearance of the skin, especially of the face', but also 'the combination of the four "humours" of the body in a certain proportion', and hence also 'Constitution or habit of mind, disposition, temperament'.[2] *The Touchstone of Complexions* (1576) offered the reader a manual to both 'the exact state, habit, disposition, and constitution of his own body outwardly' and 'the inclinations, affections, motions, and desires of his mind inwardly';[3] and when both the Prince of Morocco and Portia in *The Merchant of Venice* speak of the former's 'complexion', they are referring to his disposition as well as his skin tone.[4]

The deductions that Elizabethans drew about the minds of Africans from their skin colour were not always what we might expect. Nor were they consistent; and these inconsistencies were compounded by conflicting information from diverse sources, including ancient but persistent myths, new information from the growing corpus of travel narratives, and direct contact with the increasing numbers of Africans within England. Exploring these sources and contexts helps to explain why and how, towards the end of the period, African characters came to be given presence, voice, and subjectivity in plays by English authors. Yet it is also important to note a trenchant statement by the editors of a recent critical anthology, *Early Modern Black Diaspora Studies*, that 'Blackness is not alterity'.[5] Of course, Africans were not Others to themselves, and we must seek evidence of their own minds – their agency, interiority, and sense of identity – in Elizabethan texts. Unfortunately, there are few written records by Africans from the period, so their voices and points of view are usually mediated to us by non-African writers. Nevertheless, even in these indirect representations there are moments of dialogue, reports of actions, and glimpses of experiences that may enable us to look further than literary versions of Africans onto whom English writers projected assumptions and fantasies, and to gain at least some sense of the thoughts and feelings of the real Africans of the period.

'The ablest philosophers, mathematicians, prophets': Elizabethan ideas about African minds

The assertions about Africa of the ancient author Pliny the Elder (23/4–79 CE) continued to be reprinted through the Elizabethan period. Readers learned that apparently some Africans were 8 feet tall, some were cannibals, some had heads like dogs, some walked on their hands, and some 'have no heads, but have their mouth and their eyes in their breasts'.[6] Similarly fantastical was the fourteenth-century narrative of the supposed travels of Sir John Mandeville, also reprinted in the Elizabethan period, which reported among other wonders that 'In Ethiopia are such men that have but one foot, and they go so fast that it is a great marvel, and that is a large foot that the shadow thereof covereth the body from sun or rain when they lie upon their backs'.[7] These mythical works had extraordinary persistence, continuing to be quoted and cited even in new travel narratives based on real journeys and observations.[8] They presented the varieties of humanity in Africa as bizarre and monstrous, in keeping with the exotic flora and fauna of the continent. According to such 'authorities', Africans were a distinctly different order of humanity – or perhaps not fully human at all.

Fortunately, a more recent and reliable authority was also available: *A Geographical History of Africa* by John Leo Africanus. Written in the 1520s, this work circulated widely in Latin, Italian, and French, and was often referred to in English works about Africa even before the publication of an English translation by John Pory in 1600.[9] Leo was of North African heritage and had travelled widely in Africa. He was born a Muslim in Granada, with the given name al-Hasan ibn Muhammad ibn Ahmad al-Wazzan, and grew up in Fez. According to Pory's preface, he underwent various adventures (drawn upon by Shakespeare when constructing Othello's backstory) before being captured by Italian pirates who presented him to the Pope, and converting to Christianity. Leo offered European readers both an insider's account of Africa and an example of a gifted, educated African: Pory extolled him as 'a most accomplished and absolute man', possessing 'natural sharpness and vivacity of wit', who had been trained at the University of Fez in 'Grammar, Poetry, Rhetoric, Philosophy, History', and other disciplines.[10] His biography also illustrates the relative familiarity of North Africans, known as Moors, in southern Europe. Not only were their territories just across the Strait of Gibraltar, but they had ruled Al-Andalus, covering much of the Iberian Peninsula, until 1492. Many Moors still lived in Spain, while engagement in trade, piracy, and conflict around the Mediterranean by both Europeans and Moors brought them into frequent contact.[11]

Leo divided Africa into four regions: Barbary in the north-west; the central northern area of Numidia; Libya, corresponding to the Sahara Desert; and what Pory's translation called the 'Land of the Negros', encompassing everything south of the Sahara, including

147

Guinea and the River Niger in West Africa. Ethiopia in the east, around the Nile, was also a 'land of Negros', but not, according to Leo, part of Africa (though Pory in his additions to the volume *did* include Ethiopia in Africa).[12] Each region was divided into kingdoms (Barbary, for instance, comprised the four kingdoms of Morocco, Fez, Telensin, and Tunis),[13] which in turn were subdivided into cities, towns, and other districts. Leo gave detailed descriptions of the northern areas he knew best, charting a complex patchwork of diverse local populations and their cultures. Unsurprisingly, Barbary, where he had grown up, received most attention and praise, as 'the most noble and worthy region of all Africa, the inhabitants whereof are of a brown or tawny colour, being a civil people, and prescribe wholesome laws and constitutions unto themselves'.[14] A long description of Fez catalogued its numerous stately palaces, temples, colleges, grammar schools, and hospitals.[15] Yet praise was balanced with criticism: even a section on 'The commendable actions and virtues of the Africans', praising the people of Barbary as 'greatly addicted unto the study of good arts and sciences', added that their past excellence in mathematics, philosophy, and astrology had been destroyed 400 years ago under Islamic laws. A subsequent section on the vices of Africans listed various failings even in those of the north, but most harshly condemned 'the Negros' who 'lead a beastly kind of life, being utterly destitute of the use of reason, of dexterity of wit, and of all arts. Yea, they so behave themselves, as if they had continually lived in a forest among wild beasts.'[16] For Leo as a North African, the southern parts of the continent were remote and unfamiliar, peopled by savages; and writing now as a Christian based in Rome, his attitude even to his own North African heritage was ambivalent.

The title-page of Pory's translation of the *Geographical History* named its author as 'John Leo, a Moor', a customary designation for North Africans deriving from the ancient regional name of Mauretania.[17] Sub-Saharan Africans tended to be referred to as 'Negros', as in Pory's version of Leo, as 'blackamoors', or as

'Ethiopians' (despite Leo's exclusion of Ethiopia from the continent).[18] Some Elizabethans were precise in their choice of terms for Africans from different parts of the continent, locating 'white' or 'tawny' Moors in the north and 'blackamoors' and 'Negros' to the south; but often terminology was flexible or even confused.[19] Andrew Boorde wrote in 1555 that in Barbary 'there be white Moors and black Moors';[20] but *Batman upon Bartholome* stated that the term 'Moor' derived from the Greek for 'black', and distinguished between Africans from the north and south only in their being 'black' or 'very black' respectively.[21] In 1589, Sir Arthur Throckmorton described his African servant Anthony as 'the Moor [...] of Guinea', conflating terms for North and West Africans.[22] Conversely, another African servant in Elizabethan England, Mary Fillis, was recorded by a parish clerk as 'of Morisco', that is, North African, but also a 'blackamoor', a term usually denoting a sub-Saharan African.[23] For many Elizabethans, 'Moors' and 'Negros', northern and southern Africans, were much the same, and were simply black.[24] Other conflations added further confusions: 'Moor' was sometimes used as equivalent to 'Muslim', and the designations 'Moor' and 'Turk' were sometimes used interchangeably.[25]

Generalisation is often accompanied by disparagement and stigmatisation. Some modern scholars question whether racism, as we understand it today, existed in the sixteenth century, since it was not until the later seventeenth century that global colonialism and the Atlantic slave trade became fully established, along with the pernicious ideologies that supported them.[26] Some sixteenth-century travellers and writers presented news of encounters with non-white peoples in an open-minded spirit of wonder and curiosity. Francisco Lopez de Gomara (in an English translation of 1555) marvelled at the 'variety of colours' of different populations around the world, and concluded that 'we be all born of Adam and Eve, and know not the cause why God hath so ordained it', unless 'to declare his omnipotency and wisdom in such diversities of colours'.[27] Elsewhere, however, there is extensive evidence of negative associations with the colour black, including black skin. William Cuningham's 1559 work on geography and navigation dismissed Pliny's stories of strange African physiques as 'rather fables than any truth', but nevertheless vilified Africans as 'black, savage, monstrous, and rude'.[28] As we saw in Chapter 3, the Geneva Bible glossed the verses of *The Song of Songs* where the speaker says, 'I am black [...] but comely [...] Regard ye me not because I am black', as meaning: 'The Church confesseth her spots and sin, but hath confidence in the favour of Christ'.[29] Superstitions critiqued by Reginald Scot included the belief that the Devil had black skin and that 'a damned soul may and dooth take the shape of a black Moor, or of a beast, or of a serpent'.[30] While the abhorrent modern ideology of racism had yet to be fully elaborated and institutionalised, evidently prejudice against those with darker skin already existed.

Skin colour mattered, not only because it made Africans visibly different from native English people, but also because of the ways in which Elizabethans connected body and mind. Yet their humoral theories in some ways contradicted prejudices against dark skin. Medical authorities taught that the environment (comprising a particular combination of heat or cold, dryness or moisture) affected the balance of humours in a person's physical constitution, which in turn determined their temperament, a framework dubbed 'geo-humoralism' by the modern scholar Mary Floyd-Wilson.[31] According to Hippocrates, inhabitants of southern regions were themselves hot and dry, like the climate; but for Aristotle, whose teachings gained wider currency, Africans were cool within, because the sun drew out their inner heat.[32] The latter theory was articulated and disseminated in Jean Bodin's widely influential *Method for the Easy Comprehension of History* (1565).[33] Bodin explained that the hot climate made people of the south, including Africans, 'swarthy and deeply black'. They suffered from an excess of black bile, or melancholy, and the hotter the climate, the more this humour predominated in the tempera-ment of the people.[34] It followed that Africans were blessed with the gifts of genial melancholy (see Chapter 1 above), making them intellectual and spiritual. The world owed the origins of its learning and religion to them:

> They have revealed the secrets of nature; they have discovered the mathematical disciplines; finally, they first observed the nature and the power of religion and the celestial bodies [. . .] the ablest philosophers, mathematicians, prophets, and finally all religions in the world have poured forth from those regions as from the most plenteous spring. (111, 113)

Yet Bodin, as a Frenchman, was reluctant to concede superiority to southerners, and balanced his praise with criticism. He asserted that their gifts of melancholy were accompanied by its afflictions: 'disturbances of the intellect' which made them 'sad, with downcast face, slow step, and thoughtful' (102, 107). Moreover, their cleverness was combined with a 'cruel and perfidious' character, 'foxlike cunning', and a desire to 'inflict horribly painful torture' on their enemies (100–2).

Among the many authors who adopted and developed Bodin's geohumoral ideas was André Thevet, for whom they explained the dark skin of Africans. The sun's heat drew black bile, the earthy humour, to the surface of their bodies, where it left a dark residue: 'to the skin of this people so burned, there resteth but the earthly part of the humour'.[35] Timothy Bright concurred that dark skin was produced by melancholy: 'Of colour they [melancholics] be black, according to the humour whereof they are nourished, and the skin always receiving the black vapours, which insensibly do pass from the inward parts, taketh die and stain thereof'.[36] Meanwhile, many North European writers followed Bodin in conceding the cleverness of Africans and other melancholic southerners, but set it against the phlegmatic integrity and reliability of their own people. William Harrison granted 'that in pregnancy of wit, nimbleness of limbs, and politic inventions, they generally exceed us: notwithstanding that otherwise these gifts of theirs do often degenerate into mere subtlety, instability, unfaithfulness, and cruelty'.[37] We are familiar from early modern drama with the English stereotype of Spaniards and Italians as ingenious but duplicitous, sadistic, and deviant; this characterisation was based in geohumoralism and extended to Africans in even more intense terms.

Geohumoral theory was disrupted by the discovery of populations around the globe who lived in similar heat but had different skin colours. George Best, a travel writer, was baffled that people who lived on the equator in America and the East Indies were 'not black, but white, with long hair uncurled as we have'. He concluded 'that there is some other cause than the climate, or the sun's perpendicular reflection, that should cause the Ethiopians' great blackness' and that this was a 'curse and infection' inflicted by God on 'all these black Moors which are in Africa'.[38] Again, Best demonstrates sixteenth-century prejudice against black skin, yet his explanation for it does not seem to have achieved wide currency at this time.[39] Geohumoral theories remained prevalent, despite the challenging evidence of diverse physical characteristics in similar climates, and despite its implication – problematic for many northern writers – that Africans were intellectually superior. Beside Bodin's association of African cleverness with cunning, perfidiousness, and cruelty, another strategy was to represent African cultures as formerly world-leading, but now in decline. Louis Leroy's *Of the Variety of Things* (1594), a study of the rise and fall of civilisations informed by geohumoralism, credited the Ethiopians with the first discovery of learning, but charted its movement progressively northwards, passing to the Egyptians, then the Greeks, then the Romans.[40] The reason for the unrivalled imperial success of the Romans was that they occupied the most temperate zone, giving them a perfect balance of humours, whereas those further south had an excess of intellect which made them unstable and unworldly.[41] We have seen that Leo Africanus represented academic culture in the land of his upbringing as in decay; Pory in his additions to the text re-emphasised that the universities of Muslim cities, 'before most flourishing, have within these four hundred years

daily declined'.[42] Even so, such works acknowledged Africa's importance to the inauguration of learning and civilisation, and recognised
the superior powers of the African intellect.

Meanwhile, geohumoral ideas about African sexuality were
complicated. Bodin understood Africans as a people of extremes,
possessing both the 'greatest gifts of ability' and 'the greatest vices of
body and mind' (101, 107). Hence, they indulged in sexual excesses,
but not as spontaneous acts driven by mindless lust; instead, they
were ingeniously contrived and perverse, as Africans used their
'wisdom and reasoning power [...] that they might sin more freely
for the sake of pleasure' (105). For other writers, the inner coldness
and dryness of Africans made them weak and impotent, by contrast
with the inner heat and moisture of northerners, which made them
vigorous and virile. For Harrison, those who 'dwell toward the course
of the sun' were 'less of stature, weaker of body, more nice [fastidious],
delicate, fearful by nature'.[43] Leroy in *Of the Variety of Things* similarly described North Africans as 'commonly misshapen, meagre,
and lean, of small stature, of tawny, and duskish colour, black-eyed,
with a weak and feminine voice'.[44]

The intricacies of geohumoral thinking were not confined to
academic circles, but informed playhouse drama, as we shall see, and
even a broadside ballad known as 'The Lady and the Blackamoor'.[45]
This was first registered for publication in 1569/70 (though the
earliest surviving print copy is from the mid-seventeenth century)[46]
and belongs to a popular genre of ballads about sensational crimes. It
recounts how, in ancient Rome, an African servant – referred to as a
'heathenish blackamoor' – took revenge on his master for a rebuke.
While the lord was out hunting, the servant locked the doors of the
house and raped his master's wife on the roof. The lord returned and
tried to rescue her but could not enter, and was forced to watch
powerlessly while the servant dashed out the brains of one of his
children and cut off the head of the other. The servant then played a
sadistic trick on the lord: he offered to spare the lady's life if the lord
cut off his nose, which he did, but then threw her down from the

tower anyway. The ballad mentions the servant's 'lust' and his violent physical actions, yet there is striking emphasis on his mind: he 'call[s] to mind' his chastisement by his lord, and demands that the lady yield to him 'his mind for to fulfil'. At the same time, the ballad insistently foregrounds the hearts of non-Africans, including the victims ('His lady's cries did pierce [the lord's] heart'), the narrator ('now my trembling heart it quakes / to think what I must write'), and the audience (the tale 'will make sad the hardest heart'). Non-Africans, the ballad tells us, feel grief and pity, but the African is heartless, driven by a vicious, vengeful ingenuity. His rape of the lady is not a spontaneous carnal act but a calculated atrocity, driven by self-assertive resentment of his master, designed to cause him maximum injury, and performed in public view on the rooftop. In representing a 'blackamoor' protagonist who is duplicitous and ruthless, and uses sexual transgression in a controlled way for purposes beyond physical gratification, this ballad demonstrates the wide reach of geohumoral characterisations of Africans.

'He had so slightly considered of it before': global encounters

Ancient myths and abstract theories about African minds increasingly came up against encounters with real Africans. There were sixteen English voyages to the West African coast between 1531 and 1567, and others through following decades (though various obstacles to English trade in the region made them less frequent).[47] Some of the earlier voyages were slaving ventures. England was not yet a global colonial power with overseas plantations worked by slaves,[48] but Spanish and Portuguese trade in African slaves was well established by the mid-sixteenth century.[49] Some were brought to work in Europe: Boorde reported in 1555, 'There be many Moors brought into Christendom, into great cities and towns, to be sold, and Christian men do buy them [...] they be set most commonly to vile things; they be called slaves'.[50] However, increasing numbers were transported to Spanish and Portuguese territories in the Americas, such that the English mariner John Hawkins heard on his travels 'that Negros were very good merchandise in Hispaniola [one of the earliest Spanish colonies in the West Indies], and that store of Negros might easily be had upon the coast of Guinea', and so 'resolved with himself to make trial thereof'.[51] His three voyages of 1562, 1564–65, and 1567–68 resulted in the capture and transatlantic displacement of some 1,500 Africans.[52] Unsurprisingly (though repulsively), the published accounts of these voyages treat Africans as less than human; this was the whole premise on which the enterprise was founded. Their style is often correspondingly abrupt and casual: 'In this island we stayed certain days, going every day ashore to take the inhabitants, with burning and spoiling their towns'. Once in the West Indies, the Africans were traded for 'commodities' and 'merchandise' that the English could sell at home.[53]

The accounts of the Hawkins voyages are horrifying; yet narratives of other English trading expeditions to Africa, especially the north, record relations of mutual amity and respect. In 1585, Henry Roberts arrived in Morocco as Elizabeth I's ambassador and was received 'with all humanity and honour, according to the custom of the country'. He met the established communities of English, French, and Flemish merchants, and stayed for three years, enjoying regular audiences with the King or his viceroy, 'a very wise and discreet person'.[54] His embassy was just one episode in ongoing trade and diplomatic negotiations between England and Morocco that took place throughout Elizabeth's reign and became increasingly active, fuelled by English desire for sugar and shared hostility to Spain.[55] Even in West Africa, not all visits were conducted in the brutal fashion of Hawkins. In 1553, the King of Benin[56] received an English party in his 'great large hall, long and wide'; they noted the extreme reverence in which he was held by his subjects and kneeled to him themselves. Speaking in Portuguese, he offered them large quantities of pepper.[57] Thirty-five years later, another trading delegation to Benin encountered a similarly gracious reception and responded with courtesy to the King and his ministers.[58] After Hawkins's last slaving voyage of 1568, English transportation of enslaved Africans across the Atlantic ceased until 1641.[59] Over this period (though, of course, things were about to change, appallingly), most English merchants tried to trade *with* Africans, not *in* them, and accordingly approached them as people with different customs from their own, but fully endowed with human minds and cultures.

The English also encountered Africans on the other side of the Atlantic. *Sir Francis Drake Revived* narrated its protagonist's raids on Spanish colonies in the Panama isthmus in 1572, including his alliance with the Cimarrons, communities of African slaves who had escaped from their Spanish masters some eighty years earlier and were waging guerilla warfare against them. Published in 1626, the book was compiled in 1593 from the notes of Drake himself and members of his crew.[60] Drake was a kinsman of Hawkins and had participated in his slaving voyages;[61] but from the outset, by this account at least, he sought to treat the Cimarrons decently, and developed growing respect for them as he and his men increasingly depended on their local knowledge and resourcefulness. We even gain a strong sense of the personalities and experiences of particular Cimarrons, such as Pedro, their leader. During a long trek, the Cimarrons catch an otter and prepare it to be eaten; 'our Captain marvelling at it, Pedro (our chief Cimarron) asked him, "Are you a man of war, and in want, and yet doubt whether this be meat, that hath blood?" Herewithal our Captain rebuked himself secretly that he had so slightly considered of it before.'[62] In this striking narrative moment we hear Pedro's voice (albeit mediated) and gain a sense of his agency and outlook, while Drake's assumptions and sense of self are challenged, and he is provoked to rethink his attitudes.[63] Another Cimarron who is a strong presence in the text is Diego, who initiated Cimarron contact with Drake and his crew and took a leading role in negotiations between them.[64] He eventually returned to England with Drake, then set out with him, as his manservant and interpreter, on his circumnavigation of the globe in 1577 (during which Diego died).[65]

Yet the Cimarrons are not treated as equals: they are patronised as the victims of the tyrannical Spanish, from whom the English claim to have come to deliver them; and they are instrumentalised. We are told that:

These Cimarrons during all the time that we were with them did us continually very good service [. . .] being unto us instead of intelligencers, to advertise [inform] us; of guides in our way to direct us; of purveyors to provide victuals for us; of housewrights to build our lodgings; and had indeed able and strong bodies carrying all our necessaries, yea many times when some of our company fainted with sickness or weariness, two Cimarrons would carry him with ease between them two miles together, and at other times when need was they would show themselves no less valiant than industrious and of good judgement.[66]

Their skills and judgement are recognised, but also exploited, while they are also reduced to the role of bearers, employed merely for their physical strength. The English may not enslave them, but they certainly assume that their natural role is servitude.[67] Troubling aspects to Drake's treatment of Africans are also revealed by other sources, which record that during the circumnavigation he captured a Spanish ship off the Pacific coast of Guatemala and took from it both goods and 'a proper negro wench called Maria'. The woman became pregnant on board Drake's ship, then, when 'very great' with child, was abandoned on an island in Indonesia with two African men. For Drake's contemporary the historian William Camden, the achievement of his circumnavigation was marred by his 'having most inhumanely exposed in an island that Negro or blackamoor maid, who had been gotten with child in his ship'. However, we know nothing more about Maria – including the identity of her child's father, or how she fared on the island – and we do not have even a mediated version of her voice.[68] Based on the fragmentary information we possess, we can only imagine her experiences, thoughts, and feelings. In this, sadly, she is a more typical example than Pedro and Diego of an African in Elizabethan documentary sources.

'Among us': Africans in England

Many Elizabethans did not need to travel around the world, or to read accounts of those travels, to encounter Africans, who had an increasing presence within their own shores. As mercantile and diplomatic relations with Morocco developed, ambassadors from that country came to England in 1589, 1595, and 1600–01.[69] The latter visit attracted particular attention: the delegation stayed in London for six months and Pory published his translation of Leo Africanus to capitalise on the interest that it provoked; while the chief ambassador, Abd el-Ouahed ben Messaoud ben Mohammed Anoun, was the subject of a striking portrait (fig. 8). One observer considered the Moroccan party 'very strangely attired and be-havioured', while another referred to Anoun as 'the barbarian'. However, he brought a proposal for an unprecedentedly close alliance between his country and England, whereby they would join forces against Spain, restore Muslim territories in Andalusia, and seize Spain's New World colonies.[70] Although this never materialised, the fact that such negotiations took place demonstrates that at this point in its history England looked with more friendly eyes upon Muslim Morocco than Catholic Spain.

Africans were increasingly present in England as residents too. Some were brought back from English voyages to Africa and the Americas; others were members of foreign households, such as Elizabeth, Grace, and Mary, three 'blackamoors' who worked for Hector Nunes, a Portuguese physician and merchant, between 1576 and 1590.[71] Best wrote in 1578 that 'We [. . .] among us in England have black Moors, Ethiopians';[72] while a work of 1584 referred to 'black Moors [. . .] that dwell in Guinea (whereof I suppose you have heard and seen also some in this land)'.[73] Modern scholars have debated the significance of three documents issued in the name of

1600

ABDVLGVAHID.

LEGATVS REGIS BARBARIÆ
IN ANGLIAM.

ÆTATIS:42.

8. The Moroccan ambassador painted in London during his visit of 1600–01. Humoral theory linked the darker complexions of Africans with alien qualities of mind: melancholic and clever, but devious and cruel. Even so, Anoun's delegation formed part of friendly political and trading relations between Protestant England and Muslim Morocco.

Elizabeth I in 1596 and 1601 which ordered the transportation of 'Negros and blackamoors' out of England, 'of which kind of people there are already here too many'.[74] Recent research has found that these were not, as was previously thought, general edicts of expulsion: the second and third documents were part of a shady financial deal between the English government and Caspar Van Senden, a Lübeck merchant to whom it was indebted; the third document is only a draft; and none of them seems to have taken effect, since the masters of African servants refused to hand them over.[75] Nevertheless, the documents confirm the presence of Africans in Elizabethan England and suggest growing public awareness of this, including some hostility. They also treat the Africans as a commodity that will enable Van Senden to recoup 'costs and charges' incurred in bringing back English prisoners from Spain and Portugal.[76] Van Senden wanted to transport the Africans to Spain and Portugal, where he presumably hoped to sell them.

The English attitude to slavery is important in relation to the question of how Elizabethans regarded African minds. Did they understand Africans merely as property, or as possessing subjectivity, sensibility, and agency like their own? The evidence is mixed and complex. As early as 1555, an account of a voyage to Guinea whose participants included John Lok (brother-in-law of Anne Lock, the poet discussed in Chapter 3 above)[77] stated that on their return 'They brought with them certain black slaves'.[78] When William Towerson voyaged to Guinea soon afterwards, a representative of the local people demanded

why we had not brought again their men which the last year we took away, and could tell us that there were five taken away by Englishmen; we made him answer that they were in England well used, and were there kept till they could speak the language, and then they should be brought again, to be a help to Englishmen in this country.[79]

This was not a ruse by Towerson: some of the Africans did return to Guinea with him on subsequent voyages; and bringing Africans to England to train them in the language so they could return as interpreters and trade negotiators seems to have become a regular practice. Evidently some English merchants had confidence in the intellectual abilities of Africans and their potential as useful collaborators.[80]

Slavery had no legal status in England and the country had a reputation abroad as a place free from the practice.[81] In 1587, Nunes illegally purchased an 'Ethiopian' from a Cornish mariner, but when he tried to compel him to 'tarry and serve' him an English court ruled that he had no right to do so.[82] Yet the English did engage in slave-trading outside the realm; in 1600, for instance, a ship owned by the London merchant Paul Bayning captured a Spanish vessel near Barbados with over 100 African slaves on board, whom the English sold for pearls elsewhere in the Caribbean.[83] Some historians suspect that slave-owning was also practised by the English within England, furtively and illicitly, facilitated by the lack of legal codification.[84] However, most Africans in Elizabethan England seem to have had the status of servants or other employees. Mary Fillis, a young woman of Moroccan origin, worked first for the merchant John Barker, then for his widow, then for Millicent Porter, a seamstress, suggesting freedom to move from one employer to another.[85] Others, like Reasonable Blackman, described in Southwark parish records as a silk-weaver and a 'blackamoor', lived independently, making an income from a professional skill.[86]

Recent painstaking and groundbreaking research by historians in parish records, household accounts, tax documents, and other archival materials has transformed our knowledge of the presence of Africans in Elizabethan England. Miranda Kaufmann, for instance, author of *Black Tudors*, has compiled evidence of no fewer than 360 African individuals living in England and Scotland between 1500 and 1640.[87] There was a 'little blackamoor' at the court of Elizabeth I, and other elite households using African servants included those of Robert Dudley, Earl of Leicester; Sir Walter Ralegh; William Cecil, 1st Baron Burghley; and his son Sir Robert Cecil.[88] The households of merchants involved in overseas ventures often had African servants: those dwelling with Bayning, for instance, included 'three maids, blackamoors', recorded in 1593, and 'Julyane a blackamoor servant', who was christened in 1602.[89] Beyond London, Sir John Young of Bristol had an African gardener in 1560; Sir Edward Wynter of White Cross Manor in Gloucestershire had a black porter, Edward Swarthye; and there was a 'blackamoor' at Petworth House in Sussex, home of Henry Percy, Earl of Northumberland (see fig. 2), in the late 1580s.[90] Africans were visible in various localities and occupations. Interracial marriages took place, suggesting acceptance and integration into the community: Best had seen 'an Ethiopian as black as a coal brought into England', who took 'a fair English woman to wife';[91] while various examples in parish records include the marriage in Bristol in 1600 of 'Joan Maria a Black Moor' to Thomas Smythe, a maker of weapons.[92]

The thoughts and subjective experiences of all non-elite Elizabethans are difficult for us to access, and this is especially so for Africans in England in this period, none of whom left writings of their own composition. Nevertheless, as in English accounts of global encounters, we can sometimes gain glimpses of their lives and personalities from the few documented details that we possess. Parish records tell us that Reasonable Blackman, the 'blackamoor' silk-weaver, lived in Southwark, near the playhouses, which he perhaps supplied with costumes. He was also known as John Reason and had at least three children, Edward, Edmund and Jane, of whom the two youngest died in the plague outbreak of 1592.[93] From these bare facts we can imagine some of his life experiences; while his intriguing name might suggest something of his character and how he was regarded in his community. Perhaps he was seen as a man of notable reason: if so, was this seen as unusual and noteworthy in an African? Or was it understood as in keeping with the intellectual gifts assigned to Africans by humoral theory?[94] We also gain a possible glimpse of the mind of Mary Fillis from an unusually detailed account in the parish register of St Botolph in Aldgate of her baptism, aged twenty, in 1597. This notes that she 'was desirous to become a Christian', perhaps a merely conventional phrase to cover coercion by Mary's employer or the curate who baptised her, but also potentially a truthful description of a sincere conversion and Mary's changing sense of both personal and communal identity.[95] A third African in London whose mind we can perhaps fleetingly access is Polonia, a 'blackamoor maid' who was just twelve years old when her employer, Mistress Peirs, consulted the physician and astrologer Simon Forman (see Chapter 6 below), also in 1597. As was often the case for Forman's consultations, the patient was not present, but Forman drew a diagnostic astrological chart for Polonia, noting that she had 'much pain' in her side and stomach, was 'likely to vomit' and had 'a fever in her bones, faint heart, full of melancholy and cold humours mixed with choler'.[96] As a dedicated humoralist, Forman may have regarded Polonia as especially prone to melancholy because she was African. His notes certainly provide a glimpse of a young African girl in Elizabethan London who was in physical discomfort and psychological distress. Yet it is, again, only a fleeting glimpse: although Africans were living among English Elizabethans, often in the intimate spaces of their homes, their lived experiences, states of mind, and sense of themselves remain, frustratingly, largely inaccessible to us.

'Acts of black night': African minds on stage

At least, thanks to pioneering and assiduous archival scholars, we now know more than we did about the lives and minds of Elizabethan Africans like Reasonable Blackman, Mary Fillis, and Polonia. Filling in the tantalising gaps may be work for the imagination, a task for writers of fiction and drama rather than historians. In fact, playwrights and audiences in the period were increasingly fascinated by characters of other races; scholars have identified forty-five such characters (variously referred to as 'Africans', 'Negros', 'Moors', 'moriscos', 'Ethiops', or 'Indians') in plays from 1550 to 1621.[97] Yet Elizabethan plays rarely told stories of non-elite Africans in domestic settings; one moment featuring such a character is even less than a glimpse, when Lorenzo in *The Merchant of Venice* (1596) rebuffs Lancelet's criticism of his marriage to a Jew by accusing him of 'the getting up of the negro's belly: the Moor is with child by you, Lancelet!' (3.5.33–4). This unseen, unnamed woman is even more elusive to us than Mary Fillis or Polonia. Africans represented on the Elizabethan stage were more closely related to the 'Moors' who had regularly appeared in court masques since at least as early as the reign of Henry VIII and were primarily spectacles of exoticism.[98] They also had much in common with dramatised Turks such as Bajazeth, the self-aggrandising, cruel, tyrannical Emperor of Turkey in Marlowe's *Tamburlaine* (1587). Stage Africans were located far away, in Morocco, Spain, or ancient Rome. They embodied a composite 'Otherness': although they came from North Africa and were named as Moors, they were also referred to as 'black' or 'Negro'. They were usually larger-than-life villains who stalked the stage and delivered declamatory speeches about their schemes, ambitions, and desires for revenge. At the same time, the Elizabethan stage Moor was charismatic and compelling, and usually the cleverest character on stage. He was endowed with agency and interiority, which he revealed to the audience in soliloquies. In short, the many complexities and ambiguities in Elizabethan ideas about Africans and their minds were reflected in their depiction on stage.

George Peele's *The Battle of Alcazar* (1588) was innovative in its Moroccan setting and cast of mainly Moorish characters. Its subject was a real event of 1578, more accurately referred to as the Battle of El-Ksar el-Kebir, a devastating conflict between rival claimants to the Moroccan throne, Muly Mahamet and his brother Abdelmelec, which also drew in the Sultan of Turkey and the Kings of Portugal and Spain.[99] Abdelmelec is represented as relatively civilised, a man with whom Europeans could do business, reflecting contemporary English efforts to develop their trading relations with Morocco. However, Muly Mahamet, by stark contrast, is an 'ambitious Negro Moor', devoid of redeeming features.[100] He has close relatives murdered to clear his path to the throne, and declares:

Blood be the theme whereon our time shall tread:
Such slaughter with my weapon shall I make,
As through the stream and bloody channels deep,
Our Moors shall sail in ships and pinnaces,
From Tangier shore unto the gates of Fez. (B2r)

He is a 'barbarous Moor', 'this unbelieving Moor', and 'this foul ambitious Moor' (A2r–v, B3r, E4v), whose wickedness is repeatedly connected with his skin colour: he is 'Black in his look, and bloody in his deeds' (A2r), and is referred to six times as 'Negro'. He can deploy 'wily trains' and 'smoothest course of speech' when inveigling Sebastian, King of Portugal into an alliance (E4v), but mostly departs from the geohumoral model of Africans as governed by intellect in his extreme behaviour and lack of self-control. When deposed and forced into exile he 'lives forlorn among the mountain shrubs, / And makes his food the flesh of savage beasts', as if he too is inherently savage and bestial (B3r). He is unable to summon stoical patience with which to endure his lot, instead 'Crying for battle, famine, sword, and fire' (C2r). Evidence of the success of the play suggests that Elizabethan audiences found his violent behaviour and ranting rhetoric highly entertaining.[101]

Peele may have had a hand in Shakespeare's first play with a Moorish character, *Titus Andronicus* (1592).[102] This too was a great success,[103] but while Aaron shares Muly Mahamet's ambition, ruthlessness, and vengefulness he is very different in his evil brilliance and cool self-control. He is a scheming stage Machiavel; when he masterminds the rape of Lavinia by the Goth brothers Demetrius and Chiron he extols 'policy and stratagem', later exulting that 'I was their tutor to instruct them' (2.1.105, 5.1.98). In a callous trick reminiscent of the ballad of 'The Lady and the Blackamoor', he persuades Titus that if he chops off his hand and sends it to the Emperor his sons' lives will be spared, only for a messenger to return with their severed heads, at which Aaron later recalls that he 'laughed so heartily' (3.1, 5.1.116). His gratification lies in inflicting suffering and causing political disruption, rather than in satisfying passions or bodily desires. Although he is the lover of Tamora, Queen of the Goths and Empress of Rome, the chief pleasure this brings is power, both over her personally – she is 'fettered in amorous chains' – and in the state, where it is an opportunity to 'mount aloft' (2.1.13–15).

Aaron is unresponsive to Tamora's amorous advances in the seclusion of the forest, explaining:

Madam, though Venus govern your desires,
Saturn is dominator over mine.
What signifies my deadly-standing eye,
My silence, and my cloudy melancholy,
My fleece of woolly hair that now uncurls
Even as an adder when she doth unroll
To do some fatal execution?
No, madam, these are no venereal signs;
Vengeance is in my heart, death in my hand,
Blood and revenge are hammering in my head. (2.3.30–9)

The hot sun of the south has made him melancholic, cold-hearted, and full of sinister intentions. Clearly Aaron subscribes to geohumoralism, and accordingly he presents his inner state as legible in his physical characteristics – which, to characterise him as a man of the extreme south, are represented as those of a sub-Saharan African, even though he is repeatedly referred to as a Moor. A sketch of a performance of the play in 1595 confirms that Aaron was depicted on stage just as he is described in the text, as 'raven-coloured' (2.3.83), visually emphasising his difference from the other characters (fig. 9). The sketch intensifies this difference by positioning him at the edge of the scene, visually coded as an outsider. In the play's text, Bassianus and Lavinia link outward appearance and inner nature abusively, to identify blackness with depravity, accusing Aaron of making Tamora's honour 'of his body's hue, / Spotted, detested and abominable' (2.3.83, 73–4). Far from repudiating these charges, Aaron gleefully embraces the identity of black-faced and hence evil-minded villain: 'Let fools do good and fair men call for grace, / Aaron will have his soul black like his face' (3.1.203–4).

The play's treatment of Aaron's character takes a fascinating turn when Tamora gives birth to their child and it is black. She orders

9. This sketch of a 1595 performance of *Titus Andronicus* depicts Aaron the Moor as emphatically 'raven-coloured', as described in the play (2.3.83). Aaron participates in the Elizabethan association between dark skin and a clever but evil mind when he declares: 'Aaron will have his soul black like his face' (3.1.204).

Aaron to kill the baby, and the nurse who bears it to him vituperates it as 'A devil [...] A joyless, dismal, black, and sorrowful issue' (4.2.64–6). Yet Aaron vehemently insists that his son will live, and proclaims the supremacy of blackness: 'Coal-black is better than another hue / In that it scorns to bear another hue' (98–9). It cannot be washed white by 'all the water in the ocean'; the whiteness of the Goths, by contrast, is a 'treacherous hue, that will betray with blushing / The close enacts and counsels of thy heart' (100, 116–17). This is a misrepresentation of Africans, who do blush, and underlines how Shakespeare exaggerates and intensifies Aaron's blackness to make it absolute, unqualified, and symbolic. At first sight Aaron offers a persuasive celebration of this extreme, unvarying blackness; however, it entails the repudiation of shame, since Aaron is responding to Chiron's confession that 'I blush to think upon this ignomy' of his mother's adultery and inevitable disgrace (114). Aaron's words are also, ultimately, an argument not for the authenticity of blackness and the duplicity of whiteness, as they appear, but the opposite: white skin cannot be prevented from changing colour to reveal true inner thoughts and feelings, whereas unchanging (according to him) black skin enables the concealment of 'The close enacts and counsels of thy heart', however evil they may be. This is the brilliant but specious, self-interested casuistry of a typical Machiavel.

In Act 5, captured and brought to justice, Aaron confesses gleefully to an extraordinarily long and lurid catalogue of crimes beyond the action of the play: 'I must talk of murders, rapes and massacres, / Acts of black night, abominable deeds, / Complots of mischief, treasons, villainies' (5.1.63–5). Conflating different racial 'Others' and their stereotypes, Shakespeare imitates and merges the elaborate, wide-ranging confessions of Barabas the Jew and his henchman, Ithamore the Turk, in Marlowe's *The Jew of Malta* (1589).[104] Aaron seems to have relished the ingenious contriving of crimes as much as their enactment; he claims there were few days when he did not 'kill a man or else devise his death, / Ravish a maid or plot the way to do it' (128–9). In response, Lucius repeatedly calls Aaron a 'devil' (5.1.40, 145; 5.3.4–5), and once more Aaron willingly embraces the role: 'If there be devils, would I were a devil' (5.1.147). The play has now magnified him into a supernatural, omnipresent force of evil. It ends with him buried breast-deep in earth to starve to death, an appropriate fate since earth was the element of melancholy (see Chapter 1 above).

The Prince of Morocco in *The Merchant of Venice* (1596) again conflates different 'exotic' stereotypes, this time drawing on a Turkish character, Brusor, in *Suleiman and Perseda* (1588).[105] Also emulating Marlowe's Scythian Tamburlaine and Peele's Muly Mahamet, the Prince vaunts his martial prowess in hyperbolic rhetoric:

> By this scimitar
> That slew the Sophy and a Persian prince,
> That won three fields of Sultan Suleiman,
> I would o'er-stare the sternest eyes that look,
> Outbrave the heart most daring on the earth,
> Pluck the young sucking cubs from the she-bear,
> Yea, mock the lion when 'a roars for prey,
> To win the lady. (2.1.24–31)

His pride is his downfall: because he views Portia merely as a covetable prize which only he deserves to win, he mistakenly chooses the gold casket (2.7). Although he asserts that his red-blooded ardour is equal to that of fair-skinned suitors (2.1.1–7), Portia is not keen on his 'complexion', meaning, as noted above, both his outward appearance and his inner disposition. Before she meets him, the best she expects of him is 'the condition of a saint and the complexion of a devil', hoping he will not 'wive' her (1.2.111–13); and after he fails the casket test she is emphatically relieved: 'A gentle riddance! Draw the curtains; go. / Let all of his complexion choose me so' (2.7.78–9). Portia deduces the nature of the Prince's mind from his appearance, and rejects both.

Eleazar, protagonist of *The Spanish Moor's Tragedy* (1600, later published as *Lust's Dominion*),[106] takes even further the pride and ambition of Muly Mahamet, Aaron, and the Prince of Morocco. His father lost the thrones of Fez and Barbary when defeated by Spain, and Eleazar considers himself a prisoner at the Spanish court, even though he enjoys respect as an adviser and has a Spanish wife, Maria. He is driven by a sense of superiority, an obsessive desire for revenge, and pleasure in devising artful methods to pursue it:

> true policy breeding in the brain
> Is like a bar of iron, whose ribs being broken,
> And softened in the fire, you then may forge it
> Into a sword to kill, or to a helmet, to defend life.[107]

Like Aaron, he is melancholic: at the play's opening he is 'sick, heavy, and dull as lead', and later another character describes how 'Yonder with crossed arms stands he malcontent' (B1v, B8r). Also like Aaron, he is immune to lust, but uses sexual transgression for self-advancement. Eugenia, Queen of Spain, is his mistress, but he harshly rebuffs her ardent caresses and secretly plots her destruction, along with that of most of the court. He is free from sexual jealousy too; when he discovers that Eugenia's son Fernando, who has become King of Spain, desires his wife, he merely calculates how to exploit this:

The Spaniard loves my wife, she swears to me,
She's chaste as the white moon; well if she be.
Well too if she be not; I care not, I,
I'll climb up by that love to dignity. (B12r)

The seventeenth-century title of the first print edition of the play, *Lust's Dominion*, refers to the lust not of Eleazar but of Eugenia, as made clear in its alternative title, *The Lascivious Queen*. Most of the play's Spanish characters are in the grip of passions that are out of control: like Eugenia and Fernando, Cardinal Mendoza is also over-mastered by illicit sexual desires, while Eugenia's other son, Philip, is addicted to martial violence. Eleazar coolly and astutely navigates a course between their unruly passions that takes him all the way to the throne of Spain.

As Eleazar schemes his way to the top and torments his foes, the play relentlessly emphasises his dark colouring and associates it with evil. The word 'black' is used no fewer than twenty-eight times in the text, usually for Eleazar, who is 'The Negro King of Spain' (D12v). The word 'devil' occurs with similar frequency; in an early instance, Eleazar reports that Spaniards point at him in the street and call him 'the black prince of devils' (B3r). Again resembling Aaron, he resolves to fulfil his Satanic reputation:

Who spurns the Moor, were better set his foot upon the Devil,
Do; spurn me? and this confounding arm of wrath
Shall like a thunderbolt breaking the clouds
Divide his body from his soul. (C1r)

He draws attention to, and revels in, his African physicality, again represented as sub-Saharan rather than North African: he has 'thick' hair and an 'inky' face, and like Aaron is glad that as an African he supposedly cannot blush (B5v, B11v, C4v). Towards the end of the play, when charged with crimes, he falsely protests his innocence:

Do I all this, because my face is in night's colour dyed?
Think you my conscience and my soul is so?
Black faces may have hearts as white as snow,
And 'tis a general rule in moral rolls,
The whitest faces have the blackest souls. (G8r)

Like Aaron, he is persuasive: the Spanish *are* prejudiced against his black face and are scarcely more virtuous than him. Yet he is also duplicitous, since he *is* in fact guilty as charged. He is a true liar, and in the world of the play his blackness is a true sign of both his criminality and his perfidy.

For most of the play the Spanish are helpless victims of their own passions and Eleazar's devices. However, the tide turns when Philip and Hortenzo, a Spanish lord, paint their faces black to disguise themselves as Moors and thereby entrap Eleazar in his own torture contraption. The message seems to be that to triumph over a Moor, one must become like a Moor: a clever plotter and a false performer. The play also suggests that Spain is a hotbed of lurid and horrifying deeds, where all are depraved, Machiavellian southerners, and as a Moor Eleazar is just the most extreme case of this. Strikingly, although Philip expels all Moors from Spain at the end of the play, he is still in blackface as he does so.[108]

'Arise, black vengeance': onwards to *Othello*

As a post-Elizabethan play, *Othello* (1604) draws together many conventions regarding the stage Moor that had developed through the late Elizabethan period, while also departing from them. One of its most radical innovations is assigning its scheming, malignant role not to its Moor, but to a white character, Iago, who has much in common with Aaron and Eleazar, and even compares himself to 'devils' who 'will the blackest sins put on' (2.3.322). Meanwhile, the characterisation of Othello combines and distils many of the competing and conflicting ideas that Elizabethans had developed about African minds. Othello is repeatedly referred to as a Moor, suggesting North African heritage, but is also described several times as 'black', like a sub-Saharan African, and references to the colour throughout the play invoke its negative connotations.[109] Even when Othello speaks of his own blackness, it is to account for his supposed loss of Desdemona's affection: 'Haply, for I am black' (3.3.261). He begins the play as a 'noble Moor' like Leo Africanus, eloquently relating how he wooed Desdemona with tales of adventures much like Leo's (2.3.122, 1.3.128–69). She believes that 'my noble Moor / Is true of mind', and is incapable of jealousy because 'the sun where he was born / Drew all such humours from him' (3.4.23–4, 27–8). Yet, of course, she is proved horribly wrong; under Iago's provocation and manipulation Othello becomes an obsessive, ruthless, declamatory avenger, like Muly Mahamet or Eleazar:

> Arise, black vengeance, from the hollow hell;
> Yield up, O love, thy crown and hearted throne
> To tyrannous hate. [. . .]
> Oh, blood! Blood! Blood! (3.3.442–6)

Even worse, he loses control over his mind and body: 'pish! Noses, ears, and lips! Is't possible? Confess? Handkerchief? Oh, devil! *[He] falls in a trance*' (4.1.39–40). Iago reduces Othello to the degenerate state of the 'Negros' despised by Leo who (in Pory's translation) 'lead a beastly kind of life, being utterly destitute of the use of reason'.[110] Over the course of the play he passes through most of the diverse mental states that Elizabethans attributed to Africans, from elevated and dispassionate, to self-righteously and relentlessly vengeful, to bestial. However, he lacks one quality commonly attributed to Africans: intelligence, which Shakespeare transfers to the wily Iago. Othello's downfall is his 'free and open nature', unusual in an early modern stage Moor, such that he 'will as tenderly be led by th' nose / As asses are' (1.3.377, 379–80).

Another figure in the play is possibly African. Just before her death, Desdemona tells Emilia that 'My mother had a maid called Barbary', a name that strongly suggests North African origin. Desdemona explains that Barbary 'was in love, and he she loved proved mad / And did forsake her'. She taught Desdemona the mournful willow song that she sings as she prepares for her fate; she would 'hang her head all at one side', clearly a sufferer from melancholy, and died singing her plangent song (4.3.25–32). Barbary's story is uncannily like Ophelia's, and in eight lines we learn more about her and her inner life than is the case for the other African women who feature in texts before *Othello*. However, she seems to have much in common with them: the pregnant Maria, abandoned on an island by Drake; Polonia, diagnosed with melancholy by Forman; the nameless pregnant servant in *The Merchant of Venice*. Moreover, Barbary too is unseen by us, a shadowy figure who exists only in a brief description, somewhere beyond the perimeter of the text or stage, and whose thoughts and feelings we glimpse only as reported and ventriloquised in a non-African voice. As we have seen, even when English playwrights gave African characters prominent onstage roles, these were fictional constructs fashioned from a web of complex and often contradictory myths and conventions – not revealing but obscuring the subjectivity and interiority of real Africans in the period.

PART III
Disturbances and Discipline

ᥱᥣᦁ 6 ᥱᥢᦁ

Stars and Demons
The Permeable Mind

In the last chapter we fleetingly encountered Polonia, the twelve-year-old 'blackamoor maid' whose mistress consulted the physician Simon Forman for advice on her illness. This was one of about 1,200 consultations per year recorded in Forman's manuscript casebooks.[1] Although patients flocked to him his diagnostic methods scarcely seem medical to us, since they relied heavily on astrology. Forman and his clients believed that mind and body were affected not only by material factors such as diet, temperature, medicines, and so on, but also by forces beyond human control, including evil spirits and the mysterious, invisible influences of the stars and planets.

Each planet was associated with a particular humour: Saturn, for instance, according to an astrology manual by Claude Dariot, was 'cold and dry, melancholic, an enemy and destroyer of the nature and life of man, [. . .] masculine, evil, and the greatest misfortune'.[2] The near-homophony of 'Saturn' and 'Satan' perhaps encouraged these negative associations. As we saw in the previous chapter, Aaron in *Titus Andronicus* attributed his 'cloudy melancholy' to the fact that 'Saturn is dominator' over his desires (2.3.31, 33). Likewise, the villain Don John in *Much Ado about Nothing* (1598) asserts that he

177

'must be sad when I have cause and smile at no man's jests' because he is 'born under Saturn' (1.3.9–12). Forman himself wrote a manuscript treatise that used the titles 'Of Melancholy' and 'Of Saturn' interchangeably, and explained that Saturn was 'black, dark, heavy, slow in his moving [...] a man being born under Saturn shall be melancholic by nature'.[3] Each sign of the zodiac was also affiliated with a particular humour: Gemini, Libra, and Aquarius with blood; Taurus, Virgo, and Capricorn with black bile or melancholy; Aries, Leo, and Sagittarius with choler; and Cancer, Scorpio, and Pisces with phlegm.[4] According to Thomas Moulton's widely read *Mirror of Health*, medical practitioners must 'know in what sign, or in what degree of the sign, the sun and the moon sitteth every day in any of the twelve signs', and take this into account when determining the nature and timing of treatments.[5] Not just the sun and moon but all the other planets too must be tracked in relation to the different zodiacal constellations (fig. 10). Accordingly, Forman compiled detailed tables listing 'what diseases Saturn doth cause, and how he doth alter his nature and commix himself with the other humours in the body of man' as he passed through each house of the zodiac.[6]

Forman began each consultation by establishing the patient's name and age, and what question they wished to ask.[7] The patient was not necessarily present, as we saw in the case of Polonia in Chapter 5, whose mistress consulted Forman about her case in her absence; Margaret Altham,[8] conversely, sent a servant or relation to Forman with her questions on several occasions in 1596 and 1597. Forman would then cast figures representing the position of the stars at the patient's 'geniture' (their moment of conception) or 'nativity' (moment of birth); the stars' position at the moment when the question was posed; and the 'elections' or 'inceptions', the optimum times for future action (fig. 11).[9] Finally, he would give a judgement, which might be a medical prescription, an answer to the question, or both, or neither.[10] In Altham's case, he diagnosed that she was 'much stuffed with a tough kind of phlegm, and hard of melancholy and red choler ready to stop her wind'. At one point he prescribed a course of

10. Character, mental states, and physical wellbeing were all thought to be affected by the planets and their movements in relation to the different houses of the zodiac. These conjunctions and oppositions are represented in this diagram from a manuscript miscellany compiled *c.* 1603 by Thomas Trevelyon.

treatment, but after most consultations relating to this patient he withheld medical remedies because his astrological readings told him that the timing was unpropitious for their efficacy. They also told him that Altham's death was imminent. Although it was less prompt than he expected, it did indeed follow after a few months, and he recorded the case as an example of accurate prognosis.[11]

Forman described another woman, Susan Crosbe, as suffering a 'desperate melancholy disease', but he made a different diagnosis: in her case 'the Devil would speak often-times within her, and bid her

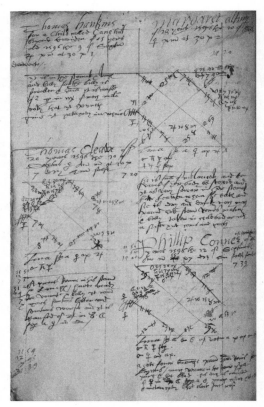

11. The physician Simon Forman cast astrological figures to diagnose the mental and physical ailments of his many patients. Here, the figure at top right is for Margaret Altham (spelled Altum), from whom Forman withheld treatment because his astrological analysis told him the timing was unpropitious and her death was imminent.

kill herself – drown or hang herself – or kill her husband. And she could abide no knives, nor pins, nor shears, nor needles, nor nails, but she must cut herself or thrust the pins into her flesh.' Forman concluded that 'all the physic in the world could not help her, for she was thoroughly purged often-times and dieted and let blood, but all would not help'.[12] This was a case of demonic possession, a recognised category of madness in medical manuals; Andrew Boorde's *Breviary of Health* (1547), for example, a frequently reprinted work, warned that sufferers 'be devilish persons and will do much harm and evil, worser than they the which be maniac, for maniac persons cometh of infirmities of the body, but demoniac persons be possessed of some evil spirit'.[13]

Forman's papers reveal that for many Elizabethans treating the troubled mind was not just a matter of managing its relations to the body, but also a matter of contending with astrological and demonic forces that were always threatening to invade its permeable boundaries, sometimes with unexpected and alarming effects.[14] However, these beliefs were also being increasingly called into question, provoking animated debates about how character and behaviour were determined, the extent and limits of human autonomy, and how far the human mind had power over itself.[15]

'A perpetual unlucky irradiation': astrology and the mind

Copernicus's revolutionary theory of a heliocentric solar system was published in 1543 and became known to some in England, particularly when the mathematician Thomas Digges added a Copernican appendix to the 1576 edition of his father Leonard's *Prognostication*, a hugely popular astrological almanac. Even so, most Elizabethans adhered to Ptolemy's geocentric cosmography, in which the earth was surrounded by the concentric spheres of the seven planets: moving outwards, the moon, Mercury, Venus, the sun, Mars, Jupiter, and Saturn. Beyond these was the sphere of fixed stars, then that of the zodiacal constellations, then finally the outermost sphere of the divine *primum mobile* or First Mover, governing the motion of all within (fig. 12).[16]

It was obvious that the sun controlled the seasons and the moon controlled the tides, so it seemed equally reasonable to Elizabethans that all the planets had an influence on earthly things.[17] *Batman upon Bartholome* explained that upon the stars 'all the virtues and properties of kinds below do depend, so that every kind hath a celestial figure agreeing unto him'.[18] This included human minds: character was widely believed to be fixed at conception or birth by the configuration of the planets. Erasmus in his *Enchiridion* affirmed that some

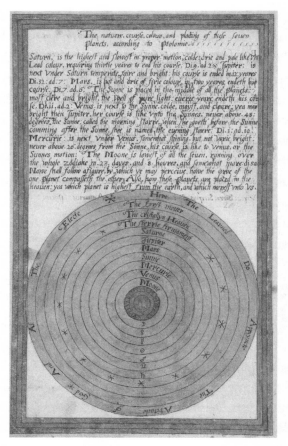

12. The Ptolemaic model of the cosmos persisted even beyond the Elizabethan period, as in this diagram from a 1608 version of Trevelyon's miscellany (see fig. 10 above). The earth was at the centre, surrounded by the spheres of the seven planets, the fixed stars, the zodiacal constellations, and the First Mover, governing the motion of all within. All these celestial bodies were believed to influence the mind.

people were more inclined towards virtue than others because of 'the influence of celestial bodies',[19] while *Batman* stated that Saturn 'maketh a man brown and foul, misdoing, slow, and heavy [...], seldom glad and merry, or laughing'.[20] This was not just an effect fixed at birth: the planets also governed short-term fluctuations in thoughts, feelings, and behaviour, especially the moon: 'in the waxing of the moon, the brain waxeth, and waneth in substance of virtue in the waning of the moon'; 'the moon maketh a man unstable, change-able, and removing about from place to place'.[21]

These beliefs were known as 'natural astrology' and were generally accepted.[22] More problematic was 'judicial astrology', which used readings of the stars and planets to predict future events. Digges's *Prognostication*, frequently reprinted after its first appearance in the 1550s,[23] instructed the reader in interpreting the heavens for prac-tical purposes ranging from weather-forecasting to choosing propi-tious dates for blood-letting, bathing, and cutting hair, but also to gain foresight of 'plenty, lack, sickness, death, wars, etc'.[24] Dariot's manual also held out the promise that through astrology the reader could manage the unpredictability of life, answering such pressing questions as 'whether any man shall have or possess riches and substance, and at what time', and 'whether a man shall obtain that woman in marriage which he desireth'.[25]

Judicial astrology was widely distrusted. Political authorities sought to suppress disruptive predictions of momentous events like the deaths of princes, while many Protestant writers regarded attempts to manipulate the future as an affront to divine authority.[26] Calvin, for example, accepted that the humoral complexions of individuals 'partly depend of the stars or at least have some agreement therewith', but objected forcefully to the claims of judicial astrologers 'to know not only the nature and complexion of men, but also all their fortunes as they call them, yea and all that they shall either do or suffer in their life'.[27] Others even questioned the relation of character to the astral influences. William Fulke in *Antiprognosticon* (1560) scoffed that those who attribute personality-traits to zodiacal birth signs

ascribe so many and so diverse qualities to every man by his nativity, that of necessity some of them must be in every man. As he which saith that a man shall be apt to anger, pride, love, pity, and such like; whereas there is no man but he shall find these and such like qualities in himself, if he enter into his own mind.[28]

Later in the period William Perkins put astrology in the same category as superstition and sorcery:

> What though the celestial bodies do cause in the terrestrial heat and cold, drought and moisture? Doth it therefore follow that these effects do declare beforehand the constitution of man's body? The disposition of men's minds? The affections of men's hearts? Or finally what success they shall have in their affairs, touching wealth, honour, and religion?[29]

Yet other authors continued to promote astrology, and clients continued to throng to Forman for astrological consultations, often for help with what we would call psychological disorders. Other Elizabethan physicians who included astrology in their methods included John Securis, William Cuningham, Thomas Twyne, and Richard Forster, who defended astrology in the preface to his *Ephemerides* (1575).[30]

For writers of literature, the language of astrology provided a taxonomy of character similar to that of humoral theory as explored in Chapter 1 above. The multiple stories in Robert Greene's *Planetomachia* (1585) illustrate how 'every man is naturally born under the influence and irradiate constellation of one of these wandering stars, and that one is always predominant in the configuration of every nativity'. Greene sought to show 'what proper qualities each particular planet doth appropriate: painting out what affectionate desires Jupiter doth allot to them that are Jovialists, and what qualities Saturn doth infuse upon them which are Saturnists, together with the diseases incident to their constitution and complexion'.[31] We still use this language today when we describe different character-types or states of mind as 'saturnine', 'jovial', or 'lunatic'. Given that most of us do not literally believe in the influence of the planets, and that even in the Elizabethan period astrology was fiercely debated, it is unclear how far Shakespeare, Greene, and other literary authors of their time actually believed in astrology when they used its language of character description. At first sight Greene looks like a believer, since *Planetomachia* included two defences of the discipline: 'A Brief Apology of the Sacred Science of Astronomy' in English and a Latin dialogue. In line with Protestant doctrine, he acknowledged some human responsibility for self-government; but at the same time, drawing on both ancient and recent sources, he asserted that 'as in the begetting or procreation of children they take some likelihood [likeness] of their parents, so being born under one of the planets they borrow of them their form, shape, valour, minds, and actions' (12). Yet matters become more complicated in the main, fictional body of *Planetomachia*, where Greene personifies the planets as the classical gods whose names they bear. As indicated by the title – which means strife among the planets – they fight among themselves: Saturn quarrels with Venus and tells a story to illustrate how love, under her influence, 'is the only plague which infecteth the minds of mortal men'; Venus retorts with a tragedy that illustrates how Saturn's 'celestial (but unfortunate) impression, joined with a perpetual unlucky irradiation, breedeth both in men's minds and bodies such hapless passions sauced with so bitter and woeful events' (21); and so on. Greene presumably did not believe in the classical gods, and by identifying them with their corresponding planets he takes astrology from the realm of science to the realm of myth. He also accentuates the arbitrariness and capriciousness of the forces that seem to govern human lives and to take our fates and fortunes out of our own control. His stories thereby become a means of exploring how far we have control over our own choices and behaviours, and how far our destinies are determined by our own characters or by higher powers. It remains indeterminate how far Greene literally believed in astrology, but he evidently found in it a useful literary device for exploring the range of human psychology and the relations between motivation and action.

John Lyly's court play *The Woman in the Moon* (1588) develops Greene's identification of the planets with their namesake gods.

185

In an alternative creation myth, Nature endows the first woman, Pandora (meaning all-gifted), with their best qualities: Saturn's 'deep conceit', Jupiter's 'high thoughts', Mars's courage, and so on.[32] The gods are jealous and offended, and conspire to take turns in ruling Pandora: Saturn makes her melancholy, Jupiter ambitious, Mars 'a vixen martialist' (2.1.181), and so on, utterly baffling three shepherds who try to woo her. Lastly, the moon, named as Luna or Cynthia, makes her mad. Pandora chooses to stay with her, because

> change is my felicity,
> And fickleness Pandora's proper form. [...]
> Cynthia made me idle, mutable,
> Forgetful, foolish, fickle, frantic, mad.
> These be the humours that content me best. (5.1.307–8, 313–15)

The play concludes as an aetiological fable – an explanation of causes and origins – like the stories in Ovid's *Metamorphoses*; in this case, an explanation of female irrationality and waywardness. Nature declares that under the lunar rule of Pandora, women will be

> mutable in all their loves,
> Fantastical, childish, and foolish in their desires,
> Demanding toys,
> And stark mad when they cannot have their will. (5.1.329–32)

The association of lunar mutability with women invokes menstruation, another way in which the earthly influence of the planets seemed manifest to Elizabethans. The play as a whole presents the female mind as particularly vulnerable to outside forces, in accordance with its usual characterisation as weak and unstable, as discussed in Chapter 4 above.

The title-page of *The Woman in the Moon* as published in 1597 specifies that it was 'presented before her Highness'.[33] In around 1588, its likely date of first performance, Elizabeth I was increasingly associated with Cynthia, the moon goddess (as in another court play of around the same date by Lyly, *Endymion*). How might she have received the play? Perhaps she chose to exempt herself from the play's satire against women, since she was generally praised as an exception to her sex, or perhaps she tacitly recognised its implicit criticism of female rule. In any case, men do not come off well either: the male gods, the shepherds, and Pandora's servant Gunophilus all behave badly, and to a large extent make Pandora what she is by competing to possess her and trying to mould her to their own desires. For Lyly, astrology, especially when the planets are personi-fied as gods, creates a dramatic space that appears playful and fantas-tical, but under this guise can address serious issues about tensions between the sexes and the unsettling nature of female power.

For Shakespeare, as well as providing a taxonomy of character, astrology offers opportunities to explore relations between higher powers of fate and human agency. We know from the start of their play that Romeo and Juliet are 'star-crossed lovers' (0.6), setting their youthful, hopeful love in a framework of tragic doom. The authority of the stars also appears beyond question in *Troilus and Cressida* as Ulysses tells a conference of Greek generals that 'when the planets / In evil mixture to disorder wander', the 'unity and married calm of states' is destroyed (1.3.93–4, 99). However, Ulysses has a rhetorical purpose – to incite his colleagues against the recalcitrant egotism of Achilles – and is using astrology to serve this, not necessarily expounding his belief-system. Cassius in *Julius Caesar* also invokes astrology rhetorically, but in the opposite way, asserting human autonomy in order to provoke Brutus to assassination and rebellion: 'Men at some time are masters of their fates. / The fault, dear Brutus, is not in our stars, / But in ourselves, that we are underlings' (1.2.139–41). These contradictory positions leave uncertain Shakespeare's view of the ongoing contemporary debate about astrology. However, he evidently found it a valuable resource for articulating the questions about relations between fate and character that are so often central to his plays, especially his tragedies.

'The Devil's mocking illusions': demonic possession

In Lyly's *The Woman in the Moon*, Pandora lurched alarmingly between extreme behaviours governed by different planets. Even more alarming to Elizabethans were the effects of another outside influence on the mind: the Devil. On the evening of 20 January 1573, at Herringswell in Suffolk, Alexander Nyndge was terrifyingly transformed, 'his chest and body swelling, with his eyes staring, and his back bending inward to his belly'. His brother Edward – a graduate, and evidently a respected figure in the household – quickly deduced that 'it was some evil spirit that so molested him'. Neighbours were summoned to assist in prayers and witnessed the spirit 'monstrously transforming [Alexander's] body, plucking his mouth awry', and 'moving him by violence' out of his chair. When questioned by Edward, the spirit declared 'in a bass sounding or hollow voice' from within Alexander that 'I come for his soul', also revealing that his name was Aubon and he came from Ireland. When Edward opened a window, Aubon suddenly left, and Alexander was himself again. However, the afflictions resumed in the early morning and for several hours Alexander was 'marvellously misformed', 'made an horrible spitting', 'was sore tormented, of all his members', and 'the voice roared exceedingly'. When Edward exhorted him to hold fast to faith, speaking 'vehemently' into his left ear, it 'was suddenly wrimpled like a clung walnut which falleth from the tree ere it be ripe'. Finally, when several of the assembled company conjured the spirit in the name of Jesus to depart, 'Alexander stood up and said, "He is gone, he is gone." '[34]

Several other cases of demonic possession were reported in the early decades of Elizabeth I's reign. In 1563, in Chester, eighteen-year-old Anne Mylner was surrounded by a 'white thing' while grazing cattle, and suffered four months of trances and convulsions, until a minister named John Lane expelled the evil spirit.[35] In 1564, in London, Edmund Kingesfielde jocularly put up a sign outside his inn depicting the Devil, whereupon his wife became 'sore troubled in mind' and suicidal; she lay ill in bed until Kingesfielde took to prayer and took the sign down.[36] Also in London, a law student in his late twenties, Robert Brigges (pronounced Bridges), became convinced in spring 1574 of his own damnation, and for several weeks passed in and out of trances in which he animatedly answered challenges from Satan.[37] In the same year, again in London, Agnes Brigges (no known relation of Robert), aged twenty, and Rachel Pinder, aged eleven, repeatedly spat out strange objects (including black silk thread, feathers, hair, lace, bent pins, and nails), disputed with churchmen in demonic voices, and accused a woman named Joan Thornton of having bewitched them.[38] Meanwhile, in Kent, also in 1574, a busy year for demons, Mildred Norrington, a seventeen-year-old servant, was afflicted with 'roaring, crying, striving, and gnashing of teeth'. A strange voice from within her body confirmed that she was possessed by Satan, who threatened to tear her in pieces, and disclosed that 'old Alice' of Westwell Street kept him in two bottles.[39]

In all these cases, physical symptoms – including distorted features, bodily contortions, shutdown of sight and hearing, and prodigious strength – were read as signs that the sufferer's mind had been invaded by an external, evil force. This mental usurpation was especially manifested in the disturbing voices, repeatedly described as deep, hollow, harsh, and much unlike their own, which emanated from demoniacs. As Bright wrote in his *Treatise of Melancholy*, 'Daily experience maketh this manifest in such as are possessed, how Satan so beareth the sway in them that their speech and phrase altereth, and their discourse is far other than before, and their whole nature at Satan's beck, and their utterance of mind as he only suggesteth.'[40] Bright's assumption (writing in 1586) that demonic possession formed part of the 'daily experience' of his readers was no doubt an exaggeration, but the cluster of recorded incidents in the 1560s and 1570s was indeed followed by many more. John Darrel, a Protestant minister who enacted a number of dispossessions in the later years of the reign, reported in 1599 that he had seen ten demoniacs and had heard of six more.[41] One historian has found documentary evidence of over 100 possessed individuals between 1550 and 1700.[42]

Just as Agnes Brigges, Rachel Pindar, and Mildred Norrington accused Joan Thornton and 'old Alice', so cases of possession were increasingly blamed upon supposed witchcraft enacted by at least one older woman of the neighbourhood. At Warboys in Huntingdonshire in 1593, ten-year-old Jane Throckmorton was struck by fits of sneezing and twitching, trances, and swellings and heavings of her belly, which she blamed on Alice Samuel, a neighbour aged nearly eighty. Jane's four sisters and seven female servants of the household became similarly afflicted. Alice's husband and daughter were accused of complicity with her in the bewitchment and in using occult means to cause the death of Lady Cromwell of Hinchingbrooke after she visited the Throckmorton household. Throughout prolonged accusations, humiliating tests, and intensifying demoniac behaviour by the Throckmorton girls, Alice protested her innocence, but eventually confessed. Her husband and daughter denied guilt to the end, but all three were tried, convicted, and hanged.[43]

As cases accumulated, more sensational symptoms were added to the demoniac repertoire and read as signs of physical and mental subjugation to a malignant outside force. The possessed had swollen, heaving bellies and strange lumps of flesh that moved around under their skin. They uttered blasphemies and obscenities, spoke in languages hitherto unknown to them, displayed clairvoyant powers, and recoiled from holy words and rituals. They lost mental control: Elizabeth, another Throckmorton daughter, reacted to a Bible reading 'like one out of her mind', while seven members of the Starkie (or Starchy) household in Lancashire who were diagnosed as possessed in the late 1590s were described as 'out of their right minds'.[44] This accorded with the *Malleus Maleficarum* (*The Hammer for Witches*, 1487), the standard manual on witchcraft across Europe, which listed among the principal powers of witches the ability to deprive their victims of reason.[45] Sufferers typically underwent cycles of dispossession and increasingly fierce repossession, until some kind of dramatic final release.

Demonic possession is an aspect of Elizabethan thinking about the mind that can seem especially remote from us and may provoke us to ask: what was really going on here? We might wonder whether some of these cases would submit to the diagnoses of modern neurological and psychiatric medicine, for example, as psychotic episodes or as instances of bipolar disorder, epilepsy, or schizophrenia.[46] Because Elizabethans lacked our scientific knowledge of such conditions, we may suppose, when faced with afflictions and behaviours that seemed to them inexplicable by natural causes, they turned to the supernatural. However, before feeling too complacent about our advanced scientific tools of analysis, we would do well to consider the modern-day cases of 'psychosomatic disorders' discussed by Suzanne O'Sullivan in *It's All in your Head* (2015). O'Sullivan, a consultant neurologist, narrates various cases from her experience in clinical practice that uncannily resemble sixteenth-century cases of demonic possession, including that of Brenda, who was afflicted with seizures: 'Brenda became increasingly unrecognisable. Her skin became waxy and pale, her stomach dramatically distended, but her seizures were not improving. [. . .] Brenda's face reddened, back arched and limbs shook violently.'[47] It's hard not to be reminded of poor Alexander Nyndge. No physiological cause could be found for Brenda's condition or for those of many other patients with symptoms including paralysis, loss of sight or hearing, loss of use of limbs, loss of sensation, and loss of or changes to the voice. As O'Sullivan explains, such cases are classified in modern medicine as 'psychomatic' or 'psychogenic' disorders – that is, physical phenomena with a source in the mind – or simply as having 'medically unexplained symptoms' (15–20). She estimates that 'Up to one-third of people seen in an average general neurology clinic have neurological symptoms that cannot be explained and, in these people, an emotional cause is often suspected' (9). Her book argues that in the here-and-now more effort is needed to take such cases seriously, to understand and treat them, and to recognise that mental states can have extreme physiological effects. Despite scientific advances, we remain perplexed by such cases; and hence, while in no way returning to the supernatural thinking of Elizabethans, we can at least appreciate its effectiveness in providing them with explanations for enduringly baffling phenomena.

Elizabethan belief-systems, combining religious and folkloric traditions, not only offered interpretations of the symptoms of sixteenth-century demoniacs, but probably had a shaping influence upon the manifestations of those symptoms. Individuals who took the lead in dealing with cases, such as Edward Nyndge and John Darrel, were often swift to diagnose possession, no doubt affecting the sufferer's understanding of their own condition and encouraging conformity to expected demoniac behaviour. The shared understanding of sufferer and exorcist that they were engaged in combat with the Devil was also often reinforced by the presence of numerous onlookers who participated in collective assent that they were witnessing Satan at work. Neighbours were summoned to join in communal prayer for Alexander Nyndge, and colleagues of the Middle Temple crowded into Robert Brigges' chamber, between twelve and twenty at a time, to behold his dialogues with the Devil.[48] In 1585 and 1586, a group of Catholic priests led by Father William Weston, a Jesuit, performed a series of spectacular exorcisms at recusant households at Denham in Buckinghamshire and elsewhere which attracted a 'great resort' of people, including an audience of over 100 for Richard Mainy's possession by seven devils representing the Seven Deadly Sins.[49] Our modern understanding of the mind suggests the force of group psychology in such incidents, as witnesses to possession perhaps carried each other along in some kind of mass delusion (accounting for strange phenomena as the work of the Devil) or mass hallucination (believing that they saw something that was not really there). Even within the Elizabethan period itself, the Church of England, perhaps surprisingly, often questioned the real presence of Satan and his cohorts in supposed possessions and exorcisms, asserting that the age of miracles was over. It instigated investigations which prompted several of the supposed demoniacs to whom John Darrel had ministered to confess to counterfeiting: William Somers, for instance, whose sensational symptoms had included running lumps of flesh under the skin and moving forms in his bed, admitted that he had created these effects by simply moving his hands and other body parts under the bedclothes. Why had onlookers been deceived by such simple tricks and testified that Somers was possessed? One of them, Master Aldridge, when asked why he had attested to demonic 'kitlings' or kittens under Somers's coverlet, acknowledged ruefully, 'I think my so affirming did proceed [...] because I had heard before that certain witches had spirits in forms of kitlings, and those forms then came to my mind'. He went on, 'I was then very greatly afraid, which is a great means to deceive a man's senses, being a mighty passion that will procure many imaginations, and cause a man to think that which is but little, to be great, that which standeth, to move, and that to be, which is not.'[50]

Cases involving charges of witchcraft also often suggest complex psychological processes in the minds of the accused. *The Most Strange and Admirable Discovery of the Three Witches of Warboys* (1593), although clearly authored by a partisan of the Throckmorton family whose daughters were supposedly possessed, also contains subtexts that evoke sympathy for the culprit they named, Alice Samuel. Following ten-year-old Jane's initial accusation – '"Grandmother, look where the old witch sits" (pointing to the same Mother Samuel) [...] "I cannot abide to look on her"'[51] – Alice is repeatedly abused by the girls, forced to come to their house or receive them at her own (to test the effects of her proximity upon them), and compelled to endure scratching by them (popular belief maintained that the bewitched could be relieved by drawing the witch's blood). Entirely understandable behaviour by Alice, such as looking 'very rueful' when first called a witch (78), or reluctance to come near the children, is read as evidence of guilt. She eventually gives way under this sustained harassment, confessing to Master Throckmorton (according to the author of the published account) that 'I have been the cause of all this trouble to your children [...] I have forsaken my maker, and given my soul to the Devil' (111). It seems highly plausible that prolonged psychological pressure had 'gaslighted' her into accepting her own culpability or that she was simply confused; the next day she retracted her confession (114). She may have been losing her wits (in Elizabethan terms) or suffering dementia (in our terms): at her trial, she sought clemency on the grounds that she was with child, despite her advanced age, causing general laughter in the courtroom (147). The author of the published account seems defensively aware that Alice, not the Throckmorton children, may appear to be the real victim: the circumstances of her confession are related in detail because it has been 'reported by some in the country [county], and those that thought themselves wise, that this Mother Samuel now in question was an old simple woman, and that one might make her by fair words confess what they would' (116).

The Warboys case not only raises fascinating questions about the psychology of those who confessed to witchcraft, but also suggests sociological explanations for witchcraft accusations. They almost invariably scapegoated the old, eccentric, and socially marginal, as when, in 1602, Mary Glover accused Elizabeth Jackson, 'an old char-woman', of having bewitched her in revenge for Glover's 'discovering to one of her mistresses a certain fashion of her subtle and importunate begging'.[52] As a poor, socially insecure older woman, Jackson was a typical Elizabethan witchcraft suspect. At the same time, Glover as a fourteen-year-old girl was a typical victim of possession; most of these were children or adolescents, also a social group with little freedom or autonomy in Elizabethan England. Such youthful demoniacs may well have enjoyed the attention, indulgence, and power gained by means of their sensational conditions.[53]

Did adolescent girls produce demoniac symptoms as an uncon-scious response to their lack of status and the traumas of adoles-cence? Or did they consciously perform their symptoms? O'Sullivan notes how, in modern medicine, classification of physical symptoms as having a psychological origin tends to lead to accusations of fakery (unfairly, she argues).[54] Elizabethan possessions too were often understood as having an element of performance. Although Alexander Nyndge's possession was not questioned as inauthentic, he was described as 'monstrously transformed [. . .] much like the picture of the Devil in a play'.[55] Satan was a familiar figure from mystery plays, and although the 1570s, when this case occurred, saw the suppression of many such plays,[56] he continued to appear on the secular stage (see below), providing a template for how the Devil, or someone possessed by him, should look and speak. As cases of possession began to proliferate and, like Nyndge's, circulated in popular print, they offered a script of demoniac behaviour not only for anyone who believed themselves possessed, but also for anyone tempted to feign possession or to coach an accomplice in feigning possession. The frequency of possession was accompanied by a growing number of confessions to deception, beginning with Agnes Brigges and Rachel Pindar, the girls who vomited up strange objects. They confessed following investigation by Matthew Parker, Archbishop of Canterbury, and their case was published as *The Disclosing of a Late Counterfeited Possession by the Devil of Two Maidens within the City of London* (1574). Performances of possession offered various kinds of advantage not only to the supposed demoniacs, but also to those who claimed the power of dispossession. Extended debates with occupying demons enabled churchmen to explicate doctrine in front of an enthralled audience, while spectacular expulsions of the Devil and his minions enabled exorcists to assert their authority as agents of God and to win converts (one of the Denham priests claimed that at least 500 converts to Catholicism had been gained by the exorcisms).[57]

'Satan's illusions': Elizabethan explanations for demonic possession

Because a number of possessions culminated in confessions of fraud, many Elizabethan writers shared our modern impulse to ask what was really going on, though their answers were not necessarily the same as ours. They often looked to the work of Johann Weyer (or Wier), a German physician whose *De praestigiis daemonum* (*On the*

Tricks of Demons, 1563) was widely read across Europe.[58] Weyer found the cause of supposed possession in imbalance of the humours and passions: sufferers were 'beset by twin diseases – that of the body, produced from the melancholic humour, and that of the spirit, such as madness, grief, fear, hatred of life, and despair' (447). Meanwhile, old women who believed themselves to have powers of bewitchment were also suffering from melancholy delusions (570–1) and Weyer therefore condemned their harsh judicial treatment. However, he was no proto-feminist, subscribing rather to the negative view of the female mind that we encountered in Chapter 4 above. Weyer asserted that self-styled witches fall into 'this rash credulity, sometimes because of the infirmity of age, but always because of the folly and weakness of their sex [...] they are destitute of a rational spirit and the power of reason [...] they lack mind, will, reason, consent, deliberation, purpose and counsel' (571–2).

Reginald Scot cites *De praestigiis daemonum* fourteen times in his sceptical *Discovery [i.e., Exposure] of Witchcraft* (1584), also discussed in Chapter 4. He elaborates upon Weyer's identification of so-called witches as older women deluded by melancholy, representing their bodies as hideously withered, 'lame, blear-eyed, pale, foul, and full of wrinkles'. He also accuses them of Catholicism or atheism: they are 'poor, sullen, superstitious, and papists; or such as know no religion'.[59] Further critiques of belief in witchcraft and possession included George Gifford's *Dialogue concerning Witches and Witchcrafts* (1593), Samuel Harsnett's *Discovery of the Fraudulent Practises of John Darrel* (1599) and *Declaration of Egregious Popish Impostures* (1603), and William Perkins's *Discourse of the Damned Art of Witchcraft*. All these English polemicists also associated witchcraft with Catholicism, extending the general Protestant view of the Catholic Church as the 'synagogue of Satan'.[60] For Scot, although many witches were superstitious self-deluders, others were knowing tricksters preying on the gullible; either way, both the superstition and the trickery aligned them with Catholicism. Just as 'All wise men understand that witches' miraculous enterprises, being contrary to nature, probability and reason, are void of truth or possibility', so 'All Protestants perceive, that popish charms, conjurations, execrations, and benedictions are not effectual, but be toys and devices only to keep the people blind, and to enrich the clergy'.[61] The Denham exorcisms of the mid-1580s by Weston and his Catholic colleagues added impetus to this line of attack: Harsnett's *Declaration* repeatedly disparaged these events as a 'play' performed by 'actors', and reproduced the later confessions of counterfeiting by those supposedly possessed.[62]

However, Harsnett's other polemic against possession and exorcism, the *Discovery* of 1599, was directed against John Darrel, a Protestant with Puritan views and affiliations who sought to demonstrate that there was no Catholic monopoly on the power to cast out devils. Although he shared the official Church of England view of Catholic exorcism rituals as idolatrous, and therefore tackled the forces of Satan instead with prayer and fasting, the cases in which Darrel acted still included many sensational scenes of affliction and dispossession. To the Church authorities he was a troublesome loose cannon, undermining the official doctrine that the age of miracles was past. Harsnett was chaplain to Richard Bancroft, Bishop of London, and campaigned against Darrel at his behest, generating an acrimonious print controversy. Darrel, his associate George More, and other anonymous supporters published defences of the authenticity of the cases in which he had been involved, while John Deacon and John Walker joined Harsnett's attack.[63] Again, under investigation a number of those supposedly possessed confessed to counterfeiting, including William Somers, as mentioned above, who claimed that Darrel had coached him in tricks to deceive spectators.

For Darrel and his supporters, it was those who denied the reality of possession and dispossession that were impious or atheistic: 'in traducing dispossession, ye traduce the kingdom of God [...] If neither possession, nor witchcraft (contrary to that hath been so long generally and confidently affirmed), why should we think that there are devils? If no devils, no God.'[64] Darrel's explanation for the confession by Somers was ingenious but mind-bending: 'Satan in his subtlety hath done in the boy some slight and trifling things at diverse times of purpose to deceive the beholders, and to bear them in hand that he did never greater things in him: thereby to induce them to think that he was a counterfeit.'[65] In other words, Satan, as the supreme master of duplicity, made Somers perform some fake symptoms of possession to create a false sense of security and distract from his real possession. As Stephen Greenblatt has observed, 'If Satan can counterfeit counterfeiting, there can be no definitive confession, and the prospect opens of an infinite regress of disclosure and uncertainty.'[66]

Attempts to debunk the appearance of possession as in fact produced simply by physiological conditions also proved bewilderingly inextricable from supernatural explanations. As early as 1580, William Fulke suggested that Anne Mylner's exorcism by John Lane 'was no miracle, but a natural work, the maid perhaps being affected with the mother or some such like disease'.[67] As mentioned in Chapter 4, 'suffocation of the mother', where the term 'mother' refers to the womb, was thought to occur when the unruly uterus moved around in the body, obstructing other organs and causing breathing difficulties. A disordered or corrupted womb could also emit rising vapours dangerous to the brain and other organs.[68] Harsnett in his *Declaration* asserted that many a so-called demoniac was an impoverished young woman taking advantage of

> a little help of the mother, epilepsy, or cramp, to teach her [to] roll her eyes, wry her mouth, gnash her teeth, startle with her body, hold her arms and hands stiff, make antic faces, girn [grimace], mow, and mop like an ape, tumble like a hedgehog, and [...] mutter out two or three words of gibberish.[69]

Partly because of confusion of its symptoms with epilepsy or the 'falling sickness', men too could suffer from the affliction, in their case arising from a disordered stomach or an excessive accumulation of semen.[70] Richard Mainy, one of the supposed Denham demoniacs, described in his confession as printed by Harsnett his realisation that 'the mother was the only disease wherewith I was vexed, and that I was free (I thanked God) from the possession of any wicked spirit'.[71] However, this condition had particularly strong associations with the disordered female body, as in Edward Jorden's *A Brief Discourse of a Disease Called the Suffocation of the Mother* (1603, see Chapter 4 above) and in his defence of Elizabeth Jackson at her trial the previous year for witch-craft, which explained the apparent signs of possession in her supposed victim, Mary Glover, as in fact symptoms of womb sickness.[72]

Jorden's attempt to exonerate Jackson failed and she was convicted, mainly because the presiding judge, Sir Edmund Anderson, was adamant that 'The land is full of witches; they abound in all places', boasting that he had sent twenty-five or twenty-six witches to the gallows himself.[73] However, Jorden's case was also impaired because Weyer, although an important authority for sceptics, and despite his emphasis on physiology and psychology, by no means excluded the supernatural from his explanation of witchcraft. For Weyer, self-styled witches 'fall into these grave mental aberrations because of the Devil's mocking illusions'.[74] They are vulnerable to these because Satan finds the physical substance of melancholy – black bile – to be a congenial host, 'into which the demon loves to insinuate himself, inasmuch as it is a material suited for his activities [. . .] penetrating the bodies of the unperceiving women by means of the special substance from which demons' bodies are composed, and blending himself into their thoughts'.[75] Stephen Bradwell, in a manuscript attack on Jorden, cited Weyer in support of the reality of demonic possession, since

the Devil may be found to have his hand in sundry bodily afflic-tions which have no supernatural symptoms to discover them [. . .] For natural and supernatural causes may concur to the production or generation of sickness [. . .] Also, Satan, the ocean-sea of subtleties, can, where leave is given him, hide his own ugly shape under the leaves of ordinary symptoms.[76]

Despite the efforts of Jorden, Harsnett, and others, for many of their contemporaries diagnosis of a medical condition by no means precluded the presence of the Devil in both body and mind.[77]

In fact, disbelievers in witchcraft and possession were no less insistent than their opponents on the dangerous presence of Satan in the world. For Scot, though supposed witches were deluded, they were women 'in whose drowsy minds the Devil hath gotten a fine seat'.[78] Although he denied 'that witches or magicians have power by words, herbs, or imprecations to thrust into the mind or conscience of man, what it shall please them', he maintained

> that the Devil, both by day and also by night, travelleth to seduce man, and to lead him from God; yea and that no way more than this, where he placeth himself as God in the minds of them that are so credulous, to attribute unto him, or unto witches that which is only in the office, nature and power of God to accomplish.[79]

The Devil could not bestow supernatural powers, but the false belief that he could do so was in itself evidence that 'the Devil indeed entereth into the mind, and that way seeketh man's confusion'.[80] Similarly, in Gifford's *Dialogue*, Daniel, the most authoritative speaker, tells Samuel, who believes he has been bewitched, 'I do not think that the old woman hath bewitched you, or that your body is bewitched, but the devil hath bewitched your mind, with blindness and unbelief, to draw you from God, even to worship himself, by seeking help at the hands of devils.'[81] For Perkins, too, the beliefs of witches that they had 'changed into other creatures, as cats, birds, mice, etc.', were 'only Satan's illusions, wherewith the minds of witches were possessed, and nothing else'; but for this very reason we should all be deeply concerned that 'the Devil deceives the mind, and makes a man think that of himself which is not true'.[82] These many polemics against belief in possession and witchcraft, far from denying the existence of the Devil, if anything gave him greater prominence and made him a more universal psychological force. He could not possess the minds of supposed demoniacs, but he was present in the weak and credulous minds of those who believed in possession, witchcraft, and exorcism, and were deceived by human pretences to supernatural powers.

'In a dark room and bound': Shakespeare on possession

Two of Shakespeare's Elizabethan plays present cases of supposed possession in a more secular fashion, barely mentioning the Devil. At the same time, though, they accord with and develop the view that evil lies less in the minds of the supposedly possessed than in the minds of those who diagnose possession and attempt exorcism. *The Comedy of Errors* was written in around 1592, not long after the sensational Catholic exorcisms by Weston and others in 1585–86. Shakespeare may also have heard about Darrel's first dispossession, also in 1586, involving the expulsion of eight demons from seventeen-year-old Katherine Wright.[83] The main source for *The Comedy of Errors* was Plautus's *Menaechmi*, but by changing the setting from Epidamnus to Ephesus, a city described in the Geneva Bible (the most widely used Bible in Elizabethan England) as inhabited by exorcists, conjurors, and practitioners of 'curious arts', Shakespeare implicitly engages with recent controversies about supposedly supernatural occurrences.[84] Antipholus of Syracuse highlights the reputation of Ephesus when he and his servant Dromio arrive there:

> They say this town is full of cozenage:
> As nimble jugglers that deceive the eye,
> Dark-working sorcerers that change the mind,
> Soul-killing witches that deform the body.

This sounds sinister, but not necessarily supernatural: Antipholus places the sorcerers and witches in the same category as not only 'nimble jugglers' but also 'Disguisèd cheaters' (1.2.97–102).

This Antipholus is repeatedly mistaken for his twin brother, Antipholus of Ephesus, hitherto unknown to him, producing increasingly bewildering confusions. He begins to feel that Ephesus may indeed be a place of magic, where he and his servant 'wander in illusions' (4.3.40). He does not exclude the Devil from his world-view: he repels the advances of a courtesan with the cry, 'Satan, avoid! I charge thee, tempt me not!' (4.3.45). However, when his apparently mad behaviour leads his 'wife' Adriana – actually his brother's wife, unaware that she is dealing with her husband's identical twin – to summon Doctor Pinch the exorcist, Antipholus of Syracuse is very clear that Pinch is no agent of God, but merely a 'doting wizard' (4.4.57). Pinch recites words of exorcism, charging Satan to depart from Antipholus, then has him bound and confined in 'a dark and dankish vault' (5.1.247). Shakespeare moves away completely from the question of whether or not supposed demoniacs are faking – indeed, Antipholus protests loudly throughout that 'I am not mad' (4.4.57) – and instead emphasises the folly and untrustworthiness of those who diagnose possession and attempt exorcism. Antipholus manages to escape from his confinement, and vigorously denounces Pinch as 'a hungry, lean-faced villain; / A mere anatomy [skeleton], a mountebank, / A threadbare juggler, and a fortune-teller' (5.1.237–9).

Shakespeare returned to this theme in *Twelfth Night*, written in about 1601 when the controversy about Darrel's dispossessions was at its height. Malvolio is tricked by Maria's forged letter into appearing before Olivia dressed in yellow stockings, cross-gartered, wreathed in smiles, and full of innuendos arising from his mistaken belief that his mistress is in love with him. Even before he arrives on stage in this condition, Maria tells Olivia: 'He's coming, madam, but in very strange manner. / He is sure possessed, madam' (3.4.8–9). This seems like a spur-of-the-moment idea, but is enthusiastically taken up by Sir Toby Belch: 'If all the devils of hell be drawn in little, and Legion himself possessed him, yet I'll speak to him' (3.4.78–80). Knowingly or unknowingly, Sir Toby echoes not only Mark 5.9, where the 'unclean spirit' possessing a demoniac tells Jesus that 'My name is Legion: for we are many', but also the supposedly Satanic voice that had emanated from the self-confessedly fraudulent demoniac Agnes Brigges in 1574, which gave his name as '"Legion, Legion," diverse times'.[85] Sir Toby resolves, 'Come, we'll have him in a dark room and bound' (3.4.122), and on Malvolio's next appearance he is 'within', according to the First Folio stage direction (4.2.19sd). This may mean that he is offstage, or in the discovery space towards the back of the stage, or, most likely, under the stage, speaking through a trapdoor.[86] Whereas the cruel confinement of Antipholus of Syracuse had been merely described, that of Malvolio is graphically presented to the audience. Feste, disguised as a foolish priest named Sir Topas, interrogates and taunts Malvolio, maddeningly interpreting everything he says as more proof of his madness, including his repeated assertions that 'I am not mad' (4.2.37). Earlier in the play, Malvolio was a deeply dislikeable character: a pompous killjoy, and exactly the kind of Puritan who wanted to close down the playhouses. Yet satisfaction at his getting his just deserts is increasingly inflected by unease as the jest goes on longer than necessary, and looks increasingly like psychological torture.

It may well be that demoniacs were habitually bound and confined in dark prisons: Boorde, for instance, advised that demoniacs should be kept 'in a sure custody' to prevent them from harming themselves and others.[87] Yet we hear little about this treatment in the published accounts of possessions; one of the reports about William Somers records that he was confined in an institution named St John's in Nottingham, and that one of his keepers, John Cooper, threatened to whip him, but these facts are mentioned only in passing.[88] The authors of such accounts were far more interested in sensational symptoms of possession, combats with Satan, and dramatic scenes of dispossession. Shakespeare's depictions of Antipholus of Syracuse and Malvolio also differ from real-life possession narratives in that there is no question of either of these supposed demoniacs counterfeiting or colluding with those ministering to them. On the contrary, they each staunchly deny that they are possessed and protest their sanity and veracity, while Shakespeare depicts those who diagnose possession as variously misguided (Adriana), foolish (Doctor Pinch), malicious (Maria and Sir Toby), or themselves counterfeiters (Feste). By creating conflict between supposed demoniacs and those who claim to treat them, and by emphasising cruelty in the treatment of demoniacs, Shakespeare suggests that belief in possession is either superstitiously perpetuated by the ignorant or artificially fomented and knowingly manipulated by mischief-makers.

'They assail them with invasions': devils in every mind

Shakespeare's depiction of possession in *The Comedy of Errors* and *Twelfth Night* strongly suggests scepticism about the Devil's presence in the minds of supposed demoniacs. Yet Satan and his ministers are not absent from Shakespeare's Elizabethan plays. In *Henry VI Part 1* (1592) Joan la Pucelle (Joan of Arc) summons '*Fiends*', which, according to the stage directions, enter, silently walk, hang their heads, shake them, and depart (5.3.1–24). *Henry VI Part 2* (1591)[89] also brings on stage a demonic spirit, Asnath, who is conjured up by the witch Margery Jordan and her confederates to serve Eleanor, Duchess of Gloucester, and makes ambiguous prophecies that anticipate those of Macbeth's witches (1.4.1–39). However, recent textual scholarship suggests that both these scenes may be by Christopher Marlowe.[90] Shakespeare seems to prefer ambiguity about the presence of Satan in the world: two characters in his early plays, Aaron in *Titus Andronicus* (1592) and the malevolent protagonist of *Richard III* (1593), are repeatedly called 'devil' by their enemies and victims, but it remains indeterminate whether they are under the supernatural direction of Satan, or merely examples of the evil potential of human nature.[91] Later, in *Hamlet* (1600), the ghost of Hamlet's father may or may not be a demonic apparition (see Chapter 10 below).

Shakespeare's discretion on this point was unusual; other dramatists enthusiastically brought devils on stage. Although after the

Reformation it was considered unacceptable for plays to represent God, Christ, the Virgin Mary, or the saints, nearly twenty of the Elizabethan plays known to us included the Devil (or Satan, Lucifer, or devils under other names) as a character, and he continued to appear until the closure of the playhouses in 1642.[92] He was also visible in woodcut book illustrations, such as those for Stephen Batman's *Crystal Glass of Christian Reformation* (1569), which vividly depict a personal Devil, with horns, claws, and wings, tempting human victims to sin (figs 13 and 14). The title-page to the news pamphlet *Sundry Strange and Inhuman Murders Lately Committed*

13. There was enduring belief in a personal Devil, with horns, claws, and wings, who continued to appear on the Elizabethan stage and in book illustrations like this one of a fool tempted into covetousness. In such depictions the human mind was led to sin by a force external to itself.

14. Another example of the personal Devil affecting the human mind from outside. In this case he tempts a woman into pride.

(1591) shows Satan in more human guise, lurking at the edge of the picture to prompt a murderer: here, he resembles a bearded man, but his true identity is indicated by his sinister black clothes and confirmed by his claws in place of hands and feet (fig. 15). His continuing cultural visibility reflects his prominence in Protestant theology. Both Luther and Calvin had written extensively of Satan and the power granted him by God to test the godly and seize the souls of the ungodly, making English Protestants perceive him as a clear and present danger.[93] Of the thirty-three homilies in the Elizabethan *Book of Homilies* – the sermons approved by the government for delivery in all parishes – no fewer than twenty-three mentioned the Devil.[94]

206

15. Here, Satan appears in slightly more human guise, as a bearded man dressed in sinister black clothes, but the claws that replace his hands and feet reveal his true identity. Again, he steers the mind from outside, in this case driving a man to murder his own children.

The question remains whether dramatic and pictorial representations reflected belief in a physical, personal Devil or were visual metaphors for abstract forces of evil in the world. As with attitudes to astrology, possession, and witchcraft, textual evidence suggests a wide spectrum of beliefs.[95] Thomas Beard's 1597 translation of Jean de Chassanion's *Theatre of God's Judgements*, a compendium of divine punishments for sinful actions in both ancient and recent times, suggests continuing belief in the material, visible existence of Satan. A carouser at an inn flippantly sells his soul to a companion for a cup of wine; in turn, the Devil, who is 'there in a man's shape (as commonly he is never far from such meetings)', buys the soul and carries the man into the air and off to hell, 'to the great astonishment and amazement of the beholders'. An habitual swearer and blasphemer in Savoy is snatched up into the air by Satan, in front of his wife and kinswoman, and carried away; in an engagingly specific detail, 'his cap tumbled from his head, and was found at Rosne, but himself no man could ever after set eye on'.[96]

However, in the popular genre of news pamphlets recounting recent sensational crimes, the Devil is more often an invisible force within the mind. In an example from 1573, told in rhyme, John Kynnestar of Bristol explained why he had stabbed his wife to death in bed:

> A thousand thoughts came in my mind;
> My wits were not mine own,
> To see how bloodily I was fed
> With seeds which the Devil had sown.[97]

Similarly, a prose pamphlet of 1591 relating how a man in Kent murdered his children to ease his way to marriage to a wealthy widow described how 'the Devil entered so far into his mind, that he cast many ways in his thought how to make them away'[98] – even though this was also the pamphlet that showed the Devil as an external, anthropomorphic figure on its title-page (fig. 15).

Scot, unsurprisingly, denied that the Devil had physical existence, since if it were so 'he should (methinks) sometimes appear unto honest and credible persons in such gross and corporal form as it is said he doth unto witches; which you shall never hear to be justified by one sufficient witness'. However, as we have seen, he did not doubt the spiritual presence of Satan, 'For the Devil indeed entereth into the mind, and that way seeketh man's confusion'.[99] Calvin had vehemently denied that Satan and his cohorts were merely metaphors for sinful human impulses: 'in this place must we confute them that fondly [foolishly] say that devils are nothing else but evil affections or perturbations of mind that are thrust into us by our flesh'. He insisted that Satan and his ministers had real existence and independent agency, but also emphasised that they were 'minds or spirits endued with sense and understanding' whose main field of attack was psychological: they 'exercise the faithful with battle, they set upon them out of ambushes, they assail them with invasions, they press them with fighting, and oftentimes worry them, trouble them, make them afraid'.[100] Perkins too emphasised the mind's vulnerability to the Devil, who 'applies himself to man's measure, and, at his own will, draws the mind into error, by his delusions, and impostures'. Satan is alert to our fallenness, 'a natural distemper in the mind of man' that predisposes us to fear, pride, revenge, curiosity, and ambition; hence, 'when the mind is possessed with these troubled passions, with care to help itself, then comes the Devil' to suggest sinful actions.[101]

Many accounts of demonic possession asserted that the evil spirit had entered the mind through a bodily orifice, such as a nostril, ear, wound, skin pore, the mouth, or the anus.[102] Even sources that emphasised the psychological operation of Satan maintained strikingly physical ideas about how he got into the mind and worked upon it. As we have seen, Weyer attributed the delusions of supposed witches to humoral imbalance, which facilitated the Devil's penetration of their minds. He went further, asserting that Satan could actively create humoral imbalance:

> just as the use of reason is impaired in persons who are drunk or delirious or melancholic (because of their humours and vapours), the Devil (with God's permission) is no less able, being a spirit, to stir up such humours and make them receptive to his illusions, and corrupt the reason so that forms of non-existent things are apprehended as real objects.[103]

Because Satan and his followers were spirits, they could enter and work through the semi-material spirits that conveyed life-force around the body and bound it to the soul (see Chapter 1 above). *The Touchstone of Complexions* warned that each human being was vulnerable to 'external spirits recoursing into his body and mind', which entered insidiously: 'for so much as spirits be without bodies, they slyly and secretly glide into the body of man, even much like as fulsome stench, or as a noisome and ill air, is inwardly drawn into the body'. Observing their victims like spies or stalkers, these malevolent spirits work out how to infiltrate their minds: 'by conjectures and tokens which they espy in the eyes, countenance, gesture, and other motions of the body of man, they slyly gather and guess the inward dispositions and thoughts of the mind'. They exploit predominant humours to provoke particular vices, inciting the sanguine 'to riot, wantonness, drunkenness, wastefulness, prodigality, filthy and detestable loves, horrible lusts, incest, and buggery', the choleric 'to testiness and anger, to brawling and chiding, contention, railing, quarrelling, fighting, murder, robbery, sedition, discord', and so on.[104]

Satan was especially implicated in melancholy. Bright's treatise on this humour addressed a friend who was suffering from an afflicted conscience and doubts of salvation. For Bright, this troubled inward state was the Devil's exploitation of 'your own conceit corrupted by melancholy'.[105] Having studied our minds since the Fall, Satan knows 'the vanity of our minds, and the secret thoughts of our heart: which after he hath found, he suggesteth (as he seeth occasion whereto we must incline) instigation of sin and disobedience against God, and his holy commandments' (228). Because of his spiritual substance, he can surreptitiously tempt us 'in the very secret thoughts of our hearts. For being a spirit [...], it is not to be doubted but that he hath a spiritual access unto our spirits, to trouble them, and to disorder all their actions' (226).

Some sources implied that Satan's intervention in the mind to incite sinful thoughts or criminal acts exonerated the human perpetrator from responsibility. This was certainly Weyer's argument against the prosecution of witches; and Bright reassured his despairing friend that he should 'not take all that your mind conceiveth of any manner of impiety whatsoever, to be from you, but from Satan [...] your own conscience bearing you witness how much repugnant they are to your desires' (230). Many Protestant writers blamed despair upon the Devil.[106] In effect, Bright asserted, his doubting friend was not himself, but was being invaded and troubled by alien thoughts in a way that resembled possession. Calvin explained, 'God suffereth not the Devil to reign over the souls of the faithful, but only delivereth him the wicked and unbelieving to govern, whom God doth not vouchsafe to have reckoned in his flock.' Everyone was assailed by Satan, but the difference between resistance and submission was the essential distinction between the elect and the damned. God allows evil spirits to attack the faithful 'and sometimes wound them, but never overcome nor oppress them. But the wicked they subdue and draw away; they reign upon their souls and bodies, and abuse them as bond-slaves to all mischievous doings.' As we saw in Chapter 3, passing through spiritual conflict and triumphing could even be a sign of election: 'the faithful can never be overcome nor oppressed by him [Satan]. They are many times stricken down, but they are never so astonied [stunned, stupefied] withal but that they recover themselves. They fall down many times with violence of strokes, but they are after raised up again.'[107] However, this was problematic as a form of spiritual consolation, not only because it turned response to the Devil's assaults into an exacting test, but also because the doctrine of predestination made states of consolation or despair self-reinforcing. An individual who was struggling to achieve conviction of salvation, with no resolution as yet in sight, might well fear that their spiritual doubts were not merely a challenge to be gloriously vanquished on the way to salvation, but a symptom of irreparable wickedness and inevitable damnation. Even more perplexingly, Satan's malicious ingenuity extended to simulating the inner experience of conversion and creating a mental and spiritual state of 'security', a false, complacent assurance of salvation.[108]

Some writers offered reassurance that the evil spirits able to enter body and mind were countered by good angels who could also enter the assailed mind and help to defend it.[109] However, most Elizabethan authors were preoccupied with the combat between the individual soul and Satan. The suppression or stripping back of Catholic rites for expelling the Devil such as baptism and exorcism shifted responsibility for fending him off from the institutional Church to the lone Christian, while the Protestant emphasis on a personal relationship with God and introspective prayer firmly located this battleground in the individual soul and mind. As the father of lies, Satan could easily conceal himself in commonplace thoughts or simulate thoughts that seemed to come from God; so that the challenge of determining one's elect or reprobate status was compounded by the challenge of identifying ideas and feelings as one's own, or planted by God, or by the Devil. Constant monitoring and evaluation of every thought was imperative.[110]

The mind, then, was a site of psychomachic struggle, not only between higher or lower impulses within the individual constitution, but also between the Christian conscience and evil forces invading from outside. Imagined debates with the Devil became a popular genre which fortified readers with model rebuttals: examples included Thomas Becon's *Governance of Virtue* (1543, with multiple later editions), John Bradford's *Godly Meditations* (1562), and Perkins's *Four Godly Treatises* (1587).[111] As John Woolton wrote in *The Christian Manual* (1576), the godly were 'afflicted, as it were, with a grievous and daily battle which is never ended before the day of death, for that deadly and crafty enemy of ours, Satan the Devil, rusheth upon us with great vehemency, and undermineth us with a thousand temptations'.[112] Every true Christian was engaged in a constant personal process of exorcism.[113]

Understanding this gives us additional tools for reading the spiritual journal of Lady Margaret Hoby. As we saw in Chapter 4, although she records many occasions of private introspection, she is mostly reticent about her inner states. However, occasionally we can detect evidence of mental and emotional turbulence when she mentions assaults by the Devil. She refers three times to the 'buffets' of Satan,[114] a term also used in Bright's *Treatise of Melancholy*, which we know she read (18): according to Bright, the melancholy mind is 'buffeted [...] and beaten with Satan on all sides'.[115] On one occasion Hoby's 'buffet' was a temptation to anger – 'after private prayers

I went about, and had occasion to chide, which I ever take to be a buffet of Satan's malice' (168) – but more frequent challenges were states of mental distraction at church or in her private devotions: 'this day, as ever, the Devil laboureth to hinder the profitable hearing of the Word and calling upon God' (10). Hoby seems to have found the summer of 1602 especially difficult: on 6 May, she recorded that God had 'suffered Satan to afflict my mind' (180), and similar entries occur intermittently for the next few months. However, mention of Satan is usually followed by a turn to God, converting the experience of the Devil's assaults into a reaffirmation of faith: 'Satan hath not ceased to cast his malice upon [me]: but temptations hath exercised me, and it hath pleased my God to deliver me from all' (181). In Chapter 4, we considered how cultural stereotypes of women as lacking emotional control, combined with Hoby's personal temperament, may explain why she seems to us to write so little about her inner state. To these we may now add other factors: for her, experiences that we would classify as personal thoughts and feelings were instead often provoked by the competing *external* forces of Satan and God; and she mostly preferred to record her struggles with Satan only once they had been resolved.[116]

The cases of demonic possession that we explored above also fall into a new perspective as simply an extreme form of a constant inner battle with the Devil and his forces in which all Christians were engaged. In fact, the case of Robert Brigges discussed above, the law student who in 1574 fell into trances and debated with Satan, is never referred to in the manuscript account as a 'possession', but rather as a 'temptation' or 'vexation'.[117] He suffered many of the same symptoms as demoniacs, including the shutting down of his senses, and unusual powers (in this case, rapid speech and an unprecedented ability to expound theology); but it may be that the eyewitness who recorded his case perceived a distinction between those taken over by the Devil, such that their identity was subsumed, and Brigges' vigorous verbal combat with an invisible Devil, retaining a distinct identity and adversarial position. Brigges' experience, though prodigious and supernatural, was closer to the inner ongoing spiritual battle of all the godly. The same is true of two later sources, Phillip Stubbes's *Crystal Glass for Christian Women* (1592), an account of his wife Katherine's deathbed struggle with the Devil, and a 1602 volume commemorating Katherine Brettergh, who also debated with Satan in her final days and overcame his temptations to despair. Again, in neither of these volumes is the case referred to as one of 'possession', and indeed in the volume on Brettergh the term 'possessed' is transferred to her spiritual victory, as she dies with 'her heart so possessed with comfort, her mouth so filled with the praises of God, her spirit so strengthened against the fear of death, her conquest so happy over her infirmities'.[118] All these cases, although unusually vocal and violent confrontations with the Devil, were simply extreme versions of everyday Protestant religious experience and practice, as the Devil passed in and out of every mind. As Perkins explained, every believer's conscience must defend the soul 'in the conflict and combat made by it against the Devil', a conflict that he imagined as inner dialogue: 'The Devil begins and disputes thus: "Thou, O wretched man, art a most grievous sinner: therefore thou art but a damned wretch." The conscience answereth and saith, "I know that Christ hath made a satisfaction for my sins, and freed me from damnation."'[119]

'Who pulls me down?': external and internal demons in *Doctor Faustus*

Unlike Robert Brigges, Katherine Stubbes, or Katherine Brettergh, the protagonist of Marlowe's *Doctor Faustus* (1588) does not fight off the Devil, but invites him in, selling his soul for twenty-four years of magical powers (including knowledge of astrology).[120] Nevertheless, his story resonates with theirs in its ambiguity as to whether Satan is an external or internal presence. *Faustus* is one of the Elizabethan plays that brings devils on stage, including in its cast list not only Mephistopheles, the spirit who serves Faustus, but also Lucifer, Beelzebub, and multiple unnamed devils. In this respect, and in its inclusion of the Seven Deadly Sins, it looks back to medieval morality plays, as also in its inclusion of a Good Angel who urges Faustus to repentance and a Bad Angel who urges him on in sin. Yet, as the play proceeds, it moves increasingly into the mind. At an early stage, Mephistopheles defines hell as not a place, but an inner state: 'Why, this is hell, nor am I out of it' (1.3.77). As Faustus himself experiences recurrent crises of conscience, the conflicting voices of the Good and Bad Angels also seem to become internalised and psychological. At the opening of Act 2, Faustus admonishes himself in soliloquy:

> Despair in God and trust in Beelzebub.
> Now go not backward. No, Faustus, be resolute.
> Why waverest thou? O, something soundeth in mine ears:
> 'Abjure this magic, turn to God again!'
> Ay, and Faustus will turn to God again.
> To God? He loves thee not. (2.1.5–10)

The two Angels appear again immediately after this and take up the debate, but their juxtaposition with such fractured, conflicted soliloquies encourages us increasingly to understand them as dramatic representations of competing forces within Faustus's mind.[121]

During this process, Faustus's speeches begin to resemble the passionate debates with Satan by Brigges, Stubbes, and Brettergh. The eyewitness who recorded Brigges' case explained that 'in the midst of his prayers the Devil would thrust into his troubled mind sometimes desperate suggestions that he had sinned against the Holy Ghost, that he was a reprobate and therefore prayed in vain, sometimes unclean thoughts, sometimes blasphemous imaginations against the majesty of God'.[122] He also explains that 'The Devil's part of the dialogue was unheard of us, but his objections do evidently appear by Brigges' answers' (98). The first of these inferred 'objections' or challenges is that 'The Devil chargeth him that he hath sold him his soul for a sum of money', to which Brigges retorts, 'Thou lyest [...] I tell thee that my name there written was not written by me. Thou shalt never have it.' He cannot sell his soul, 'for the spirit is his who gave it. Lord, do thou receive it, for to thee only I have and do bequeath it. No, no,' now addressing the Devil again, 'thou shalt never have it' (98). The single-voiced debate continues in this vein over many days, with Brigges rejecting numerous charges or temptations assumed to come from Satan. Though he is more forceful than Faustus in defying the Devil, his fluctuating address to Satan and God, both of whom are unheard and unseen by onlookers, anticipates the ambiguity of external or internal address in Faustus's soliloquies and its effect of representing a divided self.

The sense of inner, psychological conflict culminates in Faustus's anguished soliloquy as the final hour of his infernal contract runs out:

> The stars move still; time runs; the clock will strike;
> The devil will come, and Faustus must be damned.
> O, I'll leap up to my God! Who pulls me down?
> See, see where Christ's blood streams in the firmament!
> One drop would save my soul, half a drop. Ah, my Christ!
> Ah, rend not my heart for naming of my Christ! (5.2.67–73)

By now the Good and Bad Angels have disappeared; Faustus is starkly alone and profoundly divided within himself. God and the Devil represent the opposing poles between which he must choose. While intermittently drawn to repentance, he most often expresses belief that his fate is irrevocably sealed: 'My God, my God, look not so fierce on me!' (5.2.112). Is he right to feel that he is the pawn of external forces, or is he evading a choice that lies within himself? Marlowe withholds a clear answer to this question, and herein lies much of the power of the play and its continuing appeal into modern, secular times. In theological terms, Faustus commits the sin of despair: the belief that a mere human can sin enough to exceed God's mercy, which is in fact (for a believer) boundless. For a Calvinist, this would confirm that he is a reprobate, who was always predestined for hell (as Brigges, for a time, believed himself to be). However, at the same time the play and its ending have often been seen as in keeping with scandalous contemporary rumours of Marlowe's atheism, since, by contrast with the frequent visibility of devils, it feels like Faustus is abandoned by God. The emotional effect of the play is one of theological indeterminacy and psychological intensity, where our main awareness is of a man fighting inner demons, trying to decide if he is irredeemably bad or potentially good, and irresolvably conflicted within himself.

This can feel uncannily modern, but it is possible for Marlowe because he is responding to and working with the general Elizabethan belief in constant combat with evil spirits within the mind. *Doctor Faustus* is typical of the Elizabethan age in combining persistent belief in a personal, physical Devil with increasing emphasis on Satan as a threat within the mind. The mind was porous, permeable by outside forces which included evil spirits and the invisible, mysterious influences of the stars and planets. Especially vulnerable to such potent and disruptive outside influences – because it was believed to sit at the front of the brain, mediating between the mind and the world – was the faculty of imagination. This will be the subject of our next chapter.

❦ 7 ❧

'Things Feigned in the Mind'
The Unruly Imagination

In the Introduction to this book we considered the difficulty of defining the mind, now as in the sixteenth century. It is no less difficult to define one of the mind's most powerful and fascinating faculties, the imagination. For the philosopher Mary Warnock, writing in 1976, it was

> a power in the human mind which is at work in our everyday perception of the world, and is also at work in our thoughts about what is absent; which enables us to see the world, whether present or absent as significant, and also to present this vision to others, for them to share or reject.[1]

The context for this definition was a history of theories of the imagination from Hume in the eighteenth century through Kant and the Romantic poets to twentieth-century philosophy. Warnock found in Coleridge and Wordsworth particular insights into the connection 'between perception and recognizable flights of creative imagination' (10), and into the imagination's combined functions of 'Reproducing, creating, [and] understanding' (119). Wordsworth, for instance, described in *The Prelude* how youthful 'Visitings of imaginative power' enabled him as an adult to stand in Nature's presence as 'A sensitive being, a *creative* soul'.[2] Warnock's study of such works led her 'very strongly to believe that it is the cultivation of imagination which should be the chief aim of education' (9).

Warnock's is a typical modern view of imagination: as a creative power which is experienced in mystical 'visitings', which should be set free in 'flights' and which should be nurtured in children. A passage from *The French Academy* (part 2, 1594) at first seems to anticipate this. It associates the terms 'imagination' and 'fantasy', and explains that this faculty is always active, even in sleep, 'occupied [...] about those things which never have been, shall be, or can be'. It is not bound by external evidence from the senses, 'but taketh what pleaseth it, and addeth thereunto or diminisheth, changeth and rechangeth, mingleth and unmingleth, so that it cutteth asunder and seweth up again as it listeth'. However, this abundant and dynamic creativity is then deplored: 'there is nothing but the fantasy will imagine and counterfeit'. It 'forgeth and coineth' many 'new and monstrous things', 'So that in truth, fantasy is a very dangerous thing. For if it be not guided and bridled by reason, it troubleth and moveth all the sense and understanding, as a tempest doeth the sea.'[3] This view of the imagination was predominant in the sixteenth century: its inventiveness was deceptive, its energy was unruly, and it required suppression and control, an attitude of fear and suspicion with profound consequences for the Elizabethan understanding of artistic and literary creativity.

The contrast between Warnock and *The French Academy* illustrates that the imagination has a history. Elizabethan ideas about the imagination were in many ways fundamentally different from our own; beginning with the period's understanding of the location and function of this faculty in the brain.

'Three hollow places': the anatomy of the brain

In 1543, Andreas Vesalius of the world-leading anatomy school in Padua published his groundbreaking book *De humani corporis fabrica* (*On the Workings of the Human Body*). Based on observations from human dissections rather than textual traditions, it challenged many of the teachings of Galen and other authorities. In a section on the brain, Vesalius recalled his early studies at the University of Louvain, where a standard textbook, *The Philosophical Pearl*, taught that the brain had three ventricles or chambers (fig. 16). In the front chamber, *sensus communus* or common sense received impressions from the

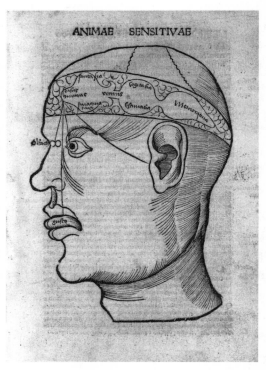

16. This textbook illustrates the standard sixteenth-century model of the brain, with three ventricles. The front chamber contained common sense (the receptor of sense-impressions), imagination, and fantasy. These passed mental images to the cogitative and estimative functions in the middle chamber, which processed them for storage in the memory at the back.

sense-organs, a process indicated by linking lines in the diagram. Imagination then turned these sense-impressions into mental images, though it could also invent its own images independently from this information about the real world and was then known as fantasy. The mental images passed to the middle chamber, the abode of reason, which distinguished humans from beasts. Here, they were processed and evaluated by the cogitative and estimative faculties, then sent for storage in the hindmost chamber, occupied by memory.[4]

'Such are the inventions of those who never look into our Maker's ingenuity in the building of the human body!' exclaimed Vesalius, promising to show 'How such people err in describing the brain' (6). His dissections had discovered *four* ventricles, illustrated in detailed woodcuts: a large one on each side (left and right), a smaller, third one in the centre, and a fourth one below this (fig. 17). Moreover, animal brains had exactly the same structure: there was no special chamber of reason in the human brain. Vesalius therefore ascribed 'no more to the ventricles than that they are cavities and spaces' in which the 'animal spirit' that powered sensation and motion was generated, boldly declaring that 'this explains nothing about the faculties of the Reigning Soul [*Princeps Anima*]'. He refrained, however, from proposing where reason or the rational soul might reside, avoiding dangerous theological territory; indeed, he was compelled to remove from the second edition a sentence disparaging the teachings of theologians on the brain (33–40).

Vesalius published a more accessible *Epitome* or summary of his rather dense *De fabrica*, but even so his empirical, surgical method and his analysis of the brain were slow to be adopted. Galen remained dominant in medicine: at least 660 editions and translations of his works appeared across Europe over the period 1473–1600, including the first English translation of his works by Thomas Gale in 1566.[5] Records of lectures on medicine in various European universities confirm that Galen, along with the Hippocratic Corpus and Avicenna, remained the principal authorities well into the seventeenth century.[6] Hence Vesalius's anatomy of the brain had limited

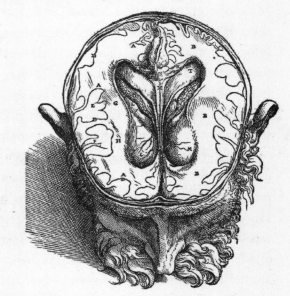

QVINTA SEPTIMI LIBRI FIGVRA·

PRAESENS figura quòd ad relictam in caluaria cerebri portionê attinet, nulla ex parte uariat: atqʒ id solũ habet proprium, quod callosum corpus hic anteriori sua sede à cerebro primùm liberauimus, ac dein eleuatum in posteriora refleximus, septum dextri ac sinistri uentriculorum diuellentes, & corporis instar testudinis extructi superiorem superficiem ob oculos ponetes. A, A, A itaqʒ & B, B, B, ac dein D, D, D, & E & F, & G & H eadem hic indicant, quæ in quarta figura. Sic quoque & L, L, & M, M, & O & P & Q eadem insinuant.

AbA ad Q.

R, R, R Notatur inferior callosi corporis superficies. est enim id à sua sede motum, atque in posteriora reflexum.

S,T,V Supe·

17. By human dissection, Vesalius discovered *four* ventricles in the brain, including these two large ones to left and right. He found that animal brains had the same structure, and suggested that the ventricles were merely cavities, with no special location in the human brain for the rational soul.

impact in Elizabethan England. In 1582, *Batman upon Bartholome* perpetuated the medieval model, representing the mind as 'divided in three cells or dens: for the brain hath three hollow places, which physicians call *ventriculos*, small wombs. In the foremost cell and womb imagination is conformed and made, in the middle, reason: in the hindermost, recordation.'[7] This is perhaps unsurprising since *Batman* was based on a medieval source, but in 1590 we also find Spenser, in his depiction of the human body as the Castle of Alma, dividing its head or topmost tower into three chambers, occupied by Phantastes (imagination) at the front, reason in the centre, and Eumnestes (memory) at the back.[8]

222

The slow acceptance of Vesalius's ideas may be attributable to his reluctance to propose clear functions for the four ventricles, or an alternative location for human reason, combined with his rather convoluted prose style. There may also have been resistance to his radical challenge to entrenched traditions, just as Copernicus's theory of a heliocentric solar system – also, coincidentally, published in 1543 – gained little purchase in England by the end of the Elizabethan era (see Chapter 6 above). Although there was a surge in anatomy books published in England in the mid- to late sixteenth century,[9] these were mostly conservative. Images from Vesalius's *De fabrica* and *Epitome* became widely known when Thomas Gemini[10] plagiarised them in his *Compendiosa totius anatomie delineatio* (*Abridged Outline of the Whole Anatomy*), 1545, accompanied by the *Epitome*'s Latin text (fig. 18). However, the 1553 English version of the *Compendiosa* by Nicholas Udall, while including these illustrations, took its text from medieval sources, as had Thomas Vicary's *Profitable Treatise of the Anatomy of Man's Body* (1548), the first anatomy book in English, which went through some ten editions.[11] Vicary may have chosen to use older sources in active rejection of Vesalius's new ideas.[12]

The French Academy (part 2, 1594) showed limited acceptance of Vesalius. A section 'Of the composition of the Brain' identified four ventricles, of which

> the two first are the greatest, having their situation before, namely on each side one, and being in fashion like to two half-moons. The third is underneath them right in the middest of the brain. The fourth and last is upon the bending down of the nape of the neck.[13]

It also echoed Vesalius's profession that 'None can here attain to a perfect knowledge of the essential power of the soul' (151n). Yet it then reverted to assertions that imagination resided 'in the former part of the brain' (155), reason – 'the principal part and virtue of the

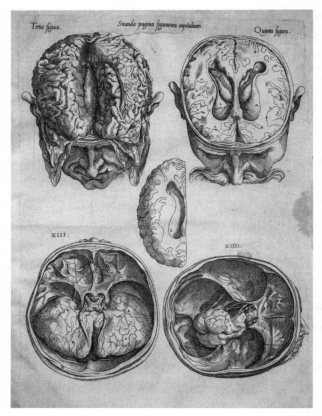

18. Vesalius's controversial ideas were slow to take hold in England. Thomas Gemini plagiarised Vesalius's illustrations in his 1545 *Compendiosa totius anatomie delineatio* (*Abridged Outline of the Whole Anatomy*), but the 1553 English version of this work by Nicholas Udall placed Vesalius's images alongside text from medieval sources.

soul' – 'in the midst of the brain' (159), and memory 'in the hinder-most part of the brain' (161). Despite the awkward fit, the medieval model of three functional ventricles was simply superimposed onto the Vesalian model of four ventricles of indistinct function. John Davies of Hereford's 1602 philosophical poem *Mirum in modum* drew extensively on *The French Academy*, including this syncretic version of brain structure: it described 'Four ventricles or concaves close conjoined', following Vesalius, but assigned them the pre-Vesalian functions of imagination in the two front ventricles, the 'royal seat' of reason in the third or 'middle region', and memory in the fourth, 'behind'.[14] Imagination continued to be located at the front of the brain, as the part of the mind most in touch with the senses and the material world, and this determined how it was understood and evaluated.

'Wicked imaginations': suspicion and fear of the imagination

In the early Tudor interlude *Hick Scorner* (*c.* 1514),[15] Imagination is an allegorical character. He is vivacious and engaging – 'I am Imagination, full of jollity. / Lord, that my heart is light!' (p. 230, ll. 892–3) – but also a criminal who has spent time in Newgate and in the stocks. He frequents brothels, commits perjury and bribery, steals, slanders, brawls and persistently leads astray his companion Free Will. His wits are agile, but applied to gain pleasure and riches, often by ruining others: 'I can imagine things subtle / For to get money plenty' (p. 175, ll. 215–16). Imagination retained this bad reputation across the century: William Perkins preached in a late Elizabethan sermon: 'The imagination and conceit [conceptual faculty] of every man is naturally evil.'[16]

Much of the hostility to imagination derived from the biblical text on which Perkins's sermon was based, 'the imagination of man's heart is evil, even from his youth' (Genesis 8.21), and many similar statements in scripture. The Book of Proverbs, for instance, taught that 'A good man getteth favour of the Lord: but the man of wicked imaginations will he condemn'.[17] 'Imagination' in this sense was a sinful thought or malicious scheme, and also had this meaning in law, which defined treason as to 'compass or imagine' the death of the monarch.[18] Hence, when, in 1601, Elizabeth I discussed the recent Essex Rebellion with the antiquary William Lambarde, he referred to it as 'Such a wicked imagination'.[19] According to the textual authorities of both church and state, the imagination was devious, furtive, and subversive.

Imagination's connection to the senses also made it the portal to the mind for bodily temptations, creating sinful appetites such as gluttony and lust. As Davies of Hereford put it, 'Fantasy being near the outward senses / Allures the soul to love things bodily'.[20] This could lead not only to sinful actions, but also to the distortion of perception by appetites and passions, deceiving reason. Thomas Wright in *The Passions of the Mind* described this effect: 'the imagination putteth green spectacles before the eyes of our wit, to make it see nothing but green, that is, serving for the consideration of the passion [...] a false imagination corrupteth the understanding'.[21]

The terms 'imagination' and 'fantasy' were sometimes used interchangeably, but often 'fantasy' specifically denoted the mind's ability to manufacture mental images autonomously, without reference to the real world.[22] This was the most wayward and deceptive aspect of the imagination. In *The Faerie Queene*, the chamber of Phantastes is full of 'idle thoughts and fantasies'. These include miscellaneous freaks and monsters – 'Infernall Hags, Centaurs, feendes, Hippodames, / Apes, Lyons, Aegles, Owles' – and dangerous falsehoods: 'Devices, dreams, opinions unsound, / Shewes, visions, soothsayes, and prophesies; / And all that fained is, as leasings, tales, and lies'.[23] A French engraving of around 1600 shows a patient undergoing a purge of fantasy's wild and overabundant inventions by having his head baked in an oven (fig. 19). As Davies of Hereford explained,

This power is powerful yet is most unstaid;
She resteth not, though sleep the corpse[24] arrest:
She dotes, and dreams, and makes the mind afraid,
With visions vain, wherewith she is oppressed,
And from things likely, things unlikely wrest.[25]

For Catholic writers, the imagination could be harnessed to spiritual purposes. Nicholas Sander justified the use of material images

19. Fantasy was the capricious and misleading power of the imagination when it made mental images from its own resources, not from sense-impressions of the real world. Here, a patient's head is baked in an oven to purge him of the wild and overabundant inventions of fantasy.

in worship on the grounds that mental images were essential to spiritual understanding:

> If [. . .] at what time I read that Christ died with his hands stretched and nailed upon the wood of the cross, I may and necessarily must devise with myself an image which showeth so much (otherwise I can never understand that which I read), how can a wise man doubt, but that thing may be lawfully set forth in an outward image, which must be necessarily conceived in an internal image?[26]

For Protestant writers, however, the human imagination was fallen and falsifying, and even making images in the mind was idolatrous. Calvin admonished that God is 'no imagined ghost or fantasy, that may be diversely fashioned after every man's liking', and that those who 'imagine him such a one as of their own rash presumption they have forged him [. . .] worship not him, but rather the device of their own heart, and their own dream instead of him'.[27] This made Protestants suspicious of the art of memory, the mnemonic use of a memory-palace or memory-theatre, described in a contemporary manual as 'a disposing or placing of sensible [sensory] things in the mind by imagination'.[28] For Perkins, the reason for the efficacy of this technique was also why it should be shunned: 'The animation of the image, which is the key of memory, is impious; because it requireth absurd, insolent and prodigious cogitations, and those especially, which set an edge upon and kindle the most corrupt affections of the flesh.'[29] In short, 'A thing feigned in the mind by imagination, is an idol'– not only an image, but a feigned or simulated image, and hence doubly false and idolatrous.[30]

Those classified as weak-minded and irrational were regarded as especially prone to the absurd feignings of the imagination. Spenser's chamber of Phantastes housed 'fooles, louers, children, Dames', and Thomas Rogers stated that 'apparitions in the night' afflicted 'no wise men' but 'only boys, women, weak, or wicked folks, whose minds being sore occupied by some strange and strong imagination suppose to see that which indeed they do not, but are merely deluded by their own conceit [thought]'.[31] Far from encouraging imagination in children, as Warnock and modern educationalists recommend, Perkins advised parents to treat it as a disease and 'to stop betimes the course of natural imagination in them, which without the special grace of God will bring eternal condemnation both to soul and body'.[32]

Melancholy was also strongly associated with a disordered imagination.[33] Bright explained that an excess of this humour 'with his vapours annoyeth the heart and passing up to the brain, counterfeiteth terrible objects to the fantasy, and polluting both the substance and spirits of the brain, causeth it without external occasion to forge monstrous fictions, and terrible to the conceit'.[34] Thomas Nashe in *The Terrors of the Night* (1594) vividly described this process:

> the grossest part of our blood is the melancholy humour, which in the spleen congealed whose office is to disperse it, with his thick

steaming fenny vapours casteth a mist over the spirit, and clean bemasketh the fantasy. And even as slime and dirt in a standing puddle engender toads and frogs, and many other unsightly creatures, so this slimy melancholy humour, still thickening as it stands still, engendereth many misshapen objects in our imaginations.[35]

As we saw in Chapter 6, black bile was thought to be a congenial habitat for Satan and his cohorts; it followed that, in the words of Du Laurens, melancholics could suffer 'the intercourse or meddling of evil angels, which cause them oftentimes to foretell and forge very strange things in their imaginations'.[36]

Many medical books invited their readers to marvel at case histories of bizarre melancholic delusions. As mentioned in Chapter 1, *The Touchstone of Complexions* recounted how one sufferer thought he had a nose as big as an elephant's trunk and another that frogs and toads were gnawing his entrails, while a third refused to sit down because he believed his buttocks were made of glass. This work also narrated ingenious treatments which manipulated the imagination in order to cure its maladies. The physician attending the man with the supposedly enormous nose somehow 'handsomely, closely, and cleanly conveyed a long pudding [sausage] into his nose; that done, he took hold of a piece of the very tip of the flesh thereof, and with a barber's razor finely cut away the nose which in imagination the party afore thought himself to have'. Similarly the patient who thought he had frogs and toads in his belly was given a laxative and an enema, while 'there was a means found to put some such crawling vermin into the basin of his close-stool [. . .] after view of his excrements taken, and seeing therein what kind of creatures swimmed, he rested satisfied in mind'.[37] Medical treatises treated the imagination as a wily enemy to be defeated on its own terms by ingenious tricks, and presented both afflictions of the imagination and their remedies as alarming and astonishing prodigies.[38]

Such prodigies of the imagination included so-called 'monstrous' births, which were blamed on things seen during conception or pregnancy which the mother's imagination imprinted on the embryo. As Lemnius explained, 'the hidden imaginations of the woman or mother [...] are of so great force and efficacy, that the things by her in mind earnestly imagined in and at the very instant time of her conception, is derived into the infant and child then begotten'. Here, 'conception' has two meanings: primarily, the conception of the child in the womb, but also, secondarily, the thought conceived by the woman at the same moment. Lemnius went on:

> For this sex being wanton, toying, and steadfastly eyeing every-thing it is offered to sight, it happeneth that the natural faculty being then in working and forming of the child directeth her cogitations and inward conceits that way, and bringeth unto the infant another foreign shape and form, in nature and condition altogether unlike the right parents.[39]

Pierre Boaistuau's *Histoires prodigieuses* (1560), translated as *Certain Secret Wonders of Nature* (1569), was among many works that narrated the case of 'a maid, rough and covered with hair like a bear', who was presented to the Emperor. Her condition was attributed to her mother's distraction at the moment of conception, when she gave 'too much regard to the picture of St John [the Baptist] clothed with a beast's skin' at the foot of her bed. Another woman, it was related, gave birth to a baby 'black like an Ethiopian', though her husband was 'of a fair and white complexion', but was exonerated from a charge of adultery because she had a picture of a Moor near her bed (fig. 20).[40]

Such case histories presented the female imagination as an alarming force with the power to imprint mental images on matter. At the same time, they associated it with women's supposed capriciousness, fickle-ness, and sensuality, and the weak rule of reason in their minds (as discussed in Chapter 4 above). These characteristics were also believed to make them particularly prone to melancholy and manipulation by the Devil, and hence to false and foolish imaginings. We saw in

20. A mother's imagination could supposedly imprint on an embryo things seen during conception. This hairy maiden's mother reportedly looked at a picture of John the Baptist in an animal skin, while the black child was born to a white mother who looked at a picture of a Moor during conception.

Chapter 4 that Ludwig Lavater, in his treatise *Of Ghosts and Spirits Walking by Night*, explained supposedly supernatural apparitions as the imaginings of timorous women; and we saw in Chapter 6 how writers such as Weyer and Scot interpreted witchcraft as the delusions of women with unbalanced humours. As Scot declared, post-menopausal women were 'the aptest persons to meet with such melancholic imaginations [...] what is it that they will not imagine[?]'[41] In short, the Elizabethan imagination was criminal, sinful, sensual, wayward, deceptive, and idolatrous; allied with the Devil, and especially active in women, Catholics, and those sick in mind.[42] It was far removed from the mystical creative power lauded by the Romantic poets and so highly esteemed in modern culture.

'Fragments of idle imaginations': the interpretation of dreams

As we have seen, the imagination, especially in its aspect of fantasy, was understood as never at rest, even in sleep. This was when it produced dreams, as Sir John Davies related in *Nosce teipsum* (1599):

> This busy power is working day and night;
>> For when the outward senses rest do take,
>> A thousand dreams fantastical and light
>> With fluttering wings do keep her still awake.[43]

Scot in *The Discovery of Witchcraft* included dreams among the foolish superstitions of the ignorant and deluded, being merely 'a looking glass' in which 'the fantasy and imagination' represent such things as the waking mind 'doth wish and hope to find'.[44] Disturbing dreams were also attributable to an impaired mind and inflamed imagination: Nashe declared in *The Terrors of the Night* that 'melancholy is the mother of dreams, and of all terrors of the night whatsoever'.[45]

As we saw in Chapter 6, there were animated Elizabethan debates about supposedly supernatural phenomena including astrological prediction, demonic possession, and witchcraft. Dreams were included in these. Were they merely the natural products of the humours and their provocation of the restless imagination, or could they have external, spiritual sources? Were they meaningless or meaningful? Ancient authorities influenced the debate, especially the *Oneirocritica* of Artemidorus (second century CE); although not translated into English until 1606, it was available in Latin and other languages and was widely known in Elizabethan England.[46] Artemidorus distinguished between the *enhypnion* – a meaningless dream, produced by random physiological or mental processes – and the *oneiros*, a predictive dream, often using cryptic symbols, to which he offered a key. Macrobius in around 400 CE developed this meaningless/meaningful distinction and broke it down into further subcategories.[47] Through the Middle Ages, more dream manuals appeared, often attributed to biblical figures associated with dream interpretation such as Daniel or Joseph. One of the most popular, *Somniale Danielis*, appeared in a short English print version in 1556 as *The Dreams of Daniel*, whose list of dream-symbols and their meanings included: 'A man that dreameth that he goeth to wed a maid, betokeneth anguish'; 'To dream to read books, betokeneth good tidings'; and 'He that dreameth to have a white head, betokeneth winning'.[48] Such confident decodings, enabling preparation for good or bad fortune, had obvious appeal for readers.

Thomas Hill wrote manuals relating to various kinds of scientific knowledge and technical skills. These included two dream manuals: *A Little Treatise of the Interpretation of Dreams, Fathered on Joseph* (1567); and *The Most Pleasant Art of the Interpretation of Dreams* (1571), a vast compendium of dream-symbols largely based on Artemidorus.[49] This latter work offered some dream interpretations that are improbably detailed and specific. For instance:

If he which is in love with a woman dreameth to have found a bird's nest, and that he reaching or putting his hand into the nest feeleth it cold, it is a token of hasty or sudden sadness and sorrow, for she shall either marry to another man, or else shall die, and he shall depart soon from that city or abiding place into another town.

Others are briefer and come thick and fast, piling up bewilderingly: 'To see a white ox, or to sit upon him, signifieth honour or advancement. To see elephants signifieth sorrow. To eat butter declareth a happy message. To see beasts make a noise within themselves signifieth the defence from enemies' – and so on.[50] There is no index or organising principle, making practical use of the volume a challenge. Nevertheless, it went through several editions and inspired various imitations.

Yet the ancient sources taught that not all dreams were meaningful. Some were merely the effects of physical processes, especially indigestion. Bullein specified foods to avoid: 'Beans among pulse be very windy, and bring grievous dreams. Pythagoras would not suffer his scholars to eat them' because 'terrible infernal dreams did follow'.[51] The humours also influenced dreams: according to Elyot, sanguine individuals dreamed of 'bloody things, or things pleasant', the phlegmatic of 'things watery, or fish', and the choleric of 'fire, fighting, or anger', while the unfortunate melancholics suffered 'dreams fearful'.[52] Dreams were therefore medically useful for diagnosis of humoral disposition, or of diseases causing humoral imbalance.[53] They could also reflect mental states, again a natural source in the internal condition of the dreamer rather than an external supernatural intervention. Some dreams were merely mundane reflections of waking activities: Du Laurens, citing Theocritus, described how 'The fisherman [...] dreameth commonly of fishes, rivers and nets; the soldier of alarums, taking of towns, and the sounding of trumpets; the amorous rave of nothing in the night but of their love's object'.[54]

More vexingly, dreams could also arise from passions of the mind. Bullein described how 'inward agony' brings

the sleeping passions of the night, with careful [care-filled] troubles of the spirits, and dreams most dreadful, of strange shapes, fearful sights, and pitiful appearing of the dead parents, friends, brethren, and old acquaintance. And sometimes the armed enemy, with frowning face, gnashing teeth, bloody hands, do merciless approach to kill me, the sleeping naked man [...] And the flesh is soon moved, through wicked lust, and in the twinkling of the eye, from dream to dream, the spirits be so variable that the night to the careful man is the very image of hell.

The diagnostic value of such dreams lay in their revelation of the dreamer's spiritual as well as physiological state: 'Mankind may soon thereby undoubtedly behold and perceive the soul, which is lively occupied when as the gross senses of the body be stopped, and in a manner dead, neither seeing, hearing, etc.'[55] It was a short step from reading dreams in this way, as symptoms of the state of the soul, to searching within them for messages from God.

Hill followed Artemidorus in acknowledging that some dreams were 'vain', caused merely by 'surfeits' of 'meats and drinks', humoral imbalances, random freaks of the imagination, or even prosaic circumstances such as the weather.[56] Yet prophetic dreams would come to the right kind of dreamer in the right conditions: 'such as be occupied in great actions and businesses, and greatly abstain from meat and drink, nor are troubled with fear nor sadness, do see and have true dreams [...] And for that cause the dreams of princes are commonly true' (D7v).[57] Dreaming meaningfully was not unlike the genial melancholy discussed in Chapter 1 above, a mark of intellectual and social distinction. Hill argued that the sensory deprivation of sleep opened the mind to profound revelations: 'a man also doth more comprehend in his dream than waking in the day time, because in a dream is more resolved than that in the day which is troubled through the doings of the outward senses' (B2v). Bright agreed:

every dream seemeth to be a kind of ecstasy, or trance, and separation of the soul from this bodily society, in which it hath been in old time instructed of God by revelation, and mysteries of secrets revealed unto it, as then more fit to apprehend such divine oracles, than altogether enjoying awake the corporal society of these earthly members.[58]

Morning dreams were believed to be most truthful. The night was thought to begin with a 'first sleep' dedicated to basic physical and mental processing: food was digested, sending vapours to the brain, where the experiences of the day were mentally digested. Then, following a period of wakefulness, in the 'second sleep' the mind was more settled and clearer, opening the imagination to divine revelation; hence, records of dreams in journals and other documents often included the time of occurrence.[59]

Yet even believers in prophetic dreams acknowledged the difficulty of distinguishing them from vain, meaningless dreams, while other Elizabethan writers dismissed dream interpretation as foolish and superstitious, along with judicial astrology and belief in witchcraft. *A Defensative against the Poison of Supposed Prophecies* (1583) by Henry Howard (later Earl of Northampton) urged the reader to 'scorn discovery by dreams, because there is no directory [authoritative] rule of distinguishing between the certain and the frivolous [...] it were a wilful oversight to measure truth by the line of imagination'.[60] Howard scoffed at lists of dream-symbols:

To dream of the yolk of an egg importeth gold, if you list to believe Artemidorus; and why so, rather than a chicken, whereunto that yolk by course of kind should have been changed? Why should dreams of water portend troubles? [...] I could say the like of falling of the salt, meeting with a dead corpse in a morning, dreaming of fire, loss of teeth, of drowning, swinging in the air, walking in a cloud, with a thousand more, which for a time encumber and disturb the fantasy with fear. (K4v)

God would not use such an ephemeral medium:

Might it not seem very strange that men should build upon the shadows of a dream, which either leaves no print at all, or such a one, as remains no longer than that of an arrow in the air, of a whale upon a quicksand, or of a ship in the water [...] For God would not have his discoveries [revelations] set forth with a pencil of pretence in a ground of fancy, but ingraven in tables of white marble with a point of diamond. (L2v)

Scot's views were similar: 'dreams, whatsoever credit is attributed unto them, proceedeth of folly; and they are fools that trust in them, for why they have deceived many'. Purported dream interpreters 'are mere cozeners [tricksters, deceivers], and worthy of great punishment'. Scot attacked Hill by name, a mark of his popularity and influence: 'He that list to see the folly and vanity thereof may read a vain treatise set out by Thomas Hill, Londoner, 1568.' For Scot, though, dreams were just the random detritus of waking thoughts and experiences; 'And therefore in mine opinion, it is time vainly employed to study about the interpretation of dreams.' Although God had communicated with Old Testament prophets through dreams, that age of miracles was past.[61]

The position of dream sceptics was pungently summarised by Nashe in *The Terrors of the Night*: 'A dream is nothing else but a bubbling scum or froth of the fancy, which the day hath left undigested; or an after-feast made of the fragments of idle imaginations'.[62] Yet Howard acknowledged one supernatural source for dreams: they could come 'from the Devil' since 'Darkness hath always been the Devil's mask'.[63] We saw in Chapter 6 that even those who denied the reality of demonic possession and witchcraft did not deny the existence of Satan and his ability to penetrate the mind. The same applied in the debate about dreams. Perkins, for instance, in his *Discourse of Witchcraft*, suggested that if dreams were 'obscure and intricate, so [that] the interpretation of them is ambiguous and uncertain', then they were likely to be of diabolical origin, since Satan 'himself cannot infallibly determine how things shall come to pass, and thereupon is constrained to give doubtful answers by dreams'.[64] However, discerning whether a dream was natural or supernatural, divine or diabolical, was 'a very hard matter, considering that the Devil in these, as well as in other things, can transform himself into an Angel of light' (100). Hence, Perkins concluded, dream interpretation should be shunned in most cases: dreams were 'not to be received, believed, or made means whereby to foretell things to come, lest by this use of them we grow into familiarity with the Devil, and before God be guilty of the sin of witchcraft' (104).

Yet the popularity of dream interpretation did not abate; if anything, it increased, with dream manuals appearing in ever greater numbers until well into the eighteenth century.[65] Dreams were even accepted as evidence by the Elizabethan judicial authorities. In the case of the witches of Warboys, discussed in Chapter 6, the Samuel family were sentenced to death not for bewitching the Throckmorton daughters – not yet a capital offence – but for causing the death by witchcraft of Lady Cromwell. This was supposedly confirmed by the fact that, immediately after accusing Alice Samuel of witchcraft, Lady Cromwell had dreamed of being tormented by a cat and had then fallen sick.[66] In 1601, shortly before the Essex Rebellion, when a London woman, Joan Notte, had two dreams of danger to Elizabeth I and her chief minister, Sir Robert Cecil, her husband felt duty-bound to report these to a justice of the peace, who in turn informed Cecil.[67]

Individuals also recorded and pondered their dreams. The astrologers John Dee and Simon Forman not only offered dream interpretations to their clients, but also transcribed in journals their own seemingly significant dreams. Dee had a vivid dream in November 1582:

> Saturday night I dreamed that I was dead, and afterward my bowels were taken out. I walked and talked with diverse, and among other with the L[ord] Treasurer [William Cecil, Lord Burghley] who was come to my house to burn my books when I was dead, and thought he looked sourly on me.[68]

Dee does not write down an interpretation, perhaps because the dream self-evidently spoke of his anxiety to gain Burghley's favour and his preoccupation with his large, valuable library, which also features in other dreams that he recorded.[69] However, when his wife dreamed in August 1578 (at around six in the morning, so with a likelihood of truth) 'that all her rings were broken', he hoped this meant that 'she is about to have as many children as there are rings' or 'that great gifts will follow'.[70]

Forman recorded a number of dreams related to his alchemical quest for the philosopher's stone, including one which vividly expressed its frustrations: a friend gave him some of the stone, but in an unstable, slippery form, which trickled away between his cupped fingers.[71] He also recorded three dreams about the Queen, in one of which she was 'a little elderly woman in a coarse white petticoat' who responded amorously when he bantered suggestively with her, suggesting Elizabeth's presence in her subjects' psyches as a symbolic object of desire.[72] Forman also recounted in a fragment of autobiography a vivid recurring childhood dream, experienced from the age of six onwards, which he interpreted as prophetic. Referring to himself in the third person, he describes how

> many mighty mountains and hills come rolling against him, as though they would overrun him and fall on him and bruise him, yet he got up always to the top of them and with much ado went over them. Then should he see many great waters like to drown him, boiling and raging against him as though they would swallow him up, yet he thought he did overpass them.

In his later career Forman was constantly in trouble with the College of Physicians and other authorities, so he interpreted these dreams retrospectively as self-vindications:

> These visions God did show him in his youth to signify unto him his troubles in his riper years. For the mighty mountains might signify the great and mighty potentates that he had controversy with afterwards. And the waters might signify the great councils that were holden against him to overthrow him. Yet God, the only defender of all that be his, would never let him be overthrown, but continually gave him always in the end the victory of all his enemies.[73]

Even if dreams were understood – as by Dee and Forman – as messages from God, they were problematic because they were encoded and because they were transmitted via the notoriously unreliable medium of the imagination. For real-life dreamers, their uncertain meaning and truth status were perplexing; but for literary authors, it was an opportunity. The genre of dream-vision, already brought to a high level of sophistication by Chaucer, not only offered creative freedom to invent fantastical alternative realities, but also gave scope to present controversial ideas in the guise of a mere dream. 'A Dream' (1593) by Thomas Churchyard combined visions of dancing fairies – 'a world of toys and trifles'[74] – with gloomy social criticism: 'In world there is such falsehood used, / The just can never thrive' (185). It presented itself as merely 'The roving thoughts of idle brain, and fancies in the head' (179), but ended with the suggestion that it was an ominous prophecy: 'would God a dream it were: / For many things I now rehearse, / Will prove too true, I fear' (191). Other late Elizabethan works, including John Lyly's *Endymion* (1588) and Spenser's *The Faerie Queene* (1590), used the ambivalence of dream worlds to profess adulation of Elizabeth as a visionary, goddess-like figure while simultaneously implying masculine frustration with female rule, Protestant frustration with the perceived incompletion of the Reformation in England, and anxieties about the Queen's advancing age and impending demise.[75]

The most accomplished work in this double-edged or layered genre is Shakespeare's *A Midsummer Night's Dream* (1595). The play's persistent references to the mutable moon, one of the most frequently used images for Elizabeth in 1590s poetry and pageantry, invoke the supposed capriciousness of the ageing Queen. There is also a sense that her stale regime is creating inertia, frustrating young men who crave change and action:

> oh, methinks, how slow
> This old moon wanes! She lingers my desires
> Like to a stepdame or a dowager
> Long withering out a young man's revenue. (1.1.3–6)

Audiences were also likely to associate Titania with Elizabeth, since the Fairy Queen had featured in a number of royal entertainments,[76] and since of course Elizabeth was identified as the eponymous central figure of Spenser's recently published *Faerie Queene*. The headstrong Titania's humiliating infatuation with an ass-headed weaver and subsequent harmonious reconciliation with Oberon convey strong implications that female powers and desires can lead to chaos, and that the world is more orderly when queens are married and governed by their husbands. Shakespeare skilfully disclaims identification between Titania and Elizabeth by introducing another Elizabeth-figure into the play, the ethereal 'fair vestal' or 'imperial votaress' who, in Oberon's vision, evades Cupid's arrow and so causes the transformation into a love charm of the flower on which it fell (2.1.155–74). Even in this guise, however, Elizabeth's repressed and displaced sexuality is responsible for the erotic turmoil of the play, including Titania's enslavement to lust for Bottom.[77]

This is potentially, then, an intensely controversial play; yet its title encourages the whole work to be dismissed as no more than a dream. Puck underlines this in his epilogue:

If we shadows have offended,
Think but this, and all is mended,
That you have but slumbered here
While these visions did appear. (5.1.409–12)

Even for modern spectators, perhaps unaware of the play's topical allusions to Elizabethan politics, the indeterminacy of dreams has an important function, since the play also explores profound ideas about love, art, and the imagination (of which more below), but does so with the lightest of touches. We can leave the theatre feeling, as Puck instructs, that 'this weak and idle theme' was 'no more yielding but a dream' (5.1.413–14); that we have simply had fun in a world of fantasy. At the same time, part of us might feel, like Bottom waking from his night in the wood, that we have experienced something revelatory and transcendental, 'a most rare vision' which 'hath no bottom' (4.1.202, 211–12). All of this is made possible by the

Elizabethan fascination with the lack of distinction between meaningful dreams – where the imagination is a conduit for divine truths – and meaningless dreams, where the imagination runs wild in its mercurial guise of fantasy.

'Feigning notable images': the imagination and literary creation

In modern thought the imagination is the source of literary and artistic creativity. For the Elizabethans, however, this was not necessarily the case. As vernacular English literature increasingly flourished in the reign of Elizabeth, it was accompanied by an emerging genre of literary theory, beginning with rhetoric manuals such as Richard Sherry's *Treatise of Schemes and Tropes* (1550) and Thomas Wilson's *Art of Rhetoric* (1553). Reflecting the rhetorical training that underpinned the humanist curriculum of grammar schools and universities, emphasis was placed upon skills of writing persuasively and for a moral purpose.[78] For Wilson, this had little to do with the imagination, a sinful faculty that distorted and defiled: 'we make that filthy by our own imagination, which of its own nature is good and godly'.[79]

Other treatises began to allow imagination a greater role in literary creation, but only as a somewhat mechanical faculty that made and organised mental images. We might not be surprised when *The Examination of Men's Wits* asserts that 'From a good imagination spring all the arts and sciences, which consist in figure, correspondence, harmony, and proportion; such are poetry, eloquence, music, and the skill of preaching'. More unexpected for us is the addition to this list of 'the practice of physic [medicine], the mathematics, astrology, and the governing of a commonwealth, the art of warfare, painting, drawing, writing, reading, to be a man gracious, pleasant, neat, witty in managing, and all the engines and devices which artificers make'.[80] The imagination bestowed skill in mental picturing, designing, and ordering. The *Examination* distinguished it from the higher faculty of judgement, noting 'how far off those who have a special gift in poetry are from understanding' (160). It also reasserted the imagination's deviousness and immorality: 'those who have much imagination are choleric, subtle, malignant, and cavillers, and always inclined to evil, which they can compass with much readiness and craft' (184–5).

George Puttenham in *The Art of English Poesy* (1589) identified two opposed forms of imagination: a disordered imagination which creates monsters, and a well-ordered imagination which is 'a representer of the best, most comely and beautiful images or appearances of things to the soul and according to their very truth'.[81] Like the passions, the imagination could be turned to good purposes if under the government of reason (see Chapter 3 above).[82] Again, for Puttenham this virtuous, controlled imagination involves skills in mental picturing and organising that belong not only to 'all good poets', but also to 'notable captains stratagematic, all cunning artificers and engineers, all legislators, politicians and counsellors of estate' (71). His conception of poetry is mainly as a technical skill, requiring a repertoire of figures and devices which he proceeds to catalogue.

Yet Puttenham also saw the poet as emulating God, the first maker, who 'without any travail to His divine imagination, made all the world of nought [. . .] even so the very poet makes and contrives out of his own brain both the verse and matter of his poem'. He also accepted that one source of poetry was 'some divine instinct – the Platonics call it *furor*' (57). This loftier, more mystical idea of the source of poetry in a kind of prophetic vision was also current in the Elizabethan period. For Thomas Lodge, poetry was 'a heavenly gift' which 'cometh from above, from a heavenly seat of a glorious God unto an excellent creature man',[83] while for Spenser it was 'a diuine instinct and vnnatural rage passing the reache of comen reason'.[84] This divine inspiration was not necessarily identified with imagination, which was rather a human mental faculty deployed in its service to give form to divinely implanted ideas. However, just as only those of the right disposition could receive meaningful dreams, so a poet needed a strong imagination in order to receive divine inspiration and turn it into art. This line of thinking drew upon the contentions of Aristotle and Ficino that melancholics, with their overactive imaginations, were often good poets (see Chapter 1 above).[85] An often-repeated maxim was *poeta nascitur, orator fit*: that is, an orator is made by training, but a poet is made by birth.[86]

However, for Puttenham divine *furor* was only one among several diverse sources of poetry,[87] while William Scott's *Model of Poesy*, a late-1590s manuscript treatise, scornfully dismissed those who claim that 'poesy is only a divine fury or inspired force [...] a thing, I know not what, poured down from heaven into their quill, I know not how, which they have no ability to order or restrain, I know not why'.[88] For Scott, poetry, like painting, required 'artificial directions which bring this natural propenseness and supernatural inspiring into actual and habitual perfection' – that is, technical skills and methods (10). These skills must be governed by reason and directed to a moral purpose. Making poetry involved 'a frame and body of rules compacted and digested by reason out of observation and experience, behoveful to some particular good end in our civil life' (7).[89]

One way of harnessing the imagination to a virtuous poetic purpose was to practise *epideixis*, the praise of a great and good historical or public figure to inspire emulation in the reader. Arguably the most important Elizabethan literary treatise was Sir Philip Sidney's *The Defence of Poesy* (composed around 1580, published in 1595). This asserts that, even if literature presents an idealised portrait of the acclaimed ancient Persian emperor Cyrus the Great, this 'is not wholly imaginative, as we are wont to say by them that build castles in the air', because it has beneficial real-world effects: 'substantially it worketh [...] to make many Cyruses' by example.[90] Similarly, in *The Faerie Queene*, Spenser takes as his muse Gloriana, an idealised version of Elizabeth I: 'Great Ladie of the greatest Isle [...] Shed thy faire beames into my feeble eyne, / And raise my thoughts'. In the Castle of Alma, true images are found not in the crazy, chaotic, crowded chamber of Phantastes, but in the well-organised chamber of reason, which is

> painted faire [. . .] with picturals
> Of Magistrates, of courts, of tribunals,
> Of commen wealthes, of states, of policy,
> Of lawes, of iudgementes, and of decretals;
> All artes, all science, all Philosophy,
> And all that in the world was ay thought wittily.[91]

Sidney's *Defence* restated a distinction made by Plato and his followers between icastic art, 'figuring forth good things', and 'phantastic' art, which 'doth contrariwise infect the fancy [a synonym for fantasy] with unworthy objects'.[92] We can infer that Spenser identifies his own poetic art not with the monsters and lies that inhabit the chamber of Phantastes – at best the raw materials of literary creation, fertile and plenitudinous, but unfashioned and ungoverned – but with the orderly, truthful, icastic representations of exemplary rulers and states found in the chamber of reason.[93]

Other processes involved in literary creation included imitation and invention, both skills in which the grammar-school curriculum gave extensive training. Imitation was not necessarily merely passive reproduction of a prior work; it was a flexible term encompassing a range of practices, and it developed skills with which a maturing writer could increasingly build upon or depart from their sources to make something new.[94] Meanwhile, 'invention' derived from the Latin verb *invenire*, to find, and in rhetorical theory denoted methodically seeking and compiling materials and arguments to make an effective case. Thomas Wilson, echoing Cicero, wrote: 'The finding out of apt matter, called otherwise invention, is a searching out of things true, or things likely, the which may reasonably set forth a matter, and make it appear probable.'[95] This, again, sounds like a rather mechanical skill; but 'invention' was also beginning to develop the modern sense of 'inventiveness', the capacity to devise something new. George Gascoigne wrote in 1575 that 'The first and most necessary point' in 'making of a delectable poem' is 'to ground it upon some fine invention', defined as 'some good and fine device showing the quick capacity of a writer'.[96] Puttenham then declared that a poet needs 'an excellent sharp and quick invention, holpen [helped] by a clear and bright fantasy and imagination'.[97]

This emerging sense of 'invention' leaned towards our modern sense of 'imagination', as did a related term, *ingenium* or 'wit'. Wit was associated with intellect and reason, and was often placed in opposition to the more impulsive, irrational faculty of will (see Chapter 8 below). In gifted individuals, wit was acute and agile, and the noun was often accompanied by the adjective 'pregnant', suggesting mental fertility.[98] Puttenham described the figure of synecdoche (using part of something to refer to the whole, or vice versa) as requiring 'a good, quick and pregnant capacity, and is not for an ordinary or dull wit so to do'.[99] 'Quick' here means 'full of life' as well as 'rapid'.[100] Similarly, when in 1598 Richard Haydock translated a treatise by Giovanni Lomazzo on the visual arts, the first treatise in this field to be published in English, he praised the 'pregnant wit' of Prometheus, the first sculptor, and his ability to make images of men that 'seemed to be endued with spirit and life'.[101] There was a related convention of representing literary creation as a male form of childbirth, as when Sidney in Sonnet 1 of *Astrophil and Stella* represents himself/Astrophil as 'great with child to speak, and helpless in my throes'.[102]

In his *Defence of Poesy*, Sidney declares that poets 'certainly in wit ought to pass all other, since all only proceedeth from their wit'.[103] He also makes frequent use of the term 'invention', often in places where we would probably use 'imagination'. Trying to avoid this controversial term is one strategy to address the problem that lies at the kernel of the *Defence*: the 'poesy' that Sidney sets out to defend is defined broadly as not just 'rhyming and versing', but all fictive writing, 'feigning notable images' (12). As such, it is open to all the same charges that were frequently brought against the imagination: that it is idle and wayward, and falsifies and corrupts. Another of Sidney's strategies is to assert that the poet (that is, the maker of fictions) 'nothing affirms, and therefore never lieth [...] the poet never maketh any circles about your imagination, to conjure you to believe for true what he writes' (34). As a self-confessed maker of fictions, the poet, paradoxically, has integrity. He is also a Neoplatonist, accessing, and allowing the reader to access, a higher, ideal world: 'lifted up with the vigour of his own invention, [he] doth grow in effect into another nature, in making things either better than nature bringeth forth or, quite anew, forms such as never were in nature [...] her world is brazen, the poets only deliver a golden' (8–9). His work expresses an '*idea* or fore-conceit' (9), at once a concept or image formed in the mind, and a Platonic ideal, the perfect essence of a moral truth.

As in this passage, the treatise often defends imaginative literature by insisting that it has moral value.[104] It is not merely feigning images that is 'the right describing note to know a poet by', but 'feigning notable images of virtues, vices, or what else, with that delightful teaching' (12). Yet at other points Sidney seems to reach beyond a moral defence towards a more radical perception that fiction might represent alternative, subversive values of aesthetic pleasure and intellectual freedom. Combined with the playful, ironic tone of the work, this makes for a treatise that is not only highly sophisticated, but also fraught with internal tensions and contradictions.[105] As such, it epitomises Elizabethan ambivalence towards the imagination and the related complexity of the period's literary theory.

'Images of absent things': the mind's eye and the 'imagine' chorus

Sidney elevates the mental picture-making of the imaginative writer above the merely mechanical operation described by some sixteenth-century writers. Drawing on Neoplatonism, he makes it a power to conceive essential truths, to give them shapes, and thereby to convey them to readers. He invokes analogies for this from the visual arts: a work of imaginative literature is 'a representing, counterfeiting, or figuring forth – to speak metaphorically, a speaking picture' (10).

Scott develops this line of thought in his *Model of Poesy*, incorporating ideas from Haydock's translation of Lomazzo's treatise on the visual arts, and even moving towards the modern literary-critical sense of the word 'image' as a metaphor or simile: the poet's business is 'drawing similitudes and images of things', and seeking 'apt comparisons and images'.[106]

Thinking about likenesses between literary and artistic creation began to raise increasingly probing questions about the powers of the imagination. In *The Passions of the Mind*, Wright listed unresolved 'Problems concerning the substance of our souls', including: 'How a corporal imagination concur[s] to a spiritual conceit [...] What is art, what the idea in the artificer's mind, by whose direction he frameth his works'.[107] This converged with increasing interest in the concept of 'the mind's eye', an expression that reached back to Plato.[108] For Sir Thomas Hoby in his 1561 translation of Castiglione, it referred to the elevated understanding of the Neoplatonic lover as he moves beyond desire for bodily beauty 'to behold the beauty that is seen with the eyes of the mind'.[109] For Henry Bull in his *Christian Prayers and Holy Meditations* (1568), it also represented spiritual insight that transcended bodily vision: 'Muse a while, how much the light and eye of the mind and soul is better than of the body [...] beasts have bodily eyes as well as men, but men only have eyes of the mind, and that, such as are godly wise.'[110] By the time of *Hamlet* (1600), however, the phrase seems to have developed the more secular sense of simply picturing in the mind a person or thing not physically present: Hamlet tells Horatio that he sees his dead father 'In my mind's eye' (1.2.185).

The concept of inner vision was important to classical rhetorical theory, which taught that an orator or writer must communicate their passions to the listener or reader by verbally recreating a visual scene in their mind. *De institutione oratoria* (*On the Education of an Orator*) by Quintilian (*c.* 35–100 CE) was widely influential in Renaissance Europe, and asserted that to achieve 'the greatest power in the expression of emotions' the 'images of absent things' must be 'presented to the mind in such a way that we seem actually to see them with our eyes and have them physically present to us'. Effective rhetoric must employ *enargeia*, 'a quality which makes us seem not so much to be talking about something as exhibiting it. Emotions will ensue just as if we were present at the event itself.' In a law court, for example,

> It is a great virtue to express our subject clearly and in such a way that it seems to be actually seen. A speech does not adequately fulfil its purpose or attain the total domination it should have if it goes no further than the ears, and the judge feels that he is merely being told the story of the matters he has to decide, without their being brought out and displayed to his mind's eye.[111]

Hence, in literature mental image-making was vital not only to creation, but also to reception. This is evident in the 1593 edition of Henry Peacham's widely known rhetorical manual *The Garden of Eloquence*, which describes metaphors as 'ready pencils pliable to line out and shadow any manner of proportion in nature. In respect of their firm impression in the mind, and remembrance of the hearer, they are as seals upon soft wax, or as deep stamps in long lasting metal.'[112] An allegory is 'a continued metaphor' which 'serveth most aptly to ingrave the lively images of things, and to present them under deep shadows to the contemplation of the mind, wherein wit and judgement take pleasure, and the remembrance receiveth a long lasting impression' (25, 27). These literary devices conveyed vivid mental images from the mind of the author to the mind of the reader, and imprinted them there.

It might appear that drama had less need of this skill of creating mental images, since it was a visual and physical as well as verbal medium. However, the mind's eye was also essential in the Elizabethan playhouses, both to transform a stage space with limited props into multiple, shifting, far-flung locations, and to evoke events occurring offstage. To address these needs, Elizabethan dramatists drew on their grammar-school training in rhetoric. *Enargeia*, combined with 'circumstances' – defined by Quintilian as details of 'motive, time, place, opportunity, means, method, and the like' – could imply offstage lives and complex psychologies for their characters, and create rich, plausible, virtual worlds for their plays.[113] Meanwhile, prologues and other choral speeches increasingly commanded spectators to 'imagine'. These began mainly as a logistical device, particularly in plays of history or travel that required rapid movement of characters between times and places. In *Thomas, Lord Cromwell* (1601), for instance, a chorus exhorts: 'Now gentlemen imagine [. . .] young Cromwell, / In Antwerp ledger for the English merchants'; and again, 'Skip some few years, that Cromwell spent in travel, / And now imagine him to be in England: / Servant unto the Master of the Rolls'.[114] Exhortations to 'imagine' could also, however, be combined with *enargeic* description, as in Thomas Heywood's *Four Prentices of London* (1602), a play about the wide-ranging chivalric adventures of four brothers. The collective imagination of the audience is mobilised to create spectacular special effects of a storm and shipwreck:

Imagine now ye see the air made thick
With stormy tempests, that disturb the sea;
And the four winds at war among themselves;
And the weak barks wherein the brothers sail
Split on strange rocks, and they enforced to swim
To save their desperate lives.[115]

Such 'imagine' choruses also developed into assertions and celebrations of the power of the imagination. In Thomas Dekker's *Old Fortunatus* (1599), a magical purse and hat enable the protagonist and his sons to travel the world. The play's choruses are full of commands to 'imagine', 'suppose', and 'think', beginning with the playhouse Prologue:[116]

for this small circumference [i.e. the playhouse] must stand
For the imagined surface of much land,

Of many kingdoms; and since many a mile
Should here be measured out, our muse entreats
Your thoughts to help poor art.

The Act 2 chorus suggests that both the playhouse stage and the mind of each spectator are capable of containing the whole turning globe through the force of imagination:

The world to the circumference of heaven
Is as a small point in geometry,
Whose greatness is so little, that a less
Cannot be made; into that narrow room
Your quick imaginations we must charm
To turn that world; and, turned, again to part it
Into large kingdoms, and within one moment
To carry Fortunatus on the wings
Of active thought, many a thousand miles.[117]

As Fortunatus's wishing hat transfers him instantaneously between distant locations it becomes a self-referential visual metaphor for the teleportational powers of the theatrical imagination.

The large commercial amphitheatre playhouses that had sprung up in London from the 1570s onwards were unprecedented both in size – with the largest, like the Globe, reportedly able to accommodate up to 3,000 people[118] – and in the significant role they rapidly assumed in urban culture. The new experience they offered of collaboration between the imaginations of playwrights, actors, and large audiences to create fictional worlds must have been mind-expanding and exhilarating for all concerned. The explicit exhortation to 'imagine' was used increasingly and with growing vigour and confidence in late Elizabethan plays, indicating that theatre was a place where suspicion and fear of the imagination were beginning to be counteracted, and where a sense was emerging of the imagination as a powerful creative force to be celebrated.[119]

'Shaping fantasies': Shakespeare on the imagination

Like other Elizabethan authors, Shakespeare regularly disparages the imagination. Hotspur 'leaped into destruction' because he was afflicted 'with great imagination, / Proper to madmen' (*Henry IV Part 2* 1.3.27–9). Master Page asks the deluded Master Ford, 'What spirit, what devil suggests this imagination?' (*Merry Wives* 3.4.181–2); and as Hamlet departs with his father's ghost, Horatio laments that 'He waxes desperate with imagination' (*Hamlet* 1.4.87).[120] Even Hamlet's statement that he sees his father 'In my mind's eye' (1.2.185) is ambiguous evidence of either his intellectual sensitivity and capacity, or his melancholy madness.

Yet Shakespeare also shows knowledge of the rhetorical theories that required the creation of visual images in the mind to engage the emotions of a listener or reader. In *The Rape of Lucrece*, his heroine is witnessed surveying a painting of the fall of Troy, an exercise in *ekphrasis*, verbal description of a visual work of art to recreate the picture in the reader's mind. At one moment this experience becomes especially intense:

For much imaginary work was there:
Conceit deceitful, so compact, so kind,
That for Achilles' image stood his spear,
Gripped in an armèd hand; himself behind
Was left unseen, save to the eye of mind.

From this suggestive fragment the whole figure of Achilles must be created in the imagination, while for other figures too 'A hand, a foot, a face, a leg, a head / Stood for the whole to be imaginèd' (1422–8). The reader must visualise in their imagination a painting not actually seen, then stretch their imaginative powers even further, joining Lucrece in completing the scene by mentally picturing details that the painting itself does not show. This draws the reader into Lucrece's compassionate and impassioned response to the painting, contributing to our imaginative participation in the fictional world of the poem and engaging our emotions with its characters and events.[121]

Shakespeare also experiments with the related dramatic convention of the 'imagine' chorus which exhorts the audience to picture in their minds things not seen on stage. He creates the most extensive, eloquent, and justly famous examples of the genre in *Henry V* (1599), where the Prologue asks:

> Can this cockpit hold
> The vasty fields of France? Or may we cram
> Within this wooden O the very casques
> That did affright the air at Agincourt?

The audience can perform feats otherwise impossible in the playhouse if they 'let us [. . .] / On your imaginary forces work', and

> Think, when we talk of horses, that you see them
> Printing their proud hooves i'th' receiving earth.
> For 'tis your thoughts that now must deck our kings,
> Carry them here and there, jumping o'er times. (Prol. 11–29)

After this opening chorus has activated our imaginations, that of Act 3 deploys potent *enargeic* description to conjure up the English fleet at sea and place us in the heart of the scene:

> think
> You stand upon the rivage [shore] and behold
> A city on th'inconstant billows dancing,
> For so appears this fleet majestical,
> Holding due course to Harfleur.

Multiple imperatives exhort the audience to 'Work, work your thoughts' (3.0.1–35).

In Act 4, Shakespeare introduces a further sophisticated use for the 'imagine' chorus in the disparity between what it describes – an idealistic vision of Henry on the eve of the battle of Agincourt dispensing to 'every wretch' throughout the camp 'A largess universal, like the sun' (4.0.43, 41) – and the ensuing dramatic action, in which Henry is disguised and, unknown to his soldiers, antagonises some of them, and bemoans the burdens of kingship. This ironic discrepancy between what the chorus asks us to imagine and what we then see take place contributes to Shakespeare's nuanced enquiry into Henry's character and into the complex relation between image and reality in monarchical identity. Here and elsewhere, Shakespeare also devises new poetic variations on the now-familiar imperative to 'imagine': 'Now entertain conjecture of a time' (4.0.1); 'But now behold, / In the quick forge and working-house of thought' (5.0.22–3).[122]

Shakespeare's most profound and influential reflections on the imagination are in *A Midsummer Night's Dream*. As discussed above, the play's title represents the whole work as dreamed by the audience, that is, formed in their imaginations. Within it, many scenes explore how the collective imagination works in the playhouse. The persistent misunderstandings of this by the mechanicals in their rehearsal scenes train the audience to exercise their collective imagination correctly. On the one hand, Bottom and his colleagues lack confidence in the imagination, insisting that a wall and moonshine must be physically represented on stage. On the other, they overtrust the imagination, fearing that ladies in the audience will believe the killing and the lion in the play are real, unless clearly told otherwise (3.1.1–60). All of this seems funny and foolish, but in rejecting the mechanicals' misconceptions, spectators implicitly consent to participation in the collective theatrical imagination and come to understand this as finely calibrated: we must invest belief in the imagined world of the play, while at the same time retaining the knowledge that it is only imaginary and illusory.

At the beginning of Act 5, the terms 'imagination', 'imagine', and 'imagining' are used seven times within some 200 lines. Theseus is

Duke of Athens and the voice of reason, so dismisses the lovers'
bizarre tales of their nocturnal adventures, reiterating the commonplace disparagement of imagination:

> I never may believe
> These antique fables, nor these fairy toys.
> [...]
> The lunatic, the lover, and the poet
> Are of imagination all compact.

His attempted diatribe undermines itself, however, not least since he
is himself just such an 'antique fable'. Moreover, as he proceeds,
poetic *furor* sounds increasingly exhilarating and becomes a power of
the poet more than a force from the gods: 'The poet's eye, in a fine
frenzy rolling, / Doth glance from heaven to earth, from earth to
heaven'. The familiar Elizabethan concept of pregnant wit is reinvig-
orated:

> as imagination bodies forth
> The forms of things unknown, the poet's pen
> Turns them to shapes and gives to airy nothing
> A local habitation and a name.

In Elizabethan theories of human fertilisation, the womb provided
raw matter which was infused with life and shape by the male seed.[123]
Likewise, here the womb-like imagination 'bodies forth' inchoate
material which is given vitality and specificity by the phallic pen.
This version of the imagination is female and bodily, but not evil;
the emphasis is on its fertility and its role as an essential partner
in the poet's act of creation. It is the source and essence of poetry
(5.1.2–22).

Textual evidence suggests that the lines of this speech that expand
upon the process of poetic creation were added by Shakespeare at
some point between composition of the play in 1595 and printing of

the quarto in 1600, as he reflected further on his own imaginative art.[124] Interestingly, it was during this period, in 1599, that he wrote *Henry V*, where, as we have seen, he was also thinking strenuously about the powers of the imagination. In Theseus's speech in *A Midsummer Night's Dream*, there is a striking absence of any moral defence of the imagination, as found in Sidney and other Elizabethan literary theorists. There is no distinction made between wrong and right kinds of imagination, or between disorderly and well-governed imagination. In subverting Theseus's scepticism to turn it into a celebration of imagination, Shakespeare does not delete lines on 'fairy toys' and the 'frantic' delusions of lovers and madmen, but unapologetically associates the lunatic, the lover, and the poet, embracing and revelling in the capriciousness of the imagination. Their 'seething brains' and 'shaping fantasies' sound far more exciting than what 'cool reason [. . .] comprehends'. The passage and the play align the imagination with fairy magic and the intoxication of love, and celebrate its energy, unpredictability, and freedom.

In line with the implicit metaphor of the imagination as a mental womb, Hippolyta seems to understand the dream-like nocturnal events in the wood more deeply than Theseus:

> all their minds transfigured so together,
> More witnesseth than fancy's images
> And grows to something of great constancy;
> But, howsoever, strange and admirable [wondrous]. (5.1.24–7)

These lines may be taken as describing the mysterious creative communion that the play seeks to create between the imaginations of the playwright, the actors, and the audience. The play's last words then fall neither to Theseus nor Hippolyta, but to the fairies whose existence Theseus has denied; it thereby suggests that the world of magic, dreams, and imagination frames the world of waking experience, rather than vice versa, and that imagination has a higher truth than the so-called reality of bare reason.

As an Elizabethan, Shakespeare understood the imagination as mercurial and potentially maddening. However, as a theatre-poet he was habituated to seeing his ideas achieve visual embodiment on stage and to using language to create disembodied pictures in his auditors' minds. He works this magic repeatedly in *A Midsummer Night's Dream*: just two examples are Titania's vivid description of the disturbance of the seasons, and Oberon's lyrical, meticulously detailed evocation of 'a bank where the wild thyme blows' (2.1.82–117, 249–56).[125] Moreover, Shakespeare evidently experienced a particular alacrity and personal pleasure in literary creation which is manifest in the effervescent brilliance of this play and its almost euphoric representation of imagination. Here and in Shakespeare's works more generally, there emerges a new understanding of imagination as an inspiring, visionary, mystical force and as the source of artistic creativity. The human mind is not just a vessel for divine visions, but has its own autonomous creative power, identified as imagination. This new thinking, eloquently expressed, had extensive influence on later writers, especially the Romantic poets, and hence contributed to our concept of the imagination today.[126] However, if we recontextualise it in the Elizabethan period, when the predominant attitude to the imagination was one of distrust, hostility, and suppression, we can fully appreciate Shakespeare's radicalism as both practitioner and philosopher of imagination.

8

Governing Self and State
The Politics of the Mind

The *Touchstone of Complexions* was one of many Elizabethan works that likened the human constitution to a state or commonwealth. It declared:

> even as in a civil tumult and seditious uproar among the common people, the magistrate hath much ado to appease and mollify the wilful people's rage and headiness, so likewise reason is not able easily to subdue the lewd affections and unbridled motions that grow by immoderate gourmandising, surfeit, and drunkenness.

Reason must rule over the unruly passions and bodily appetites, and chaos would ensue in both the mind and the state if hierarchy should break down. The *Touchstone* elaborated on the hierarchical structure of the commonwealth, which consisted of 'the poor commonalty [common people], lowest in degree', then 'merchants and traffickers', then 'the high magistrates and peers of the realm, who, by due administration of the laws and political ordinances, keep the rude multitude in due order of obedience, and see public peace and tranquillity maintained'. It then applied the analogy to the human constitution: 'The like order, comeliness and agreement is in the body of man, wherein every part doth properly and orderly execute his peculiar office'.[1] Peace and tranquillity in state and self alike depended upon members keeping to their place and fulfilling their designated function, and upon autocratic rule. The mind should govern the body; while within the mind, reason should control the disorderly forces of fantasy, the passions, and the sensual appetites. Self-government was the key to virtue.[2]

The popularity of this analogy meant that discussions of personal psychology and political ideology were closely intertwined. There was a long history behind this: hierarchical images of the mind as state and the state as mind reached back to Plato's *Republic*. However, as with other influences from classical thought, this ancient and established model of personal and political order was disrupted and adapted by new ideas and circumstances. The theological upheavals of the Reformation, combined with the unusual political situation of a woman on the throne, gave rise to intense debates and new questions about the structural management of both the individual and the state. In the mind as a state, reason was placed in authority over the passions and the imagination, but according to Calvinist theology, human reason was itself fallen and corrupt, fundamentally calling this model into question. Meanwhile, in the state as mind, the presence on the throne of a woman – a sex habitually represented as irrational, as we saw in Chapter 4 – complicated identification of the monarchy with reason. Female rule also led to debates about the nature of monarchy, including the relative powers of the Queen and her male counsellors, which were associated with more complex, less autocratic models of the mind and its faculties.

Some of these more complex models involved a mental faculty not yet considered in this book: will. Definitions of will generally associated it with personal choice and agency, but beyond this it generated radically different evaluations. Some writers associated will with the passions and bodily appetites, and hence advocated its subjugation by reason. Others, however, construed it as a faculty of moral choice that should take precedence over reason. Sometimes it was will, not reason, that was represented as monarch of the mind. All of these debates, however, took place in the context of a general assumption that the mind was like a state and the state was like a mind.

'Reason beareth the room of a king': sources for politicising the mind

Plato's *Republic* proposed that for a state to be peaceful and well ordered it must be governed by philosophers, men of wisdom and reason. They must be supported by 'auxiliaries' or military forces, and the working class must willingly submit to being ruled. Harmonious and successful functioning depended upon each class keeping to its allotted role and status; there must be no aspirations to social mobility, and no resistance or disobedience. The mind should follow the same principles: 'Since the rational part is wise and looks out for the whole of the mind, isn't it right for it to rule, and for the passionate part to be its subordinate and ally?' The rational part of the mind should make strategic decisions while the passionate part serves in its defence, and together they should control 'the desirous part, which is the major constituent of an individual's mind'; otherwise, that individual risks becoming 'saturated with physical pleasures' and falling into a degenerate condition. '[S]elf-discipline [. . .] in both a community and an individual' is achieved 'when the ruler and its two subjects unanimously agree on the necessity of the rational part being the ruler and when they don't rebel against it'. In a virtuous person, 'each of his constituent parts does its own job as ruler or subject'.[3]

In his *Enchiridion*, Erasmus blended this extended political metaphor with Christian theology. For him, the Fall had destroyed the Platonic ideal: beforehand, 'both the mind ruled the body without business [difficulty], and the body obeyed without grudging', but:

Now is it clean contrary. The order between them is so troubled, the affections or appetites of the body strive to go before reason: and reason is in a manner compelled to incline and follow the judgement of the body. Thou mayest compare therefore a man properly to a communalty [commonwealth] where is debate and part-taking in itself.

To restore order and achieve virtue, reason must regain authority: 'In man reason beareth the room of a king.' In this commonwealth, the higher affections, such as reverence for parents, brotherly love, and compassion for the afflicted, are the nobility; but the lower, sensual passions, such as 'lechery, riot, envy, and such like diseases', are 'the most rascally and vile sort of the common people'. They 'ought to obey the officers and rulers, and bear no rule nor office themselves'; if they strive to overrule their superiors, 'then ariseth perilous sedition or division in our commonwealth', leading 'to extreme mischief, and to utter destruction'.[4]

This hierarchical model of the mind blended with Aristotle's theory of the three levels of the soul, as discussed in Chapters 1 and 2 above. *Batman upon Bartholome* was among many Elizabethan works that reiterated this scheme:

In diverse bodies the soul is said to be threefold, that is to say, *Vegetabilis* that giveth life, and no feeling, and that is in plants and roots, *Sensibilis*, that giveth life and feeling, and not reason, that is in unskilful beasts, *Racionalis* that giveth life, feeling, and reason, and this is in men.[5]

This structure could be used both for thinking about hierarchy in nature, with humans ruling over the plants and beasts, and for thinking about hierarchy in the individual human constitution, with reason ruling over the sensitive and vegetative faculties. Each individual could allow themselves to sink down towards the more basic and beastly parts of their nature, or raise themselves up by cultivating their higher, rational powers. They could even aspire further towards emulation of the divine, as Annibale Romei explained in *The Courtier's Academy* (1598):

if a man addict himself only to feeding and nourishment, he becometh a plant; if to things sensual, he is as a brute beast; if to things reasonable and civil, he groweth a celestial creature; but if he exalt the beautiful gift of his mind, to things invisible and divine, he transformeth himself into an angel, and to conclude, becometh the son of God.[6]

This scheme could also map onto class hierarchy. In Shakespeare's *Love's Labour's Lost* (1596), Nathaniel the curate uses it to assert both mental and social superiority over Dull, the dim-witted constable: 'His intellect is not replenished; he is only an animal – only sensible [perceptive] in the duller parts. / And such barren plants are set before us that we thankful should be – / Which we of taste and feeling are – for those parts that do fructify in us more than he' (4.2.23–5).

Meanwhile, the Neostoic emphasis on self-government was frequently expressed in political metaphors. Sometimes these represented the individual mind as a self-contained, isolationist state, withdrawn from public politics, as in the poem 'My mind to me a kingdom is', discussed in Chapter 2 above.[7] According to Lipsius, however, in his work *Of Politics*, the virtues achieved through personal constancy should be applied in prudent political service, while rulers had a special duty to cultivate self-command. He supported his arguments with the familiar mind–state analogy: 'as the mind in man's body cannot be either whole, or diseased, but the functions thereof in like manner are either vigorous, or do languish, even so is the prince in this society'.[8]

'A most excellent and perfect order': hierarchy in the Elizabethan mind

In the late sixteenth century, Platonic, Aristotelian, and Neostoic models of the mind as a hierarchically ordered state converged with emphatic force. The mind–state analogy was frequently placed within a larger structure of macrocosmic/microcosmic analogies, organising everything into a system of linked hierarchies in which higher orders governed lower orders. These hierarchies included God's supremacy over his creation; the order of the stars and planets in the cosmos; and order in the natural world, the state, the household, marriage, the human body, and the human mind. All these forms of hierarchy mapped onto each other and reinforced each other as right and God-given. Any form of social or political hierarchy could be enforced by rhetorical appeal to its conformity to the natural order and by provoking fear of the chaos that would ensue from any disruption: as Erasmus had put it, 'extreme mischief' and 'utter destruction'.

A powerful example of this is the *Homily on Obedience* (1547, reissued 1559), one of the sermons prescribed by the Elizabethan government to be delivered in parish churches across the land. It opened with a resounding declaration: 'Almighty God hath created and appointed all things, in heaven, earth, and waters, in a most excellent and perfect order'. It continued:

man himself also hath all his parts both within and without, as soul, heart, mind, memory, understanding, reason, speech, with all and singular corporal members of his body, in a profitable, necessary, and pleasant order. Every degree of people, in their vocation, calling, and office, hath appointed to them their duty and order. Some are in high degree, some in low; some kings and princes, some inferiors and subjects.

It then warned: 'where there is no right order, there reigneth all abuse, carnal liberty, enormity, sin, and Babylonical confusion'. '[M]ind, memory, understanding, [and] reason' formed an integral part of the cosmic, natural and social order in which hierarchy must be maintained at all costs.[9]

The image of the mind as ruler over the body is found across many Elizabethan genres. The hugely influential anthology *Tottel's*

Miscellany (1557) included a poem with the title 'He ruleth not though he reign over realms that is subject to his own lusts', which warns that 'If thy desire have over thee the power, / Subject then art thou and no governor'.[10] In a very different kind of book, John Banister's 1575 *Treatise of Chirurgery* (i.e., surgery), the human body is 'worthily compared to a city or commonwealth. For in a city there is but one governor (if it be well ruled), and that in man's body is reason; the prince is placed on high, for peril of rebellion, as here reason inhabiteth the brain.' There is the usual assertion that insurrection would be disastrous: 'the inferior savage members', if not strictly controlled, 'would soon scale the tower and dislodge reason their Prince', causing 'commotions or tumults'.[11]

Many works intertwined political ideology with advice on private conduct and management of the mind. Fulke Greville's 'Letter to an Honourable Lady' at once advocates the absolute authority of rulers, the proper obedience of wives to their husbands, and the Neostoic virtues of self-government. The addressee, a wife mistreated by her husband, is instructed in the 'affinity between a wife's subjection to a husband, and a subject's obedience to his sovereign', even if that sovereign is a tyrant. Her situation is 'such a model of subjects' estates under princes, as man's little world is of the great, differing only in more or less'. Resisting her husband would be an unnatural usurpation; hence, she must 'instead of mastering him, master yourself', and 'enrich yourself upon your own stock, not looking outwardly, but inwardly for the fruit of true peace'. The hierarchical order of the state and the hierarchical order of marriage must be emulated and reinforced by the maintenance of order and self-control in her 'little world' within.[12]

Shakespeare's *The Rape of Lucrece* also moves fluidly back and forth between the personal and the political, but in ways that are more complex than the absolute rejection of rebellion in most Elizabethan works. As Lucrece resists rape, she urges Tarquin to govern his passions with reason, a particular duty for him as 'a sovereign king' (652). If he submits to 'Black lust, dishonour, shame, misgoverning', then 'So shall these slaves be king, and thou their slave'(654, 659).This abdication of authority is indeed what happens: after the rape, Tarquin's soul complains that her 'subjects with foul insurrection / Have battered down her consecrated wall' (722–3). The words 'treason' and 'traitor' resound through the poem, tracing an arc from the 'high treason' committed by Tarquin's eyes as they gaze on Lucrece's beauty and incite his lust, to her dying exhortation to the men of Rome to 'let the traitor die' (73, 369, 1686). His subordination of his reason to his passions violently disrupts not only his own internal state, but also the body politic. As Lucrece contemplates the painting of the fall of Troy, she meditates on the catastrophic consequences of Paris's 'heat of lust' for Helen: 'Why should the private pleasure of someone / Become the public plague of many moe [more]?' (1478–9).

The poem's response to this question is that when disorderly private passions disrupt the state, righteous rebellion may be necessary to restore order. Tarquin's lustful passion creates turbulent passions in Lucrece (as discussed in Chapter 4), resulting in her suicide; and this in turn creates collective passions in the people of Rome: 'the people were so moved that, with one consent and a general acclamation, the Tarquins were all exiled, and the state government changed from kings to consuls' (Argument, p. 703). We saw in Chapter 3 that the passions could be harnessed to virtuous uses; similarly here, rebellion in the state is shown to be justifiable in certain circumstances, to restore virtue and order. The uprising results in the 'everlasting banishment' of the Tarquin dynasty, and with them lust, cruelty, lawlessness, and all forces of personal and political disorder. The Roman republic is founded, with 'all our country rights in Rome maintained' (1855, 1838). The idea that passions in the mind and rebellion in the state may sometimes be necessary to restore the rule of reason and order makes *The Rape of Lucrece* unusual among Elizabethan texts. However, it maintains their usual connection between states of mind and the state of the commonwealth, and their insistence on order as the ideal state for both.[13]

'She rules alone the whole mind's commonweal': Elizabeth I as Queen of the mind

In various Elizabethan writings the traditional mind–state analogy was given topical form. Elizabeth I was often identified with reason as ruler of the mind and with the rational soul, the highest of Aristotle's three levels of the soul. In Book II of Spenser's *The Faerie Queene*, Sir Guyon, the Knight of Temperance, deplores the violent and tragic outcomes 'When raging passion with fierce tyranny / Robs reason of her due regalitie'.[14] As discussed in Chapter 3 above, he visits the House of Alma, representing the human body as the seat of the rational soul. While potentially virtuous affections occupy the parlour at the heart of Alma's castle (II.ix.34–44), a wild army of other affections – the bodily, worldly passions – are outside its walls, laying violent siege:

> What warre so cruel, or what siege so sore,
>   As that, which strong affections doe apply
>   Against the forte of reason euermore,
>   To bring the soule into captiuity. (II.xi.1)

Spenser goes on:

> But in a body which doth freely yeeld
>   His partes to reasons rule obedient,
>   And letteth her that ought the scepter weeld,
>   All happy peace and goodly gouernment
>   Is setled there in sure establishment,
>   There *Alma* like a virgin Queene most bright,
>   Doth florish in all beautie excellent. (II.xi.2)

Elizabeth I had been acclaimed as a 'virgin queen' or 'maiden queen' since the late 1570s, including in Spenser's own 'Aprill' Eclogue (1579), where she is 'The flower of Virgins [. . .] a mayden Queene'.[15]

Earlier in Book II of *The Faerie Queene*, Sir Guyon had explained that he served Gloriana, 'Great and most glorious virgin Queene aliue, / That with her soueraine powre, and scepter shene / All Faery lond does peaceably sustene' (II.ii.40). Gloriana, a persona for Elizabeth, exemplifies not only monarchical glory, but temperate rule, both in her peaceful reign over the land and in her virginity, governing her own passions with the higher powers of her mind. It follows that the Knight of Temperance is her particular servant, a member of her Order of Maidenhead who bears her portrait on his shield (II.i.28, ii.42, viii.43). The description of Alma as 'a virgin Queene most bright' at once identifies her with Elizabeth, and compares Elizabeth's authority with that of the rational soul within the mind and body.[16]

Spenser vividly describes the passions that besiege the House of Alma as a horde of savage ruffians:

> A thousand villeins rownd about them swarmd
> Out of the rockes and caues adioyning nye,
> Vile caitiue wretches, ragged, rude, deformd,
> All threatning death, all in straunge manner armd,
> Some with vnweldy clubs, some with long speares,
> Some rusty knifes, some staues in fier warmd. (II.ix.13)

This description closely matches his representation of Irish rebels against English colonial rule in his prose tract *A View of the Present State of Ireland*.[17] At this time Ireland was England's major colony, and Spenser was an English settler, administrator, and landholder in that colony. Like Alma's barbarous assailants, the native Irish in the *View* are frequently represented as 'wretched' and 'rude', pursuing 'civil broils' and 'tumultuous rebellions':

> when they so make head, no laws, no penalties can restrain, but that they do in the violence of that fury tread down and trample under foot all both divine and human things, and the laws themselves they do specially rage at and rend in pieces, as

most repugnant to their liberty and natural freedom, which in their madness they effect.[18]

For Spenser, then, the relations between mind and body are inherently political, informed by his experience of colonialism and his ideological response to that experience. For him, the properly hierarchical relation between the rational soul and the disorderly, sensual passions is a direct analogy for the need for imperial authority to be imposed on Ireland's indigenous people, perceived by Spenser as unruly and uncivilised. As with all this mind-as-state, state-as-mind imagery, the analogy works in the other direction as well, with the political hierarchy of colonialism serving as an analogy for correct mind–body relations.

In the 1590s, Sir John Davies became one of the principal poetic celebrants of the Elizabethan regime as an emblem of cosmic and natural order in his poems *Orchestra* (1596), *Nosce teipsum* (1599), and *Hymns of Astraea* (also 1599). *Nosce teipsum* is dedicated to Elizabeth as 'the divinest and the richest mind', and invokes her celebrated learning to identify her with the rational soul, which is 'this cunning [knowledgeable, learned] mistress and this Queen'.[19] The comparison is developed at length: the rational soul

> Doth as her instruments the senses use,
> To know all things that are felt, heard, or seen,
> Yet she herself doth only judge and choose.

> Even as our great wise Empress, that now reigns
> By sovereign title over sundry lands
> Borrows in mean affairs her subjects' pains,
> Sees by their eyes, and writeth by their hands. (17)

Here, the reach of the rational soul in the world, through her bodily instruments, the senses and limbs, resembles that of Elizabeth as monarch of an aspiring imperial power, sending out her agents to supply her with information, carry out her orders, and exercise authority in her name.

The rational soul also has a higher tier of advisers, the inward senses or mental faculties. They assist her decision-making like Elizabeth's Privy Council:

> But things of weight and consequence indeed
>   Herself doth in her chamber them debate,
>   Where all her counsellors she doth exceed
>   As far in judgement, as she doth in state. (17)

However, Sir John emphasises that although the queenly rational soul may gather information from her outward and inward senses, she is the executive power in the mind. She withdraws from the council chamber into the even deeper seclusion of her private closet, where she alone takes decisions:

> When she defines, argues, divides, compounds,
>   Considers virtue, vice, and general things,
>   And marrying diverse principles and grounds,
>   Out of their match a true conclusion brings;
>
> These actions in her closet all alone,
>   (Retired within herself) she doth fulfil;
>   Use of her body's organs she hath none,
>   When she doth use the powers of Wit and Will. (16)

Just as Elizabeth retreats into her closet for private contemplation, so the rational soul retreats into its inmost essence, a kind of mind within the mind, secluded from the senses and all outside influences, to consider, judge, and resolve. Ultimately, it alone is the mind's decision-maker.

This representation of the rational soul's (or Queen's) relationship with her outward and inward senses (or officers and counsellors)

269

reflects intensive debate about the politics of counsel and monarchical authority over the course of Elizabeth's reign. Many humanist writers held that a ruler who governed without taking counsel was a tyrant.[20] Concerns about female rule also led some to seek reassurance in the monarch's dependence on (male) counsellors. Just before Elizabeth ascended the throne in 1558, John Knox notoriously fulminated in his *First Blast of the Trumpet against the Monstrous Regiment [Rule] of Women* that her sex should not and could not govern because they lacked reason and self-government. Women, he declared, were 'weak, frail, impatient, feeble, and foolish [...] unconstant, variable, cruel, and lacking the spirit of counsel and regiment'.[21] John Aylmer defended Elizabeth's queenship not on the grounds of capability, but because England had a 'mixed' constitution in which the aristocracy and Parliament also held power and steered the monarch.[22] To some extent Elizabeth seems to have accepted the principle of counsel: her *Sententiae*, a collection of wise sayings published in 1563, included a section 'Of Counsel', with such entries as 'Those who do all things with counsel are ruled by wisdom'.[23] However, more often her speeches, writings, and actions expressed conviction that her authority was God-given and supreme, and that she was entitled to accept or reject counsel according to her own judgement. This frustrated some of her Privy Councillors: in 1578, one of their number, Sir Francis Knollys, expressed exasperation that she would not 'suppress and subject her own will and her own affections unto sound advice of open counsel in matters touching the preventing of her danger'.

Yet Knollys also conceded that 'it is fit for all men to give place to her estate',[24] and the politics of counsel became increasingly controversial as the concept of a 'mixed' constitution was adopted by Elizabeth's political opponents. These included parliamentarians advocating the execution of Mary, Queen of Scots, radical Protestants demanding a more democratic model of church government, and Catholics intervening in the succession debate.[25] In reaction, a 1591 legal ruling reaffirming the authority of bishops also assigned to Elizabeth the same 'imperial' authority in both secular and spiritual affairs that her father,

Henry VIII, had claimed: 'by the ancient laws of this realm this kingdom of England is an absolute empire and monarchy'.[26] Sir John Davies was an ambitious young man in pursuit of court patronage, keen to distance himself from the dissenters, extremists, and seditionaries with whom, by the 1590s, 'mixed' monarchy was associated.[27] Hence, in *Nosce teipsum*, his depiction of Elizabeth/the rational soul as accepting counsel from the outward and inward senses also asserts her sacred and absolute authority as an 'Empress', and makes clear that 'she herself doth only judge and choose'.[28]

Sir John also wrote 'A Conference between a Gentleman Usher and a Post [courier]', a dialogue performed before Elizabeth in 1602 at the London house of Sir Robert Cecil, Secretary of State.[29] A courier tries to deliver letters from the Emperor of China to Cecil, but a gentleman usher tells him to give them directly to the Queen. He echoes the imagery of *Nosce teipsum*: Elizabeth makes the same use of her servants 'as the mind makes of the senses, many things she sees and hears through them, but the judgement and election is her own'.[30] Cecil, who was becoming increasingly powerful as Elizabeth drew towards death, may have had a hand in devising the entertainment, which deftly reassures Elizabeth of his subservience while asserting his indispensability as her source of information and agent in the world. A plausible connection has been drawn between the *Rainbow Portrait* of Elizabeth (fig. 21), still owned by the Cecil family, and this entertainment, at the end of which she was presented with a 'rich mantle', perhaps the robe strikingly adorned with eyes and ears that she wears in the portrait.[31] Sir John's extensive use of the mind–state analogy suggests that these represent the organs and senses that, like Cecil, serve Elizabeth as the rational soul, Queen of the mind.

As mentioned in previous chapters, *Nosce teipsum* was imitated by another philosophical poem, *Mirum in modum* (1602), by Sir John Davies's namesake John Davies of Hereford.[32] This poem too uses political imagery for the mind: the brain is where 'the soul doth hold her parliament, / To give laws for the body's government'.[33] However, its veneration of the absolute sovereignty of reason is even more

21. Sir John Davies compared Elizabeth I to the rational soul, Queen of the mind. This portrait was commissioned by Sir John's patron, Sir Robert Cecil, Elizabeth's Secretary of State. The eyes and ears on Elizabeth's robe may symbolise Sir Robert's service to her, as the senses serve the mind.

fervent than that of *Nosce teipsum*, with no mention of counsel. Davies of Hereford instructs his muse to pause in reverence as she approaches the centre of the mind, 'Sith thou art now arrived at Reason's seat; / To whom, as to thy sovereign reconcile / Thy straying thoughts' (B4r). Reason 'as sovereign sitteth in the soul, / All perverse passions therein to control'; if she were overthrown by the passions or by fantasy, she would be 'like a queen deposed from her throne' (B4v). Her authority is sole and unqualified: 'She rules alone the whole mind's common-weal, / By wholesome hests, and laws, and judgements strict' (C1r).

The faculties of mind and body all have fixed places, as in society: 'The under-rulers thoughts and fancies are, / The citizens the outward senses be; / The rurals be the bodies rare'. Chaos ensues if 'these riff-raffs in commotion rise, / And all will have their will' (I2r).

Davies of Hereford draws extensively on *The French Academy*, but reinforces his identification of sovereign reason with Elizabeth by altering gender in some passages. *The French Academy* states of reason that '*he* hath his seat by good right assigned him in the midst of the brain, as in the highest and safest fortress of the whole frame of man, to reign amidst all the other senses, as *prince and lord* over them all' (my emphases).[34] In *Mirum in modum* this becomes:

> *she* hath her throne assigned
> Between th'extreme parts of the parted brain, [...]
> There doth *she* sit, and o'er the senses reign,
> And by *her* might doth signorise the mind,
> Whose wild and wayward moods *she* doth restrain.
> (B4v, my emphases)

Meanwhile, oppositional voices saw Elizabeth very differently, questioning her fitness to be the mind or head ruling over the body of the commonwealth. The Catholic polemicist Cardinal William Allen, in his *Admonition to the Nobility and People of England and Ireland* (1588), declared Elizabeth unfit 'to rule or reign over any human society' because of her lack of self-government. He alleged that with Leicester 'and diverse others she hath abused her body, against Gods laws, to the disgrace of princely majesty and the whole nation's reproach, by unspeakable and incredible variety of lust'.[35] Another Catholic work, *A Conference about the Next Succession to the Crown of England* (1595), asserted that an evil ruler (like Elizabeth) could be removed by the commonwealth, because 'the whole body is of more authority then the only head, and may cure the head if it be out of tune'.[36] For these authors, Elizabeth was not a personification of the rational soul, but rather guilty of misgovernment of herself and hence of the nation.

At the opposite extreme, idealisations of Elizabeth by the two Davieses as presiding over hierarchy and order in mind and state can be understood as reactions to the actual disorder of the later years of her reign, which were marked by many kinds of political, economic, and social turbulence. These included plague, failed harvests, inflation, social hardship, riots, expensive foreign conflicts, invasion fears, anxiety over the succession, and bitter rivalries and factionalism at court.[37] Celebrations of Elizabeth as the rational soul, Queen of the mind, were ideologically motivated, seeking to suppress concerns that in reality England was more like a disordered mind, overwhelmed by insurrectionary forces. Meanwhile, models of the mind also became increasingly complex, moving beyond simple hierarchy to a more nuanced relationship between the interdependent powers of wit and will.

'Will would be ruled, but Wit had no reason': will and wit

Alongside constructions of the mind as having three faculties – imagination, reason, and memory – there was an alternative bipartite structure, which set the will against the intellect (defined as reason, wisdom, or wit). In many versions of this dichotomy, will was sinful and required government. A 1557 work for children by Francis Seager instructed them:

> Let reason thee rule
>   And not will thee lead
> To follow thy fancy
>   A wrong trace to tread.
> But subdue thy lust
>   And conquer thy will
> If it shall move thee
>   To do that is ill.[38]

For Thomas Blundeville in 1570, a tyrant was a prince who refused counsel and preferred 'will before reason';[39] while Thomas

Whythorne's autobiography (see Chapter 9 below) included verses on the need for 'wretched, wilful wills' to be ruled: 'Where wilful will planteth, / Wit with wisdom wanteth'.[40]

Calvin believed that the natural inclination of the human will was to make bad choices: 'to allow vanity and to refuse perfect goodness, to will evil and to be unwilling to good, to endeavour ourselves to wickedness and to resist righteousness'.[41] The Fall was an act of 'the will of man, out of which ariseth the root of evil, wherein resteth the foundation of the kingdom of Satan, which is sin' (24v). Regeneration of the will was only possible through divine grace, which could 'govern it [. . .], correct it, reform it, and renew it', and redirect it to good (34r).[42] Many English Protestant writers reiterated and elaborated upon Calvin's view. In John Woolton's *New Anatomy of Whole Man* (1576), Adam's disobedience to God 'in the liberty of his will' is blamed for turning all human wills away from God, 'so that we feel [in] ourselves a very conspiracy and open rebellion against his majesty'. Even if regenerated by divine grace, 'yet the will is not perfectly restored in this life. For the filth and dregs of original sin (albeit they are forgiven by Christ) are yet abiding in us.'[43] William Perkins blamed will for thoughts of dishonour, murder, adultery, theft or disgrace, and for converting such thoughts into sinful actions leading to damnation:

first the mind thinketh; then that thought delighteth the affection, and from that cometh consent of will; after consent of will, cometh execution of the action; after execution cometh trade and custom by often practice; and upon custom (if the work be evil) cometh the curse, which is eternal death.[44]

Reason could struggle to master will. In a dialogue between Passion and Reason in Sidney's *Old Arcadia*, will triumphs when Reason is weak: 'Will hath his will when Reason's will doth miss.'[45] Tarquin's error in *The Rape of Lucrece* is to surrender his reason to his will: 'My will is strong, past reason's weak removing' (243). In any case, Calvin taught that human reason as well as human will were 'estranged from the righteousness of God' by the Fall, which left all humanity's natural gifts 'corrupted and defiled'.[46] Woolton lamented: 'Now what can be more unhappy than this Fall and ruin of man's estate, whereby his memory, reason, and will are so pitifully impaired, and whole man so miserably corrupted?'[47] *The French Academy* agreed that 'this reason of man is of itself wholly depraved and corrupted', leaving the will 'weakened and made feeble to all goodness'.[48]

Sometimes the term opposed to will was wit, and sometimes with an optimistic sense that wit could govern will. A 1579 moral discourse by Haly Heron listed the conflicting forces that govern human conduct: 'if Virtue draw some unto goodness, Vice driveth many more unto mischief; if Reason persuade this, Fancy forceth unto that; if Wit weigh one way, Will wresteth another way'. This aligns Virtue, Reason, and Wit as trustworthy guides.[49] Similarly, Sidney in his *Defence of Poesy* wrote that 'our erected wit makes us know what perfection is, and yet our infected will keeps us from reaching unto it'.[50] However, wit's associations with mental agility and ingenuity (discussed in Chapter 7 above) often shaded into capriciousness and levity, making it even less reliable than reason as a governor of will. Ascham's educational treatise *The Schoolmaster* (1570) avers that 'those which be commonly the wisest, the best learned, and best men also when they be old, were never commonly the quickest of wit when they were young'. The many failings of the quick-witted include rapid learning but poor retention, bold speech but shallow judgement, inquisitiveness, self-regard, frivolity, and irritability. They are

> like over-sharp tools, whose edges be very soon turned [. . .] over-quick, hasty, rash, heady, and brainsick [. . .] like trees that show forth fair blossoms and broad leaves in spring-time, but bring out small and not long-lasting fruit in harvest time, and that only such as fall and rot before they be ripe.

Ascham's preference is for 'hard wits' who are 'hard to receive, but sure to keep'; their qualities include constancy, persistence, steadiness, and honesty. Though 'not quick in speaking', they are 'deep of judgement' and 'grave, steadfast, silent of tongue, secret of heart'.[51] Quick or lively wit is likewise distrusted in *The Faerie Queene*, where 'fantasticke wit' is an attribute of the vivacious, seductive Phaedria, the personification of 'immodest Merth' whose boat flits around on the Idle Lake.[52]

There is a fascinatingly nuanced relationship between wit and will in the anonymous interlude *The Marriage of Wit and Science* (1568), which may also have had the title *Wit and Will*.[53] Wit, its protagonist, is an immature, skittish youth: 'So run I to and fro with hap such as I find, / Now fast, now loose, now hot, now cold, unconstant as the wind.'[54] His mother, Nature, describes him as 'far from wisdom sage / Till tract of time shall work and frame aright / This peerless brain' (1.1.14–16). However, under God's direction she has implanted in him 'The love of knowledge and certain seeds divine', and he has the potential to become 'A certain perfect piece of work' (1.1.113, 1.1.19), an indication that the author may be a Catholic who, unlike Calvin, believed in human perfectibility through good works.[55] These innate virtuous inclinations make Wit fall in love with Science (knowledge or wisdom), whose parents are Reason and Experience. To assist him in his courtship, Nature gives him a page, Will, a boy of between eleven and twelve who is impudent, playful, and even more skittish than his master: Will describes himself as 'quick, nimble, proper,[56] and nice'[57] whereas Wit is 'full good, gentle, sober and wise' (2.2.466, 2.1.367–8).

Wit and Will are allegorical personifications of two faculties of the mind, yet because they are characters in a play they each have their own personality and agency, and hence a will of their own, complicating their relationship.[58] Will will only comply with Wit's will 'when me list [. . .] peradventure yea, peradventure no' (1.1.190, 192). Nature exhorts him to 'Be ruled by Wit, and be obedient still', but admits that 'Force thee I cannot' (1.1.207–8) – will is free. At the same time, Wit's struggle to achieve his goal of marriage to Science is impeded not only by Will's waywardness, but also by his own. He is defeated by Tediousness, and falls asleep in the lap of Idleness, who lulls him with her beguiling song:

By musing still, what canst thou find
But wants of will and restless mind,
A mind that mars and mangles all
And breedeth jars to work thy fall? (4.4.1139–42)

She and her son Ignorance rob him of his clothes, such that Science and Reason at their next encounter fail to recognise him, thinking him 'some mad-brain, or some fool' (5.1.1222). Wit dolefully laments, 'I have lost myself, I cannot tell where' (5.1.1229) – and this is clearly his own fault, not Will's.

The deficiencies and instabilities of wit made it profoundly dependent on will as an indispensable partner. In *The Marriage of Wit and Science*, Instruction urges Wit to dismiss Will, 'this peevish elf', from service as his page, but Wit refuses, because 'my Will tells me true' (4.1.883, 887). Ultimately, it is when Wit and Will both join together with Study and Diligence, under the leadership of Instruction, that they defeat the giant Tediousness; Will holds him down while Wit beheads him, and Wit wins Science as his bride (5.4, 5.5.1514–20). Their partnership is also explored at length in Nicholas Breton's allegorical narrative *The Will of Wit* (1597), which opens with the two faculties seeking one another. Although Will misses Wit as 'my good guide, my friend, and companion', while Wit misses Will as 'my merry mate, my quick sprite, my darling, and my dearest bird', they quarrel when they meet.[59] Wit reports a dialogue he overheard about 'the virtues of Wit, and the vanities of Will': 'Wit would call for Will's help, when Will cared not for Wit's counsel; Wit would be wise, and Will would be wanton; Wit would be virtuous, and Will vain'. Will, says Wit, will only be a good boy when he is beaten (5v). Yet Will retorts that

when Wit is wayward, Will is no body [...] Will would be ruled, but Wit had no reason [...] Will had been good, had not Wit been bad; Will had not lost Wit, had Wit looked unto him; Will would do well, if Wit would do better; Will would learn, if Wit would teach him. (6r–v)

The dialogue consistently affirms that Wit should be in authority over Will, but also makes clear how often he has failed in this responsibility. There are even occasions when Will can be Wit's counsellor and guide: 'Will could bring Wit into a good order when he was quite out of course' (6r–v). Their relationship is one of symbiosis as much as hierarchy.[60]

'Will is the prince, and wit the counsellor': will as Queen of the mind

Sixteenth-century ideas about the will were informed not only by Protestant teachings about its sinful disposition, but also by debates reaching back to the classical world, to St Augustine's treatise *On the Free Choice of the Will* (*De libero arbitrio*), and to medieval theologians on the relation of the will to the other faculties of the mind and soul. While there were differences of opinion, many of these authorities regarded will as not only the most wayward human faculty, but also the most powerful. As the human power of moral choice, it determined damnation or salvation, with an independent agency that placed it beyond the authority of wit and reason.[61]

As we have seen, Calvin blamed the will for the Fall and condemned the unregenerate will for committing 'wicked deeds' and 'the works of Satan'. However, he defined salvation as the reception of divine grace to regenerate the will:

the grace of God (as the word is taken when we speak of regeneration) is the rule of the spirit to direct and govern the will of man [. . .] men's will be said to be restored when the faultiness and perverseness thereof being reformed, it is directed to the true rule of justice; and also that a new will be said to be created in man.[62]

Richard Hooker's *Of the Laws of Ecclesiastical Polity* (1593), his monumental treatise on the theology, structure, and governance of the Church of England, took an even more optimistic view of the capacity for good of human reason and will.[63] He distinguished will from 'that inferior natural desire which we call appetite' and instead defined it as a rational faculty: 'the object of will is that good which reason does lead us to seek'. Guided by reason, will chooses goodness: 'To choose is to will one thing before another. And to will is to bend our souls to the having or doing of that which they see to be good. Goodness is seen with the eye of the understanding. And the light of that eye, is reason.' Yet because will is the power of choice, it has autonomy and is at liberty to reject the guidance of reason: 'There is in the will of man naturally that freedom, whereby it is apt to take or refuse any particular object whatsoever being presented to it.'[64]

The French Academy (part 2, 1594) expounded a similar view, and in doing so put a different twist from the one we have seen previously on the metaphor of the politics of counsel. It reiterated that 'reason is set over the will', but 'not to govern and turn it from one side to another by commandment and authority, either by force or violence, as a prince or magistrate, but as a counsellor or director, to admonish and to conduct it'.[65] The will can elevate itself by accepting the counsel of reason and joining with it, or debase itself by joining with 'the sensual part' of humanity, but it has a free choice in this (598). It is 'as it were a prince among his council', and as such 'may the will stay itself from desiring and following after that which is counselled and judged to be good by reason. So that the whole consultation lieth in the liberty and choice of will' (212).

We saw that in *Nosce teipsum* the regal rational soul retires into her closet to take decisions using 'the powers of Wit and Will'. Later, Sir John Davies goes into more depth about the relative authority of these two faculties:

Will is the prince, and wit the counsellor,
    Which doth for common good in council sit;
    And when wit is resolved, will lends her power,
    To execute, what is advised by wit.

Wit is the mind's chief judge, which doth control
    Of fancy's court the judgements false and vain;
    Will holds the royal sceptre in the soul,
    And on the passions of the hart doth reign.

Will is as free as any emperor;
    Nought can restrain her gentle liberty:
    No tyrant, nor no torment hath the power
    To make us will, when we unwilling be.[66]

Here, then, it is will that has the highest, imperial authority in the mind. Wit controls fancy (or fantasy), makes judgements, and gives counsel, but it is a merely intellectual faculty, which is subservient to the will's moral supremacy.

Sir John's *Hymns of Astraea* was a series of poems on the faculties of Elizabeth's mind. 'Of her Wit' praises this faculty as the eye of her mind that 'Sees through all things everywhere' and has a 'high perfection' that her subjects may admire 'Now in her speech, now policy'. However, the next poem, 'Of her Will', elevates this faculty even higher, and particularly identifies it with royal authority. It can 'spill' or 'save', and it has moral discrimination, 'Loving goodness, loathing ill'. It is a law that Elizabeth's subjects must obey: because Elizabeth's will is queen of her own mind, it must be queen of her subjects' minds too:

Royal free will, and only free,
Each other will is slave to thee.
Glad is each will to serve thee:
In thee such princely power is seen,
No spirit but takes thee for her queen,
And thinks she must observe [respect, honour] thee.[67]

Like all the poems in *Hymns of Astraea*, it is an acrostic, so the first letters of these lines on will spell out the word REGINA.

281

Shortly after her accession, Elizabeth told a deputation of lords: 'considering I am God's creature, ordained to obey His appointment, I will thereto yield, desiring from the bottom of my heart that I may have assistance of His grace to be the minister of His heavenly will in this office now committed to me'.[68] Towards the end of her reign, in 1598, the Puritan parliamentarian Peter Wentworth accused her of failing to submit to God's will in neglecting to secure the succession. He declared that God protects those 'that prefer his will before their own', and therefore it is 'very dangerous to think that there is more safety in following our own devices and fantasies than his will and pleasure'.[69] Sir John Davies's exaltation of Elizabeth's will in two works published the following year is a reaffirmation that her will is exactly aligned with, and identical with, the will of God, and hence must govern the wills of all her subjects.

We have discovered much variety and complexity in Elizabethan models of the mind as a microcosm of the state. The simplest structure was hierarchical: mind over body, or reason in government over the passions and imagination. However, thinking about the dependence of reason on other faculties could involve the politics of counsel and the concept of a 'mixed' constitution, increasingly controversial topics over the course of Elizabeth's reign. Even more complicated was the intricate interdependence of wit and will, although loyal panegyrists like Sir John Davies drew on Protestant theology to turn this too into a hierarchy in which will, or the Queen, was pre-eminent. Throughout, despite debates and new developments in politics, theology, and psychology, the ancient tradition of understanding and representing the mind as a state or commonwealth remained firmly in place.

PART IV
Writing the Mind

Writing Thought and Self
Autobiography, Sonnets, Prose Fiction

According to Thomas Wright in *The Passions of the Mind*, 'words represent most exactly the very image of the mind and soul [...] for in words as in a glass may be seen a man's life and inclinations'.[1] As medical, philosophical, and theological writing on the nature of the mind burgeoned during the late sixteenth century, many literary authors became preoccupied with representing 'the very image of the mind' in writing.

For some, this meant continuing and developing the allegorical tradition, in which mental faculties were projected outside the mind and personified. As we have seen in earlier chapters, although this genre had medieval roots, it continued to flourish in works such as interludes of the 1560s and 1570s, *The Faerie Queene*, and Breton's *Will of Wit*. Another example is the story of Queen Cordila, daughter of Kinge Leire, in *The Mirror for Magistrates*, an anthology of verse narratives in which figures from history relate their own tragic falls. Cordila's monologue, first appearing in the 1574 edition of the *Mirror*, relates how she was defeated by her enemies, then visited in prison by Despair, who urges suicide. Despair's presence is so material and so external to Cordila's mind that when Cordila wavers,

Despair seizes a knife from her and strikes the fatal blow.[2] Allegory continued to appear in various forms throughout the next century and beyond:[3] in 1678, for instance, John Bunyan's *Pilgrim's Progress* combined allegorical characters with landscapes representing mental and spiritual states such as the Slough of Despond and the Valley of Humiliations. The popularity of allegory over a long period for representing mental states and processes is understandable: it enabled authors to translate abstractions into personal or concrete form, making them vivid and accessible, and to involve them in narratives of conflict and development.[4] At the same time, however, it worked through archetypes rather than offering detailed depictions of the unique qualities of individuals, and by projecting the workings of the mind outwards rather than looking within. As Elizabethan writers became increasingly interested in disparities between the inner, mental self and the outer, social self, and in ways of representing unfolding thought-processes *within* the mind, many of them turned away from allegory towards other kinds of writing.

We have already explored in Chapters 3 and 4 the Elizabethan expansion and development of the genres of passion literature and female complaint. This chapter will discuss three more Elizabethan genres of the mind – autobiographical writing, the sonnet sequence, and prose fiction – while Chapter 10 will explore the development of the dramatic soliloquy. Across all these genres there was an increasing sense of the mind as an interior space apart from the external world, and of division between an outer, performative, social identity and an inner place of private thoughts and true intentions. As writers attempted to look into this inner place, and the mind examined itself, their writing became increasingly self-conscious and self-reflexive. At the same time there was an awareness of self-division, of diverse thoughts, feelings, and impulses in tension or in conflict with one another and an intense interest in the mind in process. Authors sought to represent both how the mind changes over time in response to external influences and experiences, and how the mind fluctuates from moment to moment as it grapples with dilemmas and works through ethical problems.

Elizabethan authors were under no illusions about the difficulty of representing the mind in words. Can a mind ever look objectively at itself? When it tries to do so, can language articulate accurately the mind's discoveries about itself? For writers of this period, these challenges were exacerbated by the fallenness of human understanding and language. As Sir John Davies wrote in *Nosce teipsum*, 'Error chokes the windows of the mind'. In contemplating itself, the mind was both hampered by its own weakness and deterred by the spectacle of its own imperfections:

> the mind can backward cast
> Upon herself her understanding light;
> But she is so corrupt, and so defaced,
> As her own image doth herself affright.

Hence, for Sir John an essential truth of the mind was that 'with herself, herself can never meet' – yet this was no reason to give up the attempt.[5] In Sir John's case, these lines were just the prelude to a long and wide-ranging poem of enquiry into the nature of the mind and soul. He and the authors discussed in this chapter – Thomas Whythorne, Sir Philip Sidney, George Gascoigne, John Lyly, and Robert Greene – made particularly important and innovative contributions to the Elizabethan effort to capture the mind in writing, but were just a few among many engaged in this endeavour.

'What I am of mind myself': Thomas Whythorne and autobiography

Modern autobiography often presents the author's reflections on their state of mind at different points in their life, on their psychological development, and on their evolving sense of identity over time. However, 'autobiography' was not yet a defined genre for the

Elizabethans, with this term only emerging in the late eighteenth century.[6] Many of them made written records of their lives in a variety of forms, including spiritual journals (like those of Lady Margaret Hoby and Richard Rogers discussed in earlier chapters), conversion narratives (like that of William Alabaster, discussed in Chapter 3), manuscript verse miscellanies, commonplace books,[7] handwritten notes on printed almanacs, and even financial accounts.[8] Yet many of these diverse life-narratives gave little attention to inner thoughts or personal identity, as we saw in the case of Hoby's journal (in Chapter 4 above). Another example is Henry Machyn, who compiled what he called his 'chronicle' in manuscript between 1550 and 1563. He gave a vivid sense of events surrounding the death of Mary I and the accession of Elizabeth I, and of the general texture of life in mid-sixteenth-century London, but we have to work hard to read between the lines to discover anything about Machyn himself and his thoughts and feelings.[9]

Another manuscript life-narrative written around 1576 by Thomas Whythorne, a composer and music teacher, is more like a modern autobiography in its author's interest in his shifting psychological states and his sense of self. Whythorne's interest in fashioning a distinctive identity is immediately apparent from his idiosyncratic system of spelling, combining recent attempts by others to systematise English orthography with his own ideas on phonetic notation.[10] For example, his introductory explanation of his spelling system concludes: 'I hav sumwhat degressed from my purpoz in saing my fansy of þis new Orthografy'.[11] (Hereafter I will quote from a modernised edition of his autobiography, for ease of reading.) Whythorne's stated reason for writing is a confidential exchange with an unnamed intimate friend, who 'did impart unto me at our last being together some of your private and secret affairs past, and also some of the secret purposes and intents the which have lain hid and been as it were entombed in your heart'. To reciprocate, he now shares 'the most part of all my private affairs and secrets, accomplished from my childhood until the day of the date hereof'. He sends his friend some 'songs and sonnets' which in themselves express his states of mind, but he wants to go further, 'to show you the cause why I wrote them' and 'to open my secret meaning in divers of them', and this produces narrative.[12]

The title of the manuscript does not suggest intimate personal revelations. Instead, it offers discourses 'of the child's life, together with a young man's life, and entering into the old man's life' (xv). Here, and at later points in the narrative, Whythorne invokes the classical tradition of the 'ages of man', which divides every lifespan into set phases. This suggests a universality to his story, a sense that is reinforced by his frequent invocation of proverbial wisdom and by his presentation of his life as an instructive example to others:

Wherein young youths are learned lessons large
By which they may, if like chance do them charge
That happed to me, the better know to deal
Therein, and so it may be for their weal. (xvi)[13]

In its substance, however, Whythorne's narrative seems far more than just exemplary or generic, describing and analysing his psychological states in particular situations with a meticulousness that evokes a distinctive experience, personality, and sense of inwardness.[14] Much of the story concerns his employment as a music tutor in a series of gentry households, and presents him as frequently involved in erotic entanglements. In his relation of these episodes there is a preoccupation with the reservation or disclosure of inner thoughts, intensified by his awareness of the ambiguity and insecurity of his social position as a gentleman, yet still a kind of servant.

At one point Whythorne suspects that his employer, a widow, is flirting with him, but is unsure of her intentions. He resolves to respond to her ambiguous provocations in kind, partly for the pleasure of the game, and partly to advance his professional and financial interests: 'if she did dissemble, I, to requite her, thought that to dissemble with a dissembler was no dissimulation [...] And also as she so intended but to make me serve her turn, so in the meanwhile I intended to make the most of her that I could to serve my turn' (30, 33–4). In a sequence of verse exchanges between them, he strategically implies amorous interest while remaining noncommittal: 'I made this song somewhat dark and doubtful of sense, because I knew not certainly how she would take it, nor to whose hands it might come after that she had read it' (31). He is acutely aware of the possible costs of unwise revelation of private thoughts. An acquaintance who fell in love with a woman confided in her all his 'mysteries, attempts and intents', only to find that she 'blazed abroad that which he had told her to keep in secret' (19). In one of Whythorne's own early employments, a young female servant left some verses between the strings of his gittern (a musical instrument), tantalising him with glimpses of her secret thoughts:

But I wish you did know my mind,
If you would not be to me unkind.
  My mind is
  That W. shall have this.

After considering, Whythorne drafted a guardedly encouraging reply: 'When ye will show your mind / To me, even hardly, / I will not be unkind.' However, despite these careful verbal stratagems, the flirtation was noticed and became generally known in the household, 'which made me to blush, and she more so'. Embarrassment was followed by worse consequences: the young woman was dismissed (21–3).

Whythorne narrates how his past self therefore exercised caution in revealing his mind to others, attempting to maintain a screen between his outer and inner selves. At the same time he applied strenuous efforts to reading the equally concealed thoughts of his female combatants. In his verse exchanges with the flirtatious widow, his calculated ambiguity was both self-protective and an attempt to smoke out her intentions: 'This answer was as doubtful to be taken and understood now, as that was which I wrote to her at the first; the which I did so make because I would see how she would take it' (41). He sings some of his semi-revealing but noncommittal verses to her in order to observe and interpret her reaction, but 'she seemed not to be anything moved or troubled withal one whit; which made me to think that she did it as a policy to keep me still in doubt of her, and by that mean to live still in a vain hope' (43). Whythorne habitually engages in what present-day cognitive theorists call 'mind-reading': observing the expressions, gestures, and behaviours of others in an attempt to deduce their thoughts and intentions.[15] This process is fraught with unreliability – an observer may misinterpret external signs, or the person observed may deliberately present deceptive signs – but Whythorne presents it as essential to the social and erotic dance that made up his professional and personal life.

Even more than the minds of others, Whythorne is fascinated by the processes of his own mind. He charts his shifting thoughts in his past predicaments in intricate detail: 'One while I thought [. . .] And another while I thought thus unto myself'; 'when I had bethought me a little while'; 'I was debating with myself', and so on (46, 67). As we have seen, some of his poems function as strategic instruments in social interactions, but others are solely for his own use, to express troubled states of mind and give solace: 'to ease my mind in this perplexity I wrote thus'; 'to ease my mind, I wrote this sonnet following' (10, 30). Poems represent past moments of mental and emotional difficulty which Whythorne paused to process and articulate: 'At this time of writing I had become very sad and was in such a quandary and fear'; 'When I had thus made this said sonnet, there came to my mind to judge doubtfully of the intention of this preceding matter' (36, 154). The prose that surrounds the poems reanalyses these moments and organises them into a sequential narrative of psychological drama and development.[16]

Whythorne records many difficulties in mastering the passions. For instance, a long sickness embittered him and made him

wreak mine anger altogether with pen and ink upon paper [. . .]
Much like, as for example, a young, shrewish maiden would do,
who, when she was much angered, would straightways go into a
cellar that her father had, and there would she with her teeth bite
upon a post a long time, till she had digested the rage of her choleric humour. (27)

He aspires to Stoic constancy, quoting approvingly the ancient Stoic
author Marcus Aurelius on 'the virtues of the mind' (113–14), but his
interest is primarily in his *changing* mental states, both in particular
encounters and relationships, and over the whole course of his life.
He frequently recalls and contemplates how significant life events
provoked new states of mind, and hence an evolving sense of identity.
In his youth Whythorne was an apprentice in the household of the
poet and musician John Heywood, but the time came for him to
leave and embark on an independent life. He vividly evokes the new
anxieties that this aroused and attempts to account for them:

When I was a scholar and a servant, my mind was then as my state
was, for then I looked no higher nor no further than to the state
that I was then in [. . .] But when I came to be my own man [. . .]
I saw how I must seek to live of myself, for the which it behoved
me to cast my wits so many ways, and they being never troubled
so much that way before as I was almost at my wits' end. (10)

Whythorne also charts his past self, or selves, when he describes
his participation in a new trend of the early Elizabethan period: the
commissioning of portraits not only by royalty and aristocrats, but
also by members of the urban professional 'middling sort', a class
to which he belonged as a gentleman, with a family coat of arms,
who was nevertheless obliged to work for a living.[17] Whythorne
was keen to assert the dignity of his profession as a musician and
had his portrait painted no fewer than four times: first at the age
of around twenty or twenty-one (soon after the watershed event

of leaving Heywood's household), then about a year later after an illness, then at thirty-four and forty-three (12, 38, 115–17, 175–6).[18] When narrating his third sitting, Whythorne ponders why people commission portraits and identifies as the most important reason 'to see how time doth alter them from time to time'. Accordingly, he compares his new portrait with the one of twelve years before, finding 'that I was much changed from that I was at that time, as by the long and fullness of my beard, the wrinkles on my face, and the hollowness of mine eyes'. The difference is not merely superficial: 'as my face was altered so were the delights of my mind changed' (116).

Whythorne's last portrait, made in 1569, became the basis of a woodcut frontispiece to a volume of his songs published in 1571 (fig. 22). This was a radical act of self-presentation: not only was no one else publishing books of secular part-songs in England, but few printed books as yet included author portraits.[19] Whythorne explained that he included an image of himself because his books were 'as my children', and he wanted to show 'the form and favour of their parent'. He also presented the portrait as part of a package – along with his coat of arms, the etymology of his name, and his motto, 'Sharp but not too much' – which added 'outward marks' to the 'inward man' shown in his songs. This was partly a matter of asserting social identity and status, but it was also about informing the onlooker 'What I am of mind myself or in condition', an objective that Whythorne pursues further by adding a long discussion of his predisposition to anger (175–7).

However, the portraits may not be completely accurate records of either Whythorne's 'outward' or 'inward man' at different points in time. The painted portrait of 1569 gives his age as forty-one, but the woodcut based on this portrait and used in his *Songs* two years later gives it as forty. The same woodcut was used again in a volume of *Duos* that he published in 1590, so that at the age of sixty-two he retained the public face of a forty-year-old.[20] Whythorne usually calls his portraits 'counterfeits', a term commonly used in the period

22. Thomas Whythorne, a musician and composer, had his portrait painted four times. The last version was the basis of this woodcut in a volume of his songs. Whythorne also wrote an autobiography and was interested in how both writing and portraits could represent 'what I am of mind myself'.

for portraits, but which could also, as today, indicate something false or spurious.[21] It may imply a recognition that these images represent him only as approximations. They form part of a suite of artefacts – with his poems, songs, prose narrative, and even his self-devised spelling system – which Whythorne contrives to record and represent his mind to himself and to others. However, much as Sir John Davies would later aver of the mind that 'with herself, herself can never meet', Whythorne is aware of his mind as in constant motion, elusive, and only capable of partial or fleeting representation. Also like Sir John, Whythorne seems to be gripped and fascinated by this impossible quest, whose pursuit is the force that drives his autobiography.[22]

'My life melts with too much thinking': *Astrophil and Stella* and the sonnet sequence

The sonnet – a lyric poem of fourteen lines, structured by a formal rhyme scheme – emerged in Italy in the early thirteenth century, then was developed by Petrarch (1304–74).[23] From its inception it was used to represent and reflect upon states of mind, and this continued when it was introduced to England by Sir Thomas Wyatt and Henry Howard, Earl of Surrey, in the early sixteenth century. Their sonnets became widely known in the popular and influential anthology *Tottel's Miscellany* (published in 1557, and reissued many times during the Elizabethan period). However, they only wrote single sonnets; the first English poet to emulate Petrarch's *Canzoniere* by writing something like a sonnet sequence was Thomas Watson in *Hekatompathia* (1582), though at eighteen lines the poems that it contained were not exactly sonnets. Sir Philip Sidney's *Astrophil and Stella*, composed around 1581–3 and comprising 108 sonnets interspersed with eleven songs, is generally hailed as the first English sonnet sequence. It achieved vast influence following its print publication, first in an unauthorised edition of 1591, then in an edition of Sidney's works supervised by his sister the Countess of Pembroke in 1598.[24]

Several poems in *Astrophil and Stella* open by addressing allegorical personifications of moral values, mental faculties, or psychological states, including Virtue, Reason, Hope, Grief, and Thought.[25] Such figures are often placed in conflict with one another: in Sonnet 10, Astrophil, the speaker of the sonnets, complains of reason's 'brabbling' with sense and love; in Sonnet 52, 'A strife is grown between virtue and love'; while in the Sixth Song common sense struggles to resolve a debate between music and beauty over Stella's relative merits, so defers to reason (pp. 193–5). Sidney draws here on the psychomachic tradition; but because these are lyric poems, not drama, the allegorical personifications are not visibly embodied, but exist only within Astrophil's mind. This is underlined when he implores sleep: 'O make in me those civil wars to cease' (Sonnet 39).

The effect of looking within at an internal drama is intensified by use throughout of this fictional persona of Astrophil, a poet-lover who is a version of Sidney, but at the same time differentiated from him, and sometimes viewed with detachment and irony. This splitting of the subject position of the poems makes them exercises in self-reflection, while the extension of self-examination across a sequence of many poems gives a sense of Astrophil's inner being as always in flux, and his self-understanding as always in process.[26] Further literary techniques contribute to this effect of introspection and an unfolding inner life. In six sonnets, Astrophil is surrounded by observers who try, but mostly fail, to read his secret thoughts, creating division between the public and private worlds of the poem, and between levels of social and psychological activity.[27] In Sonnet 23, for instance, the 'curious wits' notice his 'dull pensiveness' and rightly diagnose 'fumes of melancholy', but wrongly seek the cause in excessive study or political ambition, remaining oblivious of his passion for Stella.

In Sonnet 34, Astrophil debates with himself whether to 'publish' his 'disease'. There is no evidence that Sidney intended *Astrophil and Stella* for print publication; it was his bereaved friends and relations who brought his works to print after his death from battle wounds in 1586. However, in this period manuscript circulation could itself constitute a form of publication, as writings passed from hand to hand, were copied and often adapted, and potentially travelled beyond the immediate social circle and the control of the author.[28] Accordingly, from its opening line – 'Come, let me write' – Sonnet 34 treats writing and publishing (that is, making public) as equivalent. The possible gains – 'To ease / A burdened heart' and 'fame' – are set against the risk that 'wise men' will 'think thy words fond [foolish] ware'. The reader is thereby positioned as one of these 'wise men' or 'curious wits' (Sonnet 23) who seek to pry into Astrophil's (or Sidney's) mind, but will never wholly see or understand what it contains, despite the privileged glimpses apparently granted by the poems.

Another technique that creates a sense of psychological depth and concentration is the setting of nine of the sonnets at night.[29] By contrast with the sonnets where Astrophil is in company but mentally alone, in these nocturnal sonnets he is in solitude (apart from abstract or inanimate entities: Sonnet 98, for instance, opens, 'Ah, bed [. . .]!'). Sometimes he is persistently wakeful, a state that brings acute perception and increased mental activity: 'With windows ope then most my mind doth lie' (Sonnet 99). In other sonnets in this group, however, sleep activates his fantasy: 'unbitted [unrestrained] thought / Doth fall to stray' and 'fancy's error brings / Unto my mind [. . .] Stella's image, wrought / By love's own self' (Sonnet 38). There is an obvious analogy here with the creation of images in the mind in the making of poetry, calling into question whether the image of Stella, Astrophil's beloved, in his poems is not also a product of 'fancy's error'.

Stella – or at least Astrophil's image of Stella – entirely dominates his mind and his writing: 'I thought all words were lost, that were not spent on thee' (p. 191, Fifth Song); 'nothing from my wit or will doth flow, / Since all my words thy beauty doth endite [dictate]' (Sonnet 90). In Petrarch's sonnets, writing obsessively about his unattainable mistress, Laura, was presented as a process whereby her virtue inspired his art and elevated him to higher virtue. Sidney's sonnets balance Petrarchism with anti-Petrarchism, sometimes emulating the master and sometimes rejecting imitation. His treatment of the Petrarchan theme of moral improvement by impossible yearning is profoundly ambiguous, and Astrophil frequently voices Petrarchan veneration of Stella's perfect beauty and chastity only to balance it with realistic recognition of sexual frustration. Sonnet 71, for instance, spends thirteen of its fourteen lines extolling Stella as the book of virtue, who embodies 'sweetest sovereignty / Of reason', and 'not content to be perfection's heir / Thy self, dost strive all minds that way to move'. This upward spiritual movement over the course of the sonnet is, however, brought crashing down by its final line: 'But ah, desire still cries: "Give me some food"'.

The persistence of desire is also starkly clear in the Tenth Song, when Astrophil's imagination ranges rapaciously all over Stella's body: 'Thought, see thou no place forbear; / Enter bravely everywhere, / Seize on all to her belonging' (p. 203). Thinking here is not cerebral, but sensual, and rises to an orgasmic climax:

> Think, think of those dallyings,
>> When with dove-like murmurings,
>> With glad moaning, passed anguish,
>> We change eyes, and heart for heart
>> Each to other do impart,
>> Joying, till joy make us languish.

However, such sexual union with Stella never happens in the 'real world' of the sonnet sequence, and the song ends with Astrophil closing down these painfully excessive imagined pleasures, lamenting that 'My life melts with too much thinking'.

The use of paradoxes and antitheses was well established in the sonnet tradition, especially in a form known as the 'Petrarchan contraries'. A typical example of this is a sonnet in *Tottel's Miscellany* headed 'Description of the Contrarious Passions of a Lover' and adapted by Wyatt from Petrarch: 'I fear, and hope; I burn, and freeze like ice: / [. . .] I love another, and I hate myself.'[30] Astrophil's particular paradoxical predicament is delineated in Sonnet 61 where he tries to woo Stella, but she replies as an orthodox Petrarchan mistress that if he loves her, he will emulate her 'chaste mind' with a 'chastened mind' of his own. This leaves him in the impossible position 'That I love not, without I leave to love' – in other words, he can only obey her and prove his love for her by ceasing to love her. Even more often than such implied dialogue with Stella, these conflicting imperatives produce self-division and vigorous debate within Astrophil himself. This is particularly intense in Sonnet 34, the sonnet that debates 'publish[ing]' his 'disease':

Come, let me write. 'And to what end?' To ease
A burdened heart. 'How can words ease, which are
The glasses [mirrors] of thy daily vexing care?'
Oft cruel fights well pictured forth do please.

It may take the reader a little time to realise that these two opposed voices are both inside Astrophil's head, an effect even stronger in the early editions of the poems where there are no quotation marks.[31] The interruption of lines as they switch between voices, combined with the use of enjambment to create tension between the flow of the verse and the flow of the sense, creates a vivid sense of inner strife.[32] Such internal debate is not only an internalisation of psychomachia, but also draws on a key element of rhetorical training that Sidney would have practised extensively during his education, the ability to debate *in utramque partem*, making the case for both sides of a dispute.[33]

Astrophil sometimes attempts to focus less on his own mind than on Stella's, looking outwards to assess the effects of his words upon her. In Sonnets 57 and 58, he invokes classical theories of the power of rhetoric, especially when grounded in deep feeling, to affect the mind of the listener: 'with his golden chain / The orator so far men's hearts doth bind / That no pace else their guided steps can find' (Sonnet 58). The 'Woe' that has conquered 'Each sense of mine, each gift, each power of mind' issues in 'words, fit for woe's self to groan' (Sonnet 57). Consequently, 'Her soul [...] / Should soon be pierced with sharpness of the moan'; his words should penetrate her mind, enabling him to penetrate her body. Yet instead, in Sonnet 57 she sings his verses back to him, and in Sonnet 58 reads them back to him, in both cases producing a perverse pleasure: 'maugre [in spite of] my speech's might, / Which wooed woe, most ravishing delight / Even those sad words even in sad me did breed' (Sonnet 58). Instead of communicating his passions to Stella, his words bounce back, intensifying his self-reflection and self-division, and ravishing only himself as the woe of unrequited desire is converted into pleasure in his own aesthetic skill.[34]

The compact and intricately structured sonnet form enables each poem to capture a particular moment in the progress of the courtship, within which it identifies and addresses a particular problem, working through a thought-process over the course of its fourteen lines.[35] Sonnet 50 is a good example. The first quatrain expresses an idea that recurs throughout the sequence, that Astrophil cannot help writing because of the force of his passions:

> Stella, the fullness of my thoughts of thee
> Cannot be stayed within my panting breast,
> But they do swell and struggle forth of me,
> Till that in words thy figure be expressed.

The second quatrain then counters this with the idea that his words are inadequate to represent Stella's perfection:

> And yet, as soon as they so formed be,
> According to my lord loves own behest,
> With sad eyes I their weak proportion see,
> To portrait that which in this world is best.

The sestet alternates between these two ideas, then draws them to a conclusion:

> So that I cannot choose but write my mind,
> And cannot choose but put out what I write,
> While those poor babes their death in birth do find:
> And now my pen these lines had dashed quite,
> But that they stopped his fury from the same,
> Because their forefront bare sweet Stella's name.

Astrophil here returns to childbirth imagery for the labour of writing, as used in the first sonnet of the sequence (mentioned in Chapter 7

300

above). He sets his uncontrollable urge to write against his equally irresistible urge to destroy the unsatisfactory lines that he produces, but finally spares them, because they represent Stella. As in most sonnets of the sequence, the ending gives a sense of having arrived at a different place from where the poem began, and a superficial sense of resolution (compounded by the neatly chiming rhymes of the final couplet), yet at the same time leaves a feeling of deadlock arising from an underlying unresolved conflict. Within the sonnet, Astrophil claims that he writes involuntarily and wants to destroy his verses, but preserves them equally involuntarily. However, looking at the poem from outside, its sonnet form creates a different kind of tension: its perfect, tightly organised structure contradicts Astrophil's claim to write in a gush of passion, and rather presents a mind paralysed in paradox and tied in an intellectual knot – a different, more complex way of being out of control.

The fact that each sonnet also, for the first time in English, forms part of a sequence adds to this sense that each ending is only provisional. As each successive sonnet opens, it either continues addressing the same problem or introduces a new one.[36] The overall shape of the whole sequence also creates a sense of onward development while undercutting this with a sense of not really getting anywhere. Events that create change tend to happen in the songs that punctuate the sequence, rather than the sonnets. One major external event is a kiss that Astrophil steals from Stella while she is sleeping, in the Second Song (pp. 182–3). This provokes Stella's anger (Sonnet 73), yet inspires a flow of sonnets – mostly addressed to the kiss, not to Stella – on the theme of its sweetness (Sonnets 74, 79–82). Another significant event that takes Astrophil outside his mind is a dialogue with Stella in the Eighth Song (pp. 195–8). They meet 'for mutual comfort', in an invitingly private location, 'a grove most rich of shade', and exchange gazes and sighs. It seems that Astrophil might be about to achieve his goal and consummate his desires, and indeed when Stella speaks, she confesses her love for him. However, at the same time she insists that, although it pains her as much as him, they must renounce each other (various clues throughout the sequence indicate that she is based on Lady Penelope Rich, who was married). Other songs remain firmly within Astrophil's mind, such as the Fifth Song, a low point of disturbing bitterness and hostility towards Stella (pp. 191–3). Astrophil vituperates her as a witch and a devil who 'man's mind destroyeth', and declares that 'Sweet babes must babies have, but shrewd girls must be beaten'– that is, compliant girls must have dolls (or, punningly, be made pregnant), but badly behaved girls must be beaten.

Each of these songs seems to present a critical moment with a before and after, but around them the sonnets loop back endlessly and obsessively to the same, mainly psychological topics: the conflicting imperatives of virtue and passion; the difficulties of converting what is in the mind and heart into writing; concealed thoughts in company; nocturnal cogitation; and so on. Late in the sequence, in Sonnet 94, Astrophil's mental state seems as troubled and melancholic as ever: 'Grief, find the words; for thou hast made my brain / So dark with misty vapours'.[37] By the final sonnet, he seems to have made little progress as either a lover or a writer, or in self-understanding. Sorrow is briefly alleviated by thoughts of Stella, only to descend again into despair. The sonnet and the sequence close, characteristically, with a paradox formed of opposed yet inextricable passions: 'So strangely, alas, thy works in me prevail, / That in my woes for thee thou art my joy, / And in my joys for thee my only annoy' (Sonnet 108, ll. 12–14). The sequence as a whole is both a narrative and an anti-narrative, and can only resolve in an irresolvable conundrum.[38]

One of *Astrophil and Stella*'s most frequently recurring themes is the division between the outer world – of court politics, of gossip, of showy and artificial versifying – and Astrophil's inner world, from which flows a poetry of true passion. The sequence begins with his muse urging him to 'look in thy heart, and write' (Sonnet 1), and continues by scorning poets who indulge in Petrarchan excesses 'Of living deaths, dear wounds, fair storms and freezing fires' (Sonnet 6, even though Astrophil/Sidney himself often borrows from Petrarch).[39] His claim is that 'I can speak what I feel' and 'My words, I know, do well set forth my mind' (Sonnets 6, 44). The publication of *Astrophil and Stella* in 1591 inspired a flood of sonnet sequences, including Henry Constable's *Diana* (1592), Samuel Daniel's *Delia* (1592), Michael Drayton's *Idea* (1593), Giles Fletcher's *Licia* (1593), Thomas Lodge's *Phillis* (1593), and Spenser's *Amoretti* (1595). Ironically, the claim to be no imitator, but to write directly from the mind, became one of Sidney's most imitated features: 'This passion is no fiction', 'My tears are true', 'My verse is the true image of my mind', protested various sonneteers, with diminishing plausibility.[40] Sidney's truest heirs as creators of psychologically intense sonnet sequences published their works after the genre's main boom, and after the Elizabethan period: Shakespeare, whose sonnets were published in 1609,[41] and Sidney's niece Lady Mary Wroth, whose *Pamphilia to Amphilanthus* was published in 1621. Sidney was a trailblazer in showing how the forms of both the individual sonnet and the sonnet sequence could evoke mental states while meditating on the difficulty of representing such states.

'Exact pictures of every posture in the mind': representing thought in prose fiction

The Elizabethan literature that is most well known today is poetry and drama, yet in the period itself one of the most popular, diverse, and experimental genres was prose fiction. As discussed in the Introduction to the present volume, the second half of the sixteenth century saw a rapid expansion in the book trade in general; this was partly fuelled by the extension of literacy to more women and non-elite readers.[42] Prose fiction fed a growing demand for pleasurable reading and spanned a wide scale of genres and readerships, from courtly romances by authors like Gascoigne, Lyly, and Sidney, to more popular narratives in cheaper formats.[43] Ninety-eight works of prose fiction were published between 1580 and 1589, then 165 such works in the period 1590–99.[44]

Although recent decades have seen an increase in critical discussion of Elizabethan prose fiction, knowledge and study of these works are still limited. The genre has also been neglected by historians and theorists of the representation of subjectivity and interiority in prose fiction, who tend to look back no earlier than the eighteenth century.[45] Yet the fictional representation of the inner thoughts of characters reaches back at least to Chaucer's Criseyde, in the late fourteenth century, who debates with herself at length how to respond to the news that Troilus is in love with her: she 'gan to caste and rollen up and down / Withinne her thought his excellent prowesse'. Just as for many characters in the novels of later centuries, her thoughts are represented as speech – 'to hireself she seyde' – as she considers the pros and cons of accepting Troilus's advances.[46] Readers of later novels came to accept self-addressed speech as a convention to represent silent, internal thought, whereas in both *Troilus and Criseyde* and sixteenth-century works it is unclear whether or not such monologues are spoken aloud. Nevertheless, they were widely used in Elizabethan prose fiction as a means of articulating inner divisions and depicting the decision-making processes that produce actions and so drive the plot.

Elizabethan prose fiction also had a close relationship with the representation of psychological states in lyric poetry. The poems of *Tottel's Miscellany* were edited from diverse manuscripts, and in the process each was assigned a title that often implied both a state of mind and a moment in a narrative. These included: 'Complaint of a lover that defied love, and was by love after the more tormented'; 'Complaint of the absence of her lover being upon the sea'; and 'The lover excuseth himself of suspected change'.[47] An early Elizabethan work of prose fiction, George Gascoigne's *The Adventures of Master F. J.* (1573), expanded upon this idea of lyric verses as implying surrounding narratives. It was presented as an anthology of private courtship poems purloined from manuscript and conveyed to print by 'H. W.', a friend of a friend of the author. The 'editor' then fills in a backstory around the verses, narrating the development of a love triangle between a gentleman named only as F. J., a married lady named Elinor, and another lady named Frances.

The narrative is purportedly only present to set the verses in context, yet takes over and comes to constitute the bulk of the work. At the same time, the verses remain important, particularly for the presentation of states of mind. Some of them are instrumental in F. J.'s courtship negotiations, strategically disclosing his feelings to a specific intended reader: 'When he had well sorted this sequence [poem], he sought opportunity to leave it where she might find it before it were lost'. Others are composed in solitude, to distil and express his emotional state:

> in the morning rising very early, although it were far before his mistress's hour, he cooled his choler by walking in the gallery near to her lodging, and there in this passion compiled these verses following.

> A cloud of care hath covered all my coast,
> And storms of strife do threaten to appear.[48]

Such poems serve rather like arias in nineteenth-century operas or songs in twentieth-century musicals, halting the narrative temporarily to linger on and delve into an intense psycho-emotional moment. Both types of poem – those directed strategically towards an intended reader within the narrative, and those that are solitary utterances of overflowing emotion – contribute to this work's insistent and tantalising play upon notions of secrecy and revelation. H. W., the mysterious editor-figure, invites the reader to enjoy in print poems supposedly intended only for private manuscript circulation, and to pry into a surrounding erotic narrative that is implied, scandalously, to concern real people. Within the narrative, characters are constantly attempting – and, in the hapless F. J.'s case, mostly failing – to read one another's erotic intentions. The reader shares in this mind-reading activity, while, in the form of the poems, enjoying a degree of

privileged access into the private thoughts that lie behind the characters' actions and form the elusive core of the story. Whythorne wrote
his autobiography in around 1576, just three years after the publication of Gascoigne's *Master F. J.*, and its influence upon him is clear.[49]

Sidney's *Arcadia* also combined prose narrative and verse to
explore and represent mental states, and thereby, according to Sidney's
friend Fulke Greville, delineated 'exact pictures of every posture in
the mind'.[50] Its first version, known as the *Old Arcadia*, was composed
between around 1577 and 1580.[51] Early in the narrative, Pyrocles
declares: 'the workings of the mind, I find, much more infinite than
can be led unto by the eye or imagined by any that distract their
thoughts without [outside] themselves'.[52] He claims that he craves
solitude only for contemplation and the pursuit of self-knowledge,
but in fact is disingenuously attempting to conceal from his curious
cousin Musidorus the fact that he is in love, ironically confirming
that the inner recesses of the mind are indeed obscure.

Sidney proceeds to use various strategies to put into writing the
'infinite' 'workings of the mind'. In some passages the narrator uses
third-person prose to describe the inner states of characters, as when
the innocent princess Philoclea struggles to understand her burgeoning
desire for the Amazon Cleophila. Philoclea has not yet detected that
her apparently female companion is in fact Pyrocles in disguise, and
so is perplexed: 'the sweet Philoclea found strange unwonted motions
[passions, agitations] in herself. And yet the poor soul could neither
discern what it was, nor whither the vehemency of it tended' (85).
Soon afterwards, Sidney uses another literary technique, what John
Ruskin would later call pathetic fallacy, to externalise her troubled
state of mind and project it onto a landscape setting. Philoclea steals
out by moonlight to visit a favourite place for solitary reflection, a
melancholy wooded glade. An ancient marble altar within the glade
functions both as a textual surface for the composition of lyric verse,
and as an emblem of Philoclea's inner state. Written upon it in ink is
a poem that she composed before Cleophila's arrival, adamantly
declaring her unwavering dedication to chastity: 'My virgin life no

spotted thought shall stain.' Her past, chaste self addressed the altar as 'Thou purest stone, whose pureness doth present / My purest mind'. However, as her feelings have changed over time, so too has the poem on the altar: 'the ink was already foreworn and in many places blotted'. Philoclea interprets this as signifying the disparity between her past and present selves under the pressure of unforeseen passion: 'well do these blots become a blotted writer,' she laments, commending the altar for 'so constantly bear[ing] the marks of my inconstancy'. Two new stanzas, a 'retractation' of her former vow of chastity, 'came into her head' and are presented in full by Sidney, although he explains that the night's darkness prevented Philoclea from writing them down, so they exist only in her mind. Finally, she speaks 'with a whispering voice to herself', delivering a monologue that is full of rhetorical questions, self-reproaches, and conflicting wishes: '"O me, unfortunate wretch," said she, "what poisonous heats be these that thus possess me? How hath the sight of this strange guest invaded my soul?"' (95–7). The passage is a concise compendium of different devices for representing interior states, including pathetic fallacy and a material text that has been blotted and eroded; poetry in writing or in the mind; and self-addressed prose monologue.

The device of the unwritten or unspoken poem that exists only in the mind of a character is used again by Sidney for Gynecia, Philoclea's mother, who has shrewdly perceived that Cleophila is a man in disguise, and is consumed by desire for him and jealousy of Philoclea. As she rushes to find them alone together and interrupt their intimacy, 'there came into her mind an old song, which she thought did well figure her fortune'. As with Philoclea's two stanzas revising her poem on chastity, Sidney reproduces this song in full, though Gynecia's 'leisure served her not as then to sing it' (108). This song exists only in the mind of the character and on the page of the *Old Arcadia*, where the special powers of fiction allow the reader to access her inner thoughts.

While Gynecia does not have leisure to sing her inner poem, another one with even more ambiguous status is assigned to Pyrocles, who does not even have leisure to run over it in his thoughts. By the end of Book 3, he has been revealed to Philoclea as a man and accepted as her lover. As he lays her on a bed and gazes appreciatively at her beauties, 'there came into his mind' a song by Philisides, Sidney's own fictional persona in Arcadia, 'What tongue can her perfections tell'. This is a blazon – a catalogue of a woman's desirable physical features, including her eyes, lips, breasts, thighs, and so on – which goes on for several pages. As it ends, the narrator remarks, 'But do not think, fair ladies, his thoughts had such leisure as to run over so long a ditty; the only general fancy of it came into his mind, fixed upon the sense of that sweet subject' (207–11). The display of Philoclea's body invites the reader to share Pyrocles's 'general fancy', his sexual arousal and pleasure, but its apparent explicitness is in fact a kind of smokescreen, standing in for and distracting us from the love-making that actually occupies Pyrocles while we enjoy the poem. At the same time this version of the device of the inner poem is a tantalising provocation: the implication that Pyrocles's thoughts and actions at this moment of consummation are too sensational to be articulated in more than 'general' terms incites the reader to imagine them in full.[53]

Although the *Old Arcadia* had only limited manuscript circulation, the posthumous print publication of an expanded version, the *New Arcadia*, had far-reaching impact. The first edition appeared in 1590, in the unfinished state in which it was left at Sidney's death, followed by a composite version in 1593 which grafted on the ending of the *Old Arcadia*. It included slightly revised versions of most of the passages discussed here, as well as further representations of interiority, and these played a significant part in its extensive influence through the 1590s and onwards through subsequent centuries. Meanwhile, John Lyly's *Euphues* had been published in print in 1578 with sensational success, going through five editions by 1581 and inspiring numerous imitations.[54] Lyly moved away from the punctuation of narrative with lyric verses, instead representing the thoughts and feelings of characters in extended dialogues and monologues whose expansive, finely crafted style came to be known as 'euphuism'. Its main features are rhetorical questions, patterns of alliteration, repetition, antithesis, and reiteration of the same idea in multiple ways, often involving long sequences of proverbs and elaborate similes drawn from natural history and mythology.[55] Equipped with these tools, Lyly's characters expatiate upon intricate details of their psychological states in virtuosic prose cadenzas.

The monologues in *Euphues* typically concern conflicting passions and ethical dilemmas, working through alternatives to determine a character's next actions.[56] Like the inner debates depicted in *Astrophil and Stella* and other sonnets of the period, they draw on the rhetorical technique of debate *in utramque partem*, arguing both sides of a case.[57] A good example of this, and of euphuistic elaboration, is a speech by Lucilla after her introduction to Euphues by his friend and her intended husband, Philautus. She begins 'to fry in the flames of love' for Euphues, producing a conflict between duty and desire; and as she finds herself alone, with 'all the company being departed to their lodgings', she enters into 'terms and contrarieties', an inner debate in which she addresses herself: 'Ah, wretched wench Lucilla, how art thou perplexed? What a doubtful fight does thou feel betwixt faith and fancy, hope and fear, conscience and concupiscence?' Both the rhetorical questions and the string of antitheses are typical of euphuism, as is the sequence of analogies in the next paragraph. Lucilla doubts that Euphues will accept her love:

well doth he know that the glass once crazed will with the least clap be cracked, that the cloth which staineth with milk will soon lose his colour with vinegar, that the eagle's wing will waste the feather as well of the Phoenix as of the pheasant, that she that hath been faithless to one will never be faithful to any.

She continues:

For as the bee that gathereth honey out of the weed when she espieth the fair flower flieth to the sweetest; or as the kind spaniel though he hunt after birds yet forsakes them to retrieve the partridge; or as we commonly feed on beef hungerly at the first, yet seeing the quail more dainty change our diet; so I, although I loved Philautus for his good properties, yet seeing Euphues to excel him I ought by nature to like him better.

This goes on for several pages.[58]

This style can seem tedious to a modern reader, but many Elizabethan readers would have encountered during their education Erasmus's *De copia* (*Of Abundance*), a manual on finding as many ways as possible of saying the same thing. For Lyly's contemporaries, there was reading pleasure in admiring the author's, or character's, ingenuity and creativity in devising multiple parallel statements to reinforce and embellish a point.[59] The effect in euphuism is a tension between two contrary movements. On the one hand, the accumulation of multiple analogies situates an individual character's dilemma within a universal system of correspondences in society and nature, often justifying their decisions by an appeal to common practice and cosmic order. On the other hand, the relentless procession of antitheses suggests that all things exist in an unending state of conflict and paradox, including the human mind.[60]

Robert Greene, one of the most prolific and successful Elizabethan authors of prose fiction, began by imitating euphuism in *Mamillia* (written *c.* 1580, published 1583), then moved on to satirise it in *Menaphon* (1589). He produced a total of twenty works of prose fiction, as well as plays and rumbustious pamphlets about urban lowlife.[61] His most popular prose fiction, *Pandosto: The Triumph of Time* (1588), enjoyed success for over two centuries, particularly in redacted and affordable chapbook versions, but is best known today as the source of Shakespeare's *The Winter's Tale*.[62] Falling towards the end of Greene's euphuistic period,[63] it was, like many works of Elizabethan prose fiction, generically hybrid, also incorporating elements from ancient Greek romances, works originally composed in the early centuries CE and revived in Elizabethan England.[64] In this context, the term 'romance' means not just a love story (though love is often a prominent driver of plot) but a narrative that is fantastical, set in a distant time and place, and often featuring far-fetched events and supernatural interventions. The Greek romances included Heliodorus's *Aethiopica* (or *Aethiopian History*), translated into English by Thomas Underdowne in 1569, which went through several editions, including one in 1587, just a year before *Pandosto*; and Angel Day's English version of *Daphnis and Chloe*, which also appeared in 1587.[65] Greene borrowed some of their standard ingredients, including an oracle, a lost child cast adrift at sea, a shepherdess who is really a princess, and a general sense of wonder as characters frequently stand 'in a maze' at miraculous turns of events.[66]

Although more plot-driven than *Euphues*, *Pandosto* is punctuated by similar self-addressed monologues. Greene is interested in both the unfolding of events and the extreme psychological states provoked by those events, which in turn produce actions and drive plot.[67] Sometimes the characters seem to be merely pawns of Fortune – a term that, including variants, is mentioned over sixty times in the text – but more often it is the interplay between Fortune and the inwardly debated choices of the characters that determines the course of the narrative.[68] At the beginning of the story, Fortune brings Egistus, King of Sicilia, to visit his childhood friend Pandosto, King of Bohemia, but it is a psychological reaction that turns this into a narrative crisis, as Pandosto is seized by suspicion that Egistus is having an affair with his wife, Bellaria. Over several pages this jealousy is characterised in diverse ways: it is an arbitrary, inexplicable occurrence (he is 'furiously incensed by causeless jealousy'); an intervention in human affairs by Fortune (who, 'willing to show some sign of her inconstancy, turned her wheel and darkened their bright sun of prosperity'); or a physical and mental illness ('a certain melancholy passion, entering the mind of Pandosto, drave him into sundry and doubtful thoughts', 155–7). From this point on, Fortune and human agency interact to generate plot, and in turn the plot serves increasingly to frame euphuistic monologues in which solitary characters voice their emotional reactions to their predicaments and debate how to act.

Such self-addressed monologues become especially frequent as the narrative moves into the next generation. Egistus's son Prince Dorastus falls in love with Pandosto's daughter Fawnia, who was abandoned as a baby and has grown up believing herself the daughter of a shepherd. Fawnia contemplates her love-problem in a style similar to that of Lyly's Lucilla, addressing herself while piling up antitheses and analogies:

> Infortunate Fawnia, and therefore infortunate because Fawnia, thy shepherd's hook showeth thy poor state, thy proud desires an aspiring mind; the one declareth thy want, the other thy pride. No bastard hawk must soar so high as the hobby [falcon], no fowl gaze against the sun but the eagle, actions wrought against nature reap despite and thoughts above fortune, disdain. (182)[69]

Her facility with rhetoric is part of the evidence that she is a princess in disguise; Dorastus is nearer the truth than he knows when he muses that 'if her birth were answerable to her wit and beauty' then she would be 'a fit mate for the most famous prince in the world' (184).

The euphuistic self-addressed monologue is related to a number of other genres. Its emphasis upon inner conflict connects it to psychomachia and debate *in utramque partem*, and thereby in turn to the sonnets of the period that were also internalising these devices. Meanwhile, the long, eloquent speeches of female characters in particular, expressing their desires and debating the claims of love and virtue, also drew upon Ovid's *Heroides* and the genre of female complaint (as discussed in Chapter 4).[70] As in female complaint, it is often ambiguous whether solitary characters in Elizabethan prose fiction are speaking aloud when they put their thoughts into words, or whether speech is a device to represent silent words uttered in the mind alone. Some critics have called their self-addressed monologues 'thought "arias"' or 'soliloquies',[71] but the latter term is itself ambiguous. Dramatic soliloquies were the primary method of representing the mind in late Elizabethan plays, but should they be considered as addressed to the audience, or spoken aloud by a character to him- or herself, or as a representation of private, silent thought? Alongside new methods for representing 'the very image of the mind' in prose and poetry, the connected and eventful story of new representations of the mind in Elizabethan drama requires a chapter of its own.

❧ 10 ❧

'That Within'
Hamlet and the Mind on Stage

Hamlet, written around 1600, is a point of convergence for many lines of thought about the mind that had developed through the Elizabethan period. As noted in the Introduction to the present volume, Hamlet is a textbook melancholic, with his black garb, inconsolable grief, and desire for solitude, as well as his incapacity for action, overactive intellect and imagination, and suicidal tendencies. He recognises himself as such, and worries that his father's ghost might be a typical example of Satan's exploitation of melancholy to disrupt the imagination and plant evil intentions; the apparition

> May be a dev'l, and the dev'l hath power
> T'assume a pleasing shape; yea, and perhaps
> Out of my weakness and my melancholy,
> As he is very potent with such spirits,
> Abuses me to damn me. (2.2.517–22)

In giving the ghost of Old Hamlet an external presence visible to other characters besides his son, Shakespeare opposes himself to writers like Weyer, Scot, and Nashe who asserted that apparitions were merely delusional projections of the mind (see Chapter 6 above). Nevertheless, Hamlet is particularly sensitive to the ghost's presence (as when he sees him, but Gertrude does not, in Act 3 Scene 4), and his mind is particularly disturbed by it, corresponding with Du Laurens's assertion (in his treatise published the year before the play) that 'The imagination of melancholic men is troubled [...] by the intercourse or meddling of evil angels, which cause them often-times to foretell and forge very strange things in their imaginations'.[1] Adding yet another dimension to his melancholy, while there can be no doubt that Hamlet is afflicted with the condition, he is also aware that it can be a stereotypical social identity that is performative, as when he resolves 'To put an antic disposition on' (1.5.173), layering affected melancholy on top of actual melancholy.

All these facets of Hamlet's melancholy reflect the Elizabethan preoccupation with this humour. He is also typically Elizabethan in separating his outer and inner selves: 'I have that within which passes show' (1.2.85). In so doing, he draws on revived classical philosophies, especially Neostoicism, while his extensive self-contemplation both complies with the ancient injunction to 'know thyself' and participates in the introspection and self-examination encouraged by new devotional practices.[2] The play also reiterates the hierarchical Elizabethan ordering of faculties that elevated reason to the highest place in the mind. Ophelia laments that Hamlet's 'noble and most sovereign reason' has been 'o'erthrown' (3.1.154, 147), while he rebukes himself that God 'gave us not / That capability and godlike reason / To fust in us unused'; to live merely 'to sleep and feed' is to be 'A beast, no more' (4.1.34–8).

When consumed by fury against his mother for her remarriage, Hamlet voices the widespread view that women lacked reason and were governed by the passions and senses (see Chapter 4): 'Frailty, thy name is woman [...] O God, a beast that wants discourse of reason / Would have mourned longer' (1.12.146, 150–1). Another aspect of the same view is Ophelia's incapacity to manage her grief and her descent into a form of madness that expresses itself in childish rhymes and sexual obsession, very different from the witty repartee and philosophising that Hamlet is capable of even when supposedly (or really?) mad. Yet for Hamlet's own numerous soliloquies, Shakespeare borrows techniques for representing the mind from female complaint, along with other genres that had become prominent in the 1590s for articulating self-contemplation, inner conflict, and thought in process: passion literature, sonnets, and the self-addressed monologues of prose fiction.

Hamlet frequently uses his soliloquies to voice self-division and inner conflict: 'break, my heart, for I must hold my tongue' (1.2.159); 'Oh, what a rogue and peasant slave am I!' (2.2.469); 'I do not know / Why yet I live to say "This thing's to do"' (4.2.42–3). His uncle Claudius does the same: 'Oh, my offence is rank, it smells to heaven [. . .] My words fly up, my thoughts remain below' (3.3.36, 97). At first sight, the 1566 play *Apius and Virginia* suggests that this is nothing new: Apius, a judge who is consumed by lust for the chaste Virginia, complains: 'But out I am wounded, how am I divided?' However, he goes on: 'Conscience he pricketh me contemned, / And Justice sayeth, Judgement would have me condemned'.[3] In this play Conscience and Justice are two characters who appear on stage, along with Haphazard, Rumour, Comfort, Reward, Fame, and Memory. Such use of allegorical personifications is typical of early Elizabethan drama, but, needless to say, no such personifications appear in *Hamlet*, which epitomises a movement away from allegory towards entirely inward-looking soliloquies as the principal means of dramatising the mind.

The predominant dramatic genre of the early Elizabethan period was the allegorical morality play or interlude (a short play for performance in the intervals of a banquet or other household entertainment). We have encountered several of these in earlier chapters: in Chapter 2, *The Trial of Treasure* (1567), *Enough Is as Good as a Feast* (1568), and *The Longer Thou Livest the More Fool Thou Art* (1569); and in Chapter 8, *The Marriage of Wit and Science* (1568). The genre continued through the 1570s, with examples including *A Marriage between Wit and Wisdom* (1575), *The Tide Tarrieth No Man*

(1576), and Thomas Lupton's *All for Money* (1577). In the early 1580s, Robert Wilson was still using allegory in *The Three Ladies of London* (1581), whose characters include Lady Conscience, Dissimulation, and Sincerity. However, towards the end of the century, as the new commercial playhouses increasingly flourished they moved away from allegory. It became mainly the preserve of private, elite drama such as *A Masque of the Nine Passions* performed by the Middle Temple at Whitehall Palace in 1598, and then the lavish masques of the Jacobean court. Allegory also continued to be used in academic settings: in Thomas Tomkis's *Lingua*, staged at Trinity College, Cambridge in around 1606, the title character – the tongue or speech – petitions the judge Common Sense to be considered a sixth sense; while *Pathomachia, or The Battle of the Affections*, also known as *Love's Lodestone*, may have been performed in a university setting in around 1616–17.[4]

The legacy of allegory remains apparent in some Elizabethan and Jacobean plays for the commercial playhouses, especially in the type-characters of humours comedies and city comedies who often resemble morality-play personifications of particular vices or states of mind.[5] However, in playhouse drama of the 1590s, soliloquy – a speech delivered by a character described in a stage direction as *solus* or *sola* (alone) on stage – became the predominant means of staging the mind, especially in tragedy.[6] It was not a new phenomenon: medieval and early Tudor drama had used soliloquy for plot exposition. Morality plays and interludes also frequently featured a character-type known as the 'Vice', a lively, impudent mischief-maker who personified sinfulness and used soliloquy to taunt the audience and make them complicit in his secret plans.[7] Soliloquies continued to be deployed in this way by characters like Marlowe's Barabas in *The Jew of Malta* (1589), Shakespeare's Aaron in *Titus Andronicus* (1592), and the protagonist of his *Richard III* (1593), conniving villains who were self-consciously duplicitous and gleefully in control of the disparity between their outward and inward selves. What was new about other 1590s soliloquies was their increasing use to depict characters who were struggling to manage conflicting forces in their minds: characters who addressed themselves rather than the audience as they strove to govern their passions, grapple with an ethical dilemma, or persuade themselves into a particular opinion or course of action.[8] Characters in earlier plays (like Apius) had sometimes used soliloquy to reflect on their situation, including their state of mind, but this now took on a new intensity that reflected the post-Calvinist emphasis on inner conflict and struggle as a necessary stage on the path to salvation.[9] In fact, the term 'soliloquy' was not applied to drama until the late seventeenth century, but the late Elizabethan tragic soliloquy resembled the original sense of the word as coined by St Augustine: solitary prayer (that is, the mind in dialogue with itself) in the presence of God.[10] Let us trace in more detail how the soliloquy developed in the late Elizabethan period and how it reached its apogee in *Hamlet*.

'Still tormented is my tortured soul': Kyd, Marlowe, and early developments in playhouse soliloquy

The new humanist curriculum of sixteenth-century grammar schools and universities introduced pupils to soliloquies in the drama of ancient Rome. In the comedies of Plautus, clever slaves confided their schemes and tricks to the audience in a similar way to the medieval Vice, but those of Terence increasingly used soliloquies to explore the thoughts and feelings of characters who were frustrated or misunderstood.[11] Even more important were the tragedies of Seneca, where solitary characters used heightened rhetoric to question themselves and reflect on their inner state.[12] They were performed in Latin in schools and universities from the 1540s onwards, and became yet more widely known and admired when they were published in English editions by various translators from 1559, then gathered together by Thomas Newton as *Ten Tragedies* in 1581.[13]

The first attempt to write a Senecan tragedy in English was *Gorboduc* (1562) by Thomas Norton and Thomas Sackville. Set in ancient Britain, it emulated its Roman models in both its revenge plot and its use of soliloquy. Act 4 Scene 1 consists entirely of Queen Videna *sola* on stage after her younger son, Porrex, has murdered the elder, Ferrex, whom she favoured. She opens with a rhetorical question: 'Why should I live and linger forth my time / In longer life to double my distress?' First she addresses herself – 'O me most woeful wight [creature]' – to lament her grief; then she moves on to rebuking at length the absent Porrex: 'Thou, Porrex, thou this damnèd deed hast wrought'. Finally she resolves to act and take vengeance: 'But whereunto waste I this ruthful speech? [...] But canst thou hope to scape my just revenge?'[14] The soliloquy partly serves to indicate to the audience the direction the plot will take and to supply a motive for this; but in doing so, it also reveals to the audience Videna's evolving state of mind as she passes from loss through grievance to vindictiveness, and works out her next steps.[15]

Gorboduc belongs to a pre-playhouse era – it was performed at the Inner Temple and at court[16] – but by the late 1580s the commercial playhouses had become established and were also drawing upon Seneca. Thomas Kyd, author of *The Spanish Tragedy* (1587), flaunted his Senecan credentials by making his protagonist, Hieronimo, quote the Roman author several times in Latin.[17] Sometimes Hieronimo, whose son has been murdered, uses soliloquy to express inner turmoil, sharing with Videna the frequent use of rhetorical questions: 'Where shall I run to breathe abroad my woes, / My woes whose weight hath wearied the earth? / [...] still tormented is my tortured soul / With broken sighs and restless passions'. At other points he addresses himself by name to give advice or instructions as he thinks through his plan of action:

Hieronimo, beware, thou art betrayed,
And to entrap thy life this train is laid.
Advise thee therefore, be not credulous: [...]
Dear was the life of my beloved son,
And of his death behoves me be revenged:
Then hazard not thine own, Hieronimo,
But live t'effect thy resolution.[18]

Such speeches resemble a dialogue between two Hieronimos: one who is alert, intelligent, and cautious; another who is bolder, more unthinking, and in need of guidance. Although the terms are only implicit here, these two aspects of his mind could be identified as his reason and passion, or his wit and will; he is undergoing an internalised psychomachia.[19] Matthew Arnold, writing in 1853, found in *Hamlet* 'the dialogue of the mind with itself', but by looking at earlier plays like *The Spanish Tragedy* we can see that Shakespeare was not the first to present such dialogue.[20]

Kyd shared a writing chamber with Christopher Marlowe, who experimented audaciously with the soliloquy in *Tamburlaine* (1587) by inserting one unexpectedly in the play's sequence of mounting atrocities. Tamburlaine heartlessly refuses the pleas for mercy of the virgins of Damascus, and receives unmoved the news that his soldiers have 'hoisted up their slaughtered carcasses' upon the city walls. Marlowe then immediately and provocatively inserts a soliloquy in which the ruthless conqueror muses sensitively on love and poetry: 'What is beauty, saith my sufferings, then?'[21] The audience's response to Tamburlaine already mingles revulsion and fascination; now we are challenged even further to comprehend and evaluate a character who combines monstrous deeds of violence with refined inner contemplation of aesthetics.

The use of soliloquy to depict what is going on in the mind involves further kinds of ambiguity in *Doctor Faustus* (1588). Some aspects of this play return to the native morality play tradition, bringing on stage the Devil and the Seven Deadly Sins, and personifying the opposed forces competing for the soul as the Good and Evil Angels. Nevertheless, as we saw in Chapter 6, the play increasingly situates this combat within rather than outside the mind, culminating in the self-questioning and self-division of Faustus's final soliloquy. Alone in his study, Faustus resembles Kyd's Hieronimo in speaking to himself to articulate inner conflict and anguish; yet as he does so, his double, debating, self-contradicting voice sounds as if he is alternately ventriloquising the Evil and Good Angels:

Now, Faustus, must thou needs be damned,
And canst thou not be saved.
What boots it then to think of God or heaven?
Away with such vain fancies and despair!
Despair in God and trust in Beelzebub.
Now go not backward. No, Faustus, be resolute.
Why waverest thou? O, something soundeth in mine ears:
'Abjure this magic, turn to God again!'
Ay, and Faustus will turn to God again.
To God? He loves you not.[22]

The speech is transitional between the medieval convention of psychomachic allegory and the developing Elizabethan convention of the soliloquy as a representation of inner conflict. Its combination of aspects of both conventions creates fundamental and provocative ambiguity as to whether Faustus is the passive and unknowing victim of external forces, or the wilful agent of his own choices and his own fate. Marlowe's blending of allegory and soliloquy is thus intrinsic to his dramatisation of the forces of the Devil as both external and internal to the mind, and hence to his play's disconcerting openness to radically divergent interpretations.[23]

'A generation of still-breeding thoughts': Shakespeare's early experiments with soliloquy

Shakespeare's early works find him learning from his peers and testing out what soliloquy can do. In the opening soliloquy of *Richard III* (1593), 'Now is the winter of our discontent', the protagonist displays his sardonic wit and confesses his evil nature to the audience like a medieval Vice: 'I am determinèd to prove a villain' (1.1.1, 30). Yet unlike most Vices, he never acknowledges the presence of the audience by addressing them directly; and by Act 5, he is more in tune with recent developments in soliloquy, breaking apart like Hieronimo or Faustus, though Shakespeare articulates this self-division and mental disintegration somewhat crudely:

> What do I fear? Myself? There's none else by.
> Richard loves Richard; that is, I and I.
> Is there a murderer here? No. Yes, I am.
> Then fly. What, from myself? (5.3.180–3)[24]

Writing *The Rape of Lucrece* (1594), and thereby participating in the development of female complaint and passion literature, evidently taught Shakespeare much about how an internal monologue can represent a mind contemplating a critical moral choice that divides it against itself. He learned also how to depict a mind in process as it passes through varying states of passion and reasons through a problem.[25] These lessons were applied in *Richard II* (1595). Just as Lucrece asserts a division between her defiled body and her pure mind – 'Though my gross blood be stained with this abuse, / Immaculate and spotless is my mind' (ll. 1655–6) – so Richard distinguishes between his outer and inner being:

> my grief lies all within;
> And these external manner of laments
> Are merely shadows to the unseen grief
> That swells with silence in the tortured soul.
> There lies the substance. (4.1.288–92)[26]

Later, alone in prison, with death inevitably looming, Richard explores this inward grief in a long soliloquy:

> I have been studying how to compare
> This prison where I live unto the world;
> And, for because the world is populous
> And here is not a creature but myself,
> I cannot do it. Yet I'll hammer't out.

My brain I'll prove the female to my soul,
My soul the father, and these two beget
A generation of still-breeding thoughts;
And these same thoughts people this little world
In humours like the people of this world,
For no thought is contented. (5.5.1–11)

Richard at first dismisses the image of his prison as a microcosm of
the world, because he is its only inhabitant. Then, however, he asserts
that it *is* a microcosm, because it is peopled by his multitudinous and
proliferating thoughts, which are as diverse as the humours, or characters, of the people of the world. He goes on to detail his 'thoughts
of things divine', his 'Thoughts tending to ambition', and his
'Thoughts tending to content' (12, 18, 23). For a few moments
Richard's tragedy turns into a kind of vast, sprawling humours
comedy, in which his fluctuating moods are the characters:

Thus play I in one prison many people,
And none contented. Sometimes am I king,
Then treason makes me wish myself a beggar,
And so I am; then crushing penury
Persuades me I was better when a king;
Then am I kinged again, and by and by
Think that I am unkinged by Bolingbroke,
And straight am nothing. (31–8)

Richard here invokes the metaphor of unruly thoughts as 'treasons' or rebels; as we saw in Chapter 8, this was commonplace in the
Elizabethan period, but it has particular force for him as a deposed
king. He is a special case of self-division: his body politic (the sacred,
eternal essence of kingship, not limited to an individual incumbent)
has become divided from his body natural (the personal humanity of
the mortal individual who temporarily holds the throne). The audience has seen this separation of selves publicly and ritualistically

enacted earlier, in the deposition scene, when Richard handed over the crown to Bolingbroke:

> Now mark me how I will undo myself:
> [...]
> With mine own tears I wash away my balm,
> With mine own hands I give away my crown. (4.1.196, 200–1)

This is the particular self-reflexive paradox of a king exercising his royal authority to resign his kingship; but when Richard calls for a mirror, we can share with him a general human sense of alienation of the inner from the outer self, and the mind from the body:

> Give me that glass, and therein will I read.
> No deeper wrinkles yet? Hath sorrow struck
> So many blows upon this face of mine
> And made no deeper wounds? (269–72)

Similarly, in his final soliloquy, Shakespeare takes the intensity of self-division felt by a deposed king and widens outwards from it to make general reflections on the human condition. Richard's perception that 'Thus play I in one prison many people' (5.5.31) expresses the performative nature of kingship and his own personal histrionic tendencies, but also anticipates the general observation of Jaques in *As You Like It* (1600) that 'All the world's a stage, / And all the men and women merely players' (2.7.139–40). The ensuing turn of Richard's thought then also prefigures Hamlet's crisis of being and desire for self-extinction:

> But whate'er I am,
> Nor I nor any man that but man is
> With nothing shall be pleased, till he be eased
> With being nothing. (*Richard II*, 5.5.38–41)[27]

Shakespeare here both takes the soliloquy further inwards and turns it outwards again, as Richard's particular predicament is used to generalise and philosophise about human existence. In part, this reflects the influence of Seneca, not only emulating his soliloquies, which sometimes combined self-reflection with wider meditations, but also importing into the soliloquy the kind of content usually found in speeches by Senecan choruses, which typically expatiated on the state of humanity, the world, and the cosmos.[28] It also reflects the influence of one of Shakespeare's sources for his history plays, *The Mirror for Magistrates*, the compilation of first-person verse narratives by historical figures mentioned in the previous chapter. First published in 1559, this work passed through multiple editions with additions by various contributors.[29] It presents figures from history who step forward one by one to narrate their rise to power and lament their fall. As the title indicates, the work's purpose is to provide exemplary warnings to rulers, so each speaker opens and closes their narrative by drawing general lessons. The *Mirror*'s version of Richard II, for instance, opens his monologue with the lines: 'Happy is the prince that hath in wealth [prosperity] the grace / To follow virtue, keeping vices under, / But woe to him whose will hath wisdom's place.'[30] The thought here is far simpler than in the soliloquy that Shakespeare gives to his Richard II, which also has far more of a sense of the speaker actively working out his ideas as he speaks, rather than making a formal oration: 'Yet I'll hammer't out' (*Richard II*, 5.5.5). Nevertheless, Shakespeare was building on the *Mirror*'s blending of first-person lament with general reflection.

At this stage in his career Shakespeare was mainly producing history plays, where this use of soliloquy for choral-style meditation was useful to pause the action and provide commentary on the significance of unfolding events.[31] The Bastard in *King John* (1596) is to some extent an old-fashioned Vice-like character in his subversive energy, satirical humour, and confessional complicity with the audience, but he is given a choral soliloquy to muse eloquently on 'Commodity [material advantage], the bias of the world' (2.1.574).[32]

In *Henry IV Part 1* (1597), Shakespeare gives another choral soliloquy, this time in prose, to another Vice-like character, Falstaff, who pauses *solus* on the battlefield at Shrewsbury to deconstruct honour: 'What is honour? A word. What is in that word "honour"? [. . .] Air' (5.1.133–4).[33]

Julius Caesar (1599) finds Shakespeare taking soliloquy further again as Brutus contemplates Caesar's assassination. The setting creates a melancholic mood: Brutus is alone in his orchard by night, and punctuates his speech with mention of the unsettled behaviour of the stars ('The exhalations whizzing in the air', 2.1.44) and his own sleeplessness ('Since Cassius first did whet me against Caesar, / I have not slept', 2.1.61–2). The careful orchestration of the scene includes several interruptions by the servant Lucius, intensifying a sense of Brutus's solitude and privacy each time Lucius leaves him, and breaking his soliloquy and hence his line of thought into sections. Beginning with the declaration 'It must be by his death', Brutus deliberates upon why this is so: 'He would be crowned'; being crowned, Caesar might become a tyrant; 'Then lest he may, prevent'. Frequent enjambment and lines broken up by caesuras create turbulence between metre and sense, suggesting a mind in uneasy motion. At the same time, a sequence of conjunctions takes us from a proposition, through arguments for and against, to a resolution: 'Crown him', 'And then', 'But', 'But', 'So', 'Then', 'And since', 'And therefore', 'kill him' (2.1.10–34).

Metaphors and similes also form part of Brutus's thought-process. At the beginning and end of the soliloquy, Caesar is a serpent: 'It is the bright day that brings forth the adder', just as crowning may bring forth his 'sting'; and he is 'as a serpent's egg / Which, hatched, would as his kind grow mischievous' (2.1.14, 16, 32–3). Comparisons of Caesar to a snake obviously render him sinister and help to justify his death. Brutus also uses the image of ambition as a ladder, whose climber looks only upwards, 'scorning the base degrees / By which he did descend' (2.1.26–7). Meanwhile, throughout the soliloquy there is a sense of two audiences. Although the spectators in the playhouse

are not explicitly addressed, there is an implicit sense that Brutus is
conscious of them eavesdropping upon him and seeks to persuade
them of the justice of his cause. Even stronger, however, is the sense
that within the fictional world of the play Brutus is entirely alone,
without auditors, and is trying to argue *himself* into a conviction that
he is doing the right thing, with a strenuousness that in itself implies
his persistent doubts.

Lucius interrupts Brutus to bring him a letter, then leaves him
alone again. In the second section of his soliloquy Brutus reads aloud
from the anonymous letter, which urges him to 'Speak, strike, redress!'
(2.1.47). Dialogue with this external voice drives Brutus to self-
questioning, then to stiffened resolve: 'Am I entreated / To speak and
strike? O Rome, I make thee promise' (2.1.55–6). After another
interruption by Lucius and a knock at the gate, a third section of the
soliloquy shifts into choral meditation: 'Between the acting of a
dreadful thing / And the first motion, all the interim is / Like a
phantasma or a hideous dream' (2.1.63–5). Combined with Brutus's
repeated confession of his sleeplessness, these lines convey at once a
universal human truth, a personal psychological state, and an intensifying of the dramatic atmosphere as the suspense builds towards
the world-changing act of violence at the centre of the play. Brutus
also applies the commonplace Elizabethan image of the mind as a
state with a profound and devastating aptness as he sums up this
moment of combined psychological and political crisis: in the interim
between intention and action,

> The genius and the mortal instruments
> Are then in council, and the state of man,
> Like to a little kingdom, suffers then
> The nature of an insurrection. (2.1.66–9).

Just as Brutus's mind unfolds in all its complexity over the course of
this soliloquy, there is also an unfolding sense of Shakespeare's realisation of what soliloquy can do, and the many dramatic and literary

techniques that can be powerfully combined within it. The stage is set for *Hamlet*.[34]

'A noble mind': *Hamlet*

Critics vary in their tally of the total number of soliloquies in *Hamlet*, depending on how they define a soliloquy. All agree that a soliloquy is a speech given by a character while alone on stage, but some include in their count some shorter solo speeches that others disregard. The maximum count is twelve: eight spoken by Hamlet, one by Ophelia, one by Lucianus in the play-within-the-play, and two by Claudius.[35] Even those who arrive at a different total mostly agree that there are five important soliloquies by Hamlet: 'Oh, that this too, too sallied flesh would melt' (1.2.129–59); 'Oh, what a rogue and peasant slave am I!' (2.2.469–524); 'To be or not to be' (3.1.55–87); 'Now might I do it, but now 'a is a-praying' (3.3.73–96); and 'How all occasions do inform against me' (4.1.31–65).[36] Critics also concur that the other most significant soliloquy is Claudius's 'Oh, my offence is rank, it smells to heaven' (3.3.36–72), an archetypal revelation of the secret self and inner division as Claudius contemplates his guilt and strives to repent and pray. Whichever way we look at it, the sheer prominence and frequency of soliloquies in this play tell us that Shakespeare at this point in his career was preoccupied with exploring the potential of the device. He certainly demonstrates the wide range of moods, styles, and functions that soliloquy can encompass, even across Hamlet's speeches alone. Here, we find not only much self-castigation, self-division, and inner debate, but also, in 'To be or not to be', choral meditation; and even, in the short soliloquy ''Tis now the very witching time of night' (3.2.359–70), confession to the dark, cruel intents of a stereotypical villain.[37] 'Now could I drink hot blood,' declares Hamlet in this speech, sounding very like Lucianus, the murderer in the old-fashioned play he has just witnessed: 'Thoughts black, hands apt, drugs fit, and time agreeing' (3.2.361, 236).

The prevalence of soliloquies in the play places at its centre the mind in general, and Hamlet's mind in particular.[38] Indeed, his sense of inwardness is present not only in his soliloquies, but also in dialogue. At his first appearance he declares, in dialogue with his mother and in front of the whole court, 'I have that within which passes show' (1.2.85), creating expectations that the rest of the play goes on to fulfil. Later, Hamlet will again allude in dialogue to 'that within', when he accuses Rosencrantz and Guildenstern of trying to 'pluck out the heart of my mystery' (3.2.339). Other characters also notice his particular interiority and self-division: Claudius observes of Hamlet that 'nor th'exterior nor the inward man / Resembles that it was', and that something 'hath put him / So much from th'understanding of himself' (2.2.6–9). Speaking here to Rosencrantz and Guildenstern, Claudius purports merely to seek the cause of Hamlet's madness. Hamlet has informed us and Horatio that this 'antic disposition' is feigned (1.5.173), but Claudius seems like the feigner here, pretending a fatherly concern for his stepson while really suspecting and seeking to expose treasonous intent. Most social interactions in the play encourage us to seek hidden purposes and concealed thoughts, framing and cohering with the many moments of soliloquy.

Hamlet's first soliloquy, 'Oh, that this too, too sallied flesh would melt' (1.2.129–59), follows immediately upon the departure of the King and court with a 'Flourish [fanfare]', according to the stage direction. Hamlet is suddenly and starkly alone on stage, and fulfils our expectation that he will show us something of 'that within' to which he has just alluded (1.2.85). His flesh, in different early editions, is either too 'sallied' (assailed or sullied) or too 'solid';[39] either way, he expresses a Neoplatonic or Neostoic contempt for the body as he withdraws into the mind. He entertains suicidal thoughts, wishing that 'the Everlasting had not fixed / His canon 'gainst self-slaughter', and laments 'How weary, stale, flat, and unprofitable / Seem to me all the uses of this world', confirming his humoral disposition as melancholic.[40] As his speech proceeds, it makes even more use than Brutus's

soliloquy of enjambment, caesuras, and rhetorical questions, especially when Hamlet contemplates his mother's remarriage:

> And yet within a month –
> Let me not think on't – Frailty, thy name is woman –
> A little month, or e'er those shoes were old
> With which she followed my poor father's body,
> Like Niobe all tears, why, she –
> O God, a beast that wants discourse of reason
> Would have mourned longer – married with my uncle.

Different modern editions punctuate this passage in diverse ways,
but the effect is the same: techniques explored in Brutus's soliloquy
are taken further to make the lines of verse and the units of syntax
pull violently against each other. Recurrent parentheses, exclama-
tions, and self-interruptions produce broken phrases; sentences are
fractured and fragmentary, barely making sense. The effect is that of
a mind captured in the act of thinking.[41]

At the same time, this mind seems to be groping to express
thoughts that lie deeply buried, and that are too troubling to be fully
brought to light and articulated. The speech dramatises Hamlet as a
character with layers: an outer social persona, an inner mind, and then
yet more layers within that mind that are increasingly obscure, even to
the speaker himself. Having established this spiralling inwardness, it
ends by returning us to the outer world: 'But break, my heart, for I
must hold my tongue'. This reminds us that Hamlet's difficulty is not
only the private psychological problem of articulating his own
thoughts and feelings, but his public situation in a court where to
speak his mind would be treason. Withdrawal into the mind and solitary utterance of what lies there is not just a personal, temperamental
preference for Hamlet, but also a political necessity.[42]

In this first soliloquy Hamlet speaks to himself about himself:
'How weary [. . .] / Seem to *me* all the uses of this world'; 'Must
I remember?' (my emphases). He dwells obsessively on his personal

and political predicament as Prince of Denmark in his insistent use of possessive pronouns: 'my mother', 'my poor father's body', 'my uncle', 'My father's brother', 'my father'. His most famous soliloquy, 'To be or not to be' (3.1.55–87), is quite different. Although this is often thought of as the moment where Hamlet most fully performs his interiority and selfhood, in fact over the whole course of the speech there is not a single use of the pronouns 'I' or 'me'. Instead, Hamlet generalises about 'we' and 'us', speculating about what happens 'When *we* have shuffled off this mortal coil', and how this 'makes *us* rather bear those ills we have / Than fly to others that *we* know not of' (my emphases). Such discourse on the human condition continues the use of soliloquy for choral meditation that Shakespeare had developed in *Richard II* and *Julius Caesar*. Here, it contributes in general terms to the play's plot, mood, and themes, and to the characterisation of its protagonist, in that it powerfully conveys Hamlet's sense of the impossibility of action, but it makes no contribution to specific events. Indeed, this may be one reason for the popularity of 'To be' over the centuries: it captures the essence of the play in some thirty lines, but is readily detachable for separate performance or anthologisation. This detachability is manifest even in early editions of the play, where the soliloquy was mobile. In the Second Quarto of 1604 (Q2) and the Folio of 1623 (F), it appears in Act 3 Scene 1, where modern editions also usually place it. However, in the First Quarto of 1603 (Q1), it occurs earlier, in the equivalent of Act 2 Scene 2, and some modern productions have found that for dramatic purposes it works best in this position.[43]

Like many other Elizabethan examples of the literary or dramatic representation of inner debate, 'To be' is underpinned by the training in rhetoric that Shakespeare and others received at grammar school. As in educational exercises, there is an initial *quaestio* (a question or proposition), in this case: 'To be or not to be[?]'; that is, to seek death, or to continue to face the challenges of life. This is followed by debate *in utramque partem*, on both sides of the question, for and against.[44] As well as being familiar with this formal structure,

Elizabethan auditors or readers with a humanist education would also have recognised allusions during the speech to Aristotle's *On Interpretation* and Cicero's *Tusculan Disputations*.[45] This reflects another staple of Elizabethan schooling: commonplacing, or the collection and redeployment of eloquent passages from esteemed authorities. Hamlet, former student of the University of Wittenberg, and Shakespeare, former pupil of the King's New School in Stratford-upon-Avon, each flaunt their learning and intellect in this soliloquy.

Yet at the same time, 'To be' is accessible to those of us who do not have the benefit of a sixteenth-century humanist education. In part this is because of the universal relevance of its argument that neither life or death is an easy option; but another reason is its use of metaphors that operate on several levels. Shakespeare was already practised in the used of vivid imagery in soliloquy: Richard II's comparison of his thoughts to a world of diverse people; Brutus's representation of Caesar as a serpent. 'To be' now moves through a sequence of metaphors: the challenges of fortune are 'slings and arrows' and 'a sea of troubles'; death is a sleep, perhaps troubled by dreams; it is also 'The undiscovered country from whose bourn / No traveler returns'. Each of these images can be traced to ancient or Renaissance sources that were popular in commonplace books (collections of useful quotations on standard topics), so that on one level the speech is an exhibition of skill in gathering and using *sententiae*, or wise sayings.[46] Yet each of these images is also readily comprehensible and accessible without knowledge of these sources.[47] Present-day theorists of cognition assert that metaphor is an essential mental tool: that we habitually process our perceptions, form concepts, and articulate them, by identifying one thing with another.[48] It has been further proposed that Renaissance rhetorical theory has some overlaps with modern cognitive theory: that authors and users of rhetoric manuals understood this discipline not merely as a means of using language to persuade listeners or readers, but also as a means of organising the thoughts of a speaker or writer, and so translating a thought-process into words.[49] Certainly, in 'To be' Shakespeare uses metaphor, as well as other rhetorical techniques in which he was well versed, to create the effect of Hamlet actively working out a complex problem in his mind, and taking us through that working-out with him. It is a problem that has for him and for all of us both intellectual interest, as a knotty conundrum, and psychological interest, going to the heart of human anxieties, doubts, and fears. The speech gives pleasure because Hamlet demonstrates the enormity and profundity of what the human mind can contemplate, and invites us to participate with him in exercising and appreciating the power of the mind.[50]

But is 'To be or not to be' even a soliloquy? Hamlet is not alone on stage: before he enters, Polonius and Claudius plant Ophelia to meet him, and conceal themselves so that they can spy on the encounter (3.1.42–54). For this reason, it has been argued that 'To be' is a feigned soliloquy; that Hamlet is fully aware of his overhearers, and delivers the speech with the intention of continuing to deceive them about his state of mind.[51] It has been further argued that all Elizabethan soliloquies were understood as literally spoken aloud, not as representations of inner thoughts.[52] Yet, as we saw in Chapter 9, Elizabethan readers were familiar with self-addressed monologues in prose fiction which represented thoughts as spoken, and hovered ambiguously between audible speech and a convention for representing silent thought. It seems appropriate, then, to understand Elizabethan dramatic soliloquies as also possessing an ambiguous status between speech and thought, and as a technique familiar to and accepted by Shakespeare and his contemporaries for making inner thoughts accessible to readers or audiences.[53]

There is further indication that most Elizabethan stage soliloquies should be understood as representations of private thought in that their speakers habitually address them to themselves, rather than to their playhouse audience.[54] Unlike the Vices of medieval and early Tudor drama who directly addressed spectators, soliloquists like Richard II, Brutus, and Hamlet never acknowledge their existence, despite the fact that in the Elizabethan playhouses, with their performances by daylight and their apron stages surrounded by groundlings, audience members were highly visible both to the actors and to each other.[55] Hamlet reinforces the sense that the audience are invisible to him and do not impinge on his world when he prefaces the soliloquy 'Oh, what a rogue and peasant slave am I!' with the patently fictive declaration 'Now I am alone' (2.2.468). Yet there is sometimes a sense, as with Brutus, that he is trying to persuade the audience as much as himself of his view of things, and many actors in modern productions have found it highly effective to address at least parts of the soliloquies to their spectators. Hamlet is, after all, performing his thinking in front of them.[56] Just as his soliloquies hover ambiguously between speech and thought, so they also blur the lines between self-address and address to the audience.[57] Even if he does not acknowledge the audience, their mere presence draws them into intimacy with him, and gives them privileged access to the thoughts and feelings that he conceals from the other characters.[58] The theological model of soliloquy as prayerful dialogue with oneself before God has now become introspective dialogue with oneself before the audience.[59] Returning to 'To be or not to be', it may not much matter if Polonius, Claudius, and Ophelia are visible on stage while Hamlet delivers this speech. Just as he makes no recognition of the offstage audience, he shows no awareness of this onstage audience either. The speech is presented as entirely within the established genre of soliloquy as a representation of private thought.

Hamlet's soliloquies, whether expressing particular personal conflicts as in 'Oh, that this too, too sallied flesh would melt', or more philosophical and general as in 'To be or not to be', simulate a mind in process. They also form part of a consistent characterisation of Hamlet throughout the play as a thinker, in dialogue as well as monologue. His meditation 'What a piece of work is a man' (2.2.264–5) is delivered in conversation with Rosencrantz and Guildenstern. Other characters recognise him not only as a melancholic, but also as an intellectual: shortly after he wonders what would be 'nobler in the mind', Ophelia grieves for his 'noble mind' (though she believes it to be 'o'erthrown'; 3.1.56, 147). Thinking is his main character trait; when he looks within, what he finds is thinking. Yet, as many critics have recognised, we never feel that we fully know Hamlet's mind. This is partly because of its discontinuities: his state of mind, and the means used to represent it, differ from one soliloquy to the next; while within individual soliloquies his mind is represented as having disparate aspects that are in conflict with each other. It is also because of that initial idea, developed over the course of the play, that he has 'that within which passes show': hidden layers of his mind, spiralling inwards to ever more buried depths, but ultimately forming an indiscernible and incomprehensible 'mystery' that no one can 'pluck out'. This includes Hamlet himself: in his last soliloquy he confesses that

> I do not know
> Why yet I live to say this thing's to do,
> Sith I have cause and will and strength and means
> To do't. (4.1.42–5)

Shakespeare mobilises soliloquy, in combination with other dramatic techniques, to endow Hamlet with a mind that is in constant flux and tumult, opaque to others and unfathomable even to Hamlet himself. In this, he comes as close as any author in the history of literature to representing how it feels to have a mind.[60]

'The inward qualities of the mind': *Hamlet* and non-dramatic genres

We have traced the development of the soliloquy through dramatic innovations of the 1580s and 1590s, but it also drew upon various non-dramatic genres. In relation to *Hamlet*, the influence most discussed by modern scholars has been that of the *Essays* of Michel de Montaigne, published in French in revised and expanded editions from 1580 to 1595. The title in French was the first application to a literary form of the term *essai*, meaning a 'trying-out' or thought-experiment, which in itself suggests an affinity with Hamlet's speeches. Sir Francis Bacon emulated Montaigne by publishing a volume of *Essays* (which he too would later revise and expand) in 1597, while Sir William Cornwallis explicitly stated his admiration for Montaigne in his *Essays* of 1600 and 1601 (discussed in Chapter 2 above), which explored the 'inward qualities of the mind'.[61] The first English translation of Montaigne's *Essays* to be published, in 1603, was by John Florio, though there is evidence that others were in preparation and possibly circulating in manuscript.[62]

There is critical consensus that Shakespeare was influenced by Florio's Montaigne in his later works: *The Tempest* (1611), for instance, includes a speech by Gonzalo that closely resembles part of Montaigne's essay 'Of the Cannibals' (2.1.138–63).[63] It is unclear whether at the time he composed *Hamlet* he had access to Florio's translation, or another translation in manuscript, or was reading Montaigne in French.[64] Some scholars question whether Shakespeare knew Montaigne at all by this time,[65] yet many others feel that *Hamlet* has a discernibly Montaignian quality. The *Essays* model taking oneself as one's subject: Montaigne announces in a preface that 'it is myself I portray [...] myself am the groundwork of my book'. At the same time he implies that this is a private discourse with himself on which he is allowing the reader to eavesdrop, again offering a potential model for soliloquy: 'in contriving the same I have proposed unto myself no other than a familiar and private end; I have had no respect or consideration at all either to thy service, or to my glory'. This at once fends off the reader and invites us into a candid intimacy which is maintained throughout the essays as Montaigne shows us himself warts-and-all: 'My imperfections shall therein be read to the life, and my natural form discerned [...] I would most willingly have portrayed myself fully and naked'.[66] This is a textual performance of self-revelation and authenticity, fore-shadowing Hamlet's dramatic performance of these properties. The mind displayed by Montaigne in this performance also resembles Hamlet's: it is capricious, variable, and conflicted; constantly seeking the truth about itself, but constantly finding that truth elusive.[67] This combination of mental flux and interminable enquiry is evoked across the whole sequence of Montaigne's essays and through the whole play of *Hamlet*, but also locally, as each essay or soliloquy uses rhetorical techniques to explore propositions, work through problems, and represent the mind in action.[68]

Hamlet also sounds like Montaigne when he philosophises about the general human condition. Shakespeare could have learned this from Bacon, whose *Essays* covered topics that would have interested Hamlet: the 1597 volume opens with essays 'Of Study', 'Of Discourse', and 'Of Ceremonies and Respects'.[69] Yet Bacon's essays were less personal and more didactic than Montaigne's, directed towards advice on correct conduct in public service, and more aphoristic in style. Montaigne is more like Hamlet in his self-analysis and his digressiveness, suggesting a free flow of thought; and also in his stance as a sceptical, dissident commentator from the margins of society.[70] Cornwallis shares some of these qualities, so might look like an intermediary between Montaigne and Shakespeare, but he was probably writing his essays at the same time as Shakespeare's composition of *Hamlet*. Rather than Cornwallis being an influence on Shakespeare, it is more likely that the two authors simultaneously discovered in Montaigne a model for combining self-examination with general reflections, for looking inwards as a means of looking outwards.[71]

While the question of Montaigne's influence on *Hamlet* has received much attention, there are also clear influences from other non-dramatic sources. These include the monologues of *The Mirror for Magistrates*, which combine personal history and self-recrimination with general moral reflection,[72] and female complaint, with its techniques for representing interiority and the mind in process.[73] Passion literature, the genre we explored in Chapter 3, was another model for representing an inward gaze, mental turmoil, and self-reproaches. Hamlet could readily say with Southwell's St Peter, 'Launch forth my soul into a main of tears, / Full fraught with grief the traffic of thy mind'.[74] The self-castigating speaker of Nicholas Breton's 'The

337

Countess of Pembroke's Love' (1592) similarly foreshadows Hamlet when she contrasts 'outward shows' with 'inward thoughts', and asks:

> What life is this, that wretches here we lead?
> Caring and carking for our fleshly lives,
> Never well filled when we are too much fed,
> Where strange conceits for true contentment strive
> Tearing our hearts, and tiring out our minds.[75]

A further recent genre on which Shakespearean soliloquy draws is the sonnet sequence. Thomas Nashe recognised this genre as a kind of performance, with dramatic potential, when in 1591 he described *Astrophil and Stella* as a 'tragicomedy of love' performed on a 'paper stage'.[76] Elizabethan sonnets often simulate a speaking voice as they put thoughts into words, while at the same time seeming self-addressed more than addressed to the beloved or the reader.[77] Like Sidney's Astrophil, Hamlet could say that 'My life melts with too much thinking';[78] also like Astrophil, the more he tries to express his mind, the less he seems to know it. Most of Shakespeare's own sonnets were not published until 1609, so are post-Elizabethan and beyond the scope of this book, but some existed in manuscript by 1598, when Francis Meres wrote of Shakespeare's 'sugared Sonnets' as circulating 'among his private friends'.[79] A few appeared in print the next year in *The Passionate Pilgrim*, including a version of what would become, in 1609, Sonnet 138: 'When my love swears that she is made of truth, / I do believe her (though I know she lies)'. The speaker of this poem contemplates multiple layers of mutual self-concealment in his relationship with his mistress: 'vainly thinking that she thinks me young, / Although I know my years be past the best: / I, smiling, credit her false-speaking tongue'.[80] It shows Shakespeare understanding the potential of the sonnet form to explore levels of inwardness and to work through an argument and thought-process, skills that he was also developing in the soliloquy.

At the same time Shakespeare was undoubtedly familiar with the self-addressed monologues of prose fiction, a genre that he plundered extensively for narrative source material. As well as offering an established literary model of solitary contemplation of inner conflict, these monologues particularly exemplified the representation of thought as speech. From a dramatist's point of view, there was useful ambiguity as to whether characters were speaking aloud or were to be imagined as speaking only in their heads, silently, when they addressed themselves. Sometimes it is stated that they are speaking aloud: in the *Old Arcadia*, for example, in the scene in which Philoclea visits the marble altar in the glade (as discussed in Chapter 9 above), she speaks 'with a whispering voice to herself'.[81] In *Pandosto*, a passionate monologue by Bellaria, Pandosto's falsely accused wife, lamenting her misfortunes, breaks off because 'gasping sighs so stopped her breath that she could not utter any mo[re] words'.[82] Yet sometimes self-addressed monologues are presented as only an approximation of the words of the character: at one point in *Euphues*, the protagonist 'uttered these or the like speeches', while the first monologue in *Pandosto*, given by Franion, the King's cupbearer, closes: 'Franion having muttered out these or such like words'.[83] The self-addressed monologue may be not only a rough guide to words spoken long ago and far away, but also a rough guide to thoughts in the mind rather than words actually spoken. This makes them similar to Sidney's device in the *Arcadia* of the inner poem that is not actually written, spoken, or (in the case of 'What tongue can her perfection's tell') even exactly thought. It may make sense to think of these inner poems and self-addressed monologues of prose fiction as an accepted but artificial convention for representing in words thoughts that are not actually uttered or even fully formed into words.

The extensive use of this complex device in late Elizabethan prose fiction can help us to understand the ambiguities of contemporary dramatic soliloquy. Self-addressed speech gave both the reader of prose fiction and the audience member in the playhouse privileged access to the inner thoughts of characters. Perhaps when an

Elizabethan actor embarked on a soliloquy – as when Hamlet announces 'Now I am alone' – his audience understood that they should consider themselves just as invisible to him as was the readership of a book to its characters, and that his speech represented thoughts not actually spoken aloud. Yet the actual audibility, visibility, and physical presence of the actor made a difference; as also did the visibility of the audience, in the shared daylit space of the Elizabethan playhouse, to the actor. If he did not directly address them, then he was required consciously to perform his unconsciousness of them. Hence, self-addressed monologues in prose fiction and on stage do not work in quite the same way. Nevertheless, the conventions of prose fiction made an important contribution to the development of dramatic soliloquy as a device poised ambiguously and flexibly between words literally spoken and the artificial representation of silent thought.

1600: a moment of the mind

Many critics have acclaimed *Hamlet* as an epoch-making breakthrough in the representation of interiority and subjectivity.[84] By placing it alongside the various other Elizabethan genres that were dedicated to exploring and representing the mind, we can see that, extraordinary as it is, it did not spring out of nowhere. It is not merely that it built upon Shakespeare's previous dramatic and literary experiments, or on more general developments on the stage; it also emerged from a swelling tide of diverse literary works preoccupied with how to make thought representable and accessible. This literary tide was itself the product of a discourse of the mind, across works of medicine, philosophy, theology, and more, that had burgeoned and flourished over the course of the Elizabethan period.

In the closing years of the century and of Elizabeth I's long reign, this expanding and dynamically evolving discourse of the mind produced a remarkable cluster of works. *Hamlet*'s earliest performances followed hard upon Ben Jonson's humours comedies *Every*

Man in his Humour (1598) and *Every Man out of his Humour* (1599). London's print shops were turning out, in rapid succession: Sir John Davies's *Nosce teipsum* (1599); the English translation of André du Laurens's discourse on melancholy (1599); works on both sides of the controversy about John Darrel's exorcisms; Nicholas Breton's *Passions of the Spirit* (1599) and *Melancholic Humours* (1600); Sir William Cornwallis's *Essays* (1600 and 1601); *The Passion of a Discontented Mind* (1601); and Thomas Wright's *Passions of the Mind* (1601). These would soon be followed by John Davies of Hereford's *Mirum in modum* (1602) and Florio's translation of Montaigne (1603). These works belong to a period when many writers were acutely conscious of the waning of the century, the mortality of the ageing, childless Queen, and uncertainty about the future.[85] It seems that as Elizabethans looked back over the period coming to a close, and looked forward with some apprehension to the future, they also looked inwards. At this anxious turning point, public events created a climate of insecurity in which the private individual may well have felt powerless in relation to portentous yet unpredictable forces beyond their control. All the thinking about the mind of the last half-century came together in a cultural moment of intense focus upon what lies within.

This chapter has been dedicated to exploring where *Hamlet* came from. When we place it in context, we may conclude that Shakespeare, writing in 1600, could scarcely *not* have written a play about the mind. Some scholars have written of a 'Hamlet moment' or 'Montaignian moment' as the sixteenth century turned into the seventeenth: a moment characterised by self-consciousness and self-examination, a sceptical and satirical sensibility, analytical enquiry, and philosophical speculation.[86] While these characteristics of the period are certainly recognisable, an overview of its literary output suggests that we should properly call it a 'moment of the mind'.

Epilogue
The Elizabethan Mind and Us

The project of this book has been mainly to explore the difference between Elizabethan ideas about the mind and our own, and to demonstrate how we can read the literature of the period with more insight if we know about these differences. Yet, of course, there are also connections between Elizabethan minds and our own: *Hamlet*, for instance, was not only shaped by its own particular historical moment, but also influential upon representations of subjectivity and interiority over subsequent centuries, as it was reread and reperformed, and became a cultural icon. Elizabethan ideas about the mind are at once remote from us and linked to us through the enduring popularity of works of literature and art from the period. Before closing, then, we should consider aspects of the Elizabethan understanding of the mind that have been perpetuated or revived.

As we have seen, Sir John Davies wrote in *Nosce teipsum* (1599) that the mind struggles to know itself: 'of herself she can no judgement give, / Nor how, nor whence, nor where, nor what, she is'.[1] Today, neuroscientists and philosophers continue to investigate the mind's complex relations with the body, including the brain; its relations with the more abstract concepts of self and consciousness; and the relations between thoughts and words.[2] Aristotle distinguished between the sensitive soul, shared by humans and animals, and the intellective soul, possessed by humans alone; similarly, many scholars today understand humans as distinguished from animals by higher faculties of language, reasoning, and self-contemplation, but the nature and operation of those faculties remain in many ways mysterious.[3] Of course, we now know far more than the Elizabethans about the intricate structures of the brain and how they relate to different sensory and motor functions; we know, for instance, that it contains about 86 billion nerve cells, or neurons, which pass on electrical signals across trillions of tiny spaces called synapses.[4] Even so, many questions about the relations between brain and mind remain unresolved.

Over the centuries between the Elizabethans and us, philosophers have debated 'the mind–body problem', tending to fall into two camps. Dualists regard the mind as separate from the body and the physical world, not reducible to organic processes; whereas materialists see the mind as integrated with the body and its physical surroundings, and seek physiological explanations for all the metaphysical properties we associate with the mind.[5] Recently, materialists have been in the ascendant, largely because of advances in the understanding of brain physiology which have offered neurological answers to some questions about the mind. It has been established for some time that the brain has three sections – the cerebrum (the largest part of the brain), below this the cerebellum, and below this again the brainstem – each with different functions. The cerebrum has left and right hemispheres, each of which controls the opposite side of the body. Each hemisphere in turn is divided into four lobes, frontal, parietal, temporal, and occipital, again each with distinct functions (fig. 23).[6] This principle of structural organisation of the brain, in which different parts do different things, is known as 'localisation'.[7] Within the areas already mentioned are yet more, smaller and more complex structures, which interact in intricate networks of communication across the brain to process sensory perceptions, solve problems, make and retrieve memories, and so on. Since the 1980s,

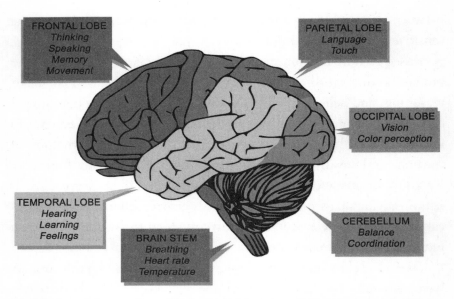

23. Modern understanding of the brain divides it into different areas with different functions. Our knowledge of the structure and operation of the brain is far more complex and sophisticated than that of the Elizabethans, but the basic principle of 'localisation' is the same.

our understanding of these structures and interconnections of the brain has been vastly increased by the development of brain-imaging techniques such as positron emission tomography (PET) and functional magnetic brain imaging (fMRI). Scientists can now undertake experiments to map the activation of different brain areas when people are subjected to particular experiences or sensory stimulations, or required to do particular tasks.[8] From this methodology a new discipline – cognitive neuroscience – has been born. It has illuminated some of the mysteries of the mind and led some brain scientists to envisage an entirely material explanation for all brain functions, including consciousness and sense of self.[9]

The Elizabethan model of the mind, with imagination at the front, understanding in the middle, and memory at the back, was far too simple (see Chapter 7 above, and fig. 16). However, the basic principle of localisation – different functions for different brain areas

– was correct. Indeed, one way in which modern scientists divide up the brain has a similar layout to the Elizabethan structure, consisting of the forebrain, midbrain, and hindbrain.[10] At the very front is one of the most powerful parts of the brain, the prefrontal cortex, which resembles the Elizabethan imagination as the receptor of sense-impressions and the seat of creative intelligence.[11] It even more closely resembles, in the accounts of modern brain scientists, the faculty that Elizabethans situated at the centre of the brain: under-standing or reason. The prefrontal cortex evaluates information, takes decisions, makes forward plans, solves problems, and manages emotions;[12] and it is far larger in humans than other animals, suggesting that it is the outcome of evolutionary enhancements and the seat of higher human faculties.[13] Modern authors describe it in terms that echo the hierarchical Elizabethan conception of reason as ruler of the mind (see Chapter 8 above). It is 'the seat of the higher functions of the brain'; it 'stands in a unique position at the top of the hierarchy of processing'; and it 'manages rational thought and logical decision-making, sending "top-down" instructions to your more primitive deep-brain centres'. In short, it is 'the CEO of the brain'.[14]

Just as the Elizabethans understood dreams as a usurpation of the powers of reason by fantasy, so too the present-day sleep scientist Matthew Walker explains that the authority of the prefrontal cortex is 'temporarily ousted each time you enter into the dreaming state of REM sleep'.[15] It is possible to draw some parallels between the early modern imagination – an unruly rebel against the government of reason – and the Freudian concept of the unconscious, which creates dreams and images that disrupt the attempts of the superego to repress and control it.[16] Neuroscientists are sceptical about many of Freud's hypotheses, but they agree that the mind is never inactive, even when apparently at rest; indeed, that some parts of the brain, such as those associated with emotions, are even more active when sensory contact with the outside world is removed.[17] Neuroscientists and psychoanalysts alike in some ways unconsciously echo *The French Academy* (1594) in its description of the irrational part of the mind:

this faculty of the fantasy is sudden, and so far from staidness, that even in the time of sleep it hardly taketh any rest, but is always occupied in dreaming and doting, yea even about those things which never have been, shall be, or can be. For it stayeth not in that which is showed unto it by the senses that serve it, but taketh what pleaseth it, and addeth thereunto or diminisheth, changeth and rechangeth, mingleth and unmingleth, so that it cutteth asunder and seweth up again as it listeth.[18]

Walker rejects Freud's dream theories as 'nonscientific' and 'unsystematic', but asserts that 'Through a combination of brain activity measures and rigorous experimental testing, we have finally begun to develop a scientific understanding of human dreams'.[19] The physiological discoveries of neuroscience have encouraged materialist frameworks for understanding the mind, generating a body of theory known as '4E cognition'. This argues that cognition – that is, mental processing or thought – is not 'brainbound', but involves interrelationships between mind, body, and world.[20] '4E' is an acronym for four aspects of cognition, defined as *embodied, embedded, extended,* and *enactive.*[21] *Embodied* cognition depends either directly or indirectly 'on dynamic interactions between the sensorimotor brain and relevant parts of the body: sense organs, limbs, sensory and motor nerves, and the like'.[22] Being *embedded* means being shaped and influenced by the surrounding material or social environment; being *extended* means exercising agency by means of objects and processes beyond the body; and being *enactive* entails engaging and interacting with the environment outside the body.[23]

Literary critics have applied these theories in their own discipline while also exploring how literature might contribute to 4E frameworks for understanding cognition.[24] 'Cognitive historicism' places a literary work in the context of the understanding of the mind that pertained in its period while placing this in dialogue with modern cognitive theories. Specialists in early modern literature have found particular resonances between their period of study and this modern theoretical framework, for reasons identified by Mary Thomas Crane in *Shakespeare's Brain* (2001): 'the cognitive concept of an embodied mind seems closer to early modern humoral physiology than the radically dualistic post-Cartesian paradigm' – that is, the separation of mind and body often attributed to Descartes in the seventeenth century (as discussed in Chapter 1 above).[25] In fact, as we have seen, Elizabethan thought was not wholly committed to the embodiment of the mind: the Aristotelian embodied soul and the organic mind of humoral medicine coexisted with intellectual frameworks that divided mind and body (see Chapter 2 above). Nevertheless, placing modern theories of 4E cognition in contact with those aspects of early modern thought that did integrate mind, body, and world has produced insightful readings of literary works by Crane and others.[26]

This approach has been accompanied by increased academic interest in the emotions. As *The Oxford Handbook of 4E Cognition* explains:

> The concept of emotion, or more generally, affect, has come to play a larger role in mainstream analyses of cognition over the past 20 years. Cognition is not the narrow, hard, cold process of ratiocinative intellect that seems to fit so well with the computational model. Affect requires a more embodied and situated conception of cognition, and we need to recognise that it permeates cognitive processes, rather than occasionally penetrating them.[27]

'Affect' is defined by the *Oxford English Dictionary* as 'A feeling or subjective experience accompanying a thought or action or occurring in response to a stimulus; an emotion, a mood'.[28] A recent 'affective turn' across a range of disciplines has included a strong historical dimension: several universities now have Centres for the History of Emotions[29] and a multivolume *Cultural History of the Emotions* has been published,[30] while numerous works have appeared specifically on the early modern emotions or passions.[31] The sixteenth-century fascination with the passions and affections seems to have been revived when the editors of *The Oxford Handbook of 4E Cognition* write: 'My anger makes me see things in specific ways; my joy leads me to ignore some of the negative factors in my environment; my fear moves me to act one way rather than another; my dark funk makes this rather than that matter.'[32] This chimes with Thomas Wright's observation in *The Passions of the Mind* (1601) that

> the passions not unfitly may be compared to green spectacles, which make all things resemble the colour of green: even so, he that loveth, hateth, or by any other passion is vehemently possessed, judgeth all things that occur in favour of that passion to be good and agreeable with reason.[33]

Meanwhile, just as the growth of the Elizabethan print trade made books on the mind available to a widening readership, so today there is a flourishing market in books that help us to understand our own minds, across a range of genres. Neurologists and neuroscientists like Suzanne O'Sullivan, Anil Seth, and Matthew Walker have illuminatingly explained their research to a general readership. Self-help books communicate the insights of psychology or promote 'mindfulness'. In the popular understanding of physiology, we have a sense of hormones as substances that mediate between body and mind not unlike Elizabethan humours, with fluctuating levels which affect our mood and behaviour.[34] We are also increasingly understanding that our gut health – our microbiome – affects our mental health, a distant echo of the Elizabethan concept of 'windy melancholy'.[35] Across other fields, too, at more of a distance from academic research, thinking about the mind in our wider culture includes some Elizabethan echoes. Like the four humoral categories, we still find it useful to classify ourselves as different personality-types, as in the Myers-Briggs and Tetramap systems for professional profiling and training: the latter even asks, 'Are you Earth, Air, Water or Fire?'[36] We are still fascinated and mystified by our dreams, with dream-symbol dictionaries continuing to be published,[37] while astrology too continues to flourish as a guide to personality and a predictive tool.

Surveying this cultural landscape, it seems that our frameworks for understanding the mind are no less eclectic and jumbled than those of the Elizabethans. Yet obviously those grounded in serious scientific disciplines seem most likely to solve the mind's mysteries. Seth in his illuminating book on consciousness, *Being You*, describes how neuroscience has made huge advances in 'the attempt to understand how the inner universe of subjective experience relates to, and can be explained in terms of, biological and physical processes unfolding in brains and bodies'. At the same time, he is clear that this endeavour has only 'reached a point at which glimmerings of answers are beginning to emerge', and that the 'mysteries' of consciousness will not 'suddenly yield to a single eureka-like insight'.[38] Many territories of the mind remain shadowy and uncharted, as evidenced by the vast number of academics currently engaged in researching them. In my own university alone – University College London – the research domain of Neuroscience has over 450 senior investigators, most with their own research teams.[39] UCL's Faculty of Brain Sciences encompasses numerous research fields, including not only cognitive neuroscience and neurology but also psychiatry, psychology, language sciences, audiology, ophthalmology, prion diseases, dementia research, and mental health,[40] while the Department of Philosophy investigates the mind using its own disciplinary methods. Richard Passingham, another eminent neuroscientist, writes: 'Now that we know so much about *where* there is activity in the brain while people perform cognitive tasks, the next stage is to find out *how* that activity makes cognition possible.'[41] Beyond that again lies the daunting question *why*. Meanwhile, different theories of consciousness have been advanced – Seth, for instance, proposes that it is a 'controlled hallucination'[42] – but are the subject of ongoing enquiry and debate. We are not yet able to say precisely what we mean by a 'thought'.[43] It can seem that the more we discover about the brain and the mind, the more we realise how much there is still to explain.[44]

Obviously understanding of the mind has changed through history. Yet some Elizabethan ideas about the mind are ancestors of our own, while there are others that we have circled back towards after centuries of divergence. Literature and drama are particular fields where Elizabethan innovations in representing the mind and its workings have had a vast legacy in subsequent centuries. Moreover, some behaviours of the mind, and some of the experiences of having a mind, have remained much the same over time. Many of the questions that the Elizabethans asked about the mind remain pertinent today, such as: how does the mind relate to the body? How can you look into your own mind, and what do you find there? How do we translate thoughts into words? Some of the answers they came up with resemble or overlap with our own, while others are very different; hence, comparing and contrasting Elizabethan ideas about the mind with the state of knowledge now can help to throw our own assumptions and attitudes into relief. This book has aimed to show that investigating Elizabethan concepts of the mind is not only a fascinating endeavour, but essential to a full and deep understanding of the works of Shakespeare and his contemporaries. It can return us to those works with fresh insights – and at the same time it can return us with new energy to the ongoing task of understanding our minds and ourselves.

ENDNOTES

Introduction

1. Du Laurens, 'Second Discourse', 82. Further references are given parenthetically.
2. Howard, *Defensative*, K3v.
3. Barnard, Introduction; Kastan, 'Print, Literary Culture'.
4. Barnard and Bell, 'Appendix 1', 781–2.
5. Pettegree, *Book in the Renaissance*, 77–82, 124–6, 259–60.
6. Charlton and Spufford, 'Literacy, Society'.
7. Slack, 'Mirrors of Health', 238–40.
8. Febvre and Martin, *Coming of the Book*, 276–7; Slack, 'Mirrors of Health', 240, 247, 256; Taavitsainen, 'Discourse and Genre Dynamics', 34–5.
9. Taavitsainen, 'Discourse and Genre Dynamics', 44; Taavitsainen et al., 'Medical Texts in 1500–1700', 10, 12–13.
10. Binns, *Intellectual Culture*, 1–3; Febvre and Martin, *Coming of the Book*, 329–31.
11. Jones, 'Medical Literacies', 37.
12. Febvre and Martin, *Coming of the Book*, 271–2, 319–32; Pahta and Taavitsainen, 'Introducing', 5; Taavitsainen, 'Discourse and Genre Dynamics', 44; Wear, *Knowledge and Practice*, 4–5, 40.
13. Bynum, *History of Medicine*, 5–23.
14. Febvre and Martin, *Coming of the Book*, 278; Lehto, Oinonen, and Pahta, 'Explorations', 152; Mikkeli and Marttila, 'Change and Continuity', 14.
15. David J. Murray, *History*, 61; Park and Kessler, 'Concept of Psychology'; Schmitt, 'Towards a Reassessment'.
16. Slack, 'Mirrors of Health', 248–50.
17. *Batman uppon Bartholome* is based on a translation by John of Trevisa of a thirteenth-century work by Bartholomaeus Anglicus, with additions by Stephen Batman (Newbold, 'General Introduction', 18). Batman's first name is sometimes given in sixteenth-century editions of his works as Stephan. His second name is sometimes given as Bateman.
18. Rodger, 'Roger Ward's Shrewsbury Stock'.
19. Milward, 'Wright, Thomas'.
20. Carew, *Examination*, 7.

21. Sir John Davies was not yet knighted when he published *Nosce teipsum* (Kelsey, 'Davies, Sir John'), but I refer to him in this form throughout to distinguish him from John Davies of Hereford, whom I refer to as 'Davies of Hereford'.
22. Duffy, *Stripping of the Altars*; Greenblatt, *Hamlet in Purgatory*; Mullaney, *Reformation of Emotions*.
23. Richard Rogers and Ward, *Two Elizabethan Puritan Diaries*, 68; Ryrie, *Being Protestant*, 99–256.
24. Barker, *Tremulous Private Body*; Belsey, *Subject of Tragedy*. For a corrective response, see Maus, *Inwardness and Theater*.
25. Prickett, *Secret Selves*.
26. Spenser, *Amoretti*, Sonnet 45, *Shorter Poems*, 410.
27. Sir John Davies, *Poems*, 11.
28. Descartes, *Discourse on Method*, IV.32–3, pp. 28–9; David Hillman, *Shakespeare's Entrails*, 54–7; Laurie Johnson, Sutton, and Tribble, Introduction, 1–2; Paster, *Humoring the Body*; Schoenfeldt, *Bodies and Selves*, 11.
29. Miranda Anderson, *Renaissance Extended Mind*; Craik and Pollard, *Shakespearean Sensations*; Crane, *Shakespeare's Brain*; Floyd-Wilson and Garrett A. Sullivan, Jr., *Environment and Embodiment*; Laurie Johnson, Sutton, and Tribble, *Embodied Cognition*; Lyne, *Shakespeare, Rhetoric and Cognition*; Tribble, *Cognition in the Globe*.
30. Mack, *Elizabethan Rhetoric*; Vickers, *In Defence*, 254–93.
31. Sherry, *Treatise of Schemes*, B2r.
32. Lehto, Oinonen, and Pahta, 'Explorations', 152; Wootton, *Invention of Science*, locs 266, 382, 1082, 1100, 1127.
33. Donne, 'First Anniversarie', pp. 27–8, ll. 205–8.
34. Wootton, *Invention of Science*, locs 194, 506, 1196, 2972.
35. Babb, *Elizabethan Malady*, 68–9; Crane, *Losing Touch*; Johns, 'Science and the Book'; Mikkeli and Marttila, 'Change and Continuity'; Pahta and Taavitsainen, 'Interdisciplinary Approach', 3–5; 'Introducing', 3–4.
36. *OED*, 'mind, n.1', 6.a, 15, 19.a(a), 21.a.
37. Seth, *Being You*, loc. 226.
38. *OED*, 'subjective, adj. and n.', A.3.
39. Churchyard, *Challenge*, 45–57.
40. Cicero, 'Scipio Hys Dream', F6r.
41. Churchyard, *Challenge*, 46.

Chapter 1: The Mind in the Body: Medical Frameworks

1. La Primaudaye, *French Academie*, 90–1.
2. Carew, *Examination*, 100–1.
3. Aristotle, *De anima*, II.1.24, II.4.29.
4. Ibid., II.2.25, II.3.27, III.9.65, III.10.67–9, III.11.70; Park, 'Organic Soul'; Robinson, *Intellectual History*, 43–60.
5. Ruth Leila Anderson, *Elizabethan Psychology*, 7; Babb, *Elizabethan Malady*, 8–9; James, *Passion and Action*, 37.
6. Elyot, *Castell*, 16. See also Bynum, *History of Medicine*, 15–16; Carrera, 'Anger', 112–13; Gowland, 'Medicine, Psychology', 197.
7. Lemnius, *Touchstone*, 8r.
8. Bright, *Treatise of Melancholie*, 62–3.
9. *OED*, 'subtle, adj. and n.', A. adj., I.3, I.6.a, II.8.a.
10. Donne, 'The Exstasie', *Elegies and Songs and Sonnets*, pp. 59–61, ll. 61–4.
11. Helms, 'To Knit the Knot'.
12. Bynum, *History of Medicine*, 5–18.
13. Elyot, *Castell*, 3–14.
14. Taavitsainen, 'Dissemination and Appropriation', 99.

15. Du Laurens, 'Second Discourse', 85, 82. See also Batman, *Batman uppon Bartholome*, Bk 4, Ch. 6, f. 29r; Carew, *Examination*, 97, 100; Chapman, *Humorous Day's Mirth*, 8–13, 16; Babb, *Elizabethan Malady*, 6, 9–11, 16–17; Hankins, *Backgrounds*, 81, 119–45.
16. Lemnius, *Touchstone*, 70r, 114v.
17. La Primaudaye, *French Academie*, 90–1.
18. Gowland, 'Medicine, Psychology', 191–2; Paster, *Humoring the Body*, 45, 49, 52, 59–60; Schoenfeldt, *Bodies and Selves*, 20, 22.
19. Carew, *Examination*, 83.
20. Ibid., 209.
21. Chapman, *Humorous Day's Mirth*, 8.208–52.
22. Jonson, *Every Man in his Humour*, 3.1.139–42.
23. Chapman, *Humorous Day's Mirth*, 2.57–63.
24. Madeleine Doran, *Endeavors*, 229–32; Wiggins, *Shakespeare and the Drama of his Time*, 70.
25. Jonson, *Case Is Altered*, 5.1.58–9.
26. Shakespeare, *Second Part of Henrie the Fourth*, title-page.
27. Dawson and Langley, 'Affective Inheritances', 150.
28. Chapman, *Blinde Begger*, A3v, ll. 114–31, B2v, l. 328. Further references are given parenthetically.
29. Jonson, *Every Man out of his Humour*, Induction, ll. 94–120.
30. Gowland, 'Problem of Early Modern Melancholy', 77–8.
31. Bright, *Treatise of Melancholie*, 1.
32. Lemnius, *Touchstone*, 151r–152r.
33. Bright, *Treatise of Melancholie*, 101.
34. Veins of the mesentery, 'a pellicle or a skin the which doth tie the guts together' (Boorde, *Breviarie*, Bk 2, B6r).
35. Bright, *Treatise of Melancholie*, 101.
36. Du Laurens, 'Second Discourse', 96–7. See also Babb, *Elizabethan Malady*, 21–72; Erin Sullivan, *Beyond Melancholy*, 25–30.
37. Chapman, *Humorous Day's Mirth*, 10.36–53.
38. Jonson, *Every Man in his Humour*, 2.3.65–8.
39. Du Laurens, 'Second Discourse', 86.
40. Aristotle, *Problems*, in Radden, *Nature of Melancholy*, 57, 58.
41. Ficino, *Three Books on Life*, 1.4.113–15, 1.5.117, 1.6.121. See also Babb, *Elizabethan Malady*, 58–67, 175, 181–4; Brann, *Debate*; Chapman, *Humorous Day's Mirth*, 23–4; Gowland, 'Melancholy, Passions', 88–9; Gowland, *Worlds*, 89–90; Klibansky, Panofsky, and Saxl, *Saturn and Melancholy*, 241–74; Erin Sullivan, *Beyond Melancholy*, 29–30, 93–4.
42. Ficino, *Three Books*, 1.5.117–18.
43. Babb, *Elizabethan Malady*, 24–6.
44. Thomas Rogers, *Anatomie*, 51v–52r.
45. Bright, *Treatise of Melancholie*, 130–1.
46. Erin Sullivan, *Beyond Melancholy*, 89.
47. Bright, *Treatise of Melancholie*, 129.
48. Lyly, *Midas*, 5.2.107–11.
49. Sidney, *Old Arcadia*, 64; Sidney, *New Arcadia*, 419. For more on the relation between the two versions of the *Arcadia*, see Ch. 9 below.
50. Goldring, *Nicholas Hilliard*, 229–32; Macleod, *Elizabethan Treasures*, 168–9, 172–3; Strong, *Elizabethan Image*, 105–6, 147–51.
51. For more melancholic portraits, see Strong, *Elizabethan Image*, 134–55.
52. Lemnius, *Touchstone*, 135v.
53. Paynell, *Regimen*, 132v; Bynum, *History of Medicine*, 23.
54. Babb, *Elizabethan Malady*, 6; Erin Sullivan, *Beyond Melancholy*, 93, 98–9, 104, 106, 111–13.
55. Bright, *Treatise of Melancholie*, 102–3, 180.

56. Du Laurens, 'Second Discourse', 88–9, 125; Babb, *Elizabethan Malady*, 26–8; *OED*, 'hypochondria, n.', 1.a. & b.
57. Du Laurens, 'Second Discourse', 129, 140.
58. Shapiro, *1599*, 245–6; Erin Sullivan, *Beyond Melancholy*, 112–20.
59. For the history of theories of the passions before the Elizabethan period, see Dixon, *From Passions to Emotions*, 26–61; James, *Passion and Action*, 29–64; Tilmouth, *Passion's Triumph*, 15–30.
60. La Primaudaye, *Second Part*, 247.
61. Elyot, *Castell*, 95–6.
62. Bullein, *Governement*, 54r–v.
63. Thomas Rogers, *Anatomie*, 3r–v.
64. Thomas Wright, *Passions*, 41. I use the 1601 edition, not the revised edition of 1604. Further references are given parenthetically. For more on taxonomies of the passions by Aristotle, Cicero, Augustine, and Aquinas, see Dixon, *From Passions to Emotions*, 40, 43, 44; James, *Passion and Action*, 4–7, 57–60; Newbold, General Introduction, 38–9; Paster, Rowe, and Floyd-Wilson, Introduction, 2.
65. Carrera, 'Anger', 99, 108–9, 143–4; Paster, *Humoring*, 45.
66. Thomas Wright, *Passions*, 13–14. Further references are given parenthetically.
67. Descartes, *Discourse on Method*, IV.32–3, pp. 28–9.
68. Paster, *Humoring*, esp. 5, 10, 12, 19, 26, 42; Paster, Rowe, and Floyd-Wilson, *Reading the Early Modern Passions*, esp. Introduction, 16.
69. Helms, 'To Knit the Knot'; Laurie Johnson, Sutton, and Tribble, *Embodied Cognition*; Kambaskovic, Introduction, 1–2; Ovens, 'Alchemy'; Tribble, *Cognition in the Globe*; Wolfe and van Esveld, 'Material Soul', esp. 374–9.
70. Craik and Pollard, *Shakespearean Sensations*; Hobgood, *Passionate Playgoing*; Ros King, 'Plays, Playing, and Make-Believe'.
71. Moulton, *Mirrour*, G1v.
72. On the popularity of Moulton's *Mirror* and Elyot's *Castell*, see Slack, 'Mirrors of Health', 237, 247–8.
73. Elyot, *Castell*, 95.
74. Ibid., 102–3.
75. E.g., Du Laurens, 'Second Discourse', 106–13; Lemnius, *Touchstone*, 51v.
76. Schoenfeldt, *Bodies and Selves*, esp. 1, 11, 22.
77. Elyot, *Castell*, 96–8.
78. Thomas Lodge, *Treatise of the Plague*, E3r; Slack, 'Mirrors of Health', 268–70.
79. Slack, 'Mirrors of Health', 268–70.
80. Montaigne, 'An Apologie of Raymond Sebond', in *Essayes*, Bk 2, Ch. 12, p. 328.
81. *ESTC*.
82. Boorde, *Compendyous Regyment*, B3v.
83. *Arden of Faversham*, 8.3–4.
84. David Hillman, *Shakespeare's Entrails*, esp. 4–11, 47, 52–3; Laurence Johnson, '"Nobler in the Mind"'; Laurie Johnson, 'Quaint Knowledge'; Laqué, 'Not Passion's Slave'.
85. Gowland, 'Medicine, Psychology', 197–208; Gowland, 'Melancholy, Passions', 83–4, 90; Meek and Erin Sullivan, *Renaissance of Emotion*; Erin Sullivan, *Beyond Melancholy*; Erin Sullivan, 'Passions of Thomas Wright'; Taylor, *Sources of the Self*, 111–42; Trevor, 'Sadness'. For a survey of recent debates and developments, see Dawson and Langley, 'Affective Inheritances'.
86. Elyot, *Castell*, 102, 99.
87. 'Originally: a solid medicinal or emollient substance spread on a bandage or dressing and applied to the skin' (*OED*, 'plaster, n.', 1.a.).
88. Bullein, *Governement*, 52v–53r.
89. Soellner, *Shakespeare's Patterns*, 15.
90. Bright, *Treatise of Melancholie*, *iii.r, 62.
91. Du Laurens, 'Second Discourse', 83–4.

Chapter 2: Mind against Body: Philosophical and Religious Frameworks

1. Sidney's *Arcadia* exists in two versions. The *Old Arcadia* was composed between around 1577 and 1580, and circulated only in manuscript. The revised and expanded *New Arcadia* was written around 1585 and first published in 1590. For more details, see Ch. 9 below.
2. Sidney, *New Arcadia*, 551–4.
3. Thomas Rogers, *Anatomie*, 'The Preface to the Friendly Reader'.
4. Whythorne, *Autobiography*, mod., 46, 82.
5. Sidney, *Astrophil*, Sonnets 23 and 27.
6. Goldring, *Nicholas Hilliard*, 163–4.
7. Cornwallis, *Essayes*, Hh2v– Hh3r.
8. Grymeston, *Miscelanea*, A3v. This work was compiled at some time between 1601 and 1604 (Levin, Bertolet, and Carney, *Biographical Encyclopedia*, 576).
9. Sidney, *Defence*, 30; Spenser, *Shorter Poems*, 410.
10. Published in several Elizabethan editions; Wiggins with Catherine Richardson, *British Drama*, 1.278, pp. 297, 299.
11. Axton, *Three Tudor Classical Interludes*, p. 78, ll. 518–19; p. 80, ll. 604–5.
12. Spenser, *Faerie Queene*, II.xii.47; Starnes, 'Figure Genius'; Ulreich, 'Genius'.
13. Sir John Davies, *Poems*, 11. For more on Sir John's *Nosce teipsum*, see Ossa-Richardson, 'Known Unknowns'; Swann, '*Nosce Teipsum*'; and Ch. 8 below.
14. Soellner, *Shakespeare's Patterns*, esp. xiii–xiv, 3–40, 405 n. 4.
15. Langley, *Narcissism and Suicide*.
16. Puttenham, *Art of English Poesy*, ed. Alexander, 169.
17. Foster, 'Against the Perjured Falsehood', 100.
18. Raymond Martin and Barresi, *Rise and Fall of Soul and Self*, 126; Erin Sullivan, 'Passions of Thomas Wright', 39.
19. Thomas Thomas, *Dictionarium*, Nn3r.
20. Davies of Hereford, *Mirum in modum*, A4r.
21. 'Know thyself', Speake, *Oxford Dictionary of Proverbs*; Plato, *Alcibiades I*, 128E–133C.
22. Bostock, *Plato*.
23. Plato, *Republic*, Ch. 6; Ch. 12, 588b–589b.
24. Raymond Martin and Barresi, *Rise and Fall of Soul and Self*, 13–21; Osmond, *Imagining the Soul*, 15–25; Sorabji, 'Soul and Self', 10–11, 12–14, 20; Taylor, *Sources of the Self*, 115–26.
25. Aristotle, *De anima*, II.2.25, II.3.27, III.9.65, III.10.67–9, III.11.70.
26. Ibid., III.4.59, p. xxxix.
27. Ibid., II.1.24, III.4.59.
28. Ibid., III.5.61. See also commentary on this passage in ibid., pp. 312–14; and Raymond Martin and Barresi, *Rise and Fall of Soul and Self*, 21–4; Osmond, *Imagining the Soul*, 25–9; Sorabji, 'Soul and Self', 8–10, 20.
29. Full name Lucius Annaeus Seneca, known as Seneca the Younger.
30. Monsarrat, *Light from the Porch*, 9–10, 25–40.
31. Ibid., 10–16.
32. Seneca, 'De tranquillitate animi', 234–5, 250–1, 266–7. See also Sorabji, *Self*, 195–6.
33. Sorabji, *Self*, 194–5.
34. Epictetus, *Discourses*, I.1.23; Sorabji, *Self*, 44, 181; Sorabji, 'Soul and Self', 17–18. For more on the classical background to Renaissance ideas of an inner self, see Gowland, 'Medicine, Psychology', 198–9; Taylor, *Sources of the Self*, 111–14.
35. *Geneva Bible*, Romans 7.22–5. See also 2 Corinthians 4.16, Galatians 5.16–17, and Ephesians 3.16.
36. Dixon, *From Passions to Emotions*, 26–61; Raymond Martin and Barresi, *Rise and Fall of Soul and Self*, 69–74; Osmond, *Imagining Soul*, 41–3; Taylor, *Sources of the Self*, 127–42.
37. Raymond Martin and Barresi, *Rise and Fall of Soul and Self*, 77–8.

38. Brljak, Introduction, 3–12.
39. On the continuance of allegory beyond the Middle Ages, see Brljak, 'Age of Allegory'.
40. Bevington, *From 'Mankind' to Marlowe*, 152–61.
41. *Triall of Treasure*, A2r, C1r. Further references are given parenthetically.
42. For more on 'contentation' or 'contentment' as terms for the apprehension of salvation by the elect, see Brian Cummings, *Mortal Thoughts*, 188–9, and Ch. 3 below.
43. Thomas Rogers, *Anatomie*, 12r–13v, 102r–103r.
44. Self-exertion or spiritual discipline; *OED*, 'exercitation, n.', 1, 3.b.
45. Thomas Rogers, *Anatomie*, 2r. See also Tilmouth, *Passions Triumph*, esp. 30–3.
46. Thomas Rogers, *Anatomie*, 31v–32v.
47. Goodrich, *Faithful Translators*, 10–11.
48. Voragine, *Golden Legend*, I.28.
49. Hackett, *Women and Romance*, 31–2, 73–4, 120, 122–9, 167–71.
50. Foxe, *Book of Martyrs*, xii–xiii, xix–xxi.
51. Hoby, *Private Life*, 22, 70.
52. Foxe, *Book of Martyrs*, xxvii; Knott, *Discourses of Martyrdom*, 40–1, 48.
53. Foxe, *Book of Martyrs*, 136–7.
54. On questions of sincerity and authentic selfhood in Foxe's narratives, their use of visual images, and their relation to medieval saints' lives, see Brian Cummings, *Mortal Thoughts*, 92–132.
55. Foxe, *Acts and Monuments*, 8.668.
56. On John Bale and Foxe as editors of Askew's narrative, see Wall, 'Editing Anne Askew's *Examinations*'.
57. Foxe, *Book of Martyrs*, 24–8; Knott, *Discourses of Martyrdom*, 55–6. For more on the protection of private thoughts by religious defendants under interrogation, see Covington, *Trail of Martyrdom*, 24, 103–53.
58. Roper, *Mirrour of Vertue*, 140.
59. William Allen, *Briefe Historie*, d6r.
60. Bettenson, *Documents of the Christian Church*, 243.
61. Batman, 'Booke of the Coppies', 19r.
62. William Allen, *Briefe Historie*, c3r. For another defence of equivocation, see Gerard, *Autobiography*, 125–7. On judicial efforts to penetrate the inner thoughts of Jesuit missionaries, see Hanson, *Discovering the Subject*, 1–6, 24–54.
63. William Allen, *Briefe Historie*, d6v.
64. On the complementarity of Protestant and Catholic discourses of martyrdom, and their mutual preoccupation with outward signs of inner truth, see Monta, *Martyrdom and Literature*, 9–78.
65. William Allen, *Briefe Historie*, f6v.
66. Ryrie, *Being Protestant*, 44–5.
67. Lewalski, *Protestant Poetics*, 13–27; Ryrie, *Being Protestant*, 2, 39–41.
68. Including an abridgement, there were ten further editions by 1599; *ESTC*.
69. Calvin, *Institution* (1561), 185v.
70. Perkins, *Golden Chaine*, C6r, Q4v; *Exposition of the Symbole*, 439.
71. Ryrie, *Being Protestant*, 110–12.
72. Griffiths, 'An Homily Wherein Is Declared That Common Prayer and Sacraments Ought to Be Ministered in a Tongue That Is Understanded of the Hearers', *Homilies*, 353–4. On the closet as the location for private prayer, see Ferry, *'Inward' Language*, 46–55; Ryrie, *Being Protestant*, 159.
73. *ESTC*; Charlton, *Women, Religion*, 168–74.
74. Bull, *Christian Praiers*, 135.
75. Warnicke, 'Lady Mildmay's Journal', 56–7, 60–1, 64; Pollock, 'Mildmay, Grace'; Ryrie, *Being Protestant*, 111, 117, 309, 314.
76. Aston, *England's Iconoclasts*, 294–342, esp. 300–3, 318–19; Porter, *Making and Unmaking*, 22–3.

77. Martz, *Poetry of Meditation*, 25–6, 121–4; O'Malley, *First Jesuits*, 37–50, 127–33, 162–4.
78. Gerard, *Autobiography*, 22, 24, 25, 72, 116, and *passim*; Questier, 'Like Locusts', 274–5.
79. Martz, *Poetry of Meditation*, 4–9; Questier, 'Like Locusts', 278–9; Ryrie, *Being Protestant*, 6, 113, 284–5.
80. Borris, *Visionary Spenser*, 5, 7, 11–14. See also Baker-Smith, 'Uses of Plato'; Hutton, 'Introduction to the Renaissance and Seventeenth Century'; Kraye, 'Transformation of Platonic Love'.
81. Erasmus, *Enchiridion*, 60, 63, 71, 106; Tilmouth, *Passion's Triumph*, 16–18. For more references to Plato in Erasmus, *Enchiridion*, see 19, 47, 55, 66, 136, 139.
82. Castiglione, *Courtyer*, Xx1v–Xx3r.
83. Hutton, 'Introduction to the Renaissance and Seventeenth Century', 68.
84. Sonnets 15 and 79, Spenser, *Shorter Poems*, 395, 427.
85. Geoff Baldwin, 'Individual and Self', 346–9; Monsarrat, *Light from the Porch*, 23–40, 45.
86. Monsarrat, *Light from the Porch*, 41–2.
87. William Baldwin, *Treatise*, M4v, and see J7r–v; *ESTC*; King, 'Baldwin, William'; Monsarrat, *Light from the Porch*, 81–2.
88. Monsarrat, *Light from the Porch*, 38–9, 45–7.
89. Guicciardini, *Garden of Pleasure*, A3v.
90. Cardano, *Cardanus Comforte*, C3r.
91. Monsarrat, *Light from the Porch*, 52.
92. Saunders, *Justus Lipsius*, 22.
93. Lipsius, *Two Bookes of Constancie*, 2–3, 9, 15, 29; McCrea, *Constant Minds*, 3–5, 12. On early modern anxieties about compassion, see Langley, *Shakespeare's Contagious Sympathies*.
94. McCrea, *Constant Minds*, 24; Stelling, *Religious Conversion*, 126–8. For more on the Protestant critique of Neostoicism, see Ch. 3 below.
95. Du Vair, *Moral Philosophie*, 149.
96. Greville, 'Letter', 154.
97. McCrea, *Constant Minds*.
98. Geoff Baldwin, 'Individual and Self', esp. 353, 360; McCrea, *Constant Minds*, 3–4.
99. Pebworth and Summers, 'Thus Friends Absent', esp. 368.
100. May, 'Authorship of "My Mind"', 385.
101. May, *Elizabethan Courtier Poets*, 283.
102. May, 'Dyer, Sir Edward'; Nelson, 'Vere, Edward de'.
103. Spenser, *Faerie Queene*, VI.ix.29–31.
104. Monsarrat, *Light from the Porch*, 109–17.
105. Cornwallis, *Essayes*, O1v, Q1r. Further references are given parenthetically.

Chapter 3: Knowing by Feeling: Writing the Passions

1. May, *Elizabethan Courtier Poets*, pp. 256–64, ll. 3, 64.
2. Cornwallis, *Essayes*, O1v, Y2r.
3. Gazzard, 'Nicholas Breton', 23–4, 36–7; May, *Poems of Oxford and Essex*, 102.
4. Roychoudhury, *Phantasmatic*, 41–2.
5. Erasmus, *First Tome*, 52r.
6. La Primaudaye, *Second Part*, 88. On the heart as the seat of spiritual conflict (with mainly seventeenth-century examples), see Erin Sullivan, *Beyond Melancholy*, 146–62.
7. Hankins, *Backgrounds of Shakespeare's Thought*, 82–3, 87, 108–9, 114–20, 149–50, 154, 195, 232.
8. Sidney, *Old Arcadia*, 167.
9. May, *Elizabethan Courtier Poets*, p. 256, ll. 2–3.
10. Gazzard, 'Nicholas Breton', 24–5; May, *Poems of Oxford and Essex*, 94–5.

11. E.g., Arab, Dowd, and Zucker, *Historical Affects*; Broomhall, *Authority, Gender and Emotions*; Broomhall, *Early Modern Emotions*; Broomhall, *Gender and Emotions*; Broomhall, *Ordering Emotions*; Carrera, *Emotions and Health*; Brian Cummings and Sierhuis, *Passions and Subjectivity*; Dawson and Langley, 'Affective Inheritances'; Meek and Erin Sullivan, *Renaissance of Emotion*; Mullaney, *Reformations of Emotion*; Erin Sullivan, *Beyond Melancholy*; R. S. White, Houlahan, and O'Loughlin, *Shakespeare and Emotions*.
12. Dixon, *Passions to Emotions*, 52; James, *Passion and Action*, 24–5; Miles, *Shakespeare and the Constant Romans*, 63–82; Sellars, 'Neo-Stoicism'.
13. Calvin, *Institution* (1561), 166v–167r; Monsarrat, *Light from the Porch*, 70–7.
14. Bullinger, *Fiftie Godlie and Learned Sermons*, 285; Monserrat, *Light from the Porch*, 74–5.
15. Thomas Rogers, *Anatomie*, 3r.
16. Thomas Rogers, *Paterne*, A8r, B5r–v.
17. Lemnius, *Touchstone*, 59v.
18. La Primaudaye, *French Academie*, 16, 309.
19. Spenser, *Faerie Queene*, II.ix.16, 17, 13. Further references are given parenthetically.
20. Calvin, *Sermons upon S. Paule too the Ephesians*, 130r; Knewstub, *Sermon*, C2r; Smith, *Benefit of Contentation*; Brian Cummings, *Mortal Thoughts*, 188–9. See also Ch. 2 above for discussion of Contentation in *The Trial of Treasure*.
21. Calvin, *Institution* (1561), 167r. On 'godly sorrow' as a stage in progress towards salvation (though with mainly seventeenth-century examples), see Erin Sullivan, *Beyond Melancholy*, 126–62.
22. Sometimes referred to as Mary Sidney or Mary Sidney Herbert, but I follow the editors of her *Collected Works* in referring to her hereafter as Pembroke.
23. Babington, *Briefe Conference*, ¶2v–¶3v.
24. Perkins, *Discourse of Conscience*, 2–3. Further references are given parenthetically.
25. Perkins, *Declaration*, 1, 5.
26. For more on prayer as struggle, see Ryrie, *Being Protestant*, 3, 239–56.
27. On the dearth of religious lyric in Protestant England between the 1540s and 1590s, see Coles, *Religion, Reform*, 115–16, 121.
28. Calvin, *Psalmes of David*, *6v; Serjeantson, 'Book of Psalms', 646–7. On the importance of the Psalms to Protestants, see Ahnert, 'Introduction'; *Book of Common Prayer*, ed. Brian Cummings, xxxv–xxxvi, lv–lvi, 783–4; Lewalski, *Protestant Poetics*, 39–53; Hannibal Hamlin, *Psalm Culture*; Pembroke, *Collected Works*, 2.6–7. For an overview of early modern English Psalm translations and paraphrases, including a discussion of Pembroke's work, see Mackenzie, 'Psalms'.
29. Pembroke, *Collected Works*, 2.3.
30. Hannibal Hamlin, 'Sobs for Sorrowful Souls'; Lewalski, *Protestant Poetics*, 46.
31. Brian Cummings, *Literary Culture*, locs 2866–971.
32. Hannibal Hamlin, 'Sobs for Sorrowful Souls', 227–8.
33. Ahnert, 'Introduction', 501; Pembroke, *Collected Works*, 2.6; *Book of Common Prayer*, ed. Brian Cummings, 512. Although Cummings gives the Psalm texts from the 1662 *Book of Common Prayer*, these were essentially unchanged from those used in the Elizabethan period; see *Book of Common Prayer*, ed. Brian Cummings, lv–lvi, 783–4. On the particular importance of Psalm 51 for the Protestant doctrine of justification by faith, and for early modern English poetry, see Hannibal Hamlin, *Psalm Culture*, 173–217.
34. Lock is sometimes spelled Locke or Lok, and Anne is also sometimes known by her maiden name of Vaughan, or her other married names of Dering or Prowse. See Collinson, 'Locke, Anne'. For the debate on Lock's authorship of the 'Meditation', see Coles, *Religion, Reform*, 126; Lock, *Collected Works*, liii–liv; May, 'Anne Lock and Thomas Norton'. For more on Lock's life and works, see Quatro, 'Hidden Life'; Stevenson, *Women Latin Poets*, 270–2.

35. Calvin, *Sermons upon Ezechias*, 38–40.
36. *OED*, 'passioned, adj.', 2.
37. Lock, *Collected Works*, 62.
38. *Geneva Bible*, 280v, 'An Excellent Song which was Salomons', 1.4–5 and note f. For more on the negative associations of blackness, see Ch. 5 below.
39. Lock, *Collected Works*, 65, 67, 70, 71. See Coles, *Religion, Reform*, 113–48; Woods, 'Body Penitent'.
40. Pembroke, *Collected Works*, 2.11, 2.21.
41. Hannay, 'Unlock my Lipps'; Pembroke, *Collected Works*, 2.7–8, 2.50.
42. Pembroke, *Collected Works*, 2.152.
43. *Book of Common Prayer*, ed. Brian Cummings, 602.
44. Pembroke, *Collected Works*, 2.234–5. On the use of metaphors of chambers, closets, or cabinets to represent withdrawal into the mind, see Ferry, *'Inward' Language*, 46–9.
45. For more on the Sidney Psalms and their context of Protestant introspective devotion, see Molekamp, *Women and the Bible*, 151–84.
46. Richard Rogers and Ward, *Two Elizabethan Puritan Diaries*, 64–5. Further references are given parenthetically.
47. On wandering thoughts as a form of Satanic temptation, see Ryrie, *Being Protestant*, 246–7, and the discussion of Lady Margaret Hoby's diary in Ch. 6 below. On writing a spiritual journal as in itself a devotional act (not just a record of devotions), see Ryrie, *Being Protestant*, 314.
48. Ryrie, *Being Protestant*, 310–11; Stewart, *Oxford History*, locs 3447–525.
49. See also Psalms 42.3, 56.8, 116.8, and 137.1. *Book of Common Prayer*, ed. Brian Cummings, 468, 501, 504, 517, 580, 601.
50. Sonnet 8, Lock, *Collected Works*, 67.
51. Ryrie, *Being Protestant*, 187–95.
52. For more tears, see Richard Rogers and Ward, *Two Elizabethan Puritan Diaries*, 68, 75.
53. For more on Richard Rogers's journal, see Stewart, *Oxford History*, locs 3291–704.
54. Brian Cummings, *Literary Culture*, loc. 4258; Martz, *Poetry of Meditation*, 25–39; Molly Murray, *Poetics of Conversion*, 7, 10–12; O'Malley, *First Jesuits*, 40–2; Sweeney, *Robert Southwell*, 50–2, 72, 75, 78–82.
55. Questier, 'Like Locusts'.
56. Persons, *Temperate Ward-word*, 66.
57. Richard Edwards, *Paradise*, M4r; and see Martz, *Poetry of Meditation*, 180–3.
58. Southwell, *Poems*, ed. McDonald and Brown, xxxii; Alison Shell, personal communication, 22 July 2019.
59. Southwell, *Collected Poems*, 43. Further references are given parenthetically.
60. Sweeney, *Robert Southwell*, 251–3, 271, 278.
61. *Biblia Sacra Vulgata, Bible Gateway*.
62. Henry, 'Salve Regina'; my translation.
63. Sweeney, *Robert Southwell*, 165–7, 180–1, 187–8.
64. Alabaster, *Unpublished Works*, xvii–xxviii; Molly Murray, *Poetics of Conversion*, 43–51.
65. Alabaster, *Unpublished Works*, 114, 106. Further references are given parenthetically. See also Molly Murray, 'Now I ame a Catholique'; *Poetics of Conversion*, 36–68; 'Radicalism of Early Modern Spiritual Autobiography', 46, 48.
66. Samuel Hartlib, quoted in Bremer, 'Alabaster, William'.
67. May, *Elizabethan Courtier Poets*, 290–4. Further references are given parenthetically by line number.
68. *CELM* DyE 25, DyE 20; Sargent, *At the Court*, 23–35, 207.
69. Marotti, '"Love Is Not Love"'.
70. Southwell, *Collected Poems*, 32–5. Further references are given parenthetically by line number.

71. Ross, 'Robert Southwell', 84.
72. See Pilarz, *Robert Southwell*, 85–9; Sweeney, *Robert Southwell*, 5, 29.
73. Southwell, *Collected Poems*, 58–60, 163; Pilarz, *Robert Southwell*, 89–90; Sweeney, *Robert Southwell*, 168, 179.
74. *ESTC*.
75. Southwell, *Marie Magdalens Funeral Teares*, A3v–A5r. Further references are given parenthetically.
76. Martz, *Poetry of Meditation*, 199–203.
77. Southwell, *Collected Poems*, 29, 40–1.
78. Ibid., 26–8, 30–1, 64–85.
79. Pilarz, *Robert Southwell*, 255.
80. May and Ringler, *Elizabethan Poetry*, 2146–50.
81. Southwell, *Collected Poems*, pp. 64–85, ll. 13–18. Further references are given parenthetically by line number.
82. Brian Cummings, *Literary Culture*, locs 4540–660; Ross, 'Robert Southwell', 96–107.
83. Jessica Martin, 'English Reformed Responses'; Ryrie, *Being Protestant*, 289–90.
84. Alison Shell, personal communications, 6 June and 22 July 2019.
85. Southwell, *Poems*, ed. McDonald and Brown, lvii. Jones printed Breton's *A Flourish upon Fancy* (c. 1585) and *Breton's Bower of Delights* (1591), having previously published two works with John Wolfe in 1583 (Copley, *Fig for Fortune*, 58 n. 269).
86. Breton, *Pilgrimage to Paradise*, 67. Further references are given parenthetically. On Breton's use of Pembroke's voice, see Trill, 'Engendering Penitence'.
87. Southwell, *Marie Magdalens Funeral Teares*, 3r–v. Southwell here follows the common practice of conflating Mary Magdalen with Mary of Bethany; see Pope, 'St. Mary Magdalen'.
88. Kerrigan, *Motives of Woe*.
89. The poem was probably written in around 1592; it was published in 1594, but the 1599 edition is the earliest to survive. Brennan, 'Nicholas Breton's *The Passions*'; Breton, *Poems*, ed. Robertson, xxv, lv–lxi; Gazzard, 'Nicholas Breton', 27.
90. Breton, *Passions of the Spirit*, 3, 40.
91. Hannay, *Philip's Phoenix*, 137–8; Lamb, *Gender and Authorship*, 47–52.
92. The family name was variously spelled Lock, Locke or Lok; see n. 34 above.
93. Lok, *Sundry Christian Passions*, title-page. Further references are given parenthetically.
94. Rienstra, 'Disorder Best Fit'.
95. Brown, 'Southwell, Robert'.
96. Brown, 'Robert Southwell'; Brian Cummings, *Literary Culture*, locs 4189–246; Sweeney, *Robert Southwell*, 17–18.
97. Kerrigan, *Motives of Woe*, 30–1; Shell, *Catholicism, Controversy*, 79–80.
98. For more examples, see Gazzard, 'Nicholas Breton'. For more on Southwell's appeal to Protestants as a poet of subjectivity, see Ross, 'Robert Southwell', 107–9.
99. Hackett, 'Art of Blasphemy?'; *Virgin Mother, Maiden Queen*, 133–62.
100. Shakespeare, *Shakespeare's Poems*, 82–91, 385–418; Shapiro, *1599*, 212–22.
101. Alabaster, *Unpublished Works*, xix–xxx, 114; Donaldson, 'Jonson, Benjamin'; Milward, 'Wright, Thomas'.
102. Wright, *Passions*, 14, 41; Tilmouth, 'Passions and Intersubjectivity', 28; *Passion's Triumph*, 26–7.
103. Wright, *Passions*, 27–34, esp. 31.
104. Erin Sullivan, 'Passions of Thomas Wright'.
105. The poem was published in print in 1604, and Ralegh's execution was in 1618, but he was also under sentence of death in 1603.
106. Philip Edwards, 'Who Wrote "The Passionate Man's Pilgrimage"?'
107. May, *Elizabethan Courtier Poets*, pp. 256–64, ll. 289–91, 3, 11–12, 23. Further references are given parenthetically by line number.
108. Ryrie, *Being Protestant*, 191.

109. Gazzard, 'Nicholas Breton', 37.
110. Breton, *Poems*, ed. Robertson, xcii–xcviii; Gazzard, 'Nicholas Breton'; May, *Poems of Oxford and Essex*, 94–5.
111. Breton, *Melancholike Humours*, B2v, B3r, C1v–C2v.
112. Trill, 'Engendering Penitence', 28.
113. Ll. 109, 217–22, 331; 63, 191–210, 337–42.
114. Southwell, *Marie Magdalens Funeral Teares*, 6v.

Chapter 4: In Other Voices: Female Minds

1. Tilney, *Flower of Friendship*, 138, and see 36, 60–3, 170–1.
2. Hoby, *Private Life*, 24. Further references are given parenthetically.
3. Garwood, *Early Modern English Noblewomen*, Ch. 9.
4. Dawson, *Lovesickness*, 46–90; Paster, *Humoring the Body*, 89–95.
5. Stuart, *Letters*, 175. Further references are given parenthetically.
6. Spenser, *Faerie Queene*, IV.ii.36.
7. Manningham, *Diary*, p. 186, f. 97b.
8. Carew, *Examination*, 282–3. Further references are given parenthetically.
9. I. T., *Haven of Pleasure*, 150–2.
10. Lavater, *Of Ghostes*, 14.
11. Scot, *Discoverie*, Bk 3, Ch. 9, pp. 52–4.
12. Payne, 'Jorden, Edward'.
13. Jorden, *Briefe Discourse*, 2r, 12v, 13v.
14. Ibid., 22v.
15. Dawson, *Lovesickness*, 72–9; Neely, *Distracted Subjects*, 50–6. On dramatic representations of female madness before Ophelia, see Richard Hillman, *Self-Speaking*, 242–5.
16. Pembroke, *Collected Works*, vol. 1.
17. Suthren, 'Iphigenia in English'.
18. Stevenson, *Women Latin Poets*, 263–8.
19. Hosington, 'Minerva and the Muses', 20, 33. For more on these and other female Elizabethan writers, see Levin, Bertolet, and Carney, *Biographical Encyclopedia*.
20. Ascham, *Scholemaster*, 21r.
21. Rhodes, Kendal, and Wilson, *English Renaissance Translation Theory*, 241.
22. Elizabeth I, *Autograph Compositions*, 168–9; *Collected Works*, 332–5.
23. Maltby, 'Queen and Scholar'; Shenk, *Learned Queen*.
24. See Frye, *Pens and Needles*, 41–5.
25. Ryrie, *Being Protestant*, 268.
26. Ascham, *Scholemaster*, 11v.
27. Mulcaster, *Positions*, 166.
28. Maltby, 'Queen and Scholar', Ch. 1.
29. Matthew Parker, 'To the Right Honorable'.
30. Mulcaster, *Positions*, 174–5.
31. Carew, *Examination*, 292.
32. Hake, *Touchestone*, 23.
33. Salter, *Mirrhor of Modestie*, C1v–C2r.
34. 'Anger', *Protection for Women*, 32, 39. Further references are given parenthetically.
35. Elizabeth D. Harvey, *Ventriloquized Voices*.
36. Bates, 'Shakespeare and the Female Voice', 59; Catty, *Writing Rape*, 62–71; Kerrigan, *Motives of Woe*.
37. Swärdh, 'From Hell', 99.
38. Bates, 'Shakespeare and the Female Voice', esp. 61.
39. Donaldson, *Rapes of Lucretia*.
40. Dubrow, 'Mirror for Complaints', 401.

41. Donaldson, *Rapes of Lucretia*, 40–56; Dubrow, 'Mirror for Complaints'; Shakespeare, *Complete Sonnets and Poems*, ed. Burrow, 55–73, esp. 73.
42. Kerrigan in *Motives of Woe* uses 'female' for works by men in female voices.
43. Calvin, *Institution* (1562), A1r.
44. Humphrey, *Interpretatio*, A4v–A5r, 170, 180–1; Rhodes, Kendal, and Wilson, *English Renaissance Translation Theory*, 276–8.
45. Robert Greene, *Penelopes Web*, title-page.
46. Matthew Parker, 'To the Right Honorable'.
47. Bentley, *Monument*, B1r.
48. Frye, *Pens and Needles*.
49. Salter, *Mirrhor of Modestie*, C1v–C2r.
50. Montaigne, *Essayes*, A2r, A5r.
51. Hosington, 'Translation as a Currency'.
52. Braden, 'Overview', 3.
53. Hosington, 'Translation as a Currency', 45. The figure is based on the *Renaissance Cultural Crossroads Catalogue*, which includes all translations out of and into all languages printed in England, Scotland, and Ireland before 1641, and all translations out of all languages into English printed abroad before 1641.
54. Micheline White, Introduction, 7–8.
55. Hosington, 'Minerva and the Muses', 33.
56. Demers, 'Nether Bitterly'; Stevenson, *Women Latin Poets*, 267.
57. Wright, 'Translating at Leisure', 60–1.
58. Frye, *Pens and Needles*, 52.
59. Hannay, *Philip's Phoenix*, 84–105.
60. Ibid., 60–3.
61. Pembroke, *Collected Works*, 1.210–20.
62. Ibid., 2.249–50.
63. Elizabeth I, *Translations, 1544–1589*, 407–21, 437–56.
64. Elizabeth I, *Translations, 1592–1598*, 203, 219.
65. Ibid., 47, 49, 53.
66. Ralegh, 'Ocean to Scinthia', ll. 203–4, 209–11.
67. For more on the politics of the mind, see Ch. 8 below.
68. Tyler, *Mirror*, 49–51.
69. Pembroke, *Collected Works*, 1.280, ll. 103–8.
70. Ibid., 1.206, ll. 1983–90.
71. For more on the diverse uses of translation by early modern women, see Clarke, 'Translation'; Uman, *Women as Translators*.
72. Stevenson, *Women Latin Poets*, 267–9 (Stevenson's translation).
73. Whitney, 'I. W. to her Unconstant Lover', ll. 81–4. Further references are given parenthetically by line number.
74. Elizabeth I, *Collected Works*, 194, speech to Parliament, 12 Nov. 1586.
75. Elizabeth I, *Selected Works*, 7–9.
76. Harington, *Nugae Antiquae*, 1.58.
77. Elizabeth I, *Selected Works*, 9.
78. For more on this poem see Summit, 'Arte of a Ladies Penne'.
79. Elizabeth I, *Selected Works*, p. 12, ll. 1–2, 5–6.
80. Axton, *Queen's Two Bodies*.
81. Marcus, 'Queen Elizabeth I', 146–8.

Chapter 5: The Minds of Africans: Imaginings and Encounters

1. See Spenser, *View*, and Ch. 8 below.
2. *OED*, 'complexion, n.', I.1.a, 3, 4.a.
3. Lemnius, *Touchstone*, title-page.

4. Shakespeare, *Merchant of Venice*, 1.2.111–12, 2.1.1, 2.7.79.
5. Cassander L. Smith, Nicholas R. Jones, and Grier, 'Chapter 1: Introduction', 4.
6. Pliny, *Summarie*, B3v–B4v.
7. Mandeville, *Voyages*, L3r–v.
8. Eden, *Decades*, 356v; Hakluyt, *Principall Navigations*, 1.77–9, 95.
9. E.g. Batman, *Batman uppon Bartholome*, Bk 15, 250v, 251v; Leroy, *Variety of Things* (English translation of a French work), 13v, 110r.
10. 'To the Reader', in Leo Africanus, *Geographical Historie*, no p. nos.
11. Bartels, *Speaking of the Moor*, 14; Brotton, *This Orient Isle*; Matar, *Turks, Moors, and Englishmen*.
12. Leo Africanus, *Geographical Historie*, Leo 2–3, Pory 12–41. Sections of the volume by Pory and Leo have their own page numbers.
13. Ibid., Leo 3.
14. Ibid., Leo 2.
15. Ibid., Leo 124–56.
16. Ibid., Leo 39–42.
17. *OED*, 'Moor, n.2'.
18. Das et al., 'Blackamoor'; *OED*, 'blackamoor, n.', 1; 'Negro, n. and adj.', A.*n*.1.a, B.1; 'Ethiopian, n. and adj.', etymology, A.n.1.a, B.adj.1.b.
19. Nubia, 'Africans'.
20. Boorde, *Fyrst Boke*, M3v.
21. Batman, *Batman uppon Bartholome*, Bk 15, Ch. 96, ff. 234r, 251r.
22. Kaufmann, 'Making the Beast', 23.
23. Habib, *Black Lives*, locs 9212–27, item 224.
24. Floyd-Wilson, *English Ethnicity*, 191 n. 33.
25. Bartels, *Speaking of the Moor*, 4; Brotton, *This Orient Isle*, 167.
26. Cassander L. Smith, *Black Africans*, 8–11; Cassander L. Smith, Nicholas R. Jones and Grier, 'Chapter 1: Introduction'.
27. Eden, *Decades*, 311r.
28. Cuningham, *Cosmographical Glasse*, 186.
29. *Geneva Bible*, 280v, 'An Excellent Song which was Salomons', 1.4–5 and note f.
30. Scot, *Discoverie*, Bk 7, Ch. 15, pp. 152–3; 'Discourse upon Divels and Spirits', Ch. 28, p. 535.
31. Floyd-Wilson, *English Ethnicity*, *passim*.
32. Ibid., 2, 25–6, 29.
33. The French edition of 1565 was followed by thirteen Latin editions between 1566 and 1650; Floyd-Wilson, *English Ethnicity*, 35, 200 n. 47.
34. Bodin, *Method*, 89, 102, 107. Further references are given parenthetically.
35. Thevet, *New Found World*, 25r.
36. Bright, *Treatise of Melancholie*, 128–9.
37. Harrison, *Historicall Description*, Bk 1, Ch. 20, p. 114. For more examples of geohumoralism, see Lemnius, *Touchstone*, 12v–13r, 38v–48v; Carew, *Examination*, 98, 166–7, 218–19.
38. Best, *True Discourse*, 28, 30–2.
39. Alden T. Vaughan and Virginia Mason Vaughan, 'Before *Othello*', 27 n. 25.
40. Leroy, *Variety of Things*, 19r, 32r, 34r, 36r, 50v.
41. Ibid., 13v–14r.
42. Leo Africanus, *Geographical Historie*, Pory 382.
43. Harrison, *Historicall Description*, Bk 1, Ch. 20, p. 114.
44. Leroy, *Variety of Things*, 13r.
45. *Lamentable Ballad*; Fumerton, *Broadside Ballad*, 269–320.
46. Fumerton, *Broadside Ballad*, 274–5. I assume for the purposes of this discussion that the seventeenth-century version of the ballad is similar to the lost Elizabethan original.
47. Habib, *Black Lives*, 65; Bartels, *Speaking of the Moor*, 50.
48. Bartels, *Speaking of the Moor*, 11; Kaufmann, *Black Tudors*, locs 52–64, 979–92.

49. Kaufmann, *Black Tudors*, loc. 89; Weissbourd, 'Those in their Possession', 15.
50. Boorde, *Fyrst Boke*, M3v–M4r.
51. Hakluyt, *Principall Navigations*, 3.521.
52. Hadfield, *Amazons, Savages and Machiavels*, 121; Kaufmann, *Black Tudors*, loc. 979.
53. Hakluyt, *Principall Navigations*, 3.526, 522.
54. Ibid., 1.237.
55. Bartels, *Speaking of the Moor*, 17, 23–4, 27; Brotton, *This Orient Isle*; Kaufmann, *Black Tudors*, Ch. 6; Matar, *Turks, Moors, and Englishmen*.
56. Further east than the present state of Benin; now in Nigeria.
57. Hakluyt, *Principall Navigations*, 1.86–7.
58. Ibid., 1.818–19. Both missions failed because of sickness among the English. See also Bartels, *Speaking of the Moor*, Ch. 2; Kaufmann, *Black Tudors*, Ch. 7.
59. Kaufmann, *Black Tudors*, loc. 3241.
60. Nichols, *Drake Revived*, title-page; Kaufmann, *Black Tudors*, loc. 1017; Cassander L. Smith, *Black Africans*, 62.
61. Kaufmann, *Black Tudors*, locs 966–92.
62. Nichols, *Drake Revived*, 55–6.
63. Cassander L. Smith, *Black Africans*, 5–6, 15.
64. Nichols, *Drake Revived*, 15, 20, 32–3.
65. Kaufmann, *Black Tudors*, Ch. 3.
66. Nichols, *Drake Revived*, 72.
67. Cassander L. Smith, *Black Africans*, Ch. 2.
68. Kaufmann, *Black Tudors*, locs 1326, 1391–1417, 1444–1510.
69. Matar, *Turks, Moors, and Englishmen*, 33–4.
70. Brotton, *This Orient Isle*, 4–5.
71. Kaufmann, *Black Tudors*, loc. 2472.
72. Best, *True Discourse*, 20.
73. *Copie of a Leter*, 13. This work was widely known as *Leicester's Commonwealth*.
74. Weissbourd, 'Those in their Possession', 2–5.
75. Kaufmann, 'Caspar Van Senden'; Weissbourd, 'Those in their Possession'.
76. Weissbourd, 'Those in their Possession', 3.
77. Collinson, 'Locke, Anne'; John Goodwin Locke, *Book of the Lockes*, 359. As explained at Ch. 3, nn. 34 and 92 above, the family name was variously spelled Lock, Locke or Lok.
78. Eden, *Decades*, 359v.
79. Hakluyt, *Principall Navigations*, 1.107–8.
80. Kaufmann, *Black Tudors*, loc. 3134; Nubia, 'Africans'.
81. Kaufmann, *Black Tudors*, locs 112–25, Ch. 2, loc. 1030.
82. Ibid., locs 853, 1666–7, 4435.
83. Ibid., loc. 2446.
84. Habib, *Black Lives*, 68–9; Ungerer, 'Presence of Africans'.
85. Kaufmann, *Black Tudors*, locs 2563–76.
86. Habib and Salkeld, 'Resonables of Boroughside', 135; Kaufmann, *Black Tudors*, loc. 6127 n. 9.
87. Kaufmann, *Black Tudors*, loc. 4456. See also Habib, *Black Lives*; Nubia, 'Africans'. Kaufmann, 'Making the Beast', 25, identifies flaws in Habib's methodology.
88. Habib, *Black Lives*, 71–6; Kaufmann, *Black Tudors*, locs 52, 554.
89. Kaufmann, *Black Tudors*, loc. 2446.
90. Ibid., loc. 1701, Ch. 4, loc. 1663.
91. Best, *True Discourse*, 19.
92. Kaufmann, 'Making the Beast', 26.
93. Habib and Salkeld, 'Resonables of Boroughside'; Kaufmann, *Black Tudors*, Ch. 5.
94. For other theories about his name, see Habib and Salkeld, 'Resonables of Boroughside', 136–7; Kaufmann, *Black Tudors*, locs 1907–21.

95. Habib, *Black Lives*, locs 9212–23, item 224; Kaufmann, *Black Tudors*, Ch. 6.
96. Habib, *Black Lives*, loc. 9212, item 223; Kassell et al., *Casebooks*, 'CASE1667: Horary consultation concerning Polonia (PERSON261)'.
97. Habib and Salkeld, 'Resonables of Boroughside', 142.
98. Wiggins with Catherine Richardson, *British Drama*, 1.117, 171, 214, 229, 313.
99. Brotton, *This Orient Isle*, 81–4.
100. Peele, *Battell of Alcazar*, D3v. Further references are given parenthetically.
101. Wiggins with Catherine Richardson, *British Drama*, 2.811, p. 433.
102. Vickers, *Shakespeare, Co-Author*, Ch. 3.
103. Habib, 'Racial Impersonation', 19; Wiggins with Catherine Richardson, *British Drama*, 3.928, p. 184.
104. Marlowe, *Jew of Malta*, 2.3.168–213.
105. Attributed to Thomas Kyd; Wiggins with Catherine Richardson, *British Drama*, 2.799, p. 403.
106. By Thomas Dekker, William Haughton and John Day; Wiggins with Catherine Richardson, *British Drama*, 4.1235, p. 206.
107. Dekker, Haughton, and Day, *Lusts Dominion*, F2r. Further references are given parenthetically.
108. Bartels, *Speaking of the Moor*, 136.
109. Shakespeare, *Othello*, 1.1.86; 1.3.287; 2.3.28; 3.3.384, 442; 5.2.128.
110. Leo Africanus, *Geographical Historie*, Leo 42.

Chapter 6: Stars and Demons: The Permeable Mind

1. Kassell, *Medicine and Magic*, 130.
2. Dariot, *Introduction*, B3r. See also Babb, *Elizabethan Malady*, 10, 57–8; Robert Greene, *Planetomachia*, xxi; Yates, *Occult Philosophy*, 51, 53.
3. Forman, 'Of Melancoly', 45r, 47v.
4. Batman, *Batman uppon Bartholome*, Bk 8, Ch. 22, f. 128v; Dariot, *Introduction*, B1v–B2r; Digges, *Prognostication*, B1v; Babb, *Elizabethan Malady*, 11; Robert Greene, *Planetomachia*, xxi; Yates, *Occult Philosophy*, 10.
5. Moulton, *Mirrour*, A2r. See also Chapman, 'Astrological Medicine'.
6. Forman, 'Of Melancoly', 48v.
7. Kassell, *Medicine and Magic*, 159.
8. Also known by her married name of Skinner.
9. Robert Greene, *Planetomachia*, xxii.
10. Kassell, *Medicine and Magic*, 159.
11. Kassell et al., *Casebooks*, 'Mrs Margaret Skinner [Altham] (PERSON6598)'; Kassell, *Medicine and Magic*, 145–7.
12. Kassell, *Medicine and Magic*, 150.
13. Boorde, *Breviarie*, Bk 2, sig. B6r.
14. On the permeability of the Renaissance self and mind, see John Jeffries Martin, *Myths of Renaissance Individualism*, 14, 83–102.
15. On early modern tensions between porous and isolationist models of self and mind, see Langley, *Contagious Sympathies*.
16. Robert Greene, *Planetomachia*, xx–xxi; Hankins, *Backgrounds*, 25.
17. Wiles, *Shakespeare's Almanac*, 131–2.
18. Batman, *Batman uppon Bartholome*, Bk 11, Ch. 11, f. 170r.
19. Erasmus, *Enchiridion*, 67.
20. Batman, *Batman uppon Bartholome*, Bk 8, Ch. 23, f. 130r.
21. Ibid., Bk 5, Ch. 3, f. 37r; Bk 8, Ch. 30, f. 134v.
22. Don Cameron Allen, *Star-Crossed Renaissance*, viii, 148.
23. *ESTC*. The earliest extant edition is from 1555, but it refers to an earlier edition, now lost.

24. Digges, *Prognostication*, title-page, D3r, E2r.
25. Dariot, *Introduction*, I3v, K1v.
26. Don Cameron Allen, *Star-Crossed Renaissance*, vii, 103–12; Robert Greene, *Planetomachia*, xxi–xxiv.
27. Calvin, *Admonicion*, A8v–B1v.
28. Fulke, *Antiprognosticon*, C4r–v.
29. Perkins, *Discourse of [. . .] Witchcraft*, 86–7; published 1608, but written some time before his death in 1602. See also Chamber, *Treatise*, 3–4.
30. Don Cameron Allen, *Star-Crossed Renaissance*, 104.
31. Robert Greene, *Planetomachia*, 2–3. Further references are given parenthetically.
32. Lyly, *Woman in the Moon*, 1.1.95–101. Further references are given parenthetically.
33. Ibid., p. 1.
34. Nyndge, *Fearfull Vexasion*. See also Almond, *Demonic Possession*, 43–57 (which reproduces the much-expanded 1615 version of the text); Sands, *Demon Possession*, 41–6.
35. Sands, *Demon Possession*, 13–28.
36. Ibid., 28–40.
37. Ibid., 57–74; Sands, *Elizabethan Lawyer's Possession*.
38. Almond, *Demonic Possession*, 58–70; Sands, *Demon Possession*, 75–89.
39. Scot, *Discoverie*, Bk 7, Ch. 1, pp. 126–8.
40. Bright, *Treatise of Melancholie*, 226.
41. Darrel, *Apologie*, D4r.
42. Almond, *Demonic Possession*, 1.
43. Ibid., 71–149.
44. Ibid., 87, 216, 219.
45. Mackay, *Hammer of Witches*, Pt II, Qn 1, Ch. 5, p. 316.
46. See Oldridge, 'Demons of the Mind', for discussion of the difficulties of interpreting early modern spiritual and psychological conditions in modern medical terms.
47. O'Sullivan, *It's All in your Head*, 11–12. Further references are given parenthetically.
48. Sands, *Elizabethan Lawyer's Possession*, 98.
49. Harsnett, *Declaration*, 226, 275.
50. Harsnett, *Discovery*, 210.
51. Almond, *Demonic Possession*, 77–8. Further references are given parenthetically.
52. Bradwell, 'Mary Glover', 3.
53. Oldridge, *Devil in Early Modern England*, 120, 126; Sands, *Demon Possession*, 86–8.
54. O'Sullivan, *It's All in your Head*, 97, 127–76.
55. Nyndge, *Fearfull Vexasion*, B1r.
56. Duffy, *Stripping of the Altars*, 579–82.
57. Oldridge, *Devil in Early Modern England*, 129–32; Harsnett, *Declaration*, 248.
58. It went through six Latin editions between 1563 and 1583, each of which was revised and expanded, and there were French and German translations. Weyer, *Witches, Devils, and Doctors*, ix, xxviii, xlv, lix, lxix. Further references are given parenthetically.
59. Scot, *Discoverie*, Bk 1, Ch. 3, p. 7.
60. Johnstone, *Devil and Demonism*, 27–59; Oldridge, *Devil in Early Modern England*, 4, 10, 35–9, 149. On the use of witchcraft and belief in the Devil to represent and process diverse forms of ideological conflict, see Stuart Clark, *Thinking with Demons*.
61. Scot, *Discoverie*, Bk 16, Ch. 7, p. 483.
62. Harsnett, *Declaration*, esp. 2.
63. D. P. Walker, *Unclean Spirits*, 66–73.
64. *Triall of Maist[er] Dorrell*, 7–8.
65. Harsnett, *Discovery*, 231.
66. Greenblatt, *Shakespearean Negotiations*, 106.
67. Fulke, *Stapleton and Martiall Confuted*, 75.

68. Brogan, 'His Belly', 3.
69. Harsnett, *Declaration*, 136.
70. Brogan, 'His Belly'.
71. Harsnett, *Declaration*, 269.
72. MacDonald, *Witchcraft and Hysteria*.
73. Bradwell, 'Mary Glover', 28.
74. Weyer, *Witches, Devils, and Doctors*, 571.
75. Ibid., 447, 569.
76. Bradwell, 'Mary Glover', 60.
77. Brogan, 'His Belly', 13–14. Oldridge, 'Demons of the Mind', discusses the persistence throughout the seventeenth century of physiological explanations for Satan's incursions into the mind.
78. Scot, *Discoverie*, Bk 1, Ch. 3, p. 7.
79. Ibid., Bk 10, Ch. 5, p. 181.
80. Ibid., Bk 1, Ch. 6, p. 13.
81. Giffard, *Dialogue*, B1v–B2r.
82. Perkins, *Discourse of [. . .] Witchcraft*, 26–7.
83. Harsnett, *Discovery*, 297 (numbered 279)–314; Sands, *Demon Possession*, 109–25.
84. *Geneva Bible*, Acts 19.13 and marginal note, 19.19.
85. Almond, *Demonic Possession*, 64.
86. Shakespeare, *Twelfth Night*, ed. Warren and Wells, 58.
87. Boorde, *Breviarie*, Bk 2, A4v.
88. Almond, *Demonic Possession*, 241, 282–3.
89. *Henry VI* and *2 Henry VI* were originally known by different names, and *2 Henry VI* was probably written first. See Wiggins with Catherine Richardson, *British Drama*, 3.888, p. 92; 3.919, p. 161.
90. Gary Taylor and Egan, *New Oxford Shakespeare: Authorship Companion*, 496, 515.
91. *Titus Andronicus*, 5.1.40; 5.2.86, 90; 5.3.5; *Richard III*, 1.2.32, 43, 48, 71, 88; 1.3.116; 4.4.335.
92. Cox, *Devil and Sacred*, 210.
93. Jeffrey Burton Russell, *Mephistopheles*, 34–7, 57.
94. Johnstone, *Devil and Demonism*, 69.
95. Ibid., 7.
96. Chassanion, *Theatre*, 145, 182.
97. [Jude Smith], *True Reporte*, A5r.
98. *Sundrye Strange [. . .] Murthers*, A3r.
99. Scot, *Discoverie*, Bk 1, Ch. 6, pp. 12–13.
100. Calvin, *Institution* (1561), 49v–50r.
101. Perkins, *Discourse of [. . .] Witchcraft*, ¶4r–¶5r.
102. Almond, *Demonic Possession*, 20; Oldridge, *Devil in Early Modern England*, 112; Sands, *Demon Possession*, 13–15.
103. Weyer, *Witches, Devils, and Doctors*, 189.
104. Lemnius, *Touchstone*, 21v–24r.
105. Bright, *Treatise of Melancholie*, 222. Further references are given parenthetically.
106. Ryrie, *Being Protestant*, 32.
107. Calvin, *Institution* (1561), 49v–50r.
108. Ryrie, *Being Protestant*, 23, 27, 46; Stachniewski, *Persecutory Imagination*.
109. Weyer, *Witches, Devils, and Doctors*, 189; Lemnius, *Touchstone*, 22r, 24r.
110. Johnstone, *Devil and Demonism*, 2–3, 23–4, 60–141, 286–93; Oldridge, *Devil in Early Modern England*, 16–57; Jeffrey Burton Russell, *Mephistopheles*, 30–1.
111. Johnstone, *Devil and Demonism*, 96–7.
112. Woolton, *Christian Manuell*, F2v.
113. Oldridge, *Devil in Early Modern England*, 123.
114. Hoby, *Private Life*, 168, 182. Further references are given parenthetically.

115. Bright, *Treatise of Melancholie*, 233.
116. Johnstone, *Devil and Demonism*, 127–8.
117. Sands, *Elizabethan Lawyer's Possession*, 38–9.
118. Harrison, 'Brief Discourse', Epistle 'To the Christian Reader', no p. no.
119. Perkins, *Discourse of Conscience*, 147–8.
120. Marlowe, *Doctor Faustus, A-Text*, 1.1.140, 2.1.168–71, 2.3.34–65, 4.0.9. Further references are given parenthetically.
121. Belsey, *Subject of Tragedy*, 43–6.
122. Sands, *Elizabethan Lawyer's Possession*, 96. Further references are given parenthetically.

Chapter 7: 'Things Feigned in the Mind': The Unruly Imagination

1. Warnock, *Imagination*, 196. Further references are given parenthetically.
2. Wordsworth, *Prelude* (1805), Bk 11, ll. 252–6. For more examples of Romantic writings on imagination, see Smid, *Imagination*, 16–17, 24.
3. La Primaudaye, *Second Part*, 155–6.
4. Vesalius, *Vesalius on the Human Brain*, 5–6. Further references are given parenthetically.
5. Durling, 'Chronological Census', esp. 231, 244.
6. Carrera, 'Anger', 98; Mikkeli and Marttila, 'Change and Continuity', 13–14; Roychoudhury, *Phantasmatic Shakespeare*, 29–35; Wear, *Knowledge and Practice*, 35.
7. Batman, *Batman uppon Bartholome*, Bk 5, Ch. 3, f. 36v, 'Of the Braine'. See also Bk 3, Ch. 10, ff. 14v–15r, 'Of the inner Sense'.
8. Spenser, *Faerie Queene*, II.ix.47–58.
9. Taavitsainen and Pahta, 'Appendix D', 262.
10. Also known as Thomas Geminus or Lambrit; Peter Murray Jones, 'Gemini, Thomas'.
11. Larkey, 'Vesalian Compendium'.
12. Norman Moore and I. G. Murray, 'Vicary, Thomas'.
13. La Primaudaye, *Second Part*, 150. Further references are given parenthetically.
14. Davies of Hereford, *Mirum in modum*, B2r–v. See also Du Laurens, 'Second Discourse', 78–9.
15. Lancashire, *Two Tudor Interludes*, 22. Further references are given parenthetically.
16. Perkins, *Treatise of Mans Imaginations*, 21–2 (published 1607 but based on a sermon given by Perkins before his death in 1602).
17. Proverbs 12.2. See also Genesis 6.5, Isaiah 55.7 and 65.2, Jeremiah 18.12, Lamentations 3.61, Luke 1.51, 2 Corinthians 10.3 and 10.5, Galatians 6.3.
18. *Statutes of the Realm*, 1: 319–20, 25o Edw.III. Stat.5. c.2; Bellamy, *Tudor Law of Treason*, 10–12, 62; Cunningham, *Imaginary Betrayals*, 7–10, 148 n. 34; Roychoudhury, *Phantasmatic Shakespeare*, 160–2.
19. Scott-Warren, 'Was Elizabeth I Richard II?', 225.
20. Davies of Hereford, *Mirum in modum*, C2v.
21. Thomas Wright, *Passions*, 92–3.
22. Lewis, *Hamlet and the Vision of Darkness*, 201–2; Roychoudhury, *Phantasmatic Shakespeare*, 7, 21.
23. Spenser, *Faerie Queene*, II.ix.50–1.
24. Here, the living body.
25. Davies of Hereford, *Mirum in modum*, B3v.
26. Sander, *Treatise of Images*, 43v.
27. Calvin, *Institution* (1561), 4v–5r.
28. Gratarolo, *Castel of Memorie*, G6v; Yates, *Art of Memory*.
29. Perkins, *Arte of Prophecying*, 130.
30. Perkins, 'Warning against Idolatrie', 841. For more on Protestant distrust of the art of memory, see Yates, *Art of Memory*, locs 4061, 4100, 4111, 4558, 4658, 4785, 4827, 4852, 5118.
31. Spenser, *Faerie Queene*, II.ix.50; Thomas Rogers, *Anatomie*, 36v.

32. Perkins, *Treatise of Mans Imaginations*, 167.
33. Roychoudhury, *Phantasmatic Shakespeare*, 139–42.
34. Bright, *Treatise of Melancholie*, 102.
35. Nashe, *Terrors*, C2v.
36. Du Laurens, 'Second Discourse', 100.
37. Lemnius, *Touchstone*, 150v–151r.
38. For similar stories of bizarre melancholy delusions and their cures, see Scot, *Discoverie*, Bk 3, Ch. 9, pp. 53–4; Du Laurens, 'Second Discourse', 100–4. See also Roychoudhury, 'Forms of Fantasy', 56; *Phantasmatic Shakespeare*, 138–9.
39. Lemnius, *Touchstone*, 40r.
40. Boaistuau, *Certaine Secrete Wonders*, 12r, 13r–v, and see 15v, 98v, 99v. See also Lupton, *Thousand Notable Things*, 26, 137, 156–7, 190; Montaigne, *Essayes*, Bk 1, Ch. 20, p. 45; Crawford, *Marvelous Protestantism*, 18–20; Huet, *Monstrous Imagination*, 19, 33; Roychoudhury, *Phantasmatic Shakespeare*, 167–8.
41. Scot, *Discoverie*, Bk 3, Ch. 9, pp. 52–4.
42. For more on sixteenth-century distrust of the imagination, see Rossky, 'Imagination in the English Renaissance', 49–64.
43. Sir John Davies, *Poems*, 41.
44. Scot, *Discoverie*, Bk 10, Ch. 2, pp. 178–9.
45. Nashe, *Terrors*, 220; Gowland, 'Melancholy, Imagination', 68–72.
46. Rivière, *Dreams*, Introduction, Ch. 2; Shakespeare, *Midsummer Night's Dream*, ed. Holland, 5–7.
47. Shakespeare, *Midsummer Night's Dream*, ed. Holland, 6–8.
48. *Dreames of Daniell*, A2r.
49. The earliest surviving edition is from 1576. Hill acknowledged Artemidorus as a source in *The Contemplation of Mankinde*, 131v. He may have used a Latin translation of Artemidorus owned by John Dee (Rivière, *Dreams*, Ch. 2).
50. Hill, *Interpretacion*, F1v, O3v.
51. Bullein, *Bulwarke*, 28r.
52. Elyot, *Castell*, 3–5.
53. Wright, *Passions*, 111; Gowland, 'Melancholy, Imagination', 65; Rivière, *Dreams*, Ch. 1.
54. Du Laurens, 'Second Discourse', 100.
55. Bullein, *Bulwarke*, 6v.
56. Hill, *Interpretacion*, D4v–D8r. Further references are given parenthetically.
57. See also Thomas Rogers, *Anatomie*, 37r–38v.
58. Bright, *Treatise of Melancholie*, 118.
59. Hill, *Interpretacion*, C1v; Ekirch, *At Day's Close*, locs 5418–48, 5799–826; E. Ruth Harvey, *Inward Wits*, 49–50; Rivière, *Dreams*, Ch. 2.
60. Howard, *Defensative*, L1r. Further references are given parenthetically.
61. Scot, *Discoverie*, Bk 10, Ch. 1, p. 177; Ch. 4, p. 180; Ch. 10, p. 187.
62. Nashe, *Terrors*, C3v.
63. Howard, *Defensative*, K3v, L1v.
64. Perkins, *Discourse of [. . .] Witchcraft*, 102. Further references are given parenthetically.
65. Rivière, *Dreams*, Ch. 2.
66. Almond, *Demonic Possession*, 89, 142, 148.
67. Keith Thomas, *Religion*, loc. 2592; Levin, *Dreaming*, 147, 152–5.
68. Dee, *Diaries*, 51–2; Dee, *Private Diary*, 17–18; Sherman, *John Dee*, 51–2.
69. Dee, *Diaries*, 240, 283.
70. Ibid., 3.
71. Forman, Ashmole MS 1472, p. 809; Kassell, *Medicine and Magic*, 33, 173.
72. Forman, dream of 23 Jan. 1597, Ashmole MS 226, f. 44r; Montrose, 'Shaping Fantasies'. For Forman's two other dreams about Elizabeth: Ashmole MS 226, f. 44v (22 Feb. 1597), f. 310r (9 Jan. 1598); Traister, *Notorious*, 176.

73. Forman, 'Bocke of the Life', 137; Rowse, *Case Books*, 273–4. For more vivid dreams by Forman, see Kassell, *Medicine and Magic*, 54, 209–10, 217–18; Traister, *Notorious*, 13, 90, 109, 114–16, 122, 148, 169.

74. Churchyard, *Challenge*, 177. Further references are given parenthetically.

75. Hackett, 'Dream-Visions'.

76. Shakespeare, *Midsummer Night's Dream*, ed. Holland, 29.

77. Hackett, *William Shakespeare: 'A Midsummer Night's Dream'*, 17–31; Hackett, Introduction to *A Midsummer Night's Dream*, xl–xlvii.

78. Crane, *Framing Authority*, 71, 79, 92, 137; Kalas, *Frame, Glass, Verse*, xvi, 54–5; Vickers, *English Renaissance Literary Criticism*, 1, 6–7.

79. Thomas Wilson, *Arte of Rhetorique*, G3v.

80. Carew, *Examination*, 156–7. Further references are given parenthetically.

81. Puttenham, *Art*, 71. Further references are given parenthetically.

82. Rossky, 'Imagination in the English Renaissance'.

83. Pollard, *Shakespeare's Theater*, 48.

84. Spenser, *Shorter Poems*, 137; Borris, *Visionary Spenser*.

85. See also Sumillera, 'From Inspiration', 21–3.

86. Pollard, *Shakespeare's Theater*, 45.

87. Puttenham, *Art*, 57–8.

88. Scott, *Model of Poesy*, 7. Further references are given parenthetically.

89. Hetherington, 'Instrument of Reason'.

90. Sidney, *Defence*, 9.

91. Spenser, *Faerie Queene*, I.0.4, II.ix.53.

92. Sidney, *Defence*, 36; Borris, *Visionary Spenser*, 60–3; Roychoudhury, *Phantasmatic Shakespeare*, 6, 184.

93. Roychoudhury, 'Forms of Fantasy', 51–3; Guillory, *Poetic Authority*, 37.

94. Thomas M. Greene, *Light in Troy*, esp. 1–2, 30–5, 46, 51; Hackett, 'He Is a Better Scholar'; Kerrigan, *Shakespeare's Originality*, 1–2, 6–7, 15, 22; Mack, 'Learning and Transforming', esp. 438; Rhodes, *Shakespeare and Origins*, locs 695, 758; Vickers, *English Renaissance Literary Criticism*, 26, 28.

95. Thomas Wilson, *Arte of Rhetorique*, A3v. See also Crane, *Framing Authority*, 17, 41–2; Kerrigan, *Shakespeare's Originality*, 7; Mack, *Elizabethan Rhetoric*, 9; Rhodes, *Shakespeare and Origins*, loc. 850; Vickers, *In Defence*, 28, 62, 263.

96. Gascoigne, 'Certain Notes', 237.

97. Puttenham, *Art*, 201. See also Crane, *Framing Authority*, 175, 180, 187–8, 192–4; Roland Greene, 'Invention'; Kerrigan, *Shakespeare's Originality*, 7, 22. On the emergence of concepts of originality in the early modern period, see Kearney, *Wake of Imagination*, 17, 155; Quint, *Origin and Originality*; Wootton, *Invention of Science*, Ch. 3, locs 1204–2212.

98. Marr, 'Pregnant Wit'.

99. Puttenham, *Art*, 159.

100. *OED*, 'quick, adj., n.1, and adv.', A.I.

101. Lomazzo, *Tracte*, 7.

102. Sidney, *Astrophil*, p. 153, Sonnet 1; Maus, 'Womb of his Own'.

103. Sidney, *Defence*, 41. Further references are given parenthetically.

104. Borris, *Visionary Spenser*, 57–8; Rhodes, *Common*, 153, 193–7; Rossky, 'Imagination in the English Renaissance'.

105. Alexander, Introduction to *Sidney's 'The Defence of Poesy'*, lvi; Bates, *On Not Defending Poetry*; Crane, *Framing Authority*, 189; Guillory, *Poetic Authority*, 9–10.

106. Scott, *Model*, 41, 45; Howe, 'Our Speaking Picture', esp. 43–4.

107. Thomas Wright, *Passions*, 240, 242.

108. Méndez, 'Shakespeare's Knowledge', 71.

109. Castiglione, *Courtyer*, Xx2v.

110. Bull, *Christian Prayers*, 135.

111. Quintilian, *Orator's Education*, pp. 58–61, 6.2.29–30, 32; pp. 374–7, 8.3.62; Hutson, 'Shakespearean Unscene', 181; Mack, 'Early Modern Ideas'; Nauta and Pätzold, Introduction, x.
112. Peacham, *Garden*, 14. Further references are given parenthetically.
113. Hutson, *Circumstantial Shakespeare*, esp. 2; Hutson, 'Shakespearean Unscene'.
114. *True Chronicle Historie of [. . .] Cromwell*, B1v, D2r.
115. Heywood, *Foure Prentises*, C1r.
116. The play was performed at the Rose playhouse as well as at court; Wiggins with Catherine Richardson, *British Drama*, 4.1217, p. 171.
117. Dekker, *Old Fortunatus*, playhouse prol., ll. 15–19; 2.0.1–9.
118. Gurr, *Shakespearean Stage*, 17, 142, 157–8, 162, 260–1, 268, 277.
119. For further examples and discussion, see Hackett, 'All their Minds'.
120. For more examples, see Méndez, 'Shakespeare's Knowledge', 73–4.
121. Hutson, *Circumstantial Shakespeare*, 87, 93–4; Hutson, 'Shakespearean Unscene', 181–2.
122. For further discussion, including the question of where the *Henry V* choruses were first performed, see Hackett, 'All their Minds'.
123. Aristotle, *Generation of Animals*, Bk I, Chs xix–xxi, pp. 101, 109, 113; Galen, *Natural Faculties*, Bk I, Chs 6, 12, 13, 14; Bk II, Chs 3, 6; Bk III, Chs 1, 3; Lemnius, *Touchstone*, 26v; Needham, *History of Embryology*, 71, 93.
124. Shakespeare, *Midsummer Night's Dream*, ed. Dover Wilson, 80–5; Shakespeare, *Midsummer Night's Dream*, ed. Holland, 257–61.
125. For more examples, see Hutson, 'Shakespearean Unscene', 182–3.
126. See Roychoudhury, *Phantasmatic Shakespeare*, 197–201.

Chapter 8: Governing Self and State: The Politics of the Mind

1. Lemnius, *Touchstone*, 10v, 11r–v.
2. See also Babb, *Elizabethan Malady*, 18–19; Geoff Baldwin, 'Individual and Self', 356–7.
3. Plato, *Republic*, pp. 152–5: 440e–443b.
4. Erasmus, *Enchiridion*, 61–3.
5. Batman, *Batman upon Bartholome*, Bk 3, Ch. 7, f. 14r.
6. Romei, *Courtiers Academie*, 47–8.
7. May, *Elizabethan Courtier Poets*, 283; Geoff Baldwin, 'Individual and Self'.
8. Lipsius, *Six Bookes of Politickes*, A4v–A5r.
9. Griffiths, *Two Books of Homilies*, 105–6.
10. *Tottel's Miscellany*, 116–17.
11. Banister, *Treatise of Chyrurgerie*, 'Epistle Dedicatorie', no p. no.
12. Greville, 'Letter', 154, 165.
13. Kaegi, 'Passionate Uprisings'.
14. Spenser, *Faerie Queene*, II.i.57. Further references are given parenthetically.
15. Spenser, *Shorter Poems*, p. 62, ll. 48, 57; Hackett, *Virgin Mother*, 97, 102, 106, 165, 172.
16. Bates, 'Images of Government'.
17. Written *c.* 1596, published 1633. Hadfield, 'Spenser, Edmund'.
18. Spenser, *View*, no p. nos.
19. Sir John Davies, *Poems*, 5, 17. Further references are given parenthetically.
20. E.g., Blundeville, *Very Briefe and Profitable Treatise*, Q2v–Q3r.
21. Knox, *First Blast*, B2r.
22. Aylmer, *Harborowe*, H2v–H3r; McLaren, *Political Culture*, 59–69; Mears, *Queenship and Political Discourse*, 73–103.
23. Elizabeth I, *Translations, 1544–1589*, 369–79, 370; Susan Doran, 'Elizabeth I and Counsel'.
24. British Library, London, Harleian MS 6992, f. 89, quoted in Mears, *Queenship and Political Discourse*, 90.

25. Whitgift, *Defense of the Aunswere*, 180–2, 650; Collinson, 'Grindal, Edmund'; Collinson, 'Monarchical Republic', 413–14; Guy, 'Elizabethan Establishment', 127–8; Guy, *Forgotten Years*, 161; Lake, 'Monarchical Republic'.
26. Guy, 'Elizabethan Establishment', 128–38; Guy, 'Introduction: The 1590s', 11–15; McLaren, *Political Culture*, 9, 238, 241.
27. He was not knighted until 1603, but is referred to here as Sir John Davies to distinguish him from John Davies of Hereford. Kelsey, 'Davies, Sir John'.
28. Sir John Davies, *Poems*, 17.
29. Dimmock, *Elizabethan Globalism*, 73–8; Goldring et al., *Nichols's 'Progresses'*, 4.205–8. See also Wiggins with Catherine Richardson, *British Drama*, 4.1372.
30. Goldring et al., *Nichols's 'Progresses'*, 4.206.
31. Dimmock, *Elizabethan Globalism*, esp. 2–3, 54, 58, 100 n. 17, 103, 113, 237, 248; Erler, 'Sir John Davies'; Strong, *Cult*, 46–54; *Elizabethan Image*, 197–8.
32. Finkelpearl, 'Davies, John'.
33. Davies of Hereford, *Mirum in modum*, B1r–v. Further references are given parenthetically.
34. La Primaudaye, *Second Part*, 159.
35. William Allen, *Admonition*, A4v, B2r.
36. 'Doleman', *Conference*, 38.
37. Guy, *Forgotten Years*; Guy, *Reign of Elizabeth I*.
38. S[eager], *Schoole of Vertue*, B8v–C1r.
39. Blundeville, *Very Briefe and Profitable Treatise*, Q3r.
40. Whythorne, *Autobiography*, mod., 38; and see 59, 221.
41. Calvin, *Institution* (1561), 33v. Further references are given parenthetically.
42. See Soellner, *Shakespeare's Patterns*, 18–19.
43. Woolton, *Newe Anatomie*, 15r–16r, 31v.
44. Perkins, *Treatise of Imaginations*, 173–4; Douglas Clark, 'Theorising the Will', 68–9.
45. Sidney, *Old Arcadia*, 119.
46. Calvin, *Institution* (1561), 35v.
47. Woolton, *Newe Anatomie*, 20v.
48. La Primaudaye, *French Academie*, 24–5.
49. Heron, *Newe Discourse*, 129–30.
50. Sidney, *Defence*, 10.
51. Ascham, *Scholemaster*, 4v–6r.
52. Spenser, *Faerie Queene*, II.vi.7, II.vi.Arg.
53. Wiggins with Catherine Richardson, *British Drama*, 2.460, 461.
54. *Marriage of Wit and Science*, 1.1.33–4. Further references are given parenthetically.
55. Whythorne, *Autobiography*, orig., xx; mod., 6, 28, 60; Lennam, *Sebastian Westcott*, 98–101, ix–xi.
56. 'Fit for purpose'; or 'his own person'; or 'excellent, perfect, handsome'. *OED*, 'proper, adj.', A.I.1, A.II.3.b, A.III.7.
57. 'Wanton'; or 'skilful'. *OED*, 'nice, adj.', A.2.b, 10.c.
58. Douglas Clark, 'Theorising the Will', 112–13, 117–18; Richard Hillman, *Self-Speaking*, 70–3.
59. Breton, *Wil of Wit*, 1r. Further references are given parenthetically.
60. See Douglas Clark, 'Nicholas Breton'; Douglas Clark, 'Theorising the Will', 78–91.
61. Escobedo, *Volition's Face*, 57–96; Soellner, *Shakespeare's Patterns*, 245, 248.
62. Calvin, *Institution* (1561), 24v, 33v, 34r.
63. For the relation between Hooker's theology and Calvin's, see Voak, *Richard Hooker*, 1–21.
64. Hooker, *Of the Laws*, Bk 1, Ch. 7, pp. 57–60; Douglas Clark, 'Theorising the Will', 61–5; Soellner, *Shakespeare's Patterns*, 245–6; Voak, *Richard Hooker*, 27, 31–2, 51–60.
65. La Primaudaye, *Second Part*, 204. Further references are given parenthetically.

66. Sir John Davies, *Poems*, 16, 44–5.
67. Ibid., 79–80.
68. Elizabeth I, *Collected Works*, 51–2.
69. Wentworth, *Pithie Exhortation*, 61, 85–6.

Chapter 9: Writing Thought and Self: Autobiography, Sonnets, Prose Fiction

1. Thomas Wright, *Passions*, 162.
2. Higgins et al., *Mirour for Magistrates*, 36v–38r.
3. Brljak, 'Age of Allegory'.
4. Escobedo, *Volition's Face*, 15–56.
5. Sir John Davies, *Poems*, 8–10.
6. *OED*, 'autobiography, n.'; Dragstra, Ottway, and Wilcox, Introduction, 12–13; Ferry, *'Inward' Language*, 35–6; Mascuch, *Origins*, 6–9; Stewart, *Oxford History*, loc. 355.
7. A commonplace book was a personal notebook of useful sayings and literary extracts.
8. Dragstra, Ottway, and Wilcox, Introduction, 4; Kelly, Davis, and Bedford, Introduction, 15; Skura, *Tudor Autobiography*, 1–2; Smyth, *Autobiography*; Stewart, *Oxford History*, loc. 363.
9. Machyn, *London Provisioner's Chronicle*; Mortimer, 'Tudor Chronicler'.
10. Whythorne, *Autobiography*, orig., lvi, lxvi, 4–6.
11. Ibid., orig., 6.
12. Ibid., mod., 1. Further references are to this modern spelling edition (unless otherwise stated) and are given parenthetically.
13. Ferry, *'Inward' Language*, 36–9; Mousley, 'Renaissance Selves'; Skura, *Tudor Autobiography*, 99, 107; Stewart, *Oxford History*, locs 2094, 2308–52, 2511; Whythorne, *Autobiography*, orig., lv–lvi, lviii–lix.
14. Skura, *Tudor Autobiography*, 100, 112–15, 124.
15. Hart, '1500–1620', 121; Herman, Introduction, 8–9, 15; Palmer, *Fictional Minds*, 11, 14–15, 22; Zunshine, *Why We Read Fiction*, 4, 6.
16. Shore, '"Autobiography" of Thomas Whythorne'.
17. Cooper, *Citizen Portrait*.
18. See also Whythorne, *Autobiography*, orig., 305–6. John Bennell has speculatively identified a 1569 miniature as another portrait of Whythorne: Bennell, 'Whithorne, Thomas'; Katie M. Nelson, 'Whythorne and Musicians', 40; Strong, *English Renaissance Miniature*, 58–60, pl. 59.
19. Bennell, 'Whithorne, Thomas'; Howe, 'Authority of Presence'; Stewart, *Oxford History*, loc. 2081; Whythorne, *Autobiography*, orig., xlii.
20. Stewart, *Oxford History*, loc. 2398; Whythorne, *Autobiography*, orig., 305–6.
21. *OED*, 'counterfeit, adj. and n.'.
22. For more on Whythorne, see Heale, 'Songs, Sonnets'; Hodgkin, 'Thomas Whythorne'; Mousley, 'Early Modern Autobiography'.
23. Oppenheimer, *Birth of the Modern Mind*.
24. See Regan, *Sonnet*, for the early history of the form (9–14) and its associations across the centuries with intimacy and interiority (4, 7).
25. Sidney, *Astrophil*, Sonnets 4, 10, 67, 94, and 96. Further references are given parenthetically.
26. Regan, *Sonnet*, 37; Wiseman, 'Introspection'.
27. Sonnets 23, 27, 30, 41, 54, and 104. Ferry, *'Inward' Language*, 156–61; Regan, *Sonnet*, 48–52.
28. Marotti, *Manuscript, Print*; Woudhuysen, *Sir Philip Sidney*.
29. Sonnets 31–2, 38–40, 96–9. Ferry, *'Inward' Language*, 149–56.
30. *Tottel's Miscellany*, 59.
31. Sokolov, *Renaissance Texts*, 122.
32. See also Sonnet 47.

33. Altman, *Tudor Play of Mind*; Lindheim, 'Lyly's Golden Legacy', 20; Mack, 'Rhetoric in Use', 126–7.
34. See also Sonnet 44.
35. Mack, 'Learning and Transforming', 438–40; Regan, *Sonnet*, 5–7, 10, 13.
36. On the tension between lyric and narrative, see Sokolov, *Renaissance Texts*, 127–8.
37. On Astrophil as melancholic, see Sokolov, *Renaissance Texts*, 117–32. On the 'intensity of emotional fluctuation' right to the end of *Astrophil and Stella*, see Regan, *Sonnet*, 52.
38. Sokolov, *Renaissance Texts*, 129; Sokolov, 'Sir Philip Sidney', 228, 233–5, 237.
39. Ferry, *'Inward' Language*, 136–41.
40. Barnes, *Parthenophil*, 66 (numbered 68); Constable, *Diana*, F5v; Drayton, *Idea*, in *Englands Heroicall Epistles*, P2v.
41. Though a few appeared in *The Passionate Pilgrim* (1599).
42. H. S. Bennett, *English Books*, 269; Charlton and Spufford, 'Literacy, Society'; Kastan, 'Print, Literary Culture'; Melnikoff and Gieskes, Introduction, 6–17.
43. Charlton and Spufford, 'Literacy, Society', 33; Mentz, *Romance for Sale*; Salzman, *English Prose Fiction*, 1–6; Katharine Wilson, *Fictions of Authorship*, 1, 4; Katharine Wilson, 'Revenge and Romance', 688.
44. Hamilton, 'Elizabethan Prose Fiction', 22–3.
45. E.g., Lodge, *Consciousness*; Palmer, *Fictional Minds*; Zunshine, *Why We Read Fiction*. An exception is Herman, *Emergence of Mind*.
46. Chaucer, *Troilus and Criseyde*, II.624–812, esp. 659–60, 650. On multiple, divided subjectivities in *Troilus and Criseyde*, see Patterson, *Chaucer and the Subject of History*, 142–50. On instances of the representation of subjectivity in late medieval non-dramatic literature, see Richard Hillman, *Self-Speaking*, 56.
47. *Tottel's Miscellany*, 11, 21, 33.
48. Gascoigne, *Adventures*, 12, 23.
49. Stewart, *Oxford History*, locs 2247, 2256; Whythorne, *Autobiography*, orig., liv–lv.
50. Greville, *Dedication*, 11.
51. Salzman, *English Prose Fiction*, 49.
52. Sidney, *Old Arcadia*, 13. Further references are given parenthetically.
53. I am indebted to the late Dennis Kay for pointing out these instances of 'non-texts' in the *Arcadia*. For more on the representation of thoughts in both *Arcadia*s, see Carey, 'Structure and Rhetoric'; Kinney, *Humanist Poetics*, 255–6.
54. Hunter, *John Lyly*, 72.
55. Barish, 'Prose Style', esp. 15; Heilman, 'Greene's Euphuism', 51; Hunter, *John Lyly*, 168, 265; Lindheim, 'Lyly's Golden Legacy', 19; Mack, 'Rhetoric in Use', 119–21; Salzman, *English Prose Fiction*, 36.
56. Barish, 'Prose Style', 24–5, 27–8; Lindheim, 'Lyly's Golden Legacy', 3–4, 12; Salzman, *English Prose Fiction*, 35–6; Katharine Wilson, 'Revenge and Romance', 689.
57. Lindheim, 'Lyly's Golden Legacy', 20; Mack, 'Rhetoric in Use', 126–7.
58. Lyly, *Euphues*, 109–12.
59. Hunter, *John Lyly*, 270–1; Mack, 'Rhetoric in Use', 121.
60. Barish, 'Prose Style', 22–3; Lindheim, 'Lyly's Golden Legacy', 7.
61. Hamilton, 'Elizabethan Prose Fiction', 26.
62. Newcomb, *Reading Popular Romance*; Salzman, *Anthology*, xvii.
63. Hunter, *John Lyly*, 281–3; Salzman, *English Prose Fiction*, 47; Katharine Wilson, *Fictions of Authorship*, 7.
64. Das, *Renaissance Romance*, 122.
65. Hackett, *Women and Romance*, 148–50; Salzman, *English Prose Fiction*, 59–60.
66. Robert Greene, *Pandosto*, 173, 179, 203. Further references are given parenthetically. See also Kinney, *Humanist Poetics*, 191–9.
67. Ewbank, 'From Narrative', 37–9; Hamilton, 'Elizabethan Prose Fiction', 27–8; Heilmann, 'Greene's Euphuism', 55–6; Lindheim, 'Lyly's Golden Legacy', 13–15; Mack, 'Rhetoric in Use', 128.

68. Margolies, 'Fortune and Agency', esp. 196.
69. On the rhetorical complexity of *Pandosto*'s self-addressed monologues, see Kinney, *Humanist Poetics*, 224–5.
70. Moore, 'Elizabethan Fiction'; Hamilton, 'Elizabethan Prose Fiction', 28.
71. Hart, '1500–1620', 123; Mack, 'Rhetoric in Use', 120.

Chapter 10: 'That Within': *Hamlet* and the Mind on Stage

1. Du Laurens, 'Second Discourse', 100.
2. Kaufman, *Prayer, Despair*, 103–49; Soellner, *Shakespeare's Patterns*, 172–94.
3. R. B., *Apius and Virginia*, C1r.
4. Boas, review of *Pathomachia*; Wiggins with Catherine Richardson, *British Drama*, 7.1825. For more examples, see David L. Russell, *Stuart Academic Drama*; H. K. Russell, *Tudor and Stuart Dramatizations*.
5. Baskervill, *English Elements*, 212–13; Chapman, *Humorous Day's Mirth*, 13–14; Madeleine Doran, *Endeavors*, 169; Jonson, *Every Man out of his Humour*, Introduction.
6. Brian Cummings, *Mortal Thoughts*, 168.
7. Clemen, *Shakespeare's Soliloquies*, 3–4; Cousins and Derrin, Introduction, 2; Hirsh, *Shakespeare and History of Soliloquies*, 19, 82, 115.
8. Ellrodt, *Montaigne and Shakespeare*, 76; Hirsh, 'Origin', 142; *Shakespeare and History of Soliloquies*, 19–20, 45–6, 106, 115, 181–3; Hussey, *Literary Language*, 177–90.
9. Falco, 'Tudor Transformations'; Kaufman, *Prayer, Despair*, 6–7. Richard Hillman finds 'only a very few' soliloquies in medieval drama that hint 'at subjectivity as elusive or fragmented' (*Self-Speaking*, 41).
10. Brian Cummings, *Mortal Thoughts*, 172, 175–80; Falco, 'Tudor Transformations', 32; Hirsh, *Shakespeare and History of Soliloquies*, 32.
11. Joseph A. Smith, 'Roman Soliloquy', 19–24.
12. Boyle, *Tragic Seneca*, 272–3; Joseph A. Smith, 'Roman Soliloquy', 25–6.
13. Braund, 'Haunted by Horror', 425, 429–30; Burrow, *Shakespeare and Classical Antiquity*, 163–5.
14. Norton and Sackville, *Gorboduc*, C5v–C6v.
15. Falco, 'Tudor Transformations', 41–2.
16. Wiggins with Catherine Richardson, *British Drama*, 1.351, p. 377.
17. Boyle, *Tragic Seneca*, 248–50.
18. Kyd, *Spanish Tragedy*, 3.7.1–2, 10–11; 3.2.38–40, 44–7.
19. Hirsh, 'Origin', 132–3; *Shakespeare and History of Soliloquies*, 85, 108.
20. Arnold, 'Preface'.
21. Marlowe, *Tamburlaine*, 1.5.2.68, 97.
22. Marlowe, *Doctor Faustus*, 2.1.1–10; and see Belsey, *Subject of Tragedy*, 42–6.
23. For more on Marlowe's soliloquies, see Semler, 'Doubtful Battle'.
24. Bevington, 'Giving Voice', 80–3; Brian Cummings, *Mortal Thoughts*, 180–2.
25. Bates, 'Shakespeare and the Female Voice'.
26. Kermode, *Shakespeare's Language*, locs 1630–9.
27. Bevington, 'Giving Voice', 85–6; Brian Cummings, *Mortal Thoughts*, 184–7; Greenblatt, *Will in the World*, 300–1; Kermode, *Shakespeare's Language*, locs 817–64.
28. Joseph A. Smith, 'Roman Soliloquy', 25–8; Miola, *Shakespeare and Classical Tragedy*, 38–9.
29. Archer and Hadfield, Introduction, 2–5.
30. Higgins et al., *Mirour for Magistrates*, 122r. The 1587 edition of the *Mirror* is quoted because this was probably the version used by Shakespeare; Archer and Hadfield, Introduction, 2.
31. See Burrow, 'Montaignian Moments'.
32. Shakespeare, *King John*, ed. Braunmuller, 68–71.
33. Bevington, 'Giving Voice', 88–9.

34. Greenblatt, *Will in the World*, 301–2; Kermode, *Shakespeare's Language*, locs 1719–27. For more on the development of soliloquy from *The Spanish Tragedy* to *Julius Caesar*, see Richard Hillman, *Self-Speaking*, 107–63.
35. Callaghan, *'Hamlet': Language and Writing*, 83, 97; Newell, *Soliloquies in 'Hamlet'*, 27. For alternative tallies, see Clemen, *Shakespeare's Soliloquies*, 119; Hussey, *Literary Language*, 184.
36. This final soliloquy appears in only one early edition of *Hamlet*, the Second Quarto of 1604 (Q2). It does not appear in the First Quarto of 1603 (Q1) or the Folio of 1623 (F). See Shakespeare, *Hamlet*, ed. Thompson and Taylor, 18–19.
37. Clemen, *Shakespeare's Soliloquies*, 122; Ellrodt, *Montaigne and Shakespeare*, 84–5.
38. Newell, *Soliloquies in 'Hamlet'*, 18–19.
39. 'Sallied' in Q1 and Q2; 'solid' in F.
40. Callaghan, *'Hamlet': Language and Writing*, 90.
41. Hussey, *Literary Language*; Kermode, *Shakespeare's Language*, locs 109, 361, 369–84.
42. Callaghan, *'Hamlet': Language and Writing*, 87–8; Grazia, *'Hamlet' without Hamlet*, 2, 89.
43. Shakespeare, *Hamlet*, ed. Thompson and Taylor, 18.
44. Altman, *Tudor Play of Mind*; Burrow, *Shakespeare and Classical Antiquity*, 42; Lewis, *Hamlet and the Vision of Darkness*, 268; Lim, 'To Be'; Newell, *Soliloquies in 'Hamlet'*, 75.
45. Lewis, *Hamlet and the Vision of Darkness*, 268–76; Lim, 'To Be', 648–9.
46. Lim, 'To Be', 646–53.
47. Charney, 'To Be'.
48. Crane, *Shakespeare's Brain*, 3–35.
49. Lyne, *Shakespeare, Rhetoric and Cognition*.
50. Newell, *Soliloquies in 'Hamlet'*, 76.
51. Hirsh, *Shakespeare and History of Soliloquies*, 32, 231–77.
52. Ibid., 18, 20, 26, 119, 124, 141, 285–7; Hirsh, 'What Were Soliloquies?', 206–7, 217–18.
53. Lyne, *Shakespeare, Rhetoric and Cognition*, 8, 27, 54, 57.
54. Hirsh maintains that Elizabethan soliloquies were understood as speeches not thoughts, but even so self-addressed, not addressed to the audience. Hirsh, 'Origin'; Hirsh, *Shakespeare and History of Soliloquies*, 19–20, 27, 106–16; Hirsh, 'What Were Soliloquies?', 208, 214–15.
55. Purcell, 'Performing the Public', 57.
56. Grazia, *'Hamlet' without Hamlet*, 185–6.
57. Callaghan, *'Hamlet': Language and Writing*, 82–4, 87; Brian Cummings, *Mortal Thoughts*, 170–1, 183; Richard Hillman, *Self-Speaking*, 30–1 n. 1.
58. Cousins and Derrin, Introduction, 10–11.
59. Brian Cummings, *Mortal Thoughts*, 182.
60. See Barker, *Tremulous Private Body*, 31–3; Belsey, *Subject of Tragedy*, 41–2; Crane, *Shakespeare's Brain*, 116–55; Brian Cummings, *Mortal Thoughts*, 180; Greenblatt, *Will in the World*, 323–4; David Hillman, *Shakespeare's Entrails*, 81–116; Hirsh, *Shakespeare and History of Soliloquies*, 189, 196; Kermode, *Shakespeare's Language*, locs 2325–33.
61. Cornwallis, *Essayes*, O1v; R. E. Bennett, 'Cornwallis's Use of Montaigne'; Lee, 'English Renaissance Essay', 443; Shapiro, *1599*, 328–33.
62. R. E. Bennett, 'Cornwallis's Use of Montaigne', 1080–1; William M. Hamlin, *Montaigne's English Journey*, 8 n. 18; William M. Hamlin, 'Montaigne and Shakespeare', 335–6; Shapiro, *1599*, 329.
63. Montaigne, 'Of the Caniballes', *Essayes*, Bk 1, Ch. 30, pp. 102–3.
64. Ellrodt, *Montaigne and Shakespeare*, 92–4; William M. Hamlin, 'Montaigne and Shakespeare', 335–6; William M. Hamlin, *Montaigne's English Journey*, 8 n. 18; Shapiro, *1599*, 329.
65. William M. Hamlin, *Montaigne's English Journey*, 110–11; Lim, 'To Be', 648–50.
66. Montaigne, 'The Author to the Reader', *Essayes*, A6v; Shapiro, *1599*, 333.
67. Ellrodt, *Montaigne and Shakespeare*, 1–24.

68. Brian Cummings, *Mortal Thoughts*, 179; Lee, *Shakespeare's 'Hamlet'*, 181–207; Mack, *Reading and Rhetoric*, 74–105.
69. Bacon, *Essayes*, A4v.
70. Boutcher, *School of Montaigne*, 2.212, 246; Lee, 'English Renaissance Essay', 439–44.
71. Shapiro, *1599*, 332. On the dramatic usefulness to Shakespeare of 'Montaignian moments' of reflective, essay-like speech rather than action, see Burrow, 'Montaignian Moments'.
72. Ellrodt, *Montaigne and Shakespeare*, 76–7.
73. Bates, 'Shakespeare and the Female Voice'.
74. Southwell, 'Saint Peter's Complaynt', *Collected Poems*, 64.
75. Breton, *Pilgrimage to Paradise*, 96, 94.
76. Nashe, 'Somewhat to Reade', A3r.
77. See Regan, *Sonnet*, on sonnets as speech-acts or soliloquies (7, 10) and on the dramatic qualities of *Astrophil and Stella* in particular (37, 40, 42).
78. Sidney, *Astrophil*, 'Tenth Song', 203.
79. Meres, *Palladis Tamia*, 281v–282r.
80. Shakespeare, Sonnet 1, *The Passionate Pilgrim*, in *Complete Sonnets and Poems*, ed. Burrow, 341; and see also p. 76 for identification of the poems in the volume by Shakespeare.
81. Sidney, *Old Arcadia*, 97.
82. Robert Greene, *Pandosto*, 165.
83. Lyly, *Euphues*, 112; Robert Greene, *Pandosto*, 160.
84. E.g., Greenblatt, *Will in the World*, 299; Kermode, *Shakespeare's Language*, locs 109, 369–77, 2325, 2333; Shapiro, *1599*, 328.
85. Hackett, 'As the Diall Hand'; Hackett, 'Dream-Visions of Elizabeth I'; Hackett, *Virgin Mother, Maiden Queen*, 176–97; Shakespeare, *Hamlet*, ed. Thompson and Taylor, 38–43.
86. E.g., Burrow, 'Montaignian Moments', 239; Ellrodt, *Montaigne and Shakespeare*, *passim*; Kiséry, *Hamlet's Moment*.

Epilogue: The Elizabethan Mind and Us

1. Sir John Davies, *Poems*, 8.
2. E.g., Damasio, *Self Comes to Mind*; Searle, 'Mystery of Consciousness'; Seth, *Being You*; Torey, *Conscious Mind*.
3. Newen, Gallagher, and De Bruin, Introduction, 10.
4. Bryson, *The Body*, 89–90; Kwint and Wingate, *Brains*, 22–31.
5. Newen, Gallagher, and De Bruin, Introduction, 3; Seth, *Being You*, loc. 265; Westphal, *Mind–Body Problem*.
6. Bryson, *The Body*, 90–4, 102; Gellatly and Zarate, *Introducing Mind*, 38, 40–6, 101.
7. Gellatly and Zarate, *Introducing Mind*, 22–6.
8. Passingham, *Cognitive Neuroscience*, esp. 3–9; Tracy, 'Life of Pain'.
9. Greenfield, 'Soul, Brain and Mind'; O'Shea, *The Brain*, 1–2; Seth, *Being You*; Torey, *Conscious Mind*.
10. Gellatly and Zarate, *Introducing Mind*, 40–3; O'Shea, *The Brain*, 51.
11. Passingham, *Cognitive Neuroscience*, 67; O'Shea, *The Brain*, 62.
12. Bryson, *The Body*, 91; Passingham, *Cognitive Neuroscience*, 63–9.
13. O'Shea, *The Brain*, 60–2; Passingham, *Cognitive Neuroscience*, 63–5.
14. Bryson, *The Body*, 91; Passingham, *Cognitive Neuroscience*, 67; Matthew Walker, *Why We Sleep*, 224.
15. Matthew Walker, *Why We Sleep*, 224.
16. Crane, *Framing Authority*, 71; David Hillman, *Shakespeare's Entrails*, 23–4.
17. Hahamy, 'Brain at Rest', and private correspondence, 29 May 2019; Leschziner, *Nocturnal Brain*.
18. La Primaudaye, *Second Part*, 155–6; see Ch. 7 above.

19. Matthew Walker, *Why We Sleep*, 221, 228, 233.
20. Andy Clark, *Supersizing the Mind*, xxv–xxix.
21. Newen, Gallagher, and De Bruin, Introduction; Robbins and Aydede, 'Short Primer'.
22. Robbins and Aydede, 'Short Primer', 4.
23. Newen, Gallagher, and De Bruin, Introduction, 6.
24. E.g., Bruhn and Wehrs, *Cognition, Literature, and History*; Hogan, *Cognitive Science*; Zunshine, *Cognitive Literary Studies*; Alan Richardson, 'Once upon a Mind'.
25. Crane, *Shakespeare's Brain*, 14.
26. E.g., Anderson, *Renaissance Extended Mind*; Craik and Pollard, *Shakespearean Sensations*; Floyd-Wilson and Garrett A. Sullivan, Jr, *Environment and Embodiment*; Laurie Johnson, Sutton, and Tribble, *Embodied Cognition*; Lyne, *Shakespeare, Rhetoric and Cognition*; Paster, *Humoring the Body*; Tribble, *Cognition in the Globe*.
27. Newen, Gallagher, and De Bruin, Introduction, 11.
28. *OED*, 'affect, n.', 5.b.
29. E.g., the History of Emotions Research Center at the Max Planck Institute for Human Development, Berlin; the Centre for the History of Emotions at Queen Mary, University of London; and the Australian Research Council Centre of Excellence for the History of Emotions, University of Western Australia.
30. Broomhall, Davidson, and Lynch, *Cultural History of Emotions*.
31. E.g., Broomhall, *Authority, Gender and Emotions*; Broomhall, *Early Modern Emotions*; Broomhall, *Gender and Emotions*; Broomhall, *Ordering Emotions*; Dixon, *From Passions to Emotions*; James, *Passion and Action*; Meek and Erin Sullivan, *Renaissance of Emotion*; Mullaney, *Reformation of Emotions*; Paster, Rowe, and Floyd-Wilson, *Reading the Early Modern Passions*.
32. Newen, Gallagher, and De Bruin, Introduction, 11.
33. Thomas Wright, *Passions*, 88; see Ch. 7 above.
34. Gellatly and Zarate, *Introducing Mind*, 37; O'Shea, *The Brain*, 3.
35. E.g., Fasano and Flaherty, *Gut Feelings*.
36. Tetramap, 'The Elements'.
37. E.g., Cheung, *Dream Dictionary*.
38. Seth, *Being You*, loc. 131.
39. 'UCL Research Domains – Neuroscience: People.'
40. 'About the Faculty', UCL Brain Sciences.
41. Passingham, *Cognitive Neuroscience*, 106–7; and see Seth, *Being You*, locs 251, 354.
42. Seth, *Being You*, locs 4673, 4699.
43. Bryson, *The Body*, 94.
44. See also O'Shea, *The Brain*, 1, 124.

BIBLIOGRAPHY

Manuscripts

Batman (Bateman), Stephen (Stephan). 'A Booke of the Coppies: Of Letters, Libells & Outher Inventions of Men.' Before 1584. Houghton Library, Harvard University, Cambridge, MA, MS Eng 1015.

Forman, Simon. 'The Bocke of the Life and Generation of Simon.' 1600. Oxford, Bodleian Library, Ashmole MS 208, ff. 136–42.

——. 'Of Melancoly.' 1594–95. Oxford, Bodleian Library, Ashmole MS 1495, ff. 45r–117v.

——. Untitled. Oxford, Bodleian Library, Ashmole MS 226.

——. Untitled. Oxford, Bodleian Library, Ashmole MS 1472.

Other Primary Works

Alabaster, William. *Unpublished Works*. Edited by Dana F. Sutton. Salzburg: University of Salzburg, 1997.

Alexander, Gavin, ed. *Sidney's 'The Defence of Poesy' and Selected Renaissance Literary Criticism*. London: Penguin, 2004.

Allen, William. *An Admonition to the Nobility and People of England and Ireland*. Antwerp, 1588.

——. *A Briefe Historie of the Glorious Martyrdom of XII. Reuerend Priests*. Rheims, 1582.

Almond, Philip C., ed. *Demonic Possession and Exorcism in Early Modern England: Contemporary Texts and their Cultural Contexts*. Cambridge: Cambridge University Press, 2004.

'Anger, Jane' (pseud.). *Jane Anger her Protection for Women* (London, 1589). In *The Women's Sharp Revenge: Five Women's Pamphlets from the Renaissance*, edited by Simon Shepherd, 29–51. London: Fourth Estate, 1985.

Arden of Faversham. Edited by Martin White. New Mermaids. 1982; London: A & C Black, 1990.

Aristotle. *De anima*. Translated by Christopher Shields. Oxford: Clarendon, 2016.

—. *Generation of Animals.* With translation by A. L. Peck. Loeb Classical Library. London: Heinemann, 1943.

Ascham, Roger. *The Scholemaster or Plaine and Perfite Way of Teachyng Children, to Understand, Write, and Speake, the Latin Tong.* London, 1570.

Axton, Marie, ed. *Three Tudor Classical Interludes: Thersites, Jacke Jugeler, Horestes.* Cambridge: D. S. Brewer, 1982.

Aylmer, John. *An Harborowe for Faithfull and Trewe Subjectes.* London (title-page states Strasbourg), 1559.

B., R. *A New Tragicall Comedie of Apius and Virginia.* London, 1575.

Babington, Gervase. *A Briefe Conference, betwixt Mans Frailtie and Faith.* London, 1583.

Bacon, Francis. *Essayes. Religious Meditations. Places of Perswasion and Disswasion. Seene and Allowed.* London, 1597.

Baldwin, William. *A Treatise of Morall Phylosophie, Contaynyng the Sayinges of the Wyse.* London, 1547.

Banister, John. *A Needefull, New, and Necessarie Treatise of Chyrurgerie.* London, 1575.

Barnes, Barnabe. *Parthenophil and Parthenophe.* London, 1593.

Batman (Bateman), Stephen (Stephan). *Batman uppon Bartholome.* London, 1582.

—. *A Christall Glasse of Christian Reformation.* London, 1569.

Bentley, Thomas, ed. *The Monument of Matrons.* London, 1582.

Best, George. *A True Discourse of the Late Voyages of Discoverie, for the Finding of a Passage to Cathaya, by the Northweast.* London, 1578.

Bettenson, Henry, ed. *Documents of the Christian Church.* 2nd edn. Oxford: Oxford University Press, 1963.

Bible Gateway. biblegateway.com

Blundeville, Thomas. *A Very Briefe and Profitable Treatise Declaring Howe Many Counsells, and What Maner of Counselers a Prince That Will Governe Well Ought to Have.* London, 1570.

Boaistuau, Pierre. *Certaine Secrete Wonders of Nature.* (*Histoires prodigieuses extraictes de plusiers fameux auteurs grecs & latins*, 1560.) Translated by Edward Fenton. London, 1569.

Bodin, Jean. *Method for the Easy Comprehension of History* (1565). Translated by Beatrice Reynolds. New York: Columbia University Press, 1945.

The Book of Common Prayer: The Texts of 1549, 1559, and 1662. Edited by Brian Cummings. Oxford: Oxford University Press, 2011.

Boorde, Andrew. *The Breviarie of Health.* 1547; London, 1587.

—. *A Compendyous Regyment or a Dyetary of Helth.* London, 1542.

—. *The Fyrst Boke of the Introduction of Knowledge.* London, 1555.

Bradwell, Stephen. 'Mary Glovers Late Woeful Case.' In MacDonald, *Witchcraft and Hysteria.*

Breton, Nicholas. *Melancholike Humours, in Verses of Diverse Natures.* London, 1600.

—. *The Passions of the Spirit.* London, 1599.

—. *The Pilgrimage to Paradise, Joyned with the Countesse of Penbrookes Love.* London, 1592.

—. *Poems Not Hitherto Reprinted.* Edited by Jean Robertson. 1952; Liverpool: Liverpool University Press, 1967.

—. *The Wil of Wit, Wits Will, or Wils Wit, Chuse You Whether.* London, 1597.

Bright, Timothy (Timothie). *A Treatise of Melancholie.* London, 1586.

Bull, Henry. *Christian Praiers and Holie Meditations.* London, 1578?

Bullein, William. *Bulleins Bulwarke of Defence against All Sicknesse, Soarenesse, and Woundes.* London, 1579.

—. *A Newe Booke Entituled the Governement of Healthe.* London, 1558.

Bullinger, Heinrich. *Fiftie Godlie and Learned Sermons Divided into Five Decades.* London, 1577.

Calvin, Jean. *An Admonicion against Astrology Judiciall.* (*Advertissement contre l'astrologie judiciaire*, 1549.) Translated by G[oddred] G[ilby]. London, 1561.

—. *The Institution of Christian Religion.* Translated by Thomas Norton. London, 1561.

—. *The Institution of Christian Religion.* Translated by Thomas Norton. London, 1562.

—. *The Psalmes of David and Others. With M. John Calvins Commentaries.* Translated by Arthur Golding. London, 1571.

—. *Sermons of John Calvin, upon the Songe That Ezechias Made after he Had Bene Sicke.* Translated by Anne Lock. London, 1560.

—. *The Sermons of M. Iohn Calvin, upon the Epistle of S. Paule too the Ephesians.* Translated by Arthur Golding. London, 1577.

Cardano, Girolamo. *Cardanus Comforte.* Translated by Thomas Bedingfeld. London, 1573.

Carew, Richard, trans. *The Examination of Mens Wits* (1594). From Juan Huarte, *Examen de ingenios para las ciencias* (1575). Edited by Rocío G. Sumillera. MHRA Tudor and Stuart Translations Vol. 17. London: MHRA, 2014.

Castiglione, Baldassare. *The Courtyer of Count Baldessar Castilio.* Translated by Sir Thomas Hoby. London, 1561.

Chamber, John. *A Treatise against Judicial Astrologie.* London, 1601.

Chapman, George. *The Blinde Begger of Alexandria* (1598). Malone Society Reprints. Edited by W. W. Greg. Oxford: Malone Society, 1928.

—. *An Humorous Day's Mirth.* Edited by Charles Edelman. Revels Plays. Manchester: Manchester University Press, 2010.

Chassanion, Jean de. *The Theatre of Gods Judgements.* Translated by Thomas Beard. London, 1597.

Chaucer, Geoffrey. *Troilus and Criseyde.* In *The Riverside Chaucer*, 3rd edn, general editor Larry D. Benson, 471–585. Oxford: Oxford University Press, 1988.

Churchyard, Thomas. *Churchyards Challenge.* London, 1593.

Cicero, Marcus Tullius. 'Scipio hys Dream.' ('Somnium Scipionis.') In *Paradoxa Stoicorum*, translated by Thomas Newton, E3v–F7r. London, 1569.

Constable, Henry. *Diana. Or, The Excellent Conceitful Sonnets of H. C.* London, 1595?

The Copie of a Leter, Wryten by a Master of Arte of Cambrige, to his Friend in London. (*Leicester's Commonwealth.*) Paris, 1584.

Copley, Anthony. *A Fig for Fortune by Anthony Copley: A Catholic Response to 'The Faerie Queene'.* Edited by Susannah Brietz Monta. Oxford: Oxford University Press, 2016.

Cornwallis the Younger, Sir William. *Essayes*, parts 1 and 2. London, 1600, 1601.

Cuningham, William. *The Cosmographical Glasse.* London, 1559.

Dariot, Claude. *A Breefe and Most Easie Introduction to the Astrologicall Iudgement of the Starres.* (*Ad astrorum judicia facilis introductio*, 1557.) Translated by Fabian Wither. London, 1583?

Darrel, John. *An Apologie, or Defence of the Possession of William Sommers, a Yong Man of the Towne Of Nottingham.* Amsterdam?, 1599?

Davies, Sir John. *Poems.* Edited by Robert Krueger and Ruby Nemser. Oxford: Oxford University Press, 1975.

Davies of Hereford, John. *Mirum in modum. A Glimpse of Gods Glorie and the Soules Shape.* London, 1602.

Dee, John. *Diaries.* Edited by Edward Fenton. Charlbury: Day Books, 1998.

—. *The Private Diary of Dr. John Dee, and the Catalogue of his Library of Manuscripts, from the Original Manuscripts.* Edited by James Orchard Halliwell. London: Camden Society, 1842.

Dekker, Thomas. *Old Fortunatus.* In *The Dramatic Works of Thomas Dekker*, edited by Fredson Bowers, I:105–205. Cambridge: Cambridge University Press, 1962.

—, William Haughton, and John Day. *Lusts Dominion, or, The Lascivious Queen a Tragedie.* London, 1657.

Descartes, René. *A Discourse on the Method.* Translated by Ian Maclean. Oxford: Oxford University Press, 2006.

Digges, Leonard. *A Prognostication of Right Good Effect.* London, 1555.

'Doleman, R.' (Robert Persons?). *A Conference about the Next Succession to the Crowne of England.* Antwerp, 1595.

Donne, John. *The Elegies and the Songs and Sonnets*. Edited by Helen Gardner. Oxford: Oxford University Press, 1965.

—. 'The First Anniversarie: An Anatomy of the World.' In *The Epithalamions, Anniversaries and Epicedes*, edited by W. Milgate, 20–38. Oxford: Oxford University Press, 1978.

Drayton, Michael. *Englands Heroicall Epistles. Newly Enlarged. With Idea*. London, 1599.

The Dreames of Daniell, Here Begynneth. London, 1556?

Du Laurens, André (Andreas Laurentius). 'The Second Discourse, Wherein Are Handled the Diseases of Melancholie, and the Meanes to Cure Them.' In *A Discourse of the Preservation of the Sight: Of Melancholike Diseases; Of Rheumes, and Of Old Age*, translated by Richard Surflet, 72–140. London, 1599.

Eden, Richard. *The Decades of the Newe Worlde or West India*. London, 1555.

Edwards, Richard, ed. *The Paradise of Daintie Devises*. London, 1585.

Elizabeth I. *Autograph Compositions and Foreign Language Originals*. Edited by Janel Mueller and Leah S. Marcus. Chicago: University of Chicago Press, 2003.

—. *Collected Works*. Edited by Leah S. Marcus, Janel Mueller, and Mary Beth Rose. Chicago: University of Chicago Press, 2000.

—. *Selected Works*. Edited by Steven W. May. New York: Washington Square Press, 2004.

—. *Translations, 1544–1589*. Edited by Janel Mueller and Joshua Scodel. Chicago: University of Chicago Press, 2009.

—. *Translations, 1592–1598*. Edited by Janel Mueller and Joshua Scodel. Chicago: University of Chicago Press, 2009.

Elyot, Sir Thomas. *The Castell of Health*. London, 1595.

Epictetus. *Discourses, Books 1–2*. With translation by W. A. Oldfather. Loeb Classical Library 131. Cambridge, MA: Harvard University Press, 1925.

Erasmus, Desiderius. *Enchiridion militis Christiani: An English Version*. Edited by Anne M. O'Donnell. Early English Text Society no. 282. Oxford: Oxford University Press, 1981.

—. *The First Tome or Volume of the Paraphrase of Erasmus upon the Newe Testamente*. Translated by Nicholas Udall. London, 1548.

Ficino, Marsilio. *Three Books on Life. (De vita libri tres.)* Translated and edited by Carol V. Kaske and John R. Clark. Tempe, AZ: Medieval and Renaissance Texts and Studies, 1998.

Foxe, John. *The Acts and Monuments of John Foxe*. 8 vols. Edited by Rev. Josiah Pratt. London, 1877.

—. *Foxe's Book of Martyrs: Select Narratives*. Edited by John King. Oxford: Oxford University Press, 2009.

Fulke, William. *Antiprognosticon That Is to Saye, an Invective agaynst the Vayne and Unprofitable Predictions of the Astrologians. (Antiprognosticon contra inutiles astrologorum prædictiones*, 1560.) Translated by William Painter. London, 1560.

—. *T. Stapleton and Martiall (Two Popish Heretikes) Confuted, and of their Particular Heresies Detected*. London, 1580.

Galen. *On the Natural Faculties*. Translated by Arthur John Brock. *The Internet Classics Archive*. classics.mit.edu/Galen/natfac.html

Gascoigne, George. *The Adventures of Master F. J.* (1573). In Salzman, *Anthology of Elizabethan Prose Fiction*, 1–81.

—. 'Certain Notes of Instruction' (1575). In Alexander, *Sidney's 'The Defence of Poesy'*, 237–47.

The Geneva Bible: A Facsimile of the 1560 Edition. Introduced by Lloyd E. Berry. Madison: University of Wisconsin Press, 1969.

Gerard, John. *The Autobiography of an Elizabethan*. Translated by Philip Caraman. 2nd edn. London: Longmans, Green, 1956.

Giffard (Gifford), George. *A Dialogue concerning Witches and Witchcraftes*. London, 1593.

Gratarolo, Guglielmo. *The Castel of Memorie Wherein Is Conteyned the Restoring, Augmenting, and Conserving of the Memorye and Remembraunce*. Translated by William Fulwood. London, 1562.

Greene, Robert *Pandosto. The Triumph of Time*. In Salzman, *Anthology of Elizabethan Prose Fiction*, 151–204.

—. *Penelopes Web*. London, 1587.

—. *Planetomachia* (1585). Edited by Nandini Das. Aldershot: Ashgate, 2007.

Greville, Fulke, Lord Brooke. 'A Dedication to Sir Philip Sidney.' In *Prose Works*, 3–135.

—. 'A Letter to an Honorable Lady.' In *Prose Works*, 137–76.

—. *The Prose Works of Fulke Greville, Lord Brooke*. Edited by John Gouws. Oxford: Clarendon, 1986.

Griffiths, John, ed. *The Two Books of Homilies Appointed to Be Read in Churches*. Oxford: Oxford University Press, 1859.

Grymeston, Elizabeth. *Miscelanea. Meditations. Memoratives*. London, 1604.

Guicciardini, Lodovico. *The Garden of Pleasure*. Translated by James Sanford. London, 1573.

Hake, Edward. *A Touchestone for this Time Present*. London, 1574.

Hakluyt, Richard, ed. *The Principall Navigations, Voiages and Discoveries of the English Nation*. London, 1589.

Harington, Sir John. *Nugae antiquae: Being a Miscellaneous Collection of Original Papers in Prose and Verse*. 2 vols. London, 1769–75.

Harrison, William. 'A Brief Discourse of the Christian Life and Death, of Mistris Katherin Brettergh.' In William Harrison and William Leigh, *Deaths Advantage Little Regarded, and the Soules Solace against Sorrow*. London, 1602.

—. 'An Historicall Description of the Iland of Britaine.' In *The First and Second Volumes of Chronicles*, edited by Raphael Holinshed, vol. 1. London, 1587. *The Holinshed Project*. cems.ox.ac.uk/holinshed/texts.shtml

Harsnett, Samuel. *A Declaration of Egregious Popish Impostures*. London, 1603.

—. *A Discovery of the Fraudulent Practises of John Darrel Bacheler of Artes*. London, 1599.

Heron, Haly. *A Newe Discourse of Morall Philosophie, Entituled, the Kayes of Counsaile*. London, 1579.

Heywood, Thomas. *The Foure Prentises of London*. London, 1615.

Higgins, John, et al. *The Mirour for Magistrates*. London, 1587.

Hill, Thomas. *The Contemplation of Mankinde Contayning a Singuler Discourse after the Art of Phisiognomie*. London, 1571.

—. *The Moste Pleasuante Arte of the Interpretacion of Dreames*. London, 1576.

Hoby, Lady Margaret. *The Private Life of an Elizabethan Lady: The Diary of Lady Margaret Hoby, 1599–1605*. Edited by Joanna Moody. Stroud: Sutton, 1998.

Hooker, Richard. *Of the Laws of Ecclesiastical Polity, Vol. 1: Preface, Books I to IV*. Edited by Arthur Stephen McGrade. Oxford: Oxford University Press, 2013.

Howard, Henry. *A Defensative against the Poyson of Supposed Prophesies*. London, 1583.

Humphrey, Laurence. *Interpretatio linguarum: seu de ratione conuertendi & explicandi autores tam sacros quam prophanos*. Basel, 1559.

Jonson, Ben. *The Cambridge Edition of the Works of Ben Jonson Online*. General editor Martin Butler. Cambridge: Cambridge University Press, 2015.

—. *The Case Is Altered* (1597), modernised. Edited by Robert Miola. In Butler, *Cambridge Ben Jonson Online*.

—. *Every Man in his Humour*, quarto version (1598), modernised. Edited by David Bevington. In Butler, *Cambridge Ben Jonson Online*.

—. *Every Man out of his Humour* (1599), modernised. Edited by Randall Martin. In Butler, *Cambridge Ben Jonson Online*.

Jorden, Edward. *A Briefe Discourse of a Disease Called the Suffocation of the Mother*. London, 1603.

Kassell, Lauren, et al., eds. *The Casebooks of Simon Forman and Richard Napier, 1596–1634: A Digital Edition*. casebooks.lib.cam.ac.uk

Knewstub, John. *A Sermon Preached at Paules Crosse the Fryday before Easter, Commonly Called Good Friday*. London, 1579.

Knox, John. *The First Blast of the Trumpet against the Monstruous Regiment of Women*. Geneva, 1558.

Kyd, Thomas. *The Spanish Tragedy*. Edited by J. R. Mulryne and Andrew Gurr. New Mermaids. London: Bloomsbury, 2009.

La Primaudaye, Pierre de. *The French Academie*. (*L'Académie française*, 1577.) Translated by Thomas Bowes. London, 1586.

—. *The Second Part of the French Academie*. (*Suite de l'Académie françoise*, 1580.) Translator unknown. London, 1594.

A Lamentable Ballad of the Tragical End of a Gallant Lord, and a Vertuous Lady, with the Untimely End of their Two Children, Wickedly Performed by a Heathenish Blackamoor their Servant, the Like Never Heard of Before. 1658–64? *English Broadside Ballad Archive*. EBBA 31955. University of Glasgow Library, Euing Ballads 197. ebba.english.ucsb.edu/ballad/31955/image

Lancashire, Ian, ed. *Two Tudor Interludes: The Interlude of Youth, Hick Scorner*. Manchester: Manchester University Press, 1980.

Lavater, Ludwig. *Of Ghostes and Spirites Walking by Nyght*. (*De spectris, lemuribus et magnis atque insolitis fragoribus*, 1569.) Translated by R[obert] H[arrison]. London, 1572.

Lemnius, Levinus. *The Touchstone of Complexions*. (*De habitu et constitutione corporis*, 1561.) Translated by Thomas Newton. London, 1576.

Leo Africanus, John. *A Geographical Historie of Africa*. Translated by John Pory. London, 1600.

Leroy, Louis. *Of the Interchangeable Course, or Variety of Things in the Whole World*. (*De la vicissitude ou variete des choses en l'univers*, 1575.) Translated by Robert Ashley. London, 1594.

Lipsius, Justus. *Sixe Bookes of Politickes or Civil Doctrine*. (*Politicorum sive civilis doctrinae libri sex*, 1589.) Translated by William Jones. London, 1594.

—. *Two Bookes of Constancie*. Translated by John Stradling. London, 1595.

Lock, Anne (Vaughan). *Collected Works*. Edited by Susan M. Felch. Tempe, AZ: Arizona Center for Medieval and Renaissance Studies, 1999.

Lodge, Thomas. *A Treatise of the Plague*. London, 1603.

Lok, Henry. *Sundry Christian Passions Contained in Two Hundred Sonnets*. London, 1593.

Lomazzo, Giovanni Paolo. *A Tracte Containing the Artes of Curious Paintinge Carvinge Buildinge*. (*Trattato dell'arte de la pittura, scultura, et architettura*, 1584.) Translated by Richard Haydock. London, 1598.

Lupton, Thomas. *A Thousand Notable Things, of Sundry Sortes*. London, 1579.

Lyly, John. *Euphues: The Anatomy of Wit*. In Salzman, *Anthology of Elizabethan Prose Fiction*, 83–150.

—. *Midas*. In *Galatea and Midas*, edited by George K. Hunter and David Bevington. The Revels Plays. Manchester: Manchester University Press, 2000.

—. *The Woman in the Moon*. Edited by Leah Scragg. Manchester: Manchester University Press, 2006.

MacDonald, Michael, ed. *Witchcraft and Hysteria in Elizabethan London: Edward Jorden and the Mary Glover Case*. London: Tavistock/Routledge, 1991.

Machyn, Henry. *A London Provisioner's Chronicle, 1550–1563*. Edited by Richard W. Bailey, Marilyn Miller, and Colette Moore. Michigan Publishing. quod.lib.umich.edu/m/machyn/

Mackay, Christopher S., trans. *The Hammer of Witches: A Complete Translation of the 'Malleus Maleficarum'*. Cambridge: Cambridge University Press, 2009.

Mandeville, Sir John. *The Voyages and Trauailes of Sir John Maundevile Knight*. London, 1582.

Manningham, John. *The Diary of John Manningham of the Middle Temple 1602–1603*. Edited by Robert Parker Sorlien. Hanover, NH: University of Rhode Island, 1976.

Marlowe, Christopher. *Doctor Faustus, A-Text*. In *Doctor Faustus and Other Plays*, 137–83.

—. *Doctor Faustus and Other Plays*. Edited by David Bevington and Eric Rasmussen. Oxford: Oxford University Press, 1995.

—. *The Jew of Malta*. In *Doctor Faustus and Other Plays*, 247–322.

—. *Tamburlaine, Parts One and Two*. Edited by Anthony B. Dawson. New Mermaids/ Methuen Drama. 1971; London: Bloomsbury, 2014.

The Marriage of Wit and Science. In Lennam, *Sebastian Westcott*.

May, Steven W., ed. *The Elizabethan Courtier Poets: The Poems and their Contexts*. Columbia, MO: University of Missouri Press, 1991.

—, ed. *The Poems of Edward DeVere, Seventeenth Earl of Oxford and of Robert Devereux, Second Earl of Essex. Studies in Philology* 77.5 (Winter 1980).

Meres, Francis. *Palladia Tamia*. London, 1598.

Montaigne, Michel de. *The Essayes or Morall, Politike and Millitarie Discourses*. Translated by John Florio. London, 1603.

Moulton, Thomas. *The Mirrour or Glasse of Health*. London, 1580.

Mulcaster, Richard. *Positions Wherin Those Primitive Circumstances Be Examined, Which Are Necessarie for the Training Up of Children, Either for Skill in their Booke, or Health in their Bodie*. London, 1581.

Nashe, Thomas. 'Somewhat to Reade for Them That List.' In Sir Philip Sidney, *Syr P.S. his Astrophel and Stella*, A3r–A4v. London, 1591.

—. *The Terrors of the Night or, A Discourse of Apparitions*. London, 1594.

Nichols, Philip. *Sir Francis Drake Revived*. London, 1626.

Norton, Thomas, and Thomas Sackville. *The Tragedie of Gorboduc*. London, 1565.

Nyndge, Edward. *A Booke Declaringe the Fearfull Vexasion, of One Alexander Nyndge*. London, 1573/78?

Parker, Matthew. 'To the Right Honorable Learned and Vertuous Ladie A. B.' In John Jewel, *An Apologie or Answere in Defence of the Churche of Englande* (*Apologia Ecclesiae Anglicanae*), translated by Anne Cooke Bacon. London, 1564.

Paynell, Thomas, trans. *Regimen sanitatis Salerni*. (*Salernitan Rule of Health*.) London, 1575.

Peacham, Henry. *The Garden of Eloquence*. 1577; rev. edn, London, 1593.

Peele, George. *The Battell of Alcazar*. London, 1594.

Pembroke, Mary Sidney Herbert, Countess of. *Collected Works: Volume I: Poems, Translations, and Correspondence*. Edited by Margaret P. Hannay, Noel J. Kinnamon, and Michael G. Brennan. Oxford: Clarendon, 1998.

—. *Collected Works: Volume II: The Psalmes of David*. Edited by Margaret P. Hannay, Noel J. Kinnamon, and Michael G. Brennan. Oxford: Clarendon, 1998.

Perkins, William. *The Arte of Prophecying*. (*Prophetica, sive, De sacra et unica ratione concionandi tractatus*, 1592.) Translated by Thomas Tuke. London, 1607.

—. *A Declaration of the True Manner of Knowing Christ Crucified*. Cambridge, 1596.

—. *A Discourse of Conscience*. Cambridge, 1596.

—. *A Discourse of the Damned Art of Witchcraft*. London, 1610.

—. *An Exposition of the Symbole or Creed of the Apostles*. Cambridge, 1595.

—. *A Golden Chaine, or The Description of Theologie*. (*Armilla aurea, id est, theologiæ descriptio*, 1590.) Translated by Robert Hill. London, 1591.

—. *A Treatise of Mans Imaginations*. Cambridge, 1607.

—. 'A Warning against the Idolatrie of the Last Times.' 1601. In *The Works of that Famous and Worthie Minister of Christ, in the Universitie of Cambridge, M. W. Perkins*, 813–67. Cambridge, 1603.

Persons, Robert. *A Temperate Ward-Word, to the Turbulent and Seditious Wach-Word of Sir Francis Hastinges Knight*. Antwerp, 1599.

Plato. *Alcibiades I*. In *Charmides. Alcibiades I and II. Hipparchus. The Lovers. Theages. Minos. Epinomis*. Translated by W. R. M. Lamb. Loeb Classical Library 201. Cambridge, MA: Harvard University Press, 1927.

—. *Republic*. Translated by Robin Waterfield. Oxford: Oxford University Press, 1993.

Pliny, the Elder. *A Summarie of the Antiquities, and Wonders of the Worlde*. Translated by I. A. London, 1566.

Pollard, Tanya, ed. *Shakespeare's Theater: A Sourcebook*. Malden, MA: Blackwell, 2004.

Puttenham, George. *The Art of English Poesy*. In Alexander, *Sidney's 'The Defence of Poesy'*, 55–203.

Quintilian. *The Orator's Education (De institutione oratoria)*, Vol. 3, Bks 6–8. Edited and translated by Donald A. Russell. Loeb Classical Library 126. Cambridge, MA: Harvard University Press, 2002.

Ralegh, Sir Walter. 'The 21th: and Last Booke of the Ocean to Scinthia.' In *The Penguin Book of Renaissance Verse 1509–1659*, edited by David Norbrook and H. R. Woudhuysen, 102–16. London: Allen Lane, 1992.

Rhodes, Neil, Gordon Kendal, and Louise Wilson, eds. *English Renaissance Translation Theory*. MHRA Tudor and Stuart Translations Vol. 9. London: MHRA, 2013.

Rogers, Richard, and Samuel Ward. *Two Elizabethan Puritan Diaries*. Edited by M. M. Knappen. Chicago: American Society of Church History, 1933.

Rogers, Thomas. *A Paterne of a Passionate Minde*. London, 1580.

—. *A Philosophicall Discourse, Entituled, The Anatomie of the Minde*. London, 1576.

Romei, Annibale. *The Courtiers Academie*. (*Discorsi cavallereschi*.) Translated by I. K. (John Keper?). London, 1598.

Roper, William. *The Mirrour of Vertue in Worldly Greatnes. Or the Life of Syr Thomas More Knight*. Saint-Omer, 1626.

Russell, David L., ed. *Stuart Academic Drama: An Edition of Three University Plays*. 1987; London: Routledge, 2017.

Salter, Thomas. *A Mirrhor Mete for All Mothers, Matrones, and Maidens, Intituled the Mirrhor of Modestie*. (Translation of Giovanni Michele Bruto, *La institutione di una fanciulla nata nobilmente*, 1555.) London, 1579.

Salzman, Paul, ed. *An Anthology of Elizabethan Prose Fiction*. Oxford: Oxford University Press, 1987.

Sander, Nicholas. *A Treatise of the Images of Christ and his Saints*. Louvain, 1567.

Scot, Reginald. *The Discoverie of Witchcraft*. London, 1584.

Scott, William. *The Model of Poesy*. Edited by Gavin Alexander. Cambridge: Cambridge University Press, 2013.

S[eager], F[rancis]. *The Schoole of Vertue*. London, 1557.

Seneca. '*De tranquillitate animi*.' ('On Tranquillity of Mind.') In *Moral Essays, Volume II*. Translated by John W. Basore. Loeb Classical Library 254. 202–85. Cambridge, MA: Harvard University Press, 1932.

Shakespeare, William. *The Complete Sonnets and Poems*. Edited by Colin Burrow. The Oxford Shakespeare. Oxford: Oxford University Press, 2002.

—. *Hamlet*. Edited by Ann Thompson and Neil Taylor. Arden Shakespeare. London: Cengage, 2006.

—. *The Life and Death of King John*. Edited by A. R. Braunmuller. Oxford: Oxford University Press, 1989.

—. *A Midsummer Night's Dream*. Edited by Peter Holland. Oxford: Oxford University Press, 1995.

—. *A Midsummer Night's Dream*. Edited by Stanley Wells. Introduced by Helen Hackett. London: Penguin, 2005.

—. *A Midsummer Night's Dream*. Edited by John Dover Wilson. Cambridge: Cambridge University Press, 1924.

—. *The Norton Shakespeare*. 3rd edn. International Student Edition. General editor Stephen Greenblatt. New York: Norton, 2016.

—. *The Second Part of Henrie the Fourth*. London, 1600.

—. *Shakespeare's Poems*. Edited by Katherine Duncan-Jones and H. R. Woudhuysen. Arden Shakespeare. London: Thomson, 2007.

—. *Twelfth Night, or What You Will*. Edited by Roger Warren and Stanley Wells. Oxford: Oxford University Press, 1994.

Sherry, Richard. *A Treatise of Schemes [and] Tropes Very Profytable for the Better Understanding of Good Authors*. London, 1550.

Sidney, Sir Philip. *Astrophil and Stella.* In *The Oxford Authors: Sir Philip Sidney*, edited by Katherine Duncan-Jones, 153–211. Oxford: Oxford University Press, 1989.

—. *The Countess of Pembroke's Arcadia (The New Arcadia)*, 1593. Edited by Maurice Evans. London: Penguin, 1977.

—. *The Countess of Pembroke's Arcadia (The Old Arcadia).* Edited by Katherine Duncan-Jones. 1985; rev. edn, Oxford: Oxford University Press, 1994.

—. *The Defence of Poesy.* In Alexander, *Sidney's 'The Defence of Poesy'*, 1–54.

Smith, Henry. *The Benefit of Contentation.* London, 1590.

[Smith, Jude.] *A True Reporte or Description of an Horrible, Wofull, and Moste Lamentable Murther.* London, 1573.

Southwell, St Robert. *Collected Poems.* Edited by Peter Davidson and Anne Sweeney. Manchester: Carcanet, 2007.

—. *Marie Magdalens Funeral Teares.* London, 1591.

—. *The Poems of Robert Southwell, S.J.* Edited by James H. McDonald and Nancy Pollard Brown. Oxford: Oxford University Press, 1967.

Spenser, Edmund. *The Faerie Queene.* Edited by A. C. Hamilton with Hiroshi Yamashita and Toshiyuki Suzuki. Harlow: Pearson, 2001.

—. *The Shorter Poems.* Edited by Richard A. McCabe. London: Penguin, 1999.

—. *A View of the Present State of Ireland. CELT: The Corpus of Electronic Texts.* University College Cork. celt.ucc.ie/published/E500000-001/

Statutes of the Realm, Vol. 1 (1810). *The Making of the Modern World.* Farmington Hills: Gale-Cengage, 2008.

Stuart, Lady Arbella. *Letters.* Edited by Sara Jayne Steen. Oxford: Oxford University Press, 1994.

Sundrye Strange and Inhumaine Murthers, Lately Committed. London, 1591.

T., I. *The Haven of Pleasure.* London, 1597.

Thevet, André. *The New Found Worlde, Or Antarctike.* (*Les singularitez de la France Antarctique*, 1558.) London, 1568.

Thomas, Thomas. *Dictionarium linguae Latinae et Anglicanae*, 1587. Facsimile. Menston: Scolar, 1972.

Tilney, Edmund. *The Flower of Friendship: A Brief and Pleasant Discourse of Duties in Marriage* (1568). Edited by Valerie Wayne. Ithaca, NY: Cornell University Press, 1992.

Tottel's Miscellany: Songs and Sonnets of Henry Howard, Earl of Surrey, Sir Thomas Wyatt and Others (1557). Edited by Amanda Holton and Tom MacFaul. London: Penguin, 2011.

The Triall of Maist[er] Dorrell, or A Collection of Defences against Allegations Not Yet Suffered to Receive Convenient Answere. Middleburg, 1599.

The Triall of Treasure, A New and Mery Enterlude, Called. London, 1567.

The True Chronicle Historie of the Whole Life and Death of Thomas Lord Cromwell. London, 1602.

Tyler, Margaret. *Mirror of Princely Deeds and Knighthood.* (Translation of Diego Ortúñez de Calahorra, *Espejo de príncipes y cavalleros*, 1555.) Edited by Joyce Boro. MHRA Tudor and Stuart Translations Vol. 11. London: MHRA, 2014.

Du Vair, Guillaume. *The Moral Philosophie of the Stoicks.* Translated by Thomas James. London, 1598.

Vesalius, Andreas. *Vesalius on the Human Brain.* Translated and edited by Charles Singer. London: Oxford University Press for the Wellcome Historical Medical Museum, 1952.

Vickers, Brian, ed. *English Renaissance Literary Criticism.* Oxford: Clarendon, 1999.

Voragine, Jacobus de. *The Golden Legend: Readings on the Saints* (*c.* 1260). Translated by William Granger Ryan. 2 vols. Princeton: Princeton University Press, 1993.

Wentworth, Peter. *A Pithie Exhortation to her Maiestie for Establishing her Successor to the Crowne.* Edinburgh, 1598.

Weyer, Johann. *Witches, Devils, and Doctors in the Renaissance.* (*De praestigiis daemonum* [*On the Tricks of Demons*], 1583.) General editor George Mora. Translated by John Shea. Binghamton, NY: Center for Medieval and Early Renaissance Studies, 1991.

Whitgift, John. *The Defense of the Aunswere to the Admonition.* London, 1574.

Whitney, Isabella. 'I. W. to her Unconstant Lover.' In Isabella Whitney, Mary Sidney, and Aemilia Lanyer, *Renaissance Women Poets*, edited by Danielle Clarke, 29–33. London: Penguin, 2000.

Whythorne, Thomas. *The Autobiography of Thomas Whythorne*. Original spelling edition. Edited by James M. Osborn. Oxford: Clarendon, 1961.

—. *The Autobiography of Thomas Whythorne*. Modern spelling edition. Edited by James M. Osborn. London: Oxford University Press, 1962.

Wilson, Thomas. *The Arte of Rhetorique*. London, 1553.

Woolton, John. *The Christian Manuell, or Of the Life and Maners of True Christians*. London, 1576.

—. *A Newe Anatomie of Whole Man aswell of his Body, as of his Soule*. London, 1576.

Wordsworth, William. '*The Prelude* of 1805, in Thirteen Books.' In *The Prelude: 1799, 1805, 1850*, edited by Jonathan Wordsworth, M. H. Abrams, and Stephen Gill. New York: Norton, 1979.

Wright, Thomas. *The Passions of the Minde*. London, 1601.

Secondary Works

'About the Faculty.' Brain Sciences. University College London. ucl.ac.uk/brain-sciences/about-faculty

Ahnert, Ruth. 'Introduction: The Psalms and the English Reformation.' *Re-forming the Psalms in Tudor England*. *Renaissance Studies* 29.4 (Sept. 2015): 493–508.

Alexander, Gavin. Introduction to Alexander, *Sidney's 'The Defence of Poesy'*, xvii–lxxix.

Allen, Don Cameron. *The Star-Crossed Renaissance: The Quarrel about Astrology and its Influence in England*. 1941; London: Frank Cass, 1966.

Altman, Joel B. *The Tudor Play of Mind: Rhetorical Inquiry and the Development of Elizabethan Drama*. Berkeley: University of California Press, 1978.

Anderson, Miranda. *The Renaissance Extended Mind*. Basingstoke: Palgrave Macmillan, 2015.

Anderson, Ruth Leila. *Elizabethan Psychology and Shakespeare's Plays*. *University of Iowa Humanistic Studies* 3.4. Iowa City: University of Iowa, 1927.

Arab, Ronda, Michelle M. Dowd, and Adam Zucker, eds. *Historical Affects and the Early Modern Theater*. New York: Routledge, 2015.

Archer, Harriet, and Andrew Hadfield, eds. Introduction to *'A Mirror For Magistrates' in Context: Literature, History and Politics in Early Modern England*, edited by Harriet Archer and Andrew Hadfield, 1–14. Cambridge: Cambridge University Press, 2016.

Arnold, Matthew. Preface to *Poems*, 0–v. Edinburgh: Mundell & Son, 1853. *Literature Online (LION)*, ProQuest.

Aston, Margaret. *England's Iconoclasts: Vol. 1, Laws against Images*. Oxford: Oxford University Press, 1988.

Axton, Marie. *The Queen's Two Bodies: Drama and the Elizabethan Succession*. London: Royal Historical Society, 1977.

Babb, Lawrence. *The Elizabethan Malady: A Study of Melancholia in English Literature from 1580 to 1642*. East Lansing: Michigan State College Press, 1951.

Baker-Smith, Dominic. 'Uses of Plato by Erasmus and More.' In Anna Baldwin and Hutton, *Platonism and the English Imagination*, 86–99.

Baldwin, Anna, and Sarah Hutton, eds. *Platonism and the English Imagination*. Cambridge: Cambridge University Press, 1994.

Baldwin, Geoff. 'Individual and Self in the Late Renaissance.' *Historical Journal* 44.2 (2001): 341–64.

Barish, Jonas A. 'The Prose Style of John Lyly.' *ELH* 23.1 (Mar. 1956): 14–35.

Barker, Francis. *The Tremulous Private Body: Essays on Subjection*. 1984; 2nd edn, Ann Arbor: University of Michigan Press, 1995.

Barnard, John. Introduction to Barnard and McKenzie, *Cambridge History of the Book*, 1–26.

—, and Maureen Bell. 'Appendix 1: Statistical Tables.' In Barnard and McKenzie, *Cambridge History of the Book*, 779–93.

—, and D. F. McKenzie, eds. *The Cambridge History of the Book in Britain: Vol. 4: 1557–1695*. Cambridge: Cambridge University Press, 2014.

Bartels, Emily. *Speaking of the Moor: From 'Alcazar' to 'Othello'*. Philadelphia: University of Pennsylvania Press, 2009.

Baskervill, Charles Read. *English Elements in Jonson's Early Comedy. Bulletin of the University of Texas* 178, *Humanistic Series* 12, *Studies in English* 1. 8 April 1911.

Bates, Catherine. 'Images of Government in *The Faerie Queene*, Book II.' *Notes and Queries* 234 (1989): 314–15.

—. *On Not Defending Poetry: Defence and Indefensibility in Sidney's 'Defence of Poesy'*. Oxford: Oxford University Press, 2017.

—. 'Shakespeare and the Female Voice in Soliloquy.' In Cousins and Derrin, *Shakespeare and Soliloquy*, 56–67.

Bellamy, John. *The Tudor Law of Treason*. London: Routledge & Kegan Paul, 1979.

Belsey, Catherine. *The Subject of Tragedy: Identity and Difference in Renaissance Drama*. London: Methuen, 1985.

Bennell, John. 'Whithorne, Thomas (c. 1528–1596), composer and autobiographer.' *ODNB*. https://doi.org/10.1093/ref:odnb/29313

Bennett, H. S. *English Books and Readers, 1558–1603*. Cambridge: Cambridge University Press, 1965.

Bennett, R. E. 'Sir William Cornwallis's Use of Montaigne.' *PMLA* 48.4 (Dec. 1933): 1080–9.

Bevington, David M. *From 'Mankind' to Marlowe: Growth of Structure in the Popular Drama of Tudor England*. Cambridge, MA: Harvard University Press, 1962.

—. 'Giving Voice to History in Shakespeare.' In Cousins and Derrin, *Shakespeare and Soliloquy*, 80–92.

Binns, J. W. *Intellectual Culture in Elizabethan and Jacobean England: The Latin Writings of the Age*. Leeds: Francis Cairns, 1990.

Boas, F. S. Review of *Pathomachia*, ed. Paul Edward Smith. *Review of English Studies* 19.75 (1 July 1943): 306–7.

Bostock, David. 'Plato (c. 428–347 BC).' In *The Oxford Companion to Philosophy*, edited by Ted Honderich. 2nd edn, Oxford: Oxford University Press, 2005. *Oxford Reference Online*.

Borris, Kenneth. *Visionary Spenser and the Poetics of Early Modern Platonism*. Oxford: Oxford University Press, 2017.

Boutcher, Warren. *The School of Montaigne in Early Modern Europe*. 2 vols. Oxford: Oxford University Press, 2017.

Boyle, A. J. *Tragic Seneca: An Essay in the Theatrical Tradition*. London: Routledge, 1997.

Braden, Gordon. 'An Overview.' In Braden, Robert Cummings, and Gillespie, *Oxford History of Literary Translation, Vol. 2*, 3–11.

—, Robert Cummings, and Stuart Gillespie, eds. *The Oxford History of Literary Translation in English: Volume 2, 1550–1660*. Oxford: Oxford University Press, 2010.

Brann, Noel L. *The Debate over the Origin of Genius during the Italian Renaissance*. Leiden: Brill, 2002.

Braund, Susanna. 'Haunted by Horror: The Ghost of Seneca in Renaissance Drama.' In *A Companion to the Neronian Age*, edited by Emma Buckley and Martin T. Dinter, 425–43. Chichester: Wiley-Blackwell, 2013.

Bremer, Francis J. 'Alabaster, William (1568–1640), Church of England clergyman and writer.' *ODNB*. https://doi.org/10.1093/ref:odnb/265

Brennan, Michael G. 'Nicholas Breton's *The Passions of the Spirit* and the Countess of Pembroke.' *Review of English Studies* 38.150 (May 1987): 221–5.

Brljak, Vladimir. 'The Age of Allegory.' *Studies in Philology* 114.4 (Fall 2017): 697–719.

—. 'Introduction: Allegory Past and Present.' In *Allegory Studies: Contemporary Perspectives*, ed. Vladimir Brljak, 1–40. New York: Routledge, 2022. Kindle.

Brogan, Boyd. 'His Belly, her Seed: Gender and Medicine in Early Modern Demonic Possession.' *Representations* 147 (Summer 2019): 1–25.

Broomhall, Susan, ed. *Authority, Gender and Emotions in Late Medieval and Early Modern England*. Basingstoke: Palgrave Macmillan, 2015.

—, ed. *Early Modern Emotions: An Introduction*. London: Routledge, 2016.

—, ed. *Gender and Emotions in Medieval and Early Modern Europe: Destroying Order, Structuring Disorder*. Farnham: Ashgate, 2015.

—, ed. *Ordering Emotions in Europe, 1100–1800*. Leiden: Brill, 2015.

—, Jane W. Davidson, and Andrew Lynch, eds. *A Cultural History of the Emotions*. 6 vols. London: Bloomsbury, 2019.

Brotton, Jerry. *This Orient Isle: Elizabethan England and the Islamic World*. London: Allen Lane, 2016. Kindle.

Brown, Nancy Pollard. 'Southwell, Robert [St Robert Southwell] (1561–1595), writer, Jesuit, and martyr.' *ODNB*. https://doi.org/10.1093/ref:odnb/26064

Bruhn, Mark J., and Donald R. Wehrs, eds. *Cognition, Literature, and History*. New York: Routledge, 2014.

Bryson, Bill. *The Body: A Guide for Occupants*. London: Transworld Digital, 2019. Kindle.

Burrow, Colin. *Shakespeare and Classical Antiquity*. Oxford: Oxford University Press, 2013.

—. 'Montaignian Moments: Shakespeare and the *Essays*.' In *Montaigne in Transit: Essays in Honour of Ian Maclean*, edited by Neil Kenny, Richard Scholar, and Wes Williams, 239–52. Cambridge: Legenda, 2016.

Bynum, William. *The History of Medicine: A Very Short Introduction*. Oxford: Oxford University Press, 2008.

Callaghan, Dympna. *'Hamlet': Language and Writing*. London: Bloomsbury Arden Shakespeare, 2015.

Carey, John. 'Structure and Rhetoric in Sidney's *Arcadia*.' In *Sir Philip Sidney: An Anthology of Modern Criticism*, edited by Dennis Kay, 245–64. Oxford: Clarendon, 1987.

Carrera, Elena. 'Anger and the Mind-Body Connection in Medieval and Early Modern Medicine.' In Carrera, *Emotions and Health*, 95–146.

—, ed. *Emotions and Health 1200–1700*. Leiden: Brill, 2013.

Catty, Jocelyn. *Writing Rape, Writing Women in Early Modern England: Unbridled Speech*. 1999; pbk, Basingstoke: Palgrave Macmillan, 2011.

Chapman, Allan. 'Astrological Medicine.' In Webster, *Health, Medicine and Mortality*, 275–300.

Charlton, Kenneth. *Women, Religion and Education in Early Modern England*. London: Routledge, 1999.

— and Margaret Spufford. 'Literacy, Society and Education.' In Loewenstein and Mueller, *Cambridge History*, 15–54.

Charney, Maurice. '"To Be, or Not to Be?": The Plain Language of Hamlet's Soliloquy.' *Shakespeare Newsletter* 58.2 (22 Sept. 2008): 47–50.

Cheung, Theresa. *The Dream Dictionary from A to Z: The Ultimate A to Z to Interpret the Secrets of your Dreams*. London: Harper Element, 2006.

Clark, Andy. *Supersizing the Mind: Embodiment, Action, and Cognitive Extension*. Oxford: Oxford University Press, 2008.

Clark, Douglas. 'Nicholas Breton and Early Modern Explorations of the Mind.' *Early Modern Voices*, edited by Dermot Cavanagh and Robert Maslen. *Journal of the Northern Renaissance* 9 (Autumn 2017), special issue in honour of Alison Thorne. northernrenaissance.org/nicholas-breton-and-early-modern-explorations-of-the-mind/

—. 'Theorising the Will in Early Modern English Literature.' Unpubl. PhD thesis, University of Strathclyde, 2015.

Clark, Stuart. *Thinking with Demons: The Idea of Witchcraft in Early Modern Europe*. Oxford: Oxford University Press, 1999.

Clarke, Danielle. 'Translation.' In *The Cambridge Companion to Early Modern Women's Writing*, edited by Laura Lunger Knoppers, 167–80. Cambridge: Cambridge University Press, 2009.

Clemen, Wolfgang. *Shakespeare's Soliloquies*. Translated by Charity Scott Stokes. London: Methuen, 1987.

Coles, Kimberly Anne. *Religion, Reform, and Women's Writing in Early Modern England*. Cambridge: Cambridge University Press 2008.

Collinson, Patrick. 'Grindal, Edmund (1516x20–1583), archbishop of York and of Canterbury.' *ODNB*. https://doi.org/10.1093/ref:odnb/11644

—. 'Locke [*née* Vaughan; *other married names* Dering, Prowse], Anne (c. 1530–1590x1607).' *ODNB*. https://doi.org/10.1093/ref:odnb/69054

—. 'The Monarchical Republic of Queen Elizabeth I.' *Bulletin of the John Rylands Library* 69.2 (1987): 394–424.

Cooper, Tarnya. *Citizen Portrait: Portrait Painting and the Urban Elite of Tudor and Jacobean England and Wales*. New Haven: Yale University Press, 2012.

Cousins, A. D., and Daniel Derrin. Introduction to *Shakespeare and Soliloquy*, 1–14.

—, eds. *Shakespeare and the Soliloquy in Early Modern English Drama*. Cambridge: Cambridge University Press, 2018.

Covington, Sarah. *The Trail of Martyrdom: Persecution and Resistance in Sixteenth-Century England*. Notre Dame, IN: University of Notre Dame Press, 2003.

Cox, John D. *The Devil and the Sacred in English Drama, 1350–1642*. Cambridge: Cambridge University Press, 2000.

Crabbe, M. James C., ed., *From Soul to Self*. London: Routledge, 1999.

Craik, Katharine A., and Tanya Pollard, eds. *Shakespearean Sensations: Experiencing Literature in Early Modern England*. Cambridge: Cambridge University Press, 2013.

Crane, Mary Thomas. *Framing Authority: Sayings, Self, and Society in Sixteenth-Century England*. Princeton: Princeton University Press, 1993.

—. *Losing Touch with Nature: Literature and the New Science in Sixteenth-Century England*. Baltimore: Johns Hopkins University Press, 2014.

—. *Shakespeare's Brain: Reading with Cognitive Theory*. Princeton: Princeton University Press, 2001.

Crawford, Julie. *Marvelous Protestantism: Monstrous Births in Post-Reformation England*. Baltimore: Johns Hopkins University Press, 2005.

Cummings, Brian. *The Literary Culture of the Reformation: Grammar and Grace*. Oxford: Oxford University Press, 2002. Kindle.

—. *Mortal Thoughts: Religion, Secularity and Identity in Shakespeare and Early Modern Culture*. Oxford: Oxford University Press, 2013.

—, and Freya Sierhuis, eds. *Passions and Subjectivity in Early Modern Culture*. Farnham: Ashgate, 2013.

Cunningham, Karen. *Imaginary Betrayals: Subjectivity and the Discourses of Treason in Early Modern England*. Philadelphia: University of Pennsylvania Press, 2002.

Damasio, Antonio. *Self Comes to Mind: Constructing the Conscious Brain*. New York: Pantheon, 2010.

Das, Nandini. *Renaissance Romance: The Transformation of English Prose Fiction, 1570–1620*. Farnham: Ashgate, 2011.

—, et al. 'Blackamoor.' In 'Keywords of Identity, Race, and Human Mobility in Early Modern England.' *TIDE: Travel, Transculturality, and Identity in England, c. 1550–1700*. tideproject.uk/keywords-home/?keyword_id=40

Dawson, Lesel. *Lovesickness and Gender in Early Modern English Literature*. Oxford: Oxford University Press, 2008.

—, and Eric Langley. 'Affective Inheritances: Review Essay.' *Early Theatre* 20.1 (2017): 133–52.

Demers, Patricia. '"Nether Bitterly Nor Brablingly": Lady Anne Cooke Bacon's Translation of Bishop Jewel's *Apologia Ecclesiae Anglicanae*.' In Micheline White, *English Women, Religion, and Textual Production*, 205–17.

Dimmock, Matthew. *Elizabethan Globalism: England, China and the Rainbow Portrait*. London: Paul Mellon, 2019.

Dixon, Thomas. *From Passions to Emotions: The Creation of a Secular Psychological Category*. Cambridge: Cambridge University Press, 2003.

Donaldson, Ian. 'Jonson, Benjamin [Ben] (1572–1637), poet and playwright.' *ODNB*. https://doi.org/10.1093/ref:odnb/15116

—. *The Rapes of Lucretia: A Myth and its Transformations*. Oxford: Clarendon, 1982.

Doran, Madeleine. *Endeavors of Art: A Study in Form in Elizabethan Drama*. Madison: University of Wisconsin Press, 1954.

Doran, Susan. 'Elizabeth I and Counsel.' In *The Politics of Counsel in England and Scotland, 1286–1707*, edited by Jacqueline Rose, 151–69. *Proceedings of the British Academy* 204. Oxford: British Academy/Oxford University Press, 2016.

Dragstra, Henk, Sheila Ottway, and Helen Wilcox, eds. *Betraying our Selves: Forms of Self-Representation in Early Modern English Texts*. Basingstoke: Macmillan, 2000.

—. Introduction to *Betraying our Selves*, 1–13.

Dubrow, Heather. 'A Mirror for Complaints: Shakespeare's *Lucrece* and Generic Tradition.' In *Renaissance Genres: Essays on Theory, History, and Interpretation*, edited by Barbara Kiefer Lewalski, 399–417. Cambridge, MA: Harvard University Press, 1986.

Duffy, Eamon. *The Stripping of the Altars: Traditional Religion in England, 1400–1580*. 2nd edn, New Haven: Yale University Press, 2005.

Durling, Richard J. 'A Chronological Census of Editions and Translations of Galen.' *Journal of the Warburg and Courtauld Institutes* 24.3–4 (Jul.–Dec. 1961): 230–305.

Edwards, Philip. 'Who Wrote "The Passionate Man's Pilgrimage"?' *English Literary Renaissance* 4.1, *Studies in Renaissance Poetry* (Winter 1974): 83–97.

Ekirch, A. Roger. *At Day's Close: A History of Nighttime*. 2005; London: Phoenix, 2013. Kindle.

Ellrodt, Robert. *Montaigne and Shakespeare: The Emergence of Modern Self-Consciousness*. 2015; pbk, Manchester: Manchester University Press, 2018.

Erler, Mary C. 'Sir John Davies and the Rainbow Portrait of Queen Elizabeth.' *Modern Philology*, 84.4 (May 1987): 359–71.

Escobedo, Andrew. *Volition's Face: Personification and the Will in Renaissance Literature*. Notre Dame, IN: University of Notre Dame Press, 2017. Kindle.

Ewbank, Inga-Stina. 'From Narrative to Dramatic Language: *The Winter's Tale* and its Source.' In *Shakespeare and the Sense of Performance*, edited by Marvin and Ruth Thompson, 29–47. Newark: University of Delaware Press, 1989.

Falco, Raphael. 'Tudor Transformations.' In Cousins and Derrin, *Shakespeare and Soliloquy*, 29–42.

Fasano, Alessio, and Susie Flaherty. *Gut Feelings: The Microbiome and our Health*. Cambridge, MA: MIT Press, 2021.

Febvre, Lucien, and Henri-Jean Martin. *The Coming of the Book: The Impact of Printing, 1450–1800*. (*L'apparition du livre*, 1958.) Translated by David Gerard. Edited by Geoffrey Nowell-Smith and David Wootton. 1976; London: Verso, 2010.

Ferry, Anne. *The 'Inward' Language: Sonnets of Wyatt, Sidney, Shakespeare, Donne*. Chicago: University of Chicago Press, 1983.

Finkelpearl, P. J. 'Davies, John (1564/5–1618), poet and writing-master.' *ODNB*. https://doi.org/10.1093/ref:odnb/7244

Floyd-Wilson, Mary, *English Ethnicity and Race in Early Modern Drama*. 2003; pbk, Cambridge: Cambridge University Press, 2006.

—, and Garrett A. Sullivan, Jr, eds. *Environment and Embodiment in Early Modern England*. Basingstoke: Palgrave Macmillan, 2007.

Foster, Donald W. '"Against the Perjured Falsehood of your Tongues": Frances Howard on the Course of Love.' *English Literary Renaissance* 24.1, *Women in the Renaissance III: Studies in Honor of Ruth Mortimer* (Winter 1994): 72–103.

Frye, Susan. *Pens and Needles: Women's Textualities in Early Modern England*. Philadelphia: University of Pennsylvania Press, 2010.

Fumerton, Patricia. *The Broadside Ballad in Early Modern England: Moving Media, Tactical Publics*. Philadelphia: University of Pennsylvania Press, 2020.

Garwood, Sasha. *Early Modern English Noblewomen and Self-Starvation: The Skull beneath the Skin*. Routledge, 2019.

Gazzard, Hugh. 'Nicholas Breton, the Earl of Essex, and Elizabethan Penitential Poetry.' *SEL Studies in English Literature 1500–1900* 56.1 (Winter 2016): 23–44.

Gellatly, Angus, and Oscar Zarate. *Introducing Mind and Brain: A Graphic Guide*. London: Icon Books, 2018.

Goldring, Elizabeth. *Nicholas Hilliard: Life of an Artist*. New Haven: Yale University Press, 2019.

—, et al., eds. *John Nichols's 'The Progresses and Public Processions of Queen Elizabeth I': A New Edition of the Early Modern Sources*. 5 vols. Oxford: Oxford University Press, 2014.

Goodrich, Jaime. *Faithful Translators: Authorship, Gender, and Religion in Early Modern England*. Evanston, IL: Northwestern University Press, 2014.

Gowland, Angus. 'Medicine, Psychology, and the Melancholic Subject in the Renaissance.' In Carrera, *Emotions and Health*, 185–219.

—. 'Melancholy, Imagination, and Dreaming in Renaissance Learning.' In *Diseases of the Imagination and Imaginary Diseases in the Early Modern Period*, edited by Yasmin Haskell, 53–102. Turnhout: Brepols, 2011.

—. 'Melancholy, Passions and Identity in the Renaissance.' In Brian Cummings and Sierhuis, *Passions and Subjectivity*, 75–93.

—. 'The Problem of Early Modern Melancholy.' *Past & Present* 191 (May 2006): 77–120.

—. *The Worlds of Renaissance Melancholy: Robert Burton in Context*. Cambridge: Cambridge University Press, 2006.

Grazia, Margreta de. *'Hamlet' without Hamlet*. Cambridge: Cambridge University Press, 2007.

Greenblatt, Stephen J. *Hamlet in Purgatory*. Princeton: Princeton University Press, 2001.

—. *Shakespearean Negotiations: The Circulation of Social Energy in Renaissance England*. Berkeley: University of California Press, 1988.

—. *Will in the World: How Shakespeare Became Shakespeare*. London: Jonathan Cape, 2004.

Greene, Roland. 'Invention.' In *Five Words: Critical Semantics in the Age of Shakespeare and Cervantes*, 15–40. Chicago: University of Chicago Press, 2013.

Greene, Thomas M. *The Light in Troy: Imitation and Discovery in Renaissance Poetry*. New Haven: Yale University Press, 1982.

Greenfield, Susan. 'Soul, Brain and Mind.' In Crabbe, *From Soul to Self*, 108–25.

Guillory, John. *Poetic Authority: Spenser, Milton, and Literary History*. New York: Columbia University Press, 1983.

Gurr, Andrew. *The Shakespearean Stage 1574–1642*. 4th edn, Cambridge: Cambridge University Press, 2009.

Guy, John. *Elizabeth: The Forgotten Years*. London: Viking, 2016.

—. 'The Elizabethan Establishment and the Ecclesiastical Polity.' In *Reign of Elizabeth I*, 126–49.

—. 'Introduction: The 1590s: The Second Reign of Elizabeth I?' In *Reign of Elizabeth I*, 1–19.

—, ed. *The Reign of Elizabeth I: Court and Culture in the Last Decade*. Cambridge: Cambridge University Press, 1995.

Habib, Imtiaz. *Black Lives in the English Archives, 1500–1677: Imprints of the Invisible*. 2008; Abingdon: Routledge, 2016. Kindle.

—. 'Racial Impersonation on the Elizabethan Stage: The Case of Shakespeare Playing Aaron.' *Medieval and Renaissance Drama in England* 20 (2007): 17–45.

— and Duncan Salkeld. 'The Resonables of Boroughside, Southwark: An Elizabethan Black Family near the Rose Theatre.' *Shakespeare* 11.2 (2015): 135–56.

Hackett, Helen. '"All their Minds Transfigured So Together": The Imagination at the Elizabethan Playhouse.' In *Playing and Playgoing in Early Modern England*, edited by Emma Whipday and Simon Smith. Cambridge: Cambridge University Press, 2022.

—. 'The Art of Blasphemy? Interfusions of the Erotic and the Sacred in the Poetry of Donne, Barnes, and Constable.' *Renaissance and Reformation / Renaissance et réforme* 28.3 (Summer 2004): 27–54.

—. '"As the Diall Hand Tells Ore": The Case for Dekker, Not Shakespeare, as Author.' *Review of English Studies* 63/258 (2012): 34–57.

—. 'Dream-Visions of Elizabeth I.' In *Reading the Early Modern Dream: The Terrors of the Night*, edited by Katharine Hodgkin, Michelle O'Callaghan, and S. J. Wiseman, 45–65. New York: Routledge, 2008.

—. '"He Is a Better Scholar Than I Thought He Was": Debating the Achievements of the Elizabethan Grammar Schools.' *Early Modern Voices*, edited by Dermot Cavanagh and Robert Maslen. *Journal of the Northern Renaissance* 9 (Autumn 2017), special issue in honour of Alison Thorne. http://www.northernrenaissance.org/he-is-a-better-scholar-than-i-thought-he-was-debating-the-achievements-of-the-elizabethan-grammar-schools/

—. Introduction to Shakespeare, *A Midsummer Night's Dream*, ed. Wells, xxi–lxxiii.

—. *Virgin Mother, Maiden Queen: Elizabeth I and the Cult of the Virgin Mary*. Basingstoke: Macmillan, 1995.

—. *William Shakespeare: 'A Midsummer Night's Dream'*. Writers and their Work. Plymouth: Northcote House, 1997.

—. *Women and Romance Fiction in the English Renaissance*. Cambridge: Cambridge University Press, 2000.

Hadfield, Andrew, ed. *Amazons, Savages and Machiavels: Travel and Colonial Writing in English, 1550–1630: An Anthology*. Oxford: Oxford University Press, 2001.

—. 'Spenser, Edmund (1552?–1599), poet and administrator in Ireland.' *ODNB*. https://doi.org/10.1093/ref:odnb/26145

Hahamy, Avital. 'The Brain at Rest.' *Packed Lunch* event, Wellcome Collection, London, 22 May 2019.

Hamilton, A. C. 'Elizabethan Prose Fiction and Some Trends in Recent Criticism.' *Renaissance Quarterly* 37.1 (Spring 1984): 21–33.

—, ed. *The Spenser Encyclopedia*. London: Routledge, 1996.

Hamlin, Hannibal. *Psalm Culture and Early Modern English Literature*. Cambridge: Cambridge University Press, 2004.

—. 'Sobs for Sorrowful Souls: Versions of the Penitential Psalms for Domestic Devotion.' In Jessica Martin and Ryrie, *Private and Domestic Devotion*, 211–36.

Hamlin, William M. 'Montaigne and Shakespeare.' In *The Oxford Handbook of Montaigne*, edited by Philippe Desan, 328–46. Oxford: Oxford University Press, 2016.

—. *Montaigne's English Journey: Reading the Essays in Shakespeare's Day*. Oxford: Oxford University Press, 2013.

Hankins, John Erskine. *Backgrounds of Shakespeare's Thought*. Hassocks: Harvester, 1978.

Hannay, Margaret P. *Philip's Phoenix: Mary Sidney, Countess of Pembroke*. New York: Oxford University Press, 1990.

—. '"Unlock my Lipps": The *Miserere mei Deus* of Anne Vaughan Lok and Mary Sidney Herbert, Countess of Pembroke.' In *Privileging Gender in Early Modern England*, edited by Jean R. Brink. *Sixteenth-Century Essays and Studies* 23 (1993): 19–36.

Hanson, Elizabeth. *Discovering the Subject in Renaissance England*. Cambridge: Cambridge University Press, 1998.

Hart, F. Elizabeth. '1500–1620: Reading, Consciousness, and Romance in the Sixteenth Century.' In Herman, *Emergence of Mind*, 103–31.

Harvey, E. Ruth. *The Inward Wits: Psychological Theory in the Middle Ages and the Renaissance*. Warburg Institute Surveys VI. London: Warburg Institute, 1975.

Harvey, Elizabeth D. *Ventriloquized Voices: Feminist Theory and English Renaissance Texts*. London: Routledge, 1992.

Heale, Elizabeth. 'Songs, Sonnets and Autobiography: Self-Representation in Sixteenth-Century Verse Miscellanies.' In Dragstra, Ottway, and Wilcox, *Betraying our Selves*, 59–75.

Heilman, Robert B. 'Greene's Euphuism and Some Congeneric Styles.' In *Unfolded Tales: Essays on Renaissance Romance*, edited by George M. Logan and Gordon Teskey, 49–73. Ithaca: Cornell University Press, 1989.

Helms, Nicholas R. 'To Knit the Knot: Embodied Mind in John Donne's "The Ecstasy".' *The Seventeenth Century* 34:4 (2019): 419–36.

Henry, Hugh. 'Salve Regina.' *The Catholic Encyclopedia*. Vol. 13. New York: Robert Appleton Company, 1912. newadvent.org/cathen/13409a.htm

Herman, David, ed. *The Emergence of Mind: Representations of Consciousness in Narrative Discourse in English*. Lincoln, NE: University of Nebraska Press, 2011.

—. 'Introduction.' In *Emergence of Mind*, 1–40.

Hetherington, Michael. '"An Instrument of Reason": William Scott's Logical Poetics.' *Review of English Studies* 67.280 (June 2016): 448–67.

Hillman, David. *Shakespeare's Entrails: Belief, Scepticism and the Interior of the Body*. Basingstoke: Palgrave Macmillan, 2007.

Hillman, Richard. *Self-Speaking in Medieval and Early Modern English Drama: Subjectivity, Discourse and the Stage*. Basingstoke: Macmillan, 1997.

Hirsh, James. 'The Origin of the Late Renaissance Dramatic Convention of Self-Addressed Speech.' *Shakespeare, Origins and Orignality*, edited by Peter Holland. *Shakespeare Survey* 68 (2015): 131–45.

—. *Shakespeare and the History of Soliloquies*. Madison: Fairleigh Dickinson University Press, 2003.

—. 'What Were Soliloquies in Plays by Shakespeare and Other Late Renaissance Dramatists? An Empirical Approach.' In *Shakespeare and Soliloquy*, edited by Cousins and Derrin, 205–24.

Hobgood, Allison P. *Passionate Playgoing in Early Modern England*. Cambridge: Cambridge University Press, 2014.

Hodgkin, Katharine. 'Thomas Whythorne and the Problems of Mastery.' *History Workshop* 29 (Spring, 1990): 20–41.

Hogan, Patrick Colm. *Cognitive Science, Literature, and the Arts: A Guide for Humanists*. New York: Routledge, 2003.

Hosington, Brenda M. '"Minerva and the Muses": Women Writers of Latin in Renaissance England.' *Humanistica Lovaniensia* 58 (2009): 3–43.

—. 'Translation as a Currency of Cultural Exchange in Early Modern England.' In *Early Modern Exchanges: Dialogues between Nations and Cultures, 1550–1750*, edited by Helen Hackett, 27–54. Farnham: Ashgate, 2015.

Howe, Sarah. 'The Authority of Presence: The Development of the English Author Portrait, 1500–1640.' *Papers of the Bibliographical Society of America* 102.4 (Dec. 2008): 465–99.

—. '"Our Speaking Picture": William Scott's *Model of Poesy* and the Visual Imagination.' *Sidney Journal* 33.1 (2015): 29–67.

Huet, Marie-Hélène. *Monstrous Imagination*. Cambridge, MA: Harvard University Press, 1993.

Hunter, G. K. *John Lyly: The Humanist as Courtier*. London: Routledge & Kegan Paul, 1962.

Hussey, S. S. *The Literary Language of Shakespeare*. 2nd edn, n. pl.: Routledge, 2018.

Hutson, Lorna. *Circumstantial Shakespeare*. Oxford: Oxford University Press, 2015.

—. 'The Shakespearean Unscene: Sexual Phantasies in *A Midsummer Night's Dream*.' *Journal of the British Academy* (2016): 169–95.

Hutton, Sarah. 'Introduction to the Renaissance and Seventeenth Century.' In *Platonism and the English Imagination*, edited by Anna Baldwin and Hutton, 67–73.

James, Susan. *Passion and Action: The Emotions in Seventeenth-Century Philosophy*. Oxford: Oxford University Press, 1999.

Johns, Adrian. 'Science and the Book.' In Barnard and McKenzie, *Cambridge History of the Book*, 274–303.

Johnson, Laurence. '"Nobler in the Mind": The Emergence of Early Modern Anxiety.' *AUMLA: Journal of the Australasian Universities Language and Literature Association, Special Issue: Refereed Proceedings of the 2009 AULLA Conference: The Human and the Humanities in Literature, Language and Culture* (Dec. 2009): 141–56.

Johnson, Laurie. 'Quaint Knowledge: A "Body-Mind" Pattern across Shakespeare's Career.' In Kambaskovic, *Conjunctions*, 279–301.

—, John Sutton, and Evelyn Tribble, eds. *Embodied Cognition and Shakespeare's Theatre: The Early Modern Body-Mind*. New York: Routledge, 2014.

—. 'Introduction: Re-cognising the Body-Mind in Shakespeare's Theatre.' In *Embodied Cognition*, 1–11.

Johnstone, Nathan. *The Devil and Demonism in Early Modern England*. Cambridge: Cambridge University Press, 2006.

Jones, Peter Murray. 'Gemini [Geminus, Lambrit], Thomas (fl. 1540–1562), engraver, printer, and instrument maker.' *ODNB*. https://doi.org/10.1093/ref:odnb/10513

—. 'Medical Literacies and Medical Culture in Early Modern England.' In Taavitsainen and Pahta, *Medical Writing in Early Modern English*, 30–43.

Kaegi, Ann. 'Passionate Uprisings in Shakespeare's *Lucrece*.' *Shakespeare* 14:3 (2018): 205–15.

Kalas, Rayna. *Frame, Glass, Verse: The Technology of Poetic Invention in the English Renaissance*. Ithaca: Cornell University Press, 2007.

Kambaskovic, Danijela, ed. *Conjunctions of Mind, Soul and Body from Plato to the Enlightenment*. Dordrecht: Springer, 2014.

—. 'Introduction.' In *Conjunctions*, 1–8.

Kassell, Lauren. *Medicine and Magic in Elizabethan London: Simon Forman: Astrologer, Alchemist, and Physician*. Oxford: Clarendon, 2005.

Kastan, David. 'Print, Literary Culture and the Book Trade.' In Loewenstein and Mueller, *Cambridge History*, 81–116.

Kaufman, Peter Iver. *Prayer, Despair, and Drama: Elizabethan Introspection*. Urbana: University of Illinois Press, 1996.

Kaufmann, Miranda. *Black Tudors: The Untold Story*. London: Oneworld, 2017. Kindle.

—. 'Caspar Van Senden, Sir Thomas Sherley and the "Blackamoor" Project.' *Historical Research* 81.212 (May 2008): 366–71.

—. '"Making the Beast with Two Backs": Interracial Relationships in Early Modern England.' *Literature Compass* 12.1 (2015): 22–37.

Kearney, Richard. *The Wake of Imagination: Ideas of Creativity in Western Culture*. London: Hutchinson, 1988.

Kelly, Philippa, Lloyd Davis, and Ronald Bedford. Introduction to *Early Modern Autobiography: Theories, Genres, Practices*, edited by Ronald Bedford, Lloyd Davis, and Philippa Kelly, 1–16. Ann Arbor: University of Michigan Press, 2006.

Kelsey, Sean. 'Davies, Sir John (bap. 1569, d. 1626), lawyer and poet.' *ODNB*. https://doi.org/10.1093/ref:odnb/7245

Kermode, Frank. *Shakespeare's Language*. London: Penguin, 2000. Kindle.

Kerrigan, John, ed. *Motives of Woe: Shakespeare and 'Female Complaint': A Critical Anthology*. Oxford: Clarendon, 1991.

—. *Shakespeare's Originality*. Oxford: Oxford University Press, 2018.

King, John N. 'Baldwin, William (d. in or before 1563), author and printer.' *ODNB*. https://doi.org/10.1093/ref:odnb/1171

King, Ros. 'Plays, Playing, and Make-Believe: Thinking and Feeling in Shakespearean Drama.' In Laurie Johnson, Sutton, and Tribble, *Embodied Cognition*, 27–45.

Kinney, Arthur F. *Humanist Poetics: Thought, Rhetoric, and Fiction in Sixteenth-Century England*. Amherst: University of Massachusetts Press, 1986.

Kiséry, András. *Hamlet's Moment: Drama and Political Knowledge in Early Modern England*. Oxford: Oxford University Press, 2016.

Klibansky, Raymond, Erwin Panofsky, and Fritz Saxl. *Saturn and Melancholy: Studies in the History of Natural Philosophy, Religion and Art*. London: Thomas Nelson, 1964.

Knott, John R. *Discourses of Martyrdom in English Literature, 1563–1694*. Cambridge: Cambridge University Press, 1993.

Kraye, Jill. 'The Transformation of Platonic Love in the Italian Renaissance.' In Anna Baldwin and Hutton, *Platonism and the English Imagination*, 76–85.

Kwint, Marius, and Richard Wingate, eds. *Brains: The Mind as Matter*. London: Wellcome Collection, 2012.

Lake, Peter. '"The Monarchical Republic of Queen Elizabeth I" (and the Fall of Archbishop Grindal) Revisited.' In *The Monarchical Republic of Early Modern England: Essays in Response to Patrick Collinson*, edited by John F. McDiarmid, 129–47. Aldershot: Ashgate, 2007.

Lamb, Mary Ellen. *Gender and Authorship in the Sidney Circle*. Madison: University of Wisconsin Press, 1990.

Langley, Eric. *Narcissism and Suicide in Shakespeare and his Contemporaries*. Oxford: Oxford University Press, 2009. Kindle.

—. *Shakespeare's Contagious Sympathies: Ill Communications*. Oxford: Oxford University Press, 2018.

Laqué, Stephan. '"Not Passion's Slave": Hamlet, Descartes and the Passions.' In Brian Cummings and Sierhuis, *Passions and Subjectivity*, 267–79.

Larkey, Sanford V. 'The Vesalian Compendium of Geminus and Nicholas Udall's Translation: Their Relation to Vesalius, Caius, Vicary and De Mondevelle.' *The Library* 4th ser., 13 (1932–33): 367–94.

Lee, John. 'The English Renaissance Essay: Churchyard, Cornwallis, Florio's Montaigne, and Bacon.' In *A New Companion to English Renaissance Literature and Culture, Vol. 1*, edited by Michael Hattaway, 437–46. Chichester: John Wiley, 2010.

Lehto, Anu, Raisa Oinonen and Päivi Pahta. 'Explorations through Early Modern English Medical Texts: Charting Changes in Medical Discourse and Scientific Thinking.' In Taavitsainen and Pahta, *Early Modern English Medical Texts*, 151–66.

Lennam, Trevor. *Sebastian Westcott, the Children of Paul's, and 'The Marriage of Wit and Science'*. Toronto: University of Toronto Press, 1975.

Leschziner, Guy. *The Nocturnal Brain: Nightmares, Neuroscience, and the Secret World of Sleep*. London: Simon & Schuster, 2019.

Levin, Carole. *Dreaming the English Renaissance: Politics and Desire in Court and Culture*. Basingstoke: Palgrave Macmillan, 2008.

—, Anna Riehl Bertolet, and Jo Eldridge Carney, eds. *A Biographical Encyclopedia of Early Modern Englishwomen: Exemplary Lives and Memorable Acts, 1500–1650*. London: Routledge, 2017.

Lewalski, Barbara Kiefer. *Protestant Poetics and the Seventeenth-Century Religious Lyric*. Princeton: Princeton University Press, 1979.

Lewis, Rhodri. *Hamlet and the Vision of Darkness*. Princeton: Princeton University Press, 2017.

Lim, Vanessa. '"To Be or Not to Be": Hamlet's Humanistic *Quaestio*.' *Review of English Studies* n.s. 70.296 (Sept. 2019): 640–58.

Lindheim, Nancy R. 'Lyly's Golden Legacy: *Rosalynde* and *Pandosto*.' *The English Renaissance, Studies in English Literature, 1500–1900* 15.1 (Winter 1975): 3–20.

Locke, John Goodwin. *Book of the Lockes: A Genealogical and Historical Record of the Descendants of William Locke, of Woburn*. Boston: James Munroe, 1853.

Lodge, David. *Consciousness and the Novel: Connected Essays*. Cambridge, MA: Harvard University Press, 2002.

Loewenstein, David, and Janel Mueller, eds. *The Cambridge History of Early Modern English Literature*. Cambridge: Cambridge University Press, 2002.

Lyne, Raphael. *Shakespeare, Rhetoric and Cognition*. Cambridge: Cambridge University Press, 2011.

Mack, Peter. 'Early Modern Ideas of Imagination: The Rhetorical Tradition.' In Nauta and Pätzold, *Imagination in the Later Middle Ages*, 59–76.

—. *Elizabethan Rhetoric: Theory and Practice*. Cambridge: Cambridge University Press, 2002.

—. 'Learning and Transforming Conventional Wisdom: Reading and Rhetoric in the Elizabethan Grammar School.' *Renaissance Studies* 32.3 (June 2018): 427–45.

—. 'Rhetoric in Use: Three Romances by Greene and Lodge.' In *Renaissance Rhetoric*, edited by Peter Mack, 119–39. Basingstoke: Macmillan, 1994.

Mackenzie, Donald. 'The Psalms.' In Braden, Robert Cummings, and Gillespie, *Oxford History of Literary Translation, Vol. 2*, 141–55.

Macleod, Catherine. *Elizabethan Treasures: Miniatures by Hilliard and Oliver*. London: National Portrait Gallery, 2019.

Maltby, Kate. 'Queen and Scholar: Elizabeth Tudor and Wisdom Imagery.' Unpubl. PhD thesis, University College London, 2021.

Marcus, Leah. 'Queen Elizabeth I as Public and Private Poet: Notes toward a New Edition.' In *Reading Monarch's Writing: The Poetry of Henry VIII, Mary Stuart, Elizabeth I, and James VI/I*, edited by Peter Herman, 135–53. Tempe, AZ: Arizona Center for Medieval and Renaissance Studies, 2002.

Margolies, David. 'Fortune and Agency in Greene's *Pandosto*.' In *Narrative Strategies in Early English Fiction*, edited by Wolfgang Görtschacher and Holger Klein, 195–206. Lewiston, NY: Edwin Mellen, 1995.

Marotti, Arthur F. '"Love Is Not Love": Elizabethan Sonnet Sequences and the Social Order.' *ELH* 49.2 (Summer 1982): 396–428.

—. *Manuscript, Print, and the English Renaissance Lyric*. Ithaca, NY: Cornell University Press, 1995.

Marr, Alexander. 'Pregnant Wit: *Ingegno* in Renaissance England.' *British Art Studies* 1 (Nov. 2015). britishartstudies.ac.uk/issues/issue-index/issue-1/pregnant-wit#000

Martin, Jessica. 'English Reformed Responses to the Passion.' In Jessica Martin and Ryrie, *Private and Domestic Devotion*, 115–34.

— and Alec Ryrie, eds. *Private and Domestic Devotion in Early Modern Britain*. Farnham: Ashgate, 2012.

Martin, John Jeffries. *Myths of Renaissance Individualism*. Basingstoke: Palgrave Macmillan, 2004.

Martin, Raymond, and John Barresi. *The Rise and Fall of Soul and Self: An Intellectual History of Personal Identity*. New York: Columbia University Press, 2006.

Martz, Louis L. *The Poetry of Meditation: A Study in English Religious Literature of the Seventeenth Century*. 2nd edn, New Haven: Yale University Press, 1962.

Mascuch, Michael. *Origins of the Individualist Self: Autobiography and Self-Identity in England, 1591–1791*. Cambridge: Polity, 1997.

Matar, Nabil. *Turks, Moors, and Englishmen in the Age of Discovery*. New York: Columbia University Press, 1999. Kindle.

Maus, Katharine Eisaman. *Inwardness and Theater in the English Renaissance*. Chicago: University of Chicago Press, 1995.

—. 'A Womb of his Own: Male Renaissance Poets in the Female Body.' In *Printing and Parenting in Early Modern England*, edited by Douglas A. Brooks, 89–108. Aldershot: Ashgate, 2005.

May, Steven W. 'Anne Lock and Thomas Norton's *Meditation of a Penitent Sinner*.' *Modern Philology* 114.4 (1 May 2017): 793–819.

—. 'The Authorship of "My Mind to Me a Kingdom Is".' *Review of English Studies*, n.s. 26.104 (Nov. 1975): 385–94.

—. 'Dyer, Sir Edward (1543–1607), courtier and poet.' *ODNB*. https://doi.org/10.1093/ref:odnb/8346

—, and William A. Ringler, Jr. *Elizabethan Poetry: A Bibliography and First-Line Index of English Verse, 1559–1603*. Vol. 3. London: Thoemmes Continuum, 2004.

McCrea, Adriana. *Constant Minds: Political Virtue and the Lipsian Paradigm in England, 1584–1650.* Toronto: University of Toronto Press, 1997.

McLaren, A. N. *Political Culture in the Reign of Elizabeth I: Queen and Commonwealth 1558–1585.* Cambridge: Cambridge University Press, 1999.

Mears, Natalie. *Queenship and Political Discourse in the Elizabethan Realms.* Cambridge: Cambridge University Press, 2005.

Meek, Richard, and Erin Sullivan, eds. *The Renaissance of Emotion: Understanding Affect in Shakespeare and his Contemporaries.* Manchester: Manchester University Press, 2015.

Melnikoff, Kirk, and Edward Gieskes. 'Introduction.' In *Writing Robert Greene: Essays on England's First Notorious Professional Writer,* edited by Kirk Melnikoff and Edward Gieskes, 1–24. Aldershot: Ashgate, 2008.

Méndez, Sigmund. 'Shakespeare's Knowledge of Imagination.' *Complutense Journal of English Studies* 24 (2016): 61–87.

Mentz, Steve. *Romance for Sale in Early Modern England: The Rise of Prose Fiction.* Aldershot: Ashgate, 2006.

Mikkeli, Heikki, and Ville Marttila. 'Change and Continuity in Early Modern Medicine (1500–1700).' In Taavitsainen and Pahta, *Early Modern English Medical Texts,* 13–27.

Miles, Geoffrey. *Shakespeare and the Constant Romans.* Oxford: Oxford University Press, 1996.

Milward, Peter. 'Wright, Thomas (c. 1561–1623), Roman Catholic priest and religious controversialist.' *ODNB.* https://doi.org/10.1093/ref:odnb/30059

Miola, Robert S. *Shakespeare and Classical Tragedy: The Influence of Seneca.* Oxford: Oxford University Press, 1992.

Molekamp, Femke. *Women and the Bible in Early Modern England: Religious Reading and Writing.* Oxford: Oxford University Press, 2013.

Monsarrat, Gilles D. *Light from the Porch: Stoicism and English Renaissance Literature.* Collection Études Anglaises 86. Paris: Didier-Érudition, 1984.

Monta, Susannah Brietz. *Martyrdom and Literature in Early Modern England.* Cambridge: Cambridge University Press, 2005.

Montrose, Louis Adrian. '"Shaping Fantasies": Figurations of Gender and Power in Elizabethan Culture.' *Representations* 2 (Spring 1983): 61–94.

Moore, Helen. 'Elizabethan Fiction and Ovid's *Heroides.*' *Translations and Literature* 9.1 (2000): 40–64.

Moore, Norman, and I. G. Murray. 'Vicary, Thomas (d. 1561), surgeon.' *ODNB.* https://doi.org/10.1093/ref:odnb/28266

Mortimer, Ian. 'Tudor Chronicler or Sixteenth-Century Diarist? Henry Machyn and the Nature of his Manuscript.' *Sixteenth Century Journal* 33.4 (Winter 2002): 981–98.

Mousley, Andrew. 'Renaissance Selves and Life Writing: The Autobiography of Thomas Whythorne.' *Forum for Modern Language Studies* 26.3 (1 July 1990): 222–30.

Mousley, Andy. 'Early Modern Autobiography, History and Human Testimony: The Autobiography of Thomas Whythorne.' *Textual Practice* 23.2 (2009): 267–87.

Mullaney, Steven. *The Reformation of Emotions in the Age of Shakespeare.* Chicago: University of Chicago Press, 2015.

Murray, David J. *A History of Western Psychology.* Englewood Cliffs, NJ: Prentice Hall, 1983.

Murray, Molly. '"Now I Ame a Catholique": William Alabaster and the Early Modern Catholic Conversion Narrative.' In *Catholic Culture in Early Modern England,* edited by Ronald Corthell et al., 189–215. Notre Dame, IN: University of Notre Dame Press, 2007.

—. *The Poetics of Conversion in Early Modern English Literature: Verse and Change from Donne to Dryden.* Cambridge: Cambridge University Press, 2009.

—. 'The Radicalism of Early Modern Spiritual Autobiography.' In *A History of English Autobiography,* edited by Adam Smyth, 41–55. Cambridge: Cambridge University Press, 2016.

Nauta, Lodi, and Detlev Pätzold, eds. *Imagination in the Later Middle Ages and Early Modern Times.* Leuven: Peeters, 2004.

—. Introduction to *Imagination in the Later Middle Ages,* ix–xiii.

Needham, Joseph. *A History of Embryology*. 2nd edn, rev. with Arthur Hughes. Cambridge: Cambridge University Press, 1959.

Neely, Carol Thomas. *Distracted Subjects: Madness and Gender in Shakespeare and Early Modern Culture*. Ithaca: Cornell University Press, 2004.

Nelson, Alan H. 'Vere, Edward de, seventeenth earl of Oxford (1550–1604), courtier and poet.' *ODNB*. https://doi.org/10.1093/ref:odnb/28208

Nelson, Katie M. 'Thomas Whythorne and Tudor Musicians.' Unpubl. PhD thesis, University of Warwick, 2010.

Newbold, William Webster. 'General Introduction', in *The Passions of the Mind* (1604, 2nd edn) by Thomas Wright, edited by William Webster Newbold, 3–50. New York: Garland, 1986.

Newcomb, Lori Humphrey. *Reading Popular Romance in Early Modern England*. New York: Columbia University Press, 2002.

Newell, Alex. *The Soliloquies in 'Hamlet': The Structural Design*. London: Associated University Presses, 1991.

Newen, Albert, Shaun Gallagher, and Leon De Bruin. 'Introduction: 4E Cognition: Historical Roots, Key Concepts, and Central Issues.' In *The Oxford Handbook of 4E Cognition*, edited by Albert Newen, Leon De Bruin, and Shaun Gallagher, 3–16. Oxford: Oxford University Press, 2018.

Nubia, Onyeka. 'Africans in England and Scotland (1485–1625).' *ODNB*. https://doi.org/10.1093/odnb/9780198614128.013.112804

O'Malley, John W. *The First Jesuits*. Cambridge, MA: Harvard University Press, 1993.

Oldridge, Darren. 'Demons of the Mind: Satanic Thoughts in Seventeenth-Century England.' *The Seventeenth Century* 35.3 (May–June 2020): 277–92.

—. *The Devil in Early Modern England*. Stroud: Sutton, 2000.

Oppenheimer, Paul. *The Birth of the Modern Mind: Self, Consciousness, and the Invention of the Sonnet*. New York: Oxford University Press, 1989.

O'Shea, Michael. *The Brain: A Very Short Introduction*. Oxford: Oxford University Press, 2005.

Osmond, Rosalie. *Imagining the Soul: A History*. Stroud: Sutton, 2003.

Ossa-Richardson, Anthony. 'Known Unknowns: Sir John Davies' *Nosce Teipsum* in Conversation.' *English Literary Renaissance* 51.3 (Autumn 2021): 383–408.

O'Sullivan, Suzanne. *It's All in your Head: True Stories of Imaginary Illness*. London: Chatto & Windus, 2015. Kindle.

Ovens, Michael. 'Alchemy and the Body/Mind Question in the Work of John Donne.' In Kambaskovic, *Conjunctions*, 325–36.

Pahta, Päivi, and Irma Taavitsainen. 'An Interdisciplinary Approach to Medical Writing in Early Modern English.' In Taavitsainen and Pahta, *Medical Writing in Early Modern English*, 1–8.

—. 'Introducing Early Modern English Medical Texts.' In Taavitsainen and Pahta, *Early Modern English Medical Texts*, 1–7.

Palmer, Alan. *Fictional Minds*. Lincoln, NE: University of Nebraska Press, 2004.

Park, Katharine. 'The Organic Soul.' In Schmitt, *Cambridge History*, 464–84.

—, and Eckhard Kessler. 'The Concept of Psychology.' In Schmitt, *Cambridge History*, 455–63.

Passingham, Richard. *Cognitive Neuroscience: A Very Short Introduction*. Oxford: Oxford University Press, 2016.

Paster, Gail Kern. *Humoring the Body: Emotions and the Shakespearean Stage*. Chicago: University of Chicago Press, 2004.

—. 'Introduction: Reading the Early Modern Passions.' In Paster, Rowe, and Floyd-Wilson, *Reading the Early Modern Passions*, 1–20.

—, Katherine Rowe, and Mary Floyd-Wilson, eds. *Reading the Early Modern Passions: Essays in the Cultural History of Emotion*. Philadelphia: University of Pennsylvania Press, 2004.

Patterson, Lee. *Chaucer and the Subject of History*. London: Routledge, 1991.

Payne, J. F., rev. by Michael Bevan. 'Jorden, Edward (d. 1632), physician and chemist.' *ODNB*. https://doi.org/10.1093/ref:odnb/15125

Pebworth, Ted-Larry, and Claude J. Summers. '"Thus Friends Absent Speake": The Exchange of Verse Letters between John Donne and Henry Wotton.' *Modern Philology* 81.4 (May 1984): 361–77.

Pettegree, Andrew. *The Book in the Renaissance*. New Haven: Yale University Press, 2010.

Pilarz, Scott R. *Robert Southwell and the Mission of Literature, 1561–1595*. Aldershot: Ashgate, 2004.

Pollock, Linda A. 'Mildmay [née Sharington], Grace, Lady Mildmay (c. 1552–1620).' *ODNB*. https://doi.org/10.1093/ref:odnb/45817

Pope, Hugh. 'St. Mary Magdalen.' *The Catholic Encyclopedia*. Vol. 9. New York: Robert Appleton Company, 1910. newadvent.org/cathen/09761a.htm

Porter, Chloe. *Making and Unmaking in Early Modern English Drama: Spectators, Aesthetics and Incompletion*. Manchester: Manchester University Press, 2013.

Prickett, Stephen. *Secret Selves: A History of our Inner Space*. London: Bloomsbury, 2021.

Purcell, Stephen. 'Performing the Public at Shakespeare's Globe.' *Shakespeare* 14.1 (2018): 51–63.

Quatro, Jamie. 'The Hidden Life of a Forgotten Sixteenth-Century Female Poet.' *The New Yorker*, 5 Aug. 2019. newyorker.com/books/page-turner/the-hidden-life-ofa-forgotten-sixteenth-century-female-poet

Questier, Michael. '"Like Locusts All over the World": Conversion, Indoctrination and the Society of Jesus in Late Elizabethan and Jacobean England.' In *The Reckoned Expense: Edmund Campion and the Early English Jesuits*, edited by Thomas M. McCoog, S. J., 265–84. Woodbridge: Boydell, 1996.

Quint, David. *Origin and Originality in Renaissance Literature: Versions of the Source*. New Haven: Yale University Press, 1983.

Radden, Jennifer, ed. *The Nature of Melancholy: From Aristotle to Kristeva*. Oxford: Oxford University Press, 2002.

Regan, Stephen. *The Sonnet*. Oxford: Oxford University Press, 2019. Kindle.

Renaissance Cultural Crossroads. Centre for the Study of the Renaissance, University of Warwick, 2010. dhi.ac.uk/rcc/index.php

Rhodes, Neil. *Common: The Development of Literary Culture in Sixteenth-Century England*. Oxford: Oxford University Press, 2018.

—. *Shakespeare and the Origins of English*. Oxford: Oxford University Press, 2004. Kindle.

Richardson, Alan. 'Once upon a Mind: Literary and Narrative Studies in the Age of Cognitive Science.' *Modern Fiction Studies* 61.2 (Summer 2015): 359–69.

Rienstra, Debra. '"Disorder Best Fit": Henry Lok and Holy Disorder in Devotional Lyric.' *Spenser Studies* 27 (2012): 249–87.

Rivière, Janine. *Dreams in Early Modern England: 'Visions of the Night'*. London: Routledge, 2017.

Robbins, Philip, and Murat Aydede. 'A Short Primer on Situated Cognition.' In *The Cambridge Handbook of Situated Cognition*, edited by Philip Robbins and Murat Aydede, 3–10. Cambridge: Cambridge University Press, 2009.

Robinson, Daniel N. *An Intellectual History of Psychology*. 3rd edn. London: Arnold, 1995.

Rodger, Alexander. 'Roger Ward's Shrewsbury Stock: An Inventory of 1585.' *The Library* s5-XIII.4 (1958): 247–68.

Ross, Shaun. 'Robert Southwell: Sacrament and Self.' *English Literary Renaissance* 47.1 (2017): 73–109.

Rossky, William. 'Imagination in the English Renaissance: Psychology and Poetic.' *Studies in the Renaissance* 5 (1958): 49–73.

Rowse, A. L. *The Case Books of Simon Forman: Sex and Society in Shakespeare's Age*. 1974; London: Picador, 1976.

Roychoudhury, Suparna. 'Forms of Fantasy: Psychology and Epistemology in the House of Alma, *De la force de l'imagination*, and *Othello*.' *Philological Quarterly* 98.1–2 (2019): 47–71.

—. *Phantasmatic Shakespeare: Imagination in the Age of Early Modern Science*. Ithaca: Cornell University Press, 2018.

Russell, H. K. 'Tudor and Stuart Dramatizations of the Doctrines of Natural and Moral Philosophy.' *Studies in Philology* 31.1 (Jan. 1934): 1–27.

Russell, Jeffrey Burton. *Mephistopheles: The Devil in the Modern World*. Ithaca: Cornell University Press, 1986.

Ryrie, Alec. *Being Protestant in Reformation Britain*. Oxford: Oxford University Press, 2013.

Salzman, Paul. *English Prose Fiction 1558–1700: A Critical History*. Oxford: Clarendon, 1985.

Sands, Kathleen R. *Demon Possession in Elizabethan England*. Westport, CT: Praeger, 2004.

—. *An Elizabethan Lawyer's Possession by the Devil: The Story of Robert Brigges*. Westport, CT: Praeger, 2002.

Sargent, Ralph M. *At The Court of Queen Elizabeth: The Life and Lyrics of Sir Edward Dyer*. London: Oxford University Press, 1935.

Saunders, Jason Lewis. *Justus Lipsius: The Philosophy of Renaissance Stoicism*. New York: Liberal Arts Press, 1955.

Schmitt, Charles B., gen. ed. *The Cambridge History of Renaissance Philosophy*. Cambridge: Cambridge University Press, 1988.

—. 'Towards a Reassessment of Renaissance Aristotelianism.' *History of Science* 11.3 (1973): 159–93.

Schoenfeldt, Michael C. *Bodies and Selves in Early Modern England: Physiology and Inwardness in Spenser, Shakespeare, Herbert, and Milton*. Cambridge: Cambridge University Press, 1999.

Scott-Warren, Jason. 'Was Elizabeth I Richard II?: The Authenticity of Lambarde's "Conversation".' *Review of English Studies* n.s. 64.264 (April 2013): 208–30.

Searle, John R. 'The Mystery of Consciousness Continues.' Review of Antonio Damasio, *Self Comes to Mind: Constructing the Conscious Brain*. New York Review of Books, 9 June 2011.

Sellars, John. 'Neo-Stoicism.' *Internet Encyclopedia of Philosophy*. iep.utm.edu/neostoic/

Semler, L. E. 'Doubtful Battle: Marlowe's Soliloquies.' In Cousins and Derrin, *Shakespeare and Soliloquy*, 43–55.

Serjeantson, Deirdre. 'The Book of Psalms and the Early Modern Sonnet.' *Re-forming the Psalms in Tudor England. Renaissance Studies* 29.4 (Sept. 2015): 632–49.

Seth, Anil. *Being You: A New Science of Consciousness*. London: Faber, 2021. Kindle.

Shapiro, James S. *1599: A Year in the Life of William Shakespeare*. London: Faber, 2005.

Shell, Alison. *Catholicism, Controversy, and the English Literary Imagination, 1558–1660*. Cambridge: Cambridge University Press, 1999.

Shenk, Linda. *Learned Queen: The Image of Elizabeth I in Politics and Poetry*. Basingstoke: Palgrave Macmillan, 2010.

Sherman, William H. *John Dee: The Politics of Reading and Writing in the English Renaissance*. Amherst: University of Massachusetts Press, 1995.

Shore, David R. 'The "Autobiography" of Thomas Whythorne: An Early Elizabethan Context for Poetry.' *Renaissance and Reformation / Renaissance et réforme* n.s. 5.2 (1981): 72–86.

Skura, Meredith Anne. *Tudor Autobiography: Listening for Inwardness*. Chicago: University of Chicago Press, 2008.

Slack, Paul. 'Mirrors of Health and Treasures of Poor Men: The Uses of the Vernacular Medical Literature of Tudor England.' In Webster, *Health, Medicine and Mortality*, 237–74.

Smid, Deanna. *The Imagination in Early Modern English Literature*. Leiden: Brill, 2017.

Smith, Cassander L. *Black Africans in the British Imagination: English Narratives of the Early Atlantic World*. Baton Rouge: Louisiana State University Press, 2016.

—, Nicholas R. Jones, and Miles P. Grier. 'Chapter 1: Introduction: The Contours of a Field.' In *Early Modern Black Diaspora Studies: A Critical Anthology*, edited by Cassander L. Smith, Nicholas R. Jones, and Miles P. Grier, 1–12. Cham, Switzerland: Palgrave Macmillan, 2018.

Smith, Joseph A. 'Roman Soliloquy.' In Cousins and Derrin, *Shakespeare and Soliloquy*, 15–28.

Smyth, Adam. *Autobiography in Early Modern England*. Cambridge: Cambridge University Press, 2010.

Soellner, Rolf. *Shakespeare's Patterns of Self-Knowledge*. Columbus: Ohio State University Press, 1972.

Sokolov, Danila. *Renaissance Texts, Medieval Subjectivities: Rethinking Petrarchan Desire from Wyatt to Shakespeare*. Pittsburgh: Duquesne University Press, 2017.

—. 'Sir Philip Sidney: *Astrophil and Stella*.' In *The Ashgate Research Companion to the Sidneys 1500–1700: Vol. 2: Literature*, edited by Margaret P. Hannay, Mary Ellen Lamb, and Michael G. Brennan, 225–40. Farnham: Ashgate, 2015.

Sorabji, Richard. *Self: Ancient and Modern Insights about Individuality, Life, and Death*. Oxford: Clarendon, 2006.

—. 'Soul and Self in Ancient Philosophy.' In Crabbe, *From Soul to Self*, 8–32.

Speake, Jennifer, ed. *The Oxford Dictionary of Proverbs*, 6th edn. Oxford: Oxford University Press, 2015. *Oxford Reference Online*.

Stachniewski, John. *The Persecutory Imagination: English Puritanism and the Literature of Religious Despair*. Oxford: Clarendon, 1991.

Starnes, D. T. 'The Figure Genius in the Renaissance.' *Studies in the Renaissance* 11 (1964): 234–44.

Stelling, Lieke. *Religious Conversion in Early Modern English Drama*. Cambridge: Cambridge University Press, 2019.

Stevenson, Jane. *Women Latin Poets: Language, Gender, and Authority from Antiquity to the Eighteenth Century*. Oxford: Oxford University Press, 2005.

Stewart, Alan. *The Oxford History of Life-Writing, Vol. 2, Early Modern*. Oxford: Oxford University Press, 2018. Kindle.

Strong, Roy. *The Cult of Elizabeth: Elizabethan Portraiture and Pageantry*. 1977; London: Pimlico, 1999.

—. *The Elizabethan Image: An Introduction to English Portraiture, 1558–1603*. New Haven: Yale University Press, 2019.

—. *The English Renaissance Miniature*. Rev. edn. London: Thames and Hudson, 1984.

Sullivan, Erin. *Beyond Melancholy: Sadness and Selfhood in Renaissance England*. Oxford: Oxford University Press, 2016.

—. 'The Passions of Thomas Wright: Renaissance Emotion across Body and Soul.' In Meek and Erin Sullivan, *Renaissance of Emotion*, 25–44.

Sumillera, Rocío G. 'From Inspiration to Imagination: The Physiology of Poetry in Early Modernity.' *Parergon* 33.3 (2016): 17–42.

Summit, Jennifer. '"The Arte of a Ladies Penne": Elizabeth I and the Poetics of Queenship.' *English Literary Renaissance* 26.3 (Sept. 1996): 395–422.

Suthren, Carla. 'Iphigenia in English: Reading Euripides with Lady Jane Lumley.' In *Acquisition through Translation: Towards a Definition of Renaissance Translation*, edited by Alessandra Petrina and Federica Masiero, 73–92. Turnhout: Brepols, 2020.

Swann, Elizabeth L. '*Nosce Teipsum*: The Senses of Self-Knowledge in Early Modern England.' In *Literature, Belief and Knowledge in Early Modern England: Knowing Faith*, edited by Subha Mukherji and Tim Stuart-Buttle, 195–214. London: Palgrave Macmillan, 2018.

Swärdh, Anna. 'From Hell: *A Mirror for Magistrates* and the Late Elizabethan Female Complaint.' In *Narrative Developments from Chaucer to Defoe*, edited by Gerd Bayer and Ebbe Klitgard, 97–115. New York: Routledge, 2011.

Sweeney, Anne. *Robert Southwell: Snow in Arcadia: Redrawing the English Lyric Landscape, 1586–95.* Manchester: Manchester University Press, 2006.

Taavitsainen, Irma. 'Discourse and Genre Dynamics in Early Modern English Medical Writing.' In Taavitsainen and Pahta, *Early Modern English Medical Texts*, 29–53.

—. 'Dissemination and Appropriation of Medical Knowledge: Humoral Theory in Early Modern English Medical Writing and Lay Texts.' In Taavitsainen and Pahta, *Medical Writing in Early Modern English*, 94–114.

Taavitsainen, Irma, and Päivi Pahta. 'Appendix D: Preliminary List of Texts in the Corpus of *Early Modern English Medical Texts* (*EMEMT*).' In Taavitsainen and Pahta, *Early Modern English Medical Texts*, 258–63.

—, eds. *Early Modern English Medical Texts: Corpus Description and Studies.* Amsterdam: John Benjamins, 2010.

—, eds. *Medical Writing in Early Modern English.* Cambridge: Cambridge University Press, 2011.

Taavitsainen, Irma, et al. 'Medical Texts in 1500–1700 and the Corpus of Early Modern English Medical Texts.' In Taavitsainen and Pahta, *Medical Writing in Early Modern English*, 9–29.

Taylor, Charles. *Sources of the Self: The Making of Modern Identity.* Cambridge: Cambridge University Press, 1989.

Taylor, Gary, and Gabriel Egan, eds. *The New Oxford Shakespeare: Authorship Companion.* Oxford: Oxford University Press, 2017.

Tetramap. 'The Elements.' tetramap.com/what-we-offer/

Thomas, Keith. *Religion and the Decline of Magic: Studies in Popular Beliefs in Sixteenth and Seventeenth-Century England.* 1971; London: Penguin, 1991. Kindle.

Tilmouth, Christopher. 'Passion and Intersubjectivity in Early Modern Literature.' In Brian Cummings and Sierhuis, *Passions and Subjectivity*, 13–32.

—. *Passion's Triumph Over Reason: A History of the Moral Imagination from Spenser to Rochester.* Oxford: Oxford University Press, 2007.

Torey, Zoltan L. *The Conscious Mind.* Cambridge, MA: MIT Press, 2014.

Tracy, Irene. 'A Life of Pain and Pleasure: Imaging the Human Brain.' Merton Society London Lecture. 19 May 2020.

Traister, Barbara Howard. *The Notorious Astrological Physician of London: Works and Days of Simon Forman.* Chicago: University of Chicago Press, 2001.

Trevor, Douglas. 'Sadness in *The Faerie Queene*.' In Paster, Rowe, and Floyd-Wilson, *Reading the Early Modern Passions*, 240–52.

Tribble, Evelyn B. *Cognition in the Globe: Attention and Memory in Shakespeare's Theatre.* New York: Palgrave Macmillan, 2011.

Trill, Suzanne. 'Engendering Penitence: Nicholas Breton and "the Countesse of Pembrooke".' In *Voicing Women: Gender and Sexuality in Early Modern Writing*, edited by Kate Chedgzoy, Melanie Hansen, and Suzanne Trill, 25–44. Edinburgh: Edinburgh University Press, 1996.

'UCL Research Domains – Neuroscience: People.' University College London. ucl.ac.uk/research/domains/neuroscience/research/people

Ulreich, Jr, John C. 'Genius.' In Hamilton, *Spenser Encyclopedia*, 327–8.

Uman, Deborah. *Women as Translators in Early Modern England.* Newark: University of Delaware Press, 2012.

Ungerer, Gustav. 'The Presence of Africans in Elizabethan England and the Performance of *Titus Andronicus* at Burley-on-the-Hill, 1595/96.' *Medieval and Renaissance Drama in England* 21 (2008): 19–55.

Vaughan, Alden T., and Virginia Mason Vaughan. 'Before *Othello*: Elizabethan Representations of Sub-Saharan Africans.' *Constructing Race. The William and Mary Quarterly* 54.1 (Jan. 1997): 19–44.

Vickers, Brian. *In Defence of Rhetoric.* 1988; Oxford: Clarendon, 1989.

—. *Shakespeare, Co-Author: A Historical Study of Five Collaborative Plays.* Oxford: Oxford University Press, 2004.

Voak, Nigel. *Richard Hooker and Reformed Theology: A Study of Reason, Will, and Grace.* Oxford: Oxford University Press, 2003.

Walker, D. P. *Unclean Spirits: Possession and Exorcism in France and England in the Late Sixteenth and Early Seventeenth Centuries.* Philadelphia: University of Pennsylvania Press, 1981.

Walker, Matthew. *Why We Sleep: The New Science of Sleep and Dreams.* London: Allen Lane, 2017.

Wall, Sarah E. 'Editing Anne Askew's *Examinations*: John Bale, John Foxe, and Early Modern Textual Practices.' In *John Foxe and his World*, edited by Christopher Highley and John N. King, 249–62. Aldershot: Ashgate, 2002.

Warnicke, Retha M. 'Lady Mildmay's Journal: A Study in Autobiography and Meditation in Reformation England.' *The Sixteenth Century Journal* 20.1 (Spring, 1989): 55–68.

Warnock, Mary. *Imagination.* London: Faber, 1976.

Wear, Andrew. *Knowledge and Practice in English Medicine, 1550–1680.* 2000; Cambridge: Cambridge University Press, 2004.

Webster, Charles, ed. *Health, Medicine and Mortality in the Sixteenth Century.* Cambridge: Cambridge University Press, 1979.

Weissbourd, Emily. '"Those in their Possession": Race, Slavery, and Queen Elizabeth's "Edicts of Expulsion".' *Huntington Library Quarterly* 78.1 (Spring 2015): 1–19.

Westphal, Jonathan. *The Mind–Body Problem.* Cambridge, MA: MIT Press, 2016.

White, Micheline, ed. *English Women, Religion, and Textual Production, 1500–1625.* Farnham: Ashgate, 2011.

—. 'Introduction: Women, Religious Communities, Prose Genres, and Textual Production.' In *English Women, Religion, and Textual Production*, 1–13.

White, R. S., Mark Houlahan, and Katrina O'Loughlin, eds. *Shakespeare and Emotions: Inheritances, Enactments, Legacies.* Basingstoke: Palgrave Macmillan, 2015.

Wiggins, Martin. *Shakespeare and the Drama of his Time.* Oxford: Oxford University Press, 2000.

—, with Catherine Richardson. *British Drama 1533–1642: A Catalogue.* 9 vols. Oxford: Oxford University Press, 2011–2018.

Wiles, David. *Shakespeare's Almanac: 'A Midsummer Night's Dream', Marriage and the Elizabethan Calendar.* Cambridge: D. S. Brewer, 1993.

Wilson, Katharine. *Fictions of Authorship in Late Elizabethan Narratives: Euphues in Arcadia.* Oxford: Oxford University Press, 2006.

—. 'Revenge and Romance.' In *The Oxford Handbook of Tudor Literature: 1485–1603*, edited by Mike Pincombe and Cathy Shrank, 687–703. Oxford: Oxford University Press, 2009.

Wiseman, Rebecca. 'Introspection and Self-Evaluation in *Astrophil and Stella*.' Special Issue: '*Astrophil and Stella*'. *Sidney Journal* 30.1 (2012): 51–77.

Wolfe, Charles T. and Michaela van Esveld. 'The Material Soul: Strategies for Naturalising the Soul in an Early Modern Epicurean Context.' In Kambaskovic, *Conjunctions*, 371–421.

Woods, Susanne. 'The Body Penitent: A 1560 Calvinist Sonnet Sequence.' *ANQ: A Quarterly Journal of Short Articles, Notes and Reviews* 5.2–3 (1992): 137–140.

Wootton, David. *The Invention of Science: A New History of the Scientific Revolution.* London: Allen Lane, 2015. Kindle.

Woudhuysen, H. R. *Sir Philip Sidney and the Circulation of Manuscripts, 1558–1640.* Oxford: Clarendon, 1996.

Wright, Gillian. 'Translating at Leisure: Gentlemen and Gentlewomen.' In Braden, Robert Cummings, and Gillespie, *Oxford History of Literary Translation Vol. 2*, 58–67.

Yates, Frances. *The Art of Memory.* 1966; London: Pimlico, 1992. Kindle.

—. *The Occult Philosophy in the Elizabethan Age.* London: Routledge & Kegan Paul, 1979.

Zunshine, Lisa, ed. *The Oxford Handbook of Cognitive Literary Studies.* Oxford: Oxford University Press, 2015.

—. *Why We Read Fiction: Theory of Mind and the Novel.* Columbus: Ohio State University Press, 2006.

INDEX

affect, 347–8
affections, *see* passions and affections
Africans: depicted on Elizabethan stage,
163–73; Elizabethan ideas about,
145–54; in England, 158–63; and the
slave trade, 154–5; trade with England,
155–6
Aggas, Edward, *The Defence of Death*
(1576), 71
Alabaster, William, 92–3
allegory, 56–8, 249, 277–8, 285–6, 295–6,
316–17, 321
Allen, Cardinal William, 62, 64–5, 273
Altham, Margaret, 178–9, 180
Anderson, Sir Edmund, 199
Anoun, Abd el-Ouahed ben Messaoud ben
Mohammed, 158, *159*
Apius and Virginia (play, 1566), 316
Aquinas, Thomas, 39, 79, 105
Arden of Faversham (1590), 44
Aristotle, 39; on Africans and humoral
theory, 150; on the embodied mind, 5, 8,
19–20, 21, 45, 52–4, 261; on genial
melancholy, 31, 32, 244; on the three
levels of the soul, 20, 54, 261, 266, 343;
De Anima, 5, 6, 19–20; *On Interpretation*,
332
Arnold, Matthew, 320
Artemidorus, *Oneirocritica*, 232, 233, 235,
236

Ascham, Roger, *The Schoolmaster* (1570),
122, 276–7
Askew, Anne, 61–2, 121
astrology, 177–87, 349
Augustine of Hippo, 39, 55, 79, 128, 279,
318
autobiography, Elizabethan, 287–95
Averroes (Ibn Rushd), 5
Avicenna (Ibn Sina), 5, 221
Aylmer, John, 270

Babington, Gervase, *A Brief Conference
betwixt Man's Frailty and Faith* (1583),
82
Bacon, Anne Cooke, 121, 123, 133, 134–5,
136
Bacon, Sir Francis, 11, 49, *50*, 336, 337
Baldwin, William, *Treatise of Moral
Philosophy* (1547), 70–1
Bancroft, Richard, Bishop of London,
197
Banister, John, *Treatise of Chirurgery*
(1575), 264
Barker, John, 161
Batman, Stephen, 63–4; *Batman upon
Bartholome* (1582), 6, 149, 181–2, 222,
261; *Crystal Glass of Christian
Reformation* (1569), 205–6
Bayning, Paul, 161
Beard, Thomas, 207

413